74987

DATE			

WITHDRAWN

BAKER & TAYLOR

Innocents Abroad

Innocents Abroad

AMERICAN TEACHERS IN THE AMERICAN CENTURY

Jonathan Zimmerman

HARVARD UNIVERSITY PRESS

Cambridge, Massachusetts
London, England   2006

Library of Congress Cataloging-in-Publication Data

Zimmerman, Jonathan, 1961–
   Innocents abroad: American teachers in the American century / Jonathan Zimmerman.
      p. cm.
   Includes bibliographical references and index.
   ISBN-13: 978-0-674-02361-1
   ISBN-10: 0-674-02361-7
   1. Educational exchanges—United States—History—20th century.   2. Teachers—
United States—History—20th century.   I. Title

   LB2283.Z56 2006
   370.116'3—dc22   2006043740

For Adam Jordan Spandorfer
June 4, 1993–February 7, 2005

and for John, Amy, David, and Julia

In memory, and with love

Contents

Acknowledgments

Books come from authors, and authors from parents. In 1966, just before my fifth birthday, my father joined the Peace Corps and took our family to Bangalore, India. Two years after that, we went to Teheran, Iran, for another Peace Corps assignment. Along the way, my mother began a long career as an international family-planning educator. Together, Paul and Margot Zimmerman exposed me to the central themes in this book: culture, teaching, and the role of America in the world. It would be a very different book—with a very different author—if not for them.

I am also grateful to my grandmother, Rose Aginsky Zimmerman, who has been my role model and occasional roommate for the past nine years in New York City. Born in 1907, during the first elected administration of Theodore Roosevelt, Grandma taught in the New York City public schools for more than four decades. And she teaches still, in her own way, about the things that matter: family, friendship, and education. She will not be here forever, I know, but I feel fortunate to have known her for as long as I have.

Most of all, I am lucky to have found a home at New York University's Steinhardt School of Education. The list of colleagues and students who have nurtured me at NYU is too long to enumerate here. But I'm especially grateful to Richard Arum, Rene Arcilla, Joan Malczewski, and Dean Mary Brabeck for their friendship and support. A generous research grant from the Steinhardt School of Education funded most of the archival research that I did for this book, while an equally generous sabbatical gave me the time to write it. Thanks also to the Institute for the Study of American Evangelicals, which helped fund my trips to the Billy Graham Center Archives in Wheaton, Illinois; Elizabeth Knoll, my superb editor at Harvard University Press; James Fraser, who filled in flawlessly for me during my leave; and Lucy Frazier, who keeps our department up and running while the professors all come and go.

The stories and arguments in this book rest almost entirely upon primary documents—letters, memoranda, diaries, and so on—in more than two dozen different archives. To research the book, then, I had to rely upon hundreds of librarians, archivists, and other friendly helpmates. I'm particularly indebted to the incredible research staff at the Presbyterian Historical Society, where I spent more days than the staff would perhaps care to count. Beth Bensman, Bridget Arthur Clancy, Ken Ross, and Eileen Sklar are the real deal: skilled, dedicated professionals who want to serve the public—and know precisely how to do it. I simply could not have written this book without their kind assistance and fellowship.

Born in the grace and good fortune of colleagues and family, this book would conclude amid horror and tragedy. On February 7, 2005, our dear friends John Spandorfer and Amy Jordan lost their beautiful eleven-year-old son, Adam Jordan Spandorfer. Adam was a person of enormous spirit, and I hope that some of his spunk and vitality permeate the pages that follow this one. But I'll never find the words to express the love I feel for Adam, for his family, and for my own. Throughout the ordeal, Susan Coffin taught me about strength, empathy, and devotion. And so did Sarah and Rebecca, our two extraordinary daughters, who keep Adam's spirit alive in other ways. One day, we'll all look back on this year and wonder how we made it through. But I already know the answer: we did it together. In memory, and with love.

Innocents Abroad

Introduction

ABOARD THE USS *THOMAS*

O_N July 23, 1901, the U.S. transport ship *Thomas* set sail from San Francisco Bay for the Philippines. On its previous voyages, a local newspaper noted, the USS *Thomas* had left the bay "laden with warriors and grim armaments." But now it carried "a peaceful army of gentle pedagogues," whose only "ammunition" would be schoolbooks, pencils, paper, and chalk. The 526 teachers aboard the *Thomas* included 346 men and 180 women, hailing from 43 different states and 193 colleges, universities, and normal schools. Ten of the teachers had served as soldiers in the Philippines, which had come under American rule three years earlier; several others had taught in Hawaii, another addition to the new American empire. For the rest, however, the trip would provide their first taste of the "tropics"—and of America's unique mission there. "Our nation has found herself confronted by a great problem dealing with a people who neither know nor understand the underlying principles of our civilization, yet who, for our mutual happiness and liberty, must be brought into accord with us," declared teacher Adeline Knapp, as the *Thomas* departed. "The American genius, reasoning from its own experience in the past, seeks a solution of the problem, a bridging of the chasm, through the common schools." Unlike other world powers, which used force to subdue their conquered populations, the United States would rely on education.[1]

1

With a whoop and a cheer, the teachers pushed out of San Francisco's placid harbor and into the rocky waves of the Pacific. By nightfall, many of them were seasick. "At 6:00 P.M. we rather pretend to eat for most of us begin to expect to feed the fish soon, some practicing stomach gymnastics most fervently already!" Frederick Behner recorded in his diary. Behner would soon join them, retching off the side of the boat for several hours. Over the next few days, as their stomachs quieted, the teachers settled into a noisy routine of social activity. Mostly recent graduates of large state universities, they sang their school songs and shouted "college yells" long into the night. Others formed chapters of their college fraternities or new "state teachers' associations," developing their own evening rituals and antics. "Yickety Yackety Yockety York—New York, New York, New York!" screamed the largest state contingent, numbering about sixty. A few men played poker and scandalized the more conservative passengers, who denounced the practice at the first meeting of the teachers' Young Men's Christian Association. Most of all, though, the teachers flirted—with the ship's army officers, with the crew, and with each other. "In the upper deck, some of the men and young ladies are working up what appear to be pretty bad 'cases,' " wrote Blaine Free Moore, three days into the journey. By the time the *Thomas* docked in Honolulu, four days after that, rumors of several impending marriages were already sweeping the boat.[2]

The rumors would escalate in Hawaii, where the teachers made a big splash during their brief layover. One local newspaper announced that thirty couples from the *Thomas* had married in Honolulu; even more salaciously, another paper claimed that some male teachers had taken wives from "the fair daughters of the Paradise of the Pacific." The accounts turned out to be a hoax, but not before they caused a small scandal back on the mainland—particularly among the fiancées that several new "grooms" had left behind. Meanwhile, the teachers met with American school officials to gain insight about the education of "brown people," to borrow the Americans' favored phrase. "The fact that so much had been done for the civilization and uplift of the Hawaiians gave us courage to believe that a similar mission would be crowned with success," wrote Anna Donaldson, recalling her "first glimpse of the Tropics." The teachers also visited the Bishop Museum, Honolulu's premier institution in the expanding science of ethnology. Then they lay down in the grass outside of the museum, under a big palm tree, and sang their college songs again.[3]

Returning reluctantly to the ship, the teachers would sail for another two weeks before they finally sighted the Philippine coast. They dropped anchor in Manila Harbor on August 21, but remained on board for another two days to receive medical inspections and vaccinations. Then a steamboat ferried the teachers onto the shore, where horse-drawn carriages took them to their temporary quarters at the Manila Exposition Grounds. Herbert and Elizabeth Priestley received an eight-by-fourteen-foot room in a thatched-roof hut, with two bamboo beds and a U.S. flag for a door. Here they would fight off new bouts of stomach distress—"no more fatal than our good old green apple malady," Herbert Priestley wrote, "but it hurts a slight more"—and await word of their school assignments. The teachers also received visits from dignitaries such as Indiana senator and imperialist firebrand Albert Beveridge, who praised them as the advance guard of a global American dominion. "There may be a question as to whether the constitution follows the flag but it is no longer a question whether or not the American teacher will follow the American flag," Beveridge told the instructors. "Cuba, Porto Rico, the Hawaiian Islands, Alaska, Guam and the Philippines all prove my statement." Wherever U.S. soldiers went, Beveridge declared, an army of schoolteachers would march behind them.[4]

This book examines the work—and especially the worldviews—of Americans who taught in the so-called Third World in the twentieth century. With the rise of the United States' overseas empire, thousands of instructors went to the Philippines and other new territories to teach in U.S.-sponsored public schools. After World War II, a second generation of teachers fanned out across the globe under the auspices of volunteer agencies like the Peace Corps. Throughout the century, a vast array of American missionaries taught in religious institutions. All told, between 150,000 and 200,000 Americans served as elementary or secondary teachers in Asia, Africa, and Latin America. Across the American Century, as *Time* publisher Henry Luce dubbed it in 1941, these teachers represented their nation to tens of millions of children, parents, and colleagues. More than diplomats or merchants or journalists, teachers put a human face on America as it assumed new powers and prominence on the global stage.

At the same time, the teachers would also come to question many of the assumptions that undergirded the American Century itself. Despite their divergent evaluations of America's role in the world, scholars have presumed a broad consensus among Americans about that same role. Wherever they went, the story goes, Americans sought to spread their allegedly universalistic values; indeed, they cast themselves as the globe's lone "powerhouse" of "the ideals of Freedom and Justice," to quote Henry Luce.[5] In the decades that followed Luce's manifesto, however, America's overseas teachers mounted a steady challenge to his providential premises. Even as politicians and media spokespeople celebrated the nation's special destiny, teachers began to ask whether America *was* special—and why, if at all, the rest of the world should imitate it. The more their leaders declared America's unique role, indeed, the more that American teachers came to doubt it.

Consider the Philippines, where thousands of missionaries and Peace Corps volunteers would serve as teachers in the post–World War II period. After writing curriculum guides for Philippine vocational schools in 1967, two Peace Corps teachers wondered aloud whether Americans "have a moral right" to design curricula for another nation's schools. Teachers learned about the *Thomas* generation in their preservice training, but mainly as a model to avoid, not to emulate. Unlike their predecessors, one trainee told a newspaper reporter, Peace Corps volunteers came at the request of the host country. "And we're not a missionary group," a second trainee emphasized. "An important part of our job is to learn what we can about the Philippine Islands." Among missionaries themselves, meanwhile, teachers flatly rejected any effort "to impose western values and standards," as one mission educator wrote. "Is it really necessary to introduce our typical Western 'contest mentality' as a means toward enthusiastic involvement of the Filipino people?" he asked. "The West, particularly the United States, has been marked by a pioneer frontierism and poetic rugged individualism. But Daniel Boone would have made a poor Filipino." He would also have made a poor teacher for the Philippines, the missionary added, because Boone's "cultural mold" did not fit the "communal" values that Filipinos held dear.[6]

Such concerns never occurred to teachers like Frederick Behner or Adeline Knapp, who wrote so blithely aboard the *Thomas* about spreading "civilization" in the "tropics." But the post–World War II era spawned a new awareness and appreciation of *culture*, a concept that would revolutionize the teachers' perceptions of America, teaching, and themselves. Reviewing several letters and memoirs from the *Thomas* era, Philippines Peace Corps director P. David Searles described the early teachers as "indistinguishable" from his own Peace Corps volunteers—except that the volunteers "had a more professional vocabulary for discussing cross-cultural matters."[7] As the actual testaments of post–World War II teachers reveal, however, the "vocabulary" of culture did more than simply rephrase old assumptions in a new language. Instead, the culture concept reflected entirely different ways of looking at the world—and, especially, of America's place within it.

The Culture Concept

In 1952, eminent American anthropologists A. L. Kroeber and Clyde Kluckhohn counted and categorized 164 different definitions of "culture" in the social sciences. Most scholars conceived of culture as a unified or holistic way of life, the shared system of symbols, values, and customs that influenced each individual in a given society. This reigning "culture-and-personality" concept had itself helped to shape and define midcentury America, as Kroeber and Kluckhohn recognized. From psychiatry and social work to economics and the law, they wrote, a wide range of professionals "tack on the qualifying phrase 'in our culture' to their generalizations . . . in the same way that mediaeval men added a precautionary 'God Willing' to their utterances." Even more, the concept had seeped into American *popular* culture, further distinguishing America from other Western nations. "Why has the concept of 'culture' had such difficulty in breaking through into public consciousness in France and England?" Kroeber and Kluckhohn asked. "Why has it rather suddenly become popular in the United States, to the point that such phrases as 'Eskimo culture' appear even in the comic strips?" Their answer is worth quoting in full:

> France and England, as colonial powers, were aware, of course, of other ways of life, but—perhaps precisely because of imperialism— the English and French were characteristically indifferent to the intellectual significance of cultural differences—perhaps resistant to them. Similarly, the heterogeneous cultural backgrounds of

Americans—plus the fact that the new speed of communication and political events forced a recognition of the variety of social traditions in the world generally—quite possibly have helped create a climate of opinion in the United States unusually congenial to the cultural idea.[8]

In their acknowledgments, Kroeber and Kluckhohn thanked a young graduate student named Clifford Geertz for his research assistance on their project. Geertz would later spearhead a broad scholarly assault upon his mentors' idea of culture, which promised too much and illuminated too little: as "an all-seasons explanation for anything human beings might contrive to do, imagine, say, be, or believe," Geertz recalled, the culture concept could not bear the burden that social science placed on it. Over the next twenty years, Geertz and his contemporaries reframed the concept as a language or idiom—a set of tools for "meaning-making"—rather than an organic entity that shaped personality or behavior. By the 1960s, meanwhile, historians had begun to challenge the image of American benevolence—and, even more, of American uniqueness—that also underlay the Kroeber/Kluckhohn analysis. Hardly an innocent bystander in the quest for empire, America was itself a colonial power that brought large swaths of the world into its economic, military, or cultural orbit. Around the globe, Americans assumed that "other people cannot *really* solve their problems and improve their lives unless they go about it in the same way as the United States," as historian William Appleman Williams famously wrote. To most Americans, it seemed, the "American Way of Life" was the *only* way to live.[9]

Perhaps so. But for America's overseas schoolteachers, the rise of the culture concept spelled the demise of American certainty, and, for some, of American superiority. In the early twentieth century, when dichotomous notions of "civilization" and "savagery" dominated their discourse, the teachers could speak confidently about transmitting "virtue" or "knowledge" to people who lacked them. By the 1930s, however, the notion of America as a distinct culture—with its own values, symbols, and beliefs—began to penetrate public consciousness. It would reach a crescendo in the early postwar period, when studies of an allegedly exceptional American "national character" crowded bestseller lists. To square the idea of a unique American culture with the nation's new global powers and responsibilities, commentators like Henry Luce hypothesized that American values were actually cultural universals: in the American Century, Luce proclaimed, the United States would help other countries achieve the self-evident truths that had bathed its own birth.[10] For American teachers in actual classrooms, though, this feat of ideological gymnastics often proved impossible. Imbued with the concept of America-as-a-culture, the teachers saw firsthand that many peoples around the globe simply did not share their own values and beliefs. So they started to ask hard questions about whose values—and whose beliefs—should govern the world, and why.

Indeed, they frequently framed these issues in the ascendant global idiom of "rights." As a score of scholars have recently shown, the American civil rights movement drew ideas and inspiration from anticolonial efforts in Africa and Asia. It also gained impetus from the successive worldwide struggles against Nazism and Communism, which each served to highlight America's own deviations from its avowedly democratic norms.[11] From the start, civil rights reformers like Martin Luther King, Jr., appealed to the allegedly universalistic ideal that animated America's Founding Fathers: liberty, freedom, and equality for all individuals. At home and abroad, however, this ideal stood in tandem—and sometimes in tension—with a more particularistic creed, which held that distinct *groups* were also endowed with "rights" to cultural recognition, respect, and preservation.[12] Not surprisingly, American teachers embraced both viewpoints in their forays around the globe. On the one hand, they declared, all children were endowed with the same human right to an education. On the other hand, though, all humans retained the right to define and perpetuate their distinct cultural traditions, especially through their schools. Unlike their confident forebears aboard the *Thomas*, then, post–World War II American teachers faced the awkward and often agonizing task of balancing the mutual and the particular, the universal and the cultural.

With rare exceptions, though, the teachers did not question the midcentury concept of culture itself. Influenced by Geertz and others, most scholars in the humanities and social sciences no longer speak of culture as a unified, organic object with independent, causal power. Instead, they assume a more semiotic or interpretive approach. If human beings are animals who spin "webs of significance" around themselves, as Geertz famously wrote, the webs constitute "culture"; and the job of the scholar is to decode their significance, not to divine laws or causes for human thought, action, or behavior. As this book demonstrates, however, post–World War II American teachers retained the older view of culture long after anthropologists and other scholars had rejected it. From the 1940s into the present, to put it differently, culture-as-a-cause remained a central thread in the teachers' own web of significance: it was a part of *their* culture, which they used to interpret other ones. Up in the academic stratosphere, scholars speak knowingly of culture as a poem, as a language, as a text, as a discourse. But most American teachers—and, I suspect, most Americans, period—see it in much more concrete, even corporeal terms. America has a singular culture, a national character, a distinctive way of life; and so does every other society, or so Americans believe. "What happens to a culture that suddenly discovers it is a culture?" historian Warren Susman asked two decades ago.[13] By examining Americans around the world—not just at home, as Susman and others have done—this book suggests several new answers.

Dilemmas and Critiques

First and foremost, the concept made Americans wary of imposing their values, customs, and symbols—in short, what Kroeber and Kluckhohn called "culture"—on other peoples. Part I of this book, "American Dilemmas," describes how the teachers grappled with these issues in three realms: instructional methods, school curriculum, and educational equality. In each case, with the rise of the culture concept, the teachers experienced profound doubt and perplexity about their role, purpose, and status overseas. Early American teachers confidently exported a teaching philosophy they called "progressive," stressing reason, activity, and persuasion over rote, repetition, and force; by midcentury, however, they started to wonder whether the philosophy itself reflected their own cultural biases instead of the universal needs of "The Child." Americans promoted vocational curricula over so-called book-learning, which the *Thomas* generation denounced as irrelevant or even harmful for "native" populations; as their students' cultural preference for academic instruction became clear, though, post–World War II teachers asked whether American definitions of useful schooling should take precedence over indigenous ones. On the issue of equality, finally, early teachers condemned their hosts for racial and gender prejudices that the teachers themselves displayed. In the second half of the century, by contrast, the Americans would struggle to shed their own biases, but sometimes balked at pressing others to do the same.

Second, the culture concept often led overseas teachers to assail their own culture—not just their "right" to transport it abroad.[14] In Part II, "American Critiques," I explain how teachers came to distrust or even reject popular American conceptions of teachers, of church–state relations, and of American foreign influence itself. Around the world, Americans found that other nations demanded much more preparation and expertise from their teachers than the United States did; especially in the post–World War II period, then, Americans denounced the "those who can't, teach" mentality that permeated their own educational system. Teachers also discovered that other countries provided government funds for parochial schools or even allowed religious instruction in public ones, causing some Americans to question their national doctrine of church–state separation. Most of all, the overseas experience led many teachers to lament the growing power of the United States in *global* culture. Living in conditions of relative poverty, teachers became appalled at the materialism and avarice of their homeland; but they were even more outraged to find their students and colleagues imitating it, from speech and dress to music and cuisine. Teachers inevitably blamed "cultural imperialism," which combined a generic critique of their own culture with a wariness of Americans—including, sometimes, of the teachers themselves—who spread it overseas.

Together, these elements of doubt and critique undermine our own dominant narrative about the role of Americans in the twentieth-century world. Most historians depict the twentieth-century United States as a "crusader" or "missionary" force, seeking to spread a given set of values—democracy, freedom, private enterprise, and so on—across the globe. Scholars differ primarily in their moral and political evaluations of this project, not about the impulse itself.[15] Moreover, most accounts presume a broad national consensus about America's overseas purpose and image: whereas domestic policy divides, the argument goes, foreign affairs unite.[16] The letters, diaries, and memoirs of American teachers tell a different and more complicated story. In the early 1900s, to be sure, the teachers reflected a fairly consensual certitude about American goals and ideals. But consensus as well as certainty fell apart in midcentury, when American teachers began to ask whether their culture was the "right" one—and whether they owned the right to promote it in other places. Their responses were as diverse, jumbled, and contradictory as America itself.

Nor did these answers always follow the conventional divisions of "liberal" and "conservative" back home. In domestic politics, American liberals have often borrowed from foreign models of practice and thought: early twentieth-century Progressives looked to European welfare states, for example, while postwar civil rights activists embraced anticolonial heroes like Mahatma Gandhi and Kwame Nkrumah.[17] Conservatives have more commonly taken the nationalist or exceptionalist tack, insisting that America hold fast to its timeless, unique heritage.[18] When American teachers went abroad, however, they challenged and contradicted these ideological categories. Confronted by higher educational standards overseas, liberals condemned weak teacher preparation and student motivation in America—positions associated with the "right" back home. On church–state matters, meanwhile, conservative teachers dropped their exceptionalist mantle and urged America to mimic the European and Third World practice of public funding for religious schools. Finally, teachers across the political spectrum—even in the burgeoning "Christian Right"—condemned Americans for ethnocentrism, the shared negative referent that the culture concept wrought. "We have very often substituted the filthy rags of culture—*our* culture—for the Bread of Life," warned a self-described "evangelical" mission teacher in 1957. "Only when teaching becomes relevant both to Faith and to life (African or Indian or Asian life) will education be Christian education."[19]

One might reply that a mission teacher—whatever her or his sensitivities toward "culture"—is inevitably engaged in an act of imposition, aiming to replace one theological tradition with another. But *all* education contains an element of imposition, insofar as it seeks to refashion students in ways they might not endorse or even recognize. Assuming the superiority of Western civilization, early American schoolteachers made no bones about their wish to spread it. The West was strong, honest, and dynamic; "the Orient" was weak, dissembling, and static; so the West would seek to remake the Orient in its image. Under the spell of the culture concept, post–World War II teachers would reject or even reverse these categorical judgments: once foreign peoples possessed a "culture," they could be better, but almost never worse, than we were. What teachers retained—indeed, what they imposed— were the categories themselves. Each people possessed a single culture, not more than one; the culture imprinted itself on each individual, in more or less the same way; and the teachers could identify students' "real" culture, even if the students themselves could not. "Civilization" worked to denigrate the Orient, while "culture" served to celebrate it. But both vocabularies presumed that foreign peoples shared a given set of values or characteristics, and—most of all—that American teachers could identify or even cultivate these qualities.[20]

In the course of defending non-Western culture, then, post–World War II Americans often caricatured it. Nowhere was this clearer than in teachers' ritual condemnations of "the West," which had supposedly denuded students of their "real" or indigenous culture. True, teachers wrote, students seemed to prefer rote methods to debate, analysis, and hands-on activities; they favored academic instruction more than vocational training; they often fancied Western style and clothing over so-called native garb; and so on. But these biases simply reflected the evil influence of foreign interlopers, including the American teachers themselves. "We missionaries have brought the old Puritan notion that nothing could be good unless it was tedious, forbidding, and difficult," a teacher in the Congo worried, on the eve of World War II. "We have brought the formal conceptions of education that were accepted at home a generation or more ago . . . and our Native teachers have largely copied our own methods. Having themselves experienced dullness and boredom under our teaching they impose the same on their pupils, and do it very well."[21] By indicting the West for imposing its culture on non-Western ones, American teachers made themselves into the final arbiters of all of them. They really *knew* culture, even when others did not.

Consider the following 1985 encounter between a Peace Corps teacher and a German missionary, deep in the Himalayan foothills of western Nepal. The missionary was selling religious tracts to villagers when the American teacher accosted him, demanding to know why the Nepalese needed such literature. "Because Hindus are thieves and murderers," the missionary replied. Unless they received Christ, he added, they were going to hell. Then, as the teacher recalled in an article many years later, "things got ugly":

I told him that I hoped *he* went to hell. He said he was going to heaven; hell was reserved for "infidels" like Hindus and, yes, Jews. In a truly cheap shot, I asked him why his own church had rolled over and played dead for Hitler. He told me the Holocaust was a tragedy, but mostly because of the Christians who had perished.

I told him to be fruitful and multiply, but not exactly in those words.

Since religious proselytizing was illegal in Nepal, the teacher threatened to call a police officer. The missionary hoisted his backpack and walked off, no doubt to peddle his wares elsewhere. By that time, the teacher remembered, a small crowd of villagers had gathered. None of them spoke English, so the teacher had to describe what had happened:

> "That guy hates your religion," I explained, as the missionary disappeared into the hills, "and he wants you to follow his own."
> "He told me that anyone who believes in Jesus goes to heaven," one of the villagers responded. "I like that." Another pointed approvingly to colored drawings—the Virgin Mary, the Baby Jesus and so on—in the booklet he had bought. "I wish the guy had stayed," he said. Others murmured in agreement.[22]

That teacher was I. More than two decades ago, I spent two years as a Peace Corps volunteer and English teacher in Pyuthan, Nepal. To my ears, the missionary's overt ethnocentrism reeked of early twentieth-century, pith-helmeted imperialism. But now, I wonder: wasn't I just as "imperial" as he was? His bigotries were more explicit, of course: Hindus were thieves and murderers, and that was that. Beneath a cloak of cultural sensitivity, however, my own behavior betrayed a similar bias. I never asked the villagers what they thought of the missionary or his message. Just like my German foe, I presumed that I knew what was best for them. I presumed that I knew their "real" culture, in other words, whether *they* knew it or not.

So this book has also become a journey into my own past, a "personal history" of sorts, with all of the excitement and danger that the term implies.[23] The excitement comes from placing one's life in a much broader historical narrative, which casts new light into the dark hallways of memory. The danger lies in shaping the narrative to fit the memory, so that the story of America's overseas teachers simply recapitulates my own. During the four years that I researched this project, I purposely ignored the letters and memorabilia that I collected from my Peace Corps years. Then, at the very end, I sat down and read them. I hope that I have interpreted my personal experiences through the lens of my research, and not the other way around. And I hope that my readers will forgive me in the places where I failed.

America's Overseas Teachers: A Brief Portrait

The other danger in a project of this scope is overgeneralization. America's overseas teachers were a vast and variegated lot, drawn from an enormous range of social types. They included a sixty-year-old Colorado suffragist in Puerto Rico, where she wore her white hair short to signal support for the cause back home; a young black graduate of Hampton University, working at a school in Hawaii and proudly tracing the steps of Hampton founder Samuel Chapman Armstrong; a Philadelphia-area Quaker and forty-year mission teacher to Japan, who was evacuated during World War II, but returned afterwards to tutor the Crown Prince; and a blind Peace Corps volunteer in Ecuador, where he started the country's first Special Olympics. The pioneering black historian Carter G. Woodson taught in the Philippines before starting his scholarly pursuits; educational statistician Leonard P. Ayres, author of an influential 1909 study on "laggards" in the schools, began his career as an instructor in Puerto Rico; and several future political leaders taught in the Peace Corps, most notably U.S. Senator and presidential aspirant Paul Tsongas. A college swim champion, Tsongas spent many hours in the pool at his Ethiopia school, but "manages to emerge long enough to teach the 9th grades some history and math," as another volunteer jokingly observed in 1962.[24]

Despite this diversity, the teachers did share several broad characteristics. First of all, almost all of them were white. In 1903, Woodson was one of just seven blacks out of 800 American teachers in the Philippines; for many years, America's government schools in Puerto Rico and Hawaii had no black teachers at all. After a burst of African-American hires in the late 1800s, most white-controlled missions stopped enlisting blacks around the turn of the century. Colonial regimes in Africa feared the allegedly seditious influence of African-Americans on the continent, while mission leaders worried that blacks lacked the moral fortitude to resist Africa's sensuous temptations. After midcentury, missions and volunteer agencies both mounted new campaigns to recruit African-American teachers. But most of these efforts came to naught, leaving America's teaching force nearly as monochrome as it was before. Even in the Peace Corps, where race liberals like Sargent Shriver dominated the Washington staff, blacks made up just 2 to 4 percent of teachers in the field. Nor was the agency able to attract many Hispanics or Native Americans, despite its zealous attempts to do so.

Second, most overseas teachers, like teachers at home, came from the middle class, the massive and miscellaneous bulk of Americans who defined themselves largely in terms of what they were not: rich or poor. As Hawaiian school principal Thomas Vance wrote in 1928, with perhaps more imagination than accuracy, European nations possessed only two classes: the "aristocracy" and the "laboring class." But America also boasted a third group, positioned between the other two, which gave birth to the nation's teaching force—and so much more. "Teachers are proudly enough members of the great middle class; the class that makes up 'the backbone of our American civilization,' " Vance wrote. "To make our social status still more pleasing we consider the aristocracy 'social and economic parasites.' " Nevertheless, Vance quickly added, many teachers were also plotting ways they might enter the hated upper tier. "Strange as it may seem," he quipped, "there is not an individual among us who would fail to welcome an opportunity to join this class of so-called parasites." However proud of their class position, most teachers hoped to transcend it—by leaving teaching.[25]

Third, as Vance's last comment illustrated, the majority of the teachers did not pursue education as a profession or career. As in the United States, only a small fraction of the overseas teachers in the early years had any formal training for the job. For most of them, teaching was a way station on the road to larger goals: men aimed to move into other professional or business opportunities, while women taught briefly before marriage. The exceptions were female mission teachers, who more often possessed formal training and who tended to stay for longer periods at their posts. The professional profile of teachers in the United States would shift later in the century, as expanding school systems required teachers to obtain college degrees and certification in education. But America's global teaching force would remain largely untrained and inexperienced, belying the professionalization that took place back home. In the Peace Corps, especially, volunteers often signed up to teach precisely *because*, unlike domestic situations, overseas positions did not require any teaching background or formal preparation.

Last, these largely inexperienced teachers were also very young. Government schools in America's territories generally barred candidates who were older than forty, while the vast majority of teachers were considerably younger than that. Here, too, early twentieth-century missions provided an exception: although most of their new recruits were just out of college, some teachers remained at their posts into their middle years or even into old age. In the post–World War II era, however, youth ruled. The average age of Peace Corps volunteers in the 1960s was twenty-five, as was that of the teachers who joined the host of smaller, privately operated volunteer organizations that sprouted during the decade. Within missions, meanwhile, recent college graduates came to dominate the teaching force. As so-called evangelical or fundamentalist churches entered the educational field for the first time, both mainline missions and their evangelical competitors devised "short-term" opportunities to lure new teachers overseas. Often modeled explicitly after the Peace Corps, these organizations sent untrained, novice teachers overseas for two- or three-year stints. Some groups restricted membership to people under thirty; others barred recruits from getting married during their service, which discouraged all but the very youngest candidates from applying.

Colonials, Volunteers, and Missionaries

White, middle-class, inexperienced, and young: at first glance, most American teachers in the American Century looked a lot like me. I was twenty-one years old when I joined the Peace Corps, fresh out of college, with no formal background in teaching. But looks can deceive. A Peace Corps volunteer in Nepal in the 1980s is not a missionary in India in the 1930s, or a teacher in Puerto Rico in 1901. In each of the ensuing chapters, I tell a century-long story that explains how the concept of culture altered teachers' perceptions of education, America, and the world. The strategy risks collapsing very different cohorts of teachers, from very different eras, into a single, imaginary whole. To keep them distinct in space and time, then, I have divided the teachers into three large categories: Colonials, Volunteers, and Missionaries. Each category contains its own diversity, of course, but each one also has a special character and, to some degree, a special history.

Colonials taught in government schools in the overseas American empire, primarily during the first three decades of the twentieth century. By "empire," I mean the territories that were formally annexed and administered by the United States: the Philippines, Puerto Rico, Hawaii, Guam, American Samoa, the Canal Zone, and the Virgin Islands. The largest contingent taught in the Philippines, where 4,000 Americans served as teachers before World War II; about the same number taught in all of the other colonies combined. The United States generally did not send public-school teachers to the countries that it occupied militarily without formal annexation, such as Cuba, Nicaragua, and the Dominican Republic; an important exception was Haiti, where the army hired teams of Americans as vocational instructors. Only a handful of colonial teachers would remain in American territories after 1940. The Philippines won its independence, of course, while Hawaii and Puerto Rico passed measures favoring locally born teachers over "mainlanders."

Volunteers refer to the waves of teachers who crisscrossed the globe after World War II under the auspices of secular agencies, especially the Peace Corps. Founded in 1961, the Peace Corps would send roughly 70,000 Americans abroad as teachers over the next four decades. As historians have recently reminded us, the Peace Corps was part of a much larger international youth movement that touched nearly every industrialized nation.[26] But so were dozens of other, much smaller volunteer organizations in the United States itself. The first secular American teachers in postwar Africa went to Ghana and Nigeria in 1955 under the auspices of a small private group, the African-American Institute. Over 400 Americans went to the African continent between 1961 and 1967 with Teachers for East Africa, which was conceived and administered by Teachers College at Columbia University. Undergraduates at Harvard formed their own organization, Volunteer Teachers for Africa, sending more than 100 students and recent graduates into African classrooms by 1970. About 200 Americans taught in Laos and Vietnam for International Voluntary Services, which removed the teachers in 1972 because of security problems, and because local officials said that volunteers were criticizing the U.S. war effort there.[27]

As these statistics suggest, none of these groups constituted a formidable presence on their own. Taken as a whole, however, they formed a large, but largely unknown, volunteer teacher force alongside the Peace Corps in the Third World.

Missionaries taught on behalf of American religious organizations throughout the century, straddling the colonial era and the volunteer one. During the early years, nearly all of America's missionary teachers hailed from mainline Protestant denominations or from the Catholic Church. By the 1930s, perhaps 4,000 Protestants and 1,000 Catholic American missioners taught in overseas mission schools; by 1958, their numbers had risen to 8,000 and 2,000, respectively. After that, so-called "independent" or "evangelical" churches would come to dominate the Protestant teaching force. Abandoning their old antipathy to formal education and other kinds of "institutionalism," evangelicals sent thousands of career missionaries as well as short-term teachers into Third World schools; by the 1980s, the short-termers would outnumber their brethren in the ministry. A similar development occurred in the Catholic Church, where a 1960 appeal by the Pope unleashed a flood of lay teachers as well as priests and nuns. By 1967, a single lay group, Papal Volunteers for Latin America, boasted over 1,000 members; probably half of them taught in schools.[28] As in the case of secular volunteer groups, none of these organizations of short-term missionaries sent out huge numbers of teachers by itself. Together, though, they represented a burgeoning new force—and new face—for American mission education.

Innocents Abroad

This book is about Americans who went overseas, not about the various peoples whom they encountered when they got there. In that sense it resembles its namesake, *The Innocents Abroad*, the 1869 travelogue by a young journalist named Mark Twain. *Innocents Abroad* was Twain's first book and also his most popular one, selling many more copies during his own lifetime than future classics like *Huckleberry Finn* and *Tom Sawyer*. Touring Europe and the Middle East with a group of well-to-do Americans, Twain provided rich and often caustic descriptions of the hoteliers, tour guides, and other local characters who assisted, harangued, or cheated their American visitors. But Twain's real interest lay in the Americans themselves, whose overseas experiences under-scored their shared attributes. Skewering some of his countrymen for their sycophantic imitation of all things European, he praised others for their vigor, idealism, and common-sense wisdom. Against a panorama of different peoples and nations, Twain believed, Americans' own strengths and foibles would come into sharp relief.[29]

Similarly, my own book focuses upon American teachers rather than their irreducibly diverse hosts; when these other peoples appear in the text, we see them mainly through the teachers' eyes. Even on the occasions where indigenous peoples or European expatriates comment about the teachers, these observations serve to illuminate Americans instead of the countries and cultures they crisscrossed. Like Twain, meanwhile, I have also tried to render an evenhanded judgment of overseas Americans. Despite our shared title, neither Twain nor I depict our subjects as purely innocent—or, for that matter, as uniformly guilty. American teachers displayed complex mixtures of knowledge and ignorance, compassion and cruelty, civility and boorishness, and so on. Although I cannot lay claim to Twain's wit or style, of course, I hope I have captured some of the nuance and balance of his work in my own.

But my book is also a work of history, so, like any good history, it seeks to explain change over time. Whereas Twain produced a snapshot of a single touring group in the 1800s, I chronicle thousands of teachers across the wide span of the ensuing century. Most of all, I try to assess how—and why—their beliefs, attitudes, and sensibilities shifted during this period. To highlight these new ideas, I have organized the book thematically rather than chronologically. Twain's account followed a fairly traditional narrative arc, from the beginning of his journey to the midpoint to the end, but my own book examines six different topics through the entire century, underscoring the key changes within each one. I hope that this somewhat unorthodox structure lends power and clarity to the argument, letting readers witness the important shifts in a variety of contexts. Since readers will inevitably find more interest in certain topics than in others, I also hope that my thematic organization will allow them to delve into any chapter that they choose without missing my larger claims about teachers' changing views of the world.

At the dawn of the twentieth century, this book argues, most American teachers shared a common "civilizational" impulse. Whether they taught as missionaries in European colonies or as state-paid instructors in America's own empire, the teachers presumed that whites possessed Truth, indigenous peoples toiled in darkness, and the duty of the former was to enlighten the latter. After World War II, however, teachers increasingly dissented from this simple dichotomy. Even as America developed into a global power, the emerging concept of culture made Americans wary of imposing their values and beliefs on the rest of the globe. Here they added a welcome dose of skepticism to the smug arrogance, duplicity, and ethnocentrism that permeated so much of the American Century. But "culture" imposed distortions, too, especially the fallacious idea that members of a given culture were all similar to each other—and all different from us. This book tells the story of these shifting portraits: of other peoples and other cultures, and of our own.

✎ I

American Dilemmas

*I*N HIS CLASSIC 1944 STUDY of American race relations, the Swedish sociologist Gunnar Myrdal underlined a huge contradiction at the heart of American life. On the one hand, Myrdal wrote, white Americans proudly professed their enduring faith in human equality, while on the other hand, they demonstrated a profound prejudice against their black countrymen. Over time, Myrdal confidently asserted, this "American Dilemma" would dissipate. White Americans would abandon overt racial discrimination, bringing their practices into closer accord with their principles. Meanwhile, black Americans would lose their own distinct cultural traits. "American negro culture" was a "distorted development," Myrdal wrote, "a pathological condition" born of a society that refused to accord blacks their full humanity. As racism melted away, so would the grotesque cultural variations that it had spawned.[1]

As many critics would later note, Myrdal underestimated the powerful hold of racism on the white American mind. Even more, though, his blithe dismissal of black culture would bring sharp accusations of racism against Myrdal himself. Black culture was not simply a deviant strain of "American culture" writ large, as Myrdal had supposed; instead, blacks insisted, they possessed a cultural beauty, unity, and integrity of their own. Here African-Americans would be joined by other racial minorities, by so-called white ethnics, by women, by the disabled, and by gays, each laying claim to its own "culture," and each rejecting forced assimilation into a larger national one. These developments would

21

spawn what historian John Higham would call "Another American Dilemma," pitting unity against diversity. In the balance lay the identity of America itself, Higham wrote in 1974, "what we are and what we wish to be."[2]

For America's overseas teachers, meanwhile, the concept of culture would generate yet a third dilemma: the question of America in the world. At the outset of the century, teachers rarely paused to consider if their presence and actions might insult, compromise, or weaken other cultures. But post–World War II teachers did exactly that, wondering whether they should impose their values and beliefs on peoples who did not seem to share them. Others asked if such a process was even possible, given the enormous power that culture exerted on *everyone*. "It's very difficult to get behind the cultural barriers and become just people doing things together," wrote a Peace Corps teacher from the Philippines in 1962, bemoaning her students' shy behavior. "Culture does permeate every aspect of our lives . . . Even if my skin suddenly became another color, I would have American stamped all over me."[3] From classroom instruction and curriculum to ideas about gender and disability, teachers feared that their own culture was *too* American to export abroad. Well before racial unrest and ethnic revivals made "culture" into a household word back home, then, the concept made teachers wary of American influence overseas.

The concept also imposed distortions of its own, starting with the dubious proposition that every person in a given society shared the same culture. Even more, the culture concept could blind American teachers to the ideas and beliefs that they *shared* with their hosts. "There seems to be a great gap between Quaker ways of life and Japanese ways of life," wrote a missionary teacher from Tokyo in 1970, in a typical remark. "I do not feel I am in the best position to pass judgment here."[4] By underscoring her Quaker heritage, the teacher distinguished herself from other Americans, both at home and abroad. The "Japanese" remained undifferentiated, however, an organic and entirely foreign entity that no American could rightly assess or impugn. Amid the bombast and outright bigotry that marked so much of the American Century, teachers substituted a welcome dose of doubt about America's role and purpose in a culturally diverse world. But their skepticism rarely extended to the idea of culture itself, which too often concealed the shared humanity that unites us all.

~ 1

The American Method

CLASSROOM INSTRUCTION, DISCIPLINE, AND THE DILEMMAS OF CULTURE

*I*N NOVEMBER 1901, Harry Cole sent two bitter letters from his post in the Philippines to his home in Michigan. After arriving in the islands three months earlier aboard the transport ship USS *Thomas,* Cole had tried to teach Filipinos via the "American Method": rather than simply drilling dry facts from the blackboard or a textbook, he used objects in the room to demonstrate and discuss new concepts. But the American Method simply did not suit his non-American charges. "I find this work very monotonous trying to teach these monkeys," Cole wrote. "I would give something to see a bright American child again." Having grown up under the "Spanish system" of rote instruction, Filipino children could memorize and recite well enough. But they could not comprehend or analyze what they were saying, Cole wrote, no matter how much effort—and money—that Americans expended. "It seems indeed very foolish to send 2,000 or 3,000 teachers out here on high salaries to spend their time on such work," Cole wailed. He was already counting the days until he could leave.[1]

Sixty years later, Peace Corps volunteer David King came to a nearly identical conclusion: the American Method could not succeed in the Philippines. Whereas Cole blamed Filipinos and their former Spanish rulers for an ancient system of rote, however, King blamed himself—and his fellow Americans—for trying to alter it. "We say, 'Free the child from traditional forms. Allow him to be imaginative, original,

23

creative,' " wrote King, summarizing American goals in the classroom. "This just doesn't work with Filipino kids." The informal and egalitarian nature of American instruction threatened to upset customary classroom authority in the Philippines, where the teacher reigned supreme. Most of all, King argued, the very urge to change Philippine educational patterns reflected Americans' own ethnocentric arrogance. "I've adopted some of the methods that Filipino teachers use," King reported. "And I still wonder if I'm teaching as well as [they] are."[2]

Together, these comments encapsulate the key continuities as well as the most important shifts in Americans' overseas instruction. Across an entire century and an enormous range of countries, Americans spread the gospel of "pedagogical progressivism"; rhetorically, at least, progressivism *was* the American Method. Education should be child-centered, progressives said, not teacher-centered; active, not passive; based in experience, not just in books; and focused on the community, not simply on the classroom.[3] Some American teachers did insert elements of this system into their overseas instruction, invoking John Dewey and even Jesus Christ on its behalf: to liberal missionaries, especially, Christ became the penultimate progressive educator. As in the United States, however, most American teaching did not follow the official American script.[4] Adopting the same rote methods that they reviled, early twentieth-century teachers argued that their students were too infected by "European" doctrines—and, sometimes, too impaired by racial deficiencies—to change. After World War II by contrast, Americans increasingly questioned the American Method itself. Imbued with new ideals of cultural tolerance and "rights," teachers asked why *they* had the right to foist an alien educational program on their unwilling hosts.

On the contentious issue of classroom discipline, Americans embraced the "foreign" practices they encountered. As David King correctly surmised, progressive instructional methods favored an egalitarian, easygoing rapport between teachers and students. In their official statements and policies, then, Americans reserved their greatest ire for so-called strict or dictatorial discipline, especially corporal punishment, which stamped out students' natural love of learning. As in the case of rote teaching, however, rhetoric and reality diverged. Citing the allegedly sinful or stubborn nature of their foreign pupils, early twentieth-century Americans inflicted the same harsh punishments and penalties that prevailed in the United States.[5] But so did overseas Americans in the post–World War II period, when a new "cultural" rationale sustained old classroom practices. "This isn't suburbia USA," explained a Peace Corps volunteer in Nigeria, in a typical mid-1960s defense of corporal punishment. "We have to teach according to the customs of the system, and beating kids who misbehave is part of that system." I struck a similar note in a letter from Nepal in 1984, published in an anthology of Peace Corps writers, explaining why I too had decided to strike my students:

> I think I may have solved, or at least partially solved, the problem of students making disruptive noise while I teach. The other teachers told me how to do it. *'Tapaille lei bademas haru lie pitnu parcha,'* they said, which roughly translates as 'You have to hit the bastards.' The mere mention of corporal punishment promoted in me the proper amount of Northeastern-white-liberal-public-school-educator reaction, as I informed my colleagues that I *never* hit students. It's just not necessary, I said. Boy, was I a stooge. It *is* necessary. People respond here only to punishments they've been conditioned to expect . . . Adaptation isn't a matter of choice out here. You simply have to do it, and this includes the adaptation (adulteration?) of your most strongly held principles.[6]

Twenty years after the fact, I am not particularly proud of the adaptation (adulteration?) of my principles. But I think I can explain it. The postwar American gospel of education actually contained two very *different* principles, which often came into conflict when Americans went abroad. On the one hand, teachers were urged to introduce new, child-centered methods of instruction, and on the other hand, they were instructed to respect and even preserve the venerable culture of their hosts. Yet the very doctrines of the American Method frequently clashed with local cultures, where rote learning—and strict discipline—predominated. Prefiguring recent theories of ethnic "learning styles," some Americans argued that progressive methods were in fact indigenous, not foreign, to non-American peoples.[7] But teachers discovered otherwise, experiencing a profound and often painful tension between their twin goals. In their quest for cultural sensitivity, the teachers sometimes forsook the intellectual rigor that true intercultural communication requires.

The Attack on Rote

In 1911, T. H. P. Sailer sent a letter around the world condemning "rote and mechanical methods" in the classroom. Hired by the Presbyterian Board of Foreign Missions to correspond with its teachers in the field, Sailer acknowledged that too much of American schooling still relied on simple recall. But the problem was even more pronounced among "Oriental students" abroad, who were "strong in memorizing" but "weak in reasoning ability and mental initiative." The blame for these habits lay not in "heredity," Sailer stressed, but in schools themselves. "Memorizing is an essential part of study, although it has occupied much too prominent a place," Sailer wrote. "It is important that we encourage children to think their own thoughts and develop their own individuality." Here he cited John Dewey and other American tribunes of the so-called new education, who would lead the world out of the wilderness of rote and into the promised land of reason.[8]

Around the globe, American teachers echoed Sailer's attack on rote instruction in school. Like the methods they maligned, ironically, their critique often assumed a mechanical and lockstep quality. Wherever Americans taught, it seemed, they routinely denounced rote. Human beings were defined by the capacity for reason, teachers said; rote inhibited this capacity; hence, rote made students less than human. Americans in the Philippines described their pupils as ducks and gramophones as well as monkeys; in Puerto Rico, as parrots; and in Korea, as simple machines.[9] As the metaphors suggested, some Americans attributed students' mimetic behavior to their supposedly inherent deficiencies; like Sailer, others blamed misguided doctrines of education. Yet teachers stood united in their antipathy toward rote instruction, which dampened students' character as well as their intellects. "There is very little that develops individuality and personality," complained a Baptist missionary to Japan, in a typical jeremiad against rote methods. "In fact, the purpose and the goal of the whole [Japanese] system is to throw everyone into the same mold."[10]

More than anything else, Americans despised the tradition of group reading and recitation that they encountered around the globe. Approaching her school in the Philippines for the first time, teacher Mary Fee heard a sound like "the din of a boiler factory" emanating from it. "The noise was the vociferous outcry of 189 Filipino youths," Fee wrote, "engaged in study or at least in a high, throaty clamor, over and over again, of their assigned lessons." To George Kindley, a former teacher at a Native American boarding school, his Philippine students sounded like "ten thousand wild geese in an Indian Territory corn field." When his pleas for silence fell on deaf ears, Kindley whittled several wooden paddles and hung them in his classrooms; any child who continued to read aloud received a "motherly blessing" on the behind. Likewise, teachers in Hawaii and Puerto Rico struck children for studying in concert. In British Palestine, meanwhile, a Quaker missionary shunned corporal punishment, but struggled to bring quiet to her classroom by other means. "The Eastern method of teaching is all right I guess," she wrote, in a small concession to local practice, "but our western nervous systems would soon be wrecked if we allowed our English classes to follow the same plan."[11]

Choral study was more than simply a psychological nuisance, a plague on teachers' ears and minds. It was also a pedagogical calamity, because children who studied out loud simply could not learn for themselves.[12] The same went for "copybook methods," the other major target of American wrath. Whenever students were not reciting lessons in concert, Americans groused, the pupils were transcribing information from the blackboard—or, worse, from the teacher's mouth—into their notebooks. In Bolivia, an appalled Catholic missionary watched children copy an entire lesson from the blackboard into their "crasable" (*en borrador*) notebooks; for homework, they would record the same lesson into their "clean" (*en limpio*) books. "The Bolivian system of teaching is one of copying," surmised another American Catholic. "It does not matter what goes into the head as long as it is all in the notebook."[13]

Elsewhere in Latin America, ironically, Protestant missionaries attributed this system to a "Jesuit" penchant for "memory and tradition" over "initiative and self-reliance."[14] In the Philippines and Puerto Rico, similarly, American teachers often faulted Catholic priests for imposing the "Spanish method" of rote on the islands.[15] In areas under European rule, finally, Americans blamed colonial examination systems for rote instruction. "The cramming of textbooks and memorizing of notes fills most of the scene," Presbyterian Alice Van Doren griped in 1936, after surveying 177 mission schools in India, "and the grinding of the examination machine is everywhere heard in the land." A Baptist teacher in the Assam hill country agreed. "The main aim of students in India is to pass examinations," Maza R. Evans told a colleague. "They are so formal and impractical that it is hard to try to put across . . . the more modern methods."[16] Yet across India—and around the world— Americans like Evans *did* try to employ new methods. They called the techniques "modern," "progressive," and "scientific"—or, simply, American.

The American Method

"I have always desired to be a progressive in my educational theories and practices, as what educator has not?" So asked Henry S. Townsend in 1935, looking back on a long career overseas. Townsend went to Hawaii in the 1880s, serving as teacher and principal in several institutions before becoming territorial Inspector General of Schools. Along the way, he took a correspondence course at the newly established School of Pedagogy of New York University; started a teachers' journal, which he pointedly named *Progressive Educator*; and hosted visits from famed progressive theorists Francis Parker and John Dewey. To Townsend, Parker was "the Commander in Chief of the storm troops of the educational army" that swept across the world. Describing Dewey, meanwhile, Townsend drew on a religious metaphor rather than a military one. "He was our Great High Priest," Townsend recalled, "and what he said had a tendency to be accepted without further consideration." Townsend returned to the continental United States in 1900, but was back in the tropics the following year, joining the 525 other Americans aboard the *Thomas* en route to the Philippines. He would remain there for three decades, occupying a variety of school posts but always promoting the same goal: progressive education. Returning to Hawaii in 1935, shortly before his death, he was gratified to find progressivism in full flower. "We are Deweyites, dyed in the wool," one teacher told him.[17]

Townsend's simple rhetorical query—what educator has *not* wished to be progressive?—illustrates the enormous sway of this doctrine among overseas Americans in the early twentieth century. As in the United States, of course, progressivism meant different things to different teachers. The term also resonated more strongly with educational leaders like Townsend than it did with rank-and-file classroom instructors, most of whom lacked any formal pedagogical training. But no one could escape the influence of progressivism, no matter how one defined it. When missionaries in Cuba designed a school to showcase the best educational thought in the United States, they unhesitatingly named it *La Progresiva*.[18] To American teachers—and, often, to their non-American hosts—"progressive" and "American" education were one and the same.

Most commonly, teachers characterized progressivism in terms of its opposite: rote instruction. Rote methods were formal, passive, and boring; progressive ones were spontaneous, active, and centered on the natural interests of children. "We must not make a fetish of mere abstract information," warned George W. Carpenter, a Baptist in the Congo. "The most effective way to learn facts is to use them . . . Hence the emphasis of our schools ought constantly to be on *doing* rather than on *knowing*."[19] By the mid-1930s, "learning by doing" became the most popular adage of the American teacher overseas, just like it was at home.[20] Next came "experience," another favored educational cliché in the United States. "The Aim of Education is the harmonious development of the whole individual through experience," stated a missionary's eleventh-grade students in Iran, on the endpiece of their first school newsletter. The newsletter itself represented progressivism in action, engaging children in an enterprise that was relevant, purposeful, and self-directed. But the manifesto about education was cosigned by their American "faculty advisor," leaving little doubt about who had inspired the statement, or who was really in charge.[21]

In general, progressives said, the proper job of the teacher was to demonstrate a concept rather than merely to drill it. So they placed a special premium upon the so-called "object" method for teaching English, especially in the Philippines and other new protectorates. A lecturer aboard the *Thomas* urged America's new educational pioneers to illustrate terms with pictures or items from the classroom, instead of translating the words into Spanish. As much out of necessity as philosophy, many teachers embraced this technique when they reached the other shore. Few Americans spoke Spanish, recalled one veteran of the *Thomas*, so "the *only* possible method was by the use of objects"—or of actions. Teachers demonstrated verbs like "run" by charging across the classroom, as their delighted students looked on or joined in the fray. By 1920, one teacher would boast that his English students did not open a book for the first twelve weeks of class. They learned the language exactly the same way that American children did: via activity and experience, in real-life settings.[22]

To advocates of the "project method," meanwhile, every subject—not just English—was best taught through concrete life situations. Its most prominent advocate was Teachers College professor William Kilpatrick, who urged schools to orient instruction around tangible activities rather than abstract disciplines. Kilpatrick presented one of his earliest formulations of the project method at a 1919 conference in India; shortly thereafter, Presbyterian missionaries in the small Punjabi village of Moga took up his challenge. Second graders at Moga learned geography and mathematics by building a miniature river system, packing tiny barges with cotton and wheat for market. Sixth graders focused on their local hospital, where they investigated staff, services, and costs; eventually, they opened their own dispensary at the school. Moga missionaries studied with Kilpatrick during their furloughs back home and routinely cited his work, leading one enthusiast to label the school "a rural version of Columbia Teachers College." Kilpatrick himself would come to Moga in 1926, joining a long list of eminent educational visitors from around the world.[23]

Even as they invoked these pedagogical experts, Americans would also engage an even higher authority on behalf of "learning by doing": Jesus Christ. "He not only instructed the Twelve in the lessons of the Kingdom," Alice Van Doren explained, "but also sent them forth themselves to practice the preaching and healing which they had heard and seen while companying with Him." (Since Christ was a carpenter, she added, He demonstrated the value of "practical" and vocational skills alongside strictly "academic" ones.) Other Americans stressed that Jesus taught outside of formal classrooms, prefiguring the progressive emphasis on community-based learning. Still others noted that the "Great Teacher" employed parables and stories, which appealed to His listeners' natural interests. As overseas schools gained access to movie projectors in the early post–World War II era, missionaries noted that Jesus used powerful visual metaphors: the lilies of the field, the guests at the wedding, and so on. "God must, somehow, become visible and audible to man," declared an audiovisual (A-V) enthusiast. "Is it irreverent to say that Jesus was the ultimate in A-V Aids?"[24]

Rhetoric and Reality I: Instruction

At the same time, Americans admitted that their real-life overseas instruction frequently diverged from their worshipful progressive rhetoric. "Too many teachers . . . still seem content if pupils can recite glibly from memory," complained the Congo's George Carpenter. "We must revolutionize our own inherited ideas of what a school is and ought to be."[25] As in the United States, however, inherited ideas died hard. Teachers at one Congolese mission made children memorize Bible passages in order to advance to the next grade; another school offered a prize to the pupil who could recite the most scriptural verses. Rejecting the advice he had received aboard the *Thomas*, meanwhile, Benjamin Neal forced his Philippine students to memorize hundreds of English words alongside the Spanish translation of each one. In Puerto Rico, Leonard Ayres started off using the object method, but soon changed course. "I have classes which read English quite well, some of them with expression, but they have no idea of what it all *means*," Ayres underlined, in a letter to his sister. "They are quick to *learn* but slow to *think*." Ayres returned to the first page of his textbook and required the class to translate the entire book, word for word.[26]

Like Ayres, who would go on to study "laggards" in urban American schools, some teachers insisted that their students lacked the mental capacity to do anything *other* than memorize. Inadvertently, perhaps, *Life* magazine captured this viewpoint in a remarkable 1947 article about a "modern mission" in the Congo. Whereas earlier Americans came only with a Bible and "a trunk full of Mother Hubbards," *Life* explained, "today's missionaries are experts, especially and carefully trained for their particular job." Yet an interview with teacher Martha Bateman revealed that her own methods were anything but modern, at least in the ways that most American experts defined the term. "Miss Bateman finds that the most difficult part of her work is the limitations (sic) of the native mind, which is understandably undeveloped," *Life* reported. "But she and other mission teachers have found that the natives have an amazing talent for memory work." Similarly, Catholic teachers in the Bahamas claimed that their "small colored folk" lacked "a very high mentality." Yet almost all of the students could recite their catechism in Latin, and that was enough.[27]

Other overseas Americans rejected progressivism by invoking its own doctrine of child-interest: students did not like it, so they would not learn. In Korea, for example, pupils protested whenever Americans asked them to read materials other than the textbook, to draw conclusions from experiments, or to study English without direct translations. Likewise, Grace Bullard's Indian pupils resisted her plea to conduct their own research: " 'You tell us,' the students urged her, " 'and we will learn.' " Bullard stuck to her guns, insisting that her pupils "dig out the truth for themselves." But many teachers surrendered, or at least gave significant ground. In Palestine, for instance, students told Christina Jones that they would learn English more quickly if she drilled them in grammar. So the young Quaker missionary forsook her "modern methods," which would never work unless the children wanted them.[28]

In some ways, ironically, these departures from progressivism reflected its spirit of "experience" as well as of child-interest. According to John Dewey and his acolytes, human beings learned through a constant process of assessment, evaluation, and experimentation. By revising progressive doctrine in light of their new circumstances, then, teachers like Christina Jones were remaining true to a vital part of the Deweyan vision. Only after World War II would a new generation of American teachers call the entire vision into question, asking not simply "what works," but whether Americans had any right to participate in the answer.

Teachers, Students, and Discipline

In 1906, William B. Freer tried to explain why his students in the Philippines liked American teachers more than Spanish or Philippine ones. The answer, Freer said, lay in the Americans' amicable, informal manner. Whereas other teachers held students at a distance, Freer noted, Americans embraced them with open arms. One teacher invited a class to her home, where boys serenaded her with a guitar; others engaged students in sports, especially baseball. Most of all, Freer wrote, Americans regarded their students as *people*—that is, as full human beings, endowed with the same feelings and capacities as adults. "Americans are wont to grant children more consideration, and, in a sense, put them more on a footing of equality than do either the Filipinos themselves or the Spaniards," Freer wrote. As another observer noted, the American teacher was not *only* a teacher. He was also a friend.[29]

From the Philippines and Chile to Iraq and Iran, the image of the teacher-as-friend dominated the published and unpublished accounts by American teachers.[30] It also served to distinguish Americans from other expatriates, who maintained a frostier relationship with their foreign charges. In Syria, where French-language study was required by the state, an American mission-school principal fired a French national for failing to "mix" with students. "She is a clever girl and a good teacher, but outside of her class work we get nothing from her," the principal explained. "She refuses all invitations when the girls are included and avoids all social occasions . . . We do not like these things, naturally." To Americans, it was "natural" for a teacher to supervise dormitories, study halls, and playgrounds, and to accompany students on walks and field trips. But such activities were anathema to the French instructor, who withdrew to her room to smoke cigarettes as soon as her classes ended. When the principal tried to slough her off on another American school, its headmistress balked. "I want teachers who are interested in the school as a whole," the second principal wrote. A third American urged missions to staff their French-language courses by hiring instructors from Switzerland, who were "more congenial and less temperamental than the French."[31]

Other Americans charged that indigenous teachers, like their European counterparts, were cold, stiff, formal, and distant.[32] But they were also violent, brutalizing their students with whips, canes, and sticks and a wide range of ritual humiliations. Philippine teachers positioned miscreants on one knee, with one hand against a wall, and made them remain there for hours at a time; anyone who moved was beaten. Other teachers enlisted children to abuse each other. In one classroom, an appalled American found two student monitors brandishing huge switches. When a child so much as "wiggled" during the class recitation, a monitor would hit him. Another Philippine teacher purposefully chose small boys to whip larger ones. If the thrashing was not "severe enough," one witness recalled, the teacher "would give the little boy a cut with a whip to show him how." To Americans, the problems of teacher formality and brutality went hand in hand. Lacking any other means of communicating with students, local teachers could not control them without recourse to physical punishment.[33]

In the long run, moreover, such methods would not work. Corporal punishment would alienate children even further from the classroom,

Americans said, reinforcing whatever problems had caused their misbehavior in the first place.[34] It also threatened to spark anti-American hostility, particularly in American territories and protectorates. Like many urban school districts in the United States, then, officials in the Philippines, Puerto Rico, Hawaii, and the Virgin Islands all placed strict limits—or outright bans—upon corporal punishment.[35] "The students, being of another race, would think they were being punished because they were not white," wrote a school superintendent in the Philippines, explaining the policy. "We take the attitude that the school work is something to be desired and if any student does not wish to abide by the rules, then he is expelled and another takes his place."[36]

Rhetoric and Reality II: Corporal Punishment

But Americans overseas continued to use corporal punishment and humiliation, just as they did at home. In Hawaii, one teacher flogged a teenage boy with a bamboo stick until his legs were purple; when the boy started crying, the teacher put him in a closet. Other Americans punished students by making them stick out their tongues, which the teachers slapped with a yardstick. Others made the pupils stand for an entire day; still others forced them to eat hot red peppers. Two teachers in a Philippine village whipped children so severely—for choral reading or simply for whispering—that parents protested to school authorities, who promptly transferred the teachers to another town. Parents also complained of teacher abuse in Puerto Rico, where the law barred anyone but a principal from administering corporal punishment. Yet when teachers slapped children on their own accord, a local newspaper charged, they did not even receive a slap on the wrist. Instead, educational officials simply sent out a circular letter reminding teachers that their behavior was illegal.[37]

Even when Americans reported abuse by each other, authorities were loath to take action. In the Hawaiian village of Honokaa, principal James H. Brayton asked school officials to fine an American teacher who had struck a student in the mouth. In reply, superintendent T. H. Gibson reminded Brayton that the law allowed teachers to administer "necessary and reasonable punishment." Brayton fought back, noting that the student's alleged infraction was failure to complete a lesson. "I did not come from Seattle to Honolulu and thence to Honokaa to pamper a notoriously insubordinate and insolent teacher," Brayton thundered. Several months later, however, Gibson assigned *Brayton* to another school, and the offending teacher stayed. In the town of Waiohinu, likewise, teacher Lillian Mesick remained on the job after district supervisor Bertha Taylor reported her for striking a student who refused to put away her dictionary at the appointed time. Mesick replied that the education department required teachers to promote a "reasonable" number of students each year; that it also allowed "reasonable" physical punishment; and that she could never fulfill the first imperative without recourse to the second one. "There must be some way of correcting children," Mesick argued, noting that her school's classes were the largest in the district. "If we cannot use corporal punishment reasonably, what are we to do?" Even more, Mesick claimed, Taylor herself had slapped children on occasion. Every teacher did, just like every parent.[38]

Around the world, indeed, Americans justified corporal punishment in much the same manner as Lillian Mesick: it was necessary to maintain order, and everyone did it. "The only kind of discipline they get at home is cuffs and thumps," explained Presbyterian Ruth Parker, describing her Indian students, "and that seems to be the only way to keep them still enough to teach them anything." Most parents never objected to corporal punishment in school, Parker said; on the contrary, they demanded it. In Assam, mothers greeted Baptist teachers with a single salutation: "Whip them more, Missahib!" In the Bahamas, Catholic missionaries received a similar plea: "Do, Sister, flog dat chile: he's jes' spoiling for want of a flogging."[39] Just as some teachers maintained that nonwhite races could not move beyond rote learning, others claimed that "lesser" peoples required physical discipline. In an angry 1923 letter, for example, Muriel Murray told her mother that students on "the dark continent" were too lazy to function without floggings. The punishments were administered by her husband Albert, who drew a portrait of himself hitting a boy with a bat. He signed the illustration with a jocular but revealing inscription: "Truthfully, ASNichols." The truth was that Africans responded only to physical coercion, no matter what whites in America wished to believe.[40]

For their own part, ironically, black American missionaries often agreed with this assessment. Indeed, they censured *white* missionaries for being too *lenient* with Africans. Whites in Africa reminded Henry

McDowell of transplanted Northern schoolteachers during the Recon-struction era, who would "sympathize and weep" over black students, whereas the "hard colored teachers" gave blacks the discipline they needed. "The natives have a proverb to the effect that 'A native knows a native and is thus harder on him,' " wrote McDowell, an African-American in Portuguese West Africa. "I am afraid it is really true and that it takes colored folks to be hard on colored folks." With the rise of Garveyism and other Pan-African movements, some students invoked racial solidarity in an appeal for more mild treatment from black Amer-ican teachers. By all evidence, their entreaties fell on deaf ears. "Boy this is some sack to hold, especially when one comes out here with this kind of dope—they are the blood of my blood and flesh of my flesh," black instructor Samuel B. Coles told McDowell, mocking Pan-African pleas. "I have layed [sic] all of that rot away. I am hitting them between the eyes." At the Booker Washington Institute in Liberia, African-Americans established student military drills along the lines of Hamp-ton and Tuskegee. Some boys regarded the drills as "a chance to indulge in playfulness," the principal admitted, but "after a bit of posterior per-cussion," they quickly changed their tune.[41]

To be sure, some American teachers refused to employ corporal pun-ishment, even when parents requested it.[42] Others expressed guilt for striking their students, underscoring the gap between American ideals and practice. To Hawaii vice-principal Hubert C. Everly, his scaled sys-tem of corporal punishment—one swat for tardiness, three swats for smoking, and so on—contradicted "progressive ideology." Like their use of rote methods, though, Americans' corporal tactics fit some di-mensions of the ideology rather well. After progressive icon Francis Parker denounced corporal punishment during his visit to Hawaii, for example, Henry Townsend confronted him with another progressive principle: experience. Against his better judgment, Townsend had ac-ceded to a parent's request that he beat a student. After that, the errant pupil became a model one. "Are there not exceptions in exceptional cases?" Townsend asked Parker. Four years later, an African-American missionary in Hawaii discovered that corporal punishment worked in most cases—not just in rare ones. "Today I *learned by experience* that a good spanking followed by a hot dinner is worth ten other punish-ments," Helen James underlined in her diary. It would take a revolution across the Third World before American teachers began to wonder whether their own experiences should matter in the first place.[43]

The Postwar Critique of Rote

In 1982, George Packer graduated from Yale and joined the Peace Corps. Assigned to a school in Togo, Packer overheard an African colleague leading a biology class about human reproduction. "What is the penis?" the teacher asked. "The penis . . . is . . . the reproductive organ . . . of males," a boy responded, tentatively. "No! No!" the teacher shouted. "Who knows? Nobody? The penis is *the reproductive and urinary organ of males which engorges with blood and achieves erection when stimulated!* You had all weekend to learn it. You're going to fail your exams if you go on like this." The teacher repeated the definition three or four times, while forty children frantically copied it into their notebooks. To an appalled George Packer, such methods reflected "a French devotion to abstraction and rote learning"—and, especially, to national examinations—that the Togolese inherited from their former colonial masters. It also contradicted the central educational lessons he had imbibed in the United States: critical thinking, self-motivation, and love of learning.[44]

At first glance, Americans' post–World War II critique of overseas education differed little from the prewar period. When they arrived in the burgeoning schools of newly independent nations, American teachers found instruction based largely upon rote. Students around the world learned multiplication by chanting their times tables; to solve even the simplest problem, they often had to "sing" until they reached the relevant part of the table. In Nigeria, Peace Corps volunteers were amazed to encounter students who had memorized entire Shakespeare plays. Even art was not immune from the insidious rot of rote. In St. Lucia, an American watched a local teacher draw a boat on the blackboard and tell the children to draw one of their own. If a child's boat deviated even slightly from the teacher's, he would erase it and make them start over—even if the child's drawing was better.[45]

But several new features marked the postwar attack on rote. With the defeat of Nazism, and the discrediting of scientific racism, overseas Americans rarely attributed rote instruction to students' mental or physical weaknesses. Instead, Americans blamed the standardized national tests that Third World countries adopted from their old European rulers. To be sure, previous generations of Americans had blasted colonial examination systems for promoting memorization and other "backwards" habits. But the critique reached a crescendo in the 1950s and 1960s, as one independent country after another embraced their colonizers' exams or devised new national tests that were just as rigid as the old ones. Missionaries in Syria and Lebanon condemned local governments for adopting a French-style *Baccalaureat* examination, contrasting the French "art of cramming" with the allegedly "Anglo-Saxon type of education" that prevailed in American schools. In the former British colony of Kenya, meanwhile, members of Teachers for East Africa (TEA) denounced the "English system" of "learning by rote" and "preparing for an all-important end-of-school examination." Whether Anglo-Saxon or not, standardized nationwide tests were clearly colonial in origin—and pernicious in effect.[46]

At the most basic level, national examinations suppressed students' natural powers of reason. "These kids do not know how to think," declared a Nigeria Peace Corps volunteer, in a typical statement, "and they'll never learn so long as everything that happens in the classroom must be directed towards passing an examination." Even worse, perhaps, the tests soured children on future education by setting them up for failure. Around the globe, schools placed strict caps on the number of students they allowed into the national examinations; among the students who did take the test, meanwhile, severe grading "curves" guaranteed that the vast majority would not succeed. At George Packer's school in Togo, only three of seventy-five students passed the national high school entrance test. In the Bahamas, where students took England's Cambridge Certificate Examination, American nuns complained that schools routinely gave pupils grades of 35 or 40, but required an 88 or 90 average to sit for the test. If students made it to the exam, more than two-thirds failed. At Sister Constance Mary's school, just four pupils were permitted to take the test—and only two of them passed. "I think these children as a group are above average," Sister Constance wrote, condemning the Cambridge system. As in Garrison Keillor's Lake Wobegon, American teachers imagined a world where *every* child was "above average." But national tests reminded them that the real world—the world beyond America—did not see it that way.[47]

Reform and Resistance

Even as they condemned national examinations for spawning rote instruction, Americans resolved to introduce different types of methods. To change the testing system, the argument went, you needed a critical mass of student dissidents; but to generate dissidents, you needed new teaching practices. "I won't write their notes on the blackboard so they can simply copy down the words and memorize them," a TEA teacher told a visitor in 1961. "I intend to get them to *think* for themselves." In Ghana, Americans taught math by making students measure their bodies and classrooms; in Nigeria, science teachers gave them different substances so they could induce the laws of chemistry; and in Madagascar, a nun required her African history students to conduct interviews of their families.[48] Like their forebears in the Philippines, Americans taught English via objects and simulations rather than through translation.[49] They also led discussions about divisive topics, including *National Geographic* magazine—a source of controversy in Africa—and gender relations. "In many ways the African classroom was for me a reverse of my American classroom," recalled a Mennonite teacher. Back home, he noted, "students often attempted to shift the class discussion off the poem or short story under consideration and on to other topics such as politics, fads, latest rock music, drugs, the whole bit about the generation gap." But in Africa, he continued, "it was I as a teacher who tried to pry the students from the narrow rut of the syllabi to let their minds follow instinctive curiosity."[50]

This goal was elusive, as the Mennonite quickly learned. "It's not on the syllabus!" his students protested, when he introduced new material. "Will this be asked on the examination?" Perhaps not, their teacher responded. "I'm trying to get you to think," he told them. "I'm not interested in pouring into your minds a jumble of facts for you to spin off later." But African students *were* interested in mastering facts, which held the key to passing their tests and to obtaining a decent job. The more that Americans pressed for "discussion" and "critical thinking," then, the more that Africans pressed back. "Give us notes!" Ethiopians urged one American teacher. "How can we learn? We have nothing to memorize," they pressed another. Other African students responded with sulks and silence, rejecting American appeals for student participation.[51] Still others voted with their feet. In at least three African countries, students went on strike to protest American methods. Likewise, pupils in Nepal boycotted class until American teachers promised to drill the expected examination questions.[52]

In the American view, students' zeal for rote reflected their laziness as well as their obsession with examinations: the pupils preferred spoonfeeding by the teacher to amassing and assessing information on their

own.[53] But the children often regarded *Americans* as lazy, concluding
that teachers designed student activities as a way to avoid working
themselves.[54] Sometimes, the children were right. In Iran, for example,
Presbyterian missionary Ruth Irwin admitted that she relied upon student discussions when she was not prepared to instruct her history
course. "I went to class today without even opening my book and what
I know about history isn't much," Irwin told her daughter. "Fortunately
my girls want pointers on how to act with the boys, how to raise children, what to do when their parents won't let them go out." So Irwin
indulged them, noting that other Americans did the same. "When a
teacher hasn't studied her lesson," Irwin wrote, "she fills the time
with lessons on conduct much to the girls [sic] joy and really they get
more out of it than history!" As its foreign critics correctly sensed, the
American doctrine of "child interest" could easily become a cover for
teacher sloth.[55]

At the same time, Americans realized, it could also justify capitulation
to rote methods. Despite their paeans to student interest, after all,
Americans had largely *failed* to interest students in progressive-style instruction. As a Peace Corps volunteer in Tanzania acknowledged, "any
teacher who diverts from fact giving is doomed not only to class room
apathy but almost complete lack of attention." Indeed, an Ethiopia volunteer added, the only way to spread the allegedly universal gospel of
progressive education—especially its doctrine of "discussion"—was to
suspend discussion about it. At first, Richard Lipez wrote, he gave his
students "patient explanations" whenever they complained about new
methods. But by the end of his first year, Lipez noted, "the reply was
more often, 'Sit down and shut up!' "[56] Elsewhere, though, Americans
refrained from this decidedly unprogressive defense of progressive education. Rather than imposing techniques that their hosts did not want,
they began to ask whether the "American Method" was appropriate for
other cultures, and whether it was appropriate for Americans to interfere with them.

From Pragmatism to Culture

In 1967, a dejected Peace Corps official wrote a scathing report on
American high school teachers in Nigeria. The teachers had arrived
two years earlier full of hope and idealism, aiming to serve as "change

agents" in Africa. Over time, however, they had changed their own views. All of the Americans seemed aware of the futility of secondary schools in Nigeria, which prepared students for irrelevant examinations and nonexistent jobs. But few of the teachers believed they could do anything about it. "I was surprised at their apparent passivity," the Peace Corps official wrote. "Our Volunteers are having difficulty teaching Nigerians how to think for themselves because the Volunteers do not think for themselves."[57]

Actually, the volunteers thought a great deal. In their letters and memoirs, Americans wrestled with the dilemmas of accommodating to an educational system that they often detested. But on one level, at least, the Peace Corps official was correct: Americans *did* change their practices, and, sometimes, their beliefs, to suit their new environment. In Turkey and Nepal, teachers abandoned the "object method" of English instruction in favor of direct translation; in Tanzania, they filled up blackboards with notes for students to copy; and in Guinea-Bissau, one American confessed, she made her pupils "repeat sentences in unison as if they were Berlitz parrots."[58] To be sure, some teachers refused to make any concessions to host traditions; others tried to combine their own techniques with local ones, introducing "side dishes," as one TEA teacher wrote, without altering the main course.[59] Overall, though, Americans adopted the educational goals and methods that they encountered overseas. "Their main work-related problem was the question of whether to teach a student to think, or to pass exams," wrote a second Peace Corps official in Nigeria, describing another group of teachers. "Most struggled with the problem for a few months and finally went with the system."[60]

Like teachers in earlier eras, post–World War II Americans often cited pragmatic reasons for this decision. Some teachers found that progressive-type tactics spawned chaos in the classroom, where students interpreted their pleas for participation as a license for mischief.[61] Conceding that test preparation spawned poor teaching, others contended that students *wanted* such instruction—and would refuse to learn any other way. "We have an obligation to help the kids get through the examinations," a Nigeria teacher contended. "Whatever we may think about this method of education we are obliged to help the kid keep from screwing up his own life and that is exactly what will happen if he fails." Moreover, any deviation from the testing script would afflict

children with undue anxiety. In Japan, where the college-entrance examination was especially competitive, a Jesuit teacher scoffed when
an interviewer asked how Americans might lessen students' acute test-
related stress. "Success in the entrance exams—there is no other," the
priest tartly replied. In a society infatuated with test scores, the only
way to feel better about a test was to improve your score.[62]

At the same time, other Americans invoked a new "culturalist" defense for adopting local practices. Rote instruction was not merely effective or useful, as previous generations of teachers had found, it
was also culturally appropriate, because it dovetailed with indigenous
values. By corollary, of course, American progressive education was culturally *in*appropriate: whether it "worked" or not, it violated the traditions and mores of other peoples. "Basically and fundamentally, we are
skeptical of current attempts to impose western educational methods
upon a non-receptive culture," wrote two members of the first Peace
Corps teaching group in Ethiopia. The key verb was "impose," which
recurred throughout teachers' postwar reports and reminisces. To the
Peace Corps teachers, Ethiopian students lived in a "pre-Biblical" and
"Solomon-Sheba" society that contrasted in every conceivable way
from the Americans' own culture. "Their perceptions are different from
western perceptions; right or wrong, they're different," the teachers
declared. So it was simply wrong—not just futile, but immoral—for
Americans to press different ideas upon them.[63]

Indeed, it was "ethnocentric." A close rhetorical cousin of "impose,"
this adjective referred to the unconscious—and unjustified—assump-
tion that American culture was exceptional or superior. Ironically, many
self-avowed progressive educators in twentieth-century America saw
their project as a universalist antidote to cultural parochialism and
ethnocentricity. To overseas American critics, however, progressive education was itself ethnocentric, precisely *because* of its claim to universalism. In East Africa, TEA teachers charged that British expatriate
headmasters perpetuated a "decadent educational system" full of test
preparation, rote methods, and overly strict discipline. Yet the American teachers "were just as ethnocentric as the headmasters," wrote one
TEA evaluator, "in expecting that their concepts of good teaching
were truly universal." Likewise, a Quaker missionary in Japan worried
that her own teaching style—especially her emphasis on discussion—
might trample on traditional Japanese reticence. So she adopted local

methods, in deference to local culture. "I suspect that many things we as Americans might judge as being less than satisfactory would not be proper in an American school, but are quite desirable in a Japanese setting," she wrote.[64]

Beneath these concerns lay a contrite, "protectionist" concept of culture: since local traditions and mores were under assault from Western influence, the West needed to guard them. Strongly linked to the discipline of anthropology, the concept was anathema to Peace Corps officials, who saw overseas American teachers as "change agents." So the agency also avoided hiring anthropologists during its early years, especially to direct its education programs. "There is . . . a certain veiled hostility between the anthropologist and the educationist," observed Lawrence W. Howard, a Peace Corps staffer in the Philippines. Howard went on to quote the prominent anthropologist Margaret Mead, who parsed this tension in her characteristically wry style. "I imagine that if a referendum were to be taken of all living anthropologists on the question, 'Do you, or do you not approve of modern education in the territory where you have worked?' the results would be a 90 to 95 percent negative answer," Mead wrote. "Among the 5 to 10 percent positive answers would presumably be those of the nationals of Africa and the Pacific and other territories who, through a modern education, have arrived at being an anthropologist."[65]

As the experience of overseas teachers demonstrates, these "anthropological" sentiments extended far beyond the academy. Indeed, the more that teachers worried about other peoples' cultures, the less confidence they would display about their own educational efforts. To many teachers, the entire progressive project—even its outward cosmopolitanism—became tainted with American arrogance. It mattered little that people in other countries sometimes sought after American-style education, as Mead correctly surmised. But when they resisted, teachers were quick to blame American ethnocentricity. In her effort to promote "critical thinking" in Ethiopia, one Peace Corps volunteer confessed, she never paused to consider whether dialogue and discussion were superior to memorization; she simply presumed it. "In this my fault lay," she recalled. "I thought about myself [and] not what the boys needed, or what was necessary for them." Across the globe, the culture concept made teachers wonder if their own educational method was right, and if *they* owned any right to promote it beyond American shores.[66]

The Teacher-as-Friend: Post–World War II Dilemmas

Like their predecessors, post–World War II American teachers often embraced a friendly, informal ideal of teacher–student relations. "The children feel free to talk and discuss anything with me," wrote a deaf educator in the Virgin Islands, in a typical passage. "They . . . have accepted me as their teacher, counselor, and friend." To Kathryn Taylor, a Quaker missionary in Japan, friendships with her pupils held the key to improving her pedagogy. When students proved too reticent to speak in her English class; Taylor hosted them for tea; they then became more comfortable in her presence, and more likely to talk. Peace Corps volunteers in Malaysia boasted that they were "making friends with their students" via scout troops and other extracurricular activities, which in turn helped promote a relaxed tone in the classroom. For other Americans, meanwhile, teacher–student camaraderie constituted an end in itself. Because she lacked any training or experience in foreign language instruction, missionary Margaret Thomson admitted that her Korean students had learned very little English from her. But she had become friends with a few of them—and that was enough. "To me the most valuable part of teaching has always been the personal relationships between students and teacher," Thomson wrote.[67]

Yet several new themes marked the drive for teacher–student friendship after World War II. Especially in the 1960s, it often reflected a wider critique of hierarchy and control in schools around the world, including in the United States. Indeed, some Americans tried to *avoid* school-based teaching because they feared its allegedly inherent authoritarianism. "Like many of our counterparts in other volunteer organizations, we had hoped to escape the constraints of highly structured, rationalized society, which schools necessarily impose," wrote two members of Volunteer Teachers for Africa (VTA), the Harvard student project. Another VTA applicant requested work anywhere *except* a school setting, so he could remain "free from restrictive, staid tradition and clearly defined hierarchies." In a more optimistic vein, other teachers took note of the growing trend toward "open" and "democratic" schools in America. Citing recent books by John Holt and Charles Silberman, a Quaker applicant to Japan resolved to export their emphasis on "informal classrooms" when she went abroad. "There are excellent teachers in the traditional methods," she conceded, "but it seems much of the joy and discovery of learning has been lost in restrictive rules and lack of flexibility."[68]

But Quaker school veterans proved less than friendly to this appeal, warning that the friendship ideal simply would not work in Japan. "I feel it is only fair to point out to you that the Friends School in Tokyo is fairly traditional in its outlook and operation," wrote Jane Rittenhouse, a former teacher at the school. "If a 'Progressive School' is the only kind of school where you see yourself teaching, then perhaps this is not the place for you to consider." Around the globe, indeed, students met American appeals for friendship with a mix of baffled discomfort, passive resistance, and outright hostility. "We are considered as foreigners rather than as persons [students] could confide in and turn to in the solving of their problems," complained Catholic nuns in the Marshall Islands. "Rather, they are always reticent and withdrawn, giving only answers that they think would please." In the Philippines, students accepted a teacher's invitation to lunch, but backed out right before the date. "They said they felt ashamed to eat with me," Peace Corps volunteer Marjorie Pfankuch wrote her parents, dejectedly. "This cultural business is much more than I realized."[69]

To other observers, meanwhile, "cultural business"—that is, differences in culture—often rendered American efforts offensive as well as ineffective. Even as some teachers invoked progressive education in pleas for informal teacher–student relations, others cited cultural reasons to challenge these same appeals. "I want very much to help dissolve the mutual distrust between students and teachers . . . but approach this with reservations and a good bit of awe in the face of Japanese culture," wrote Quaker Kathryn Taylor, questioning her own efforts to promote classroom informality. "Culture and tradition are far more a living organism here than we can fully comprehend as Americans, and we will have [to] avoid damaging delicate tissues." To Ethiopia Peace Corps teacher Richard Lipez, meanwhile, Americans adopted informal teacher–student relations—like progressive instruction methods—to "cover up" for their weak knowledge of school subjects. But the very impulse to befriend students reflected an even worse ignorance of African culture. "A persistent myth in modern America prescribes informality as a prerequisite for creativity," Lipez wrote. "This, coupled with Volunteers' fears of seeming to lord it over colored people, leads most PCVs into a chummy, un-Ethiopian relationship to students and a resulting loss of discipline." Even on the question of discipline, indeed, culture would come to trump progressivism in the practice—if not the rhetoric—of many American teachers.[70]

Discipline and Culture

To be sure, post–World War II American teachers often condemned the brutal and humiliating disciplinary tactics that they witnessed around the world. Nigerian teachers slapped students across the face, or made them kneel with their hands behind their backs in front of the class; Somali teachers paddled children before the entire student body, reminding Americans of fraternity initiations back home; and Liberians smacked children with rulers for every word they misspelled, leveling one strike for each letter in the word. To a dismayed Peace Corps volunteer in Ethiopia, such practices reflected the "deference-arrogance syndrome" that was endemic to Africans, while to a Catholic missionary in Mexico, corporal punishment contravened the laws of "child psychology." Sierra Leone teacher Jim Jackson refused to attend public canings of students or to salute the national flag at his school, claiming that "a country that caned children had not yet earned [his] respect." His principal reported him to the prime minister and to the American ambassador, who engineered Jackson's transfer to another institution. In protest, his students staged a hunger strike and burned down a school building.[71]

Such reactions were rare, however. As in the pre–World War II period, students more often defended local disciplinary methods against "soft" American ones. "Although the system of schooling in the olden days was not altogether good," wrote one Ghanaian pupil, in an essay about colonial education, "it had one good aspect . . . and that is caning." African teachers agreed, insisting that students would respond to little else. "Georges, you have an American idea about punishment," a Togolese principal told George Packer. "With your American students the soft method will work. But Africans are not self-disciplined . . . For the African, you need a stick (*Pour l'africain, il faut le baton*)." For two years, Packer heard this phrase so often that he facetiously suggested it as the motto of his school. "Sometimes the sentence came with a hint of sorrow, as if we were talking about a congenital ailment like sickle-cell anemia," Packer remembered. "Or else with scientific detachment, as an ethnography lesson. Or with a note of triumph: '*You* don't understand Africans; *we* do.' " As one teacher told Packer, colonial rulers had taught Togolese to hit their students, and now a new generation of *yovos* (whites) had come to tell them the opposite.[72]

For Americans imbued with the gospel of culture—and with a corresponding aversion to "colonialism"—the last argument was often a winning one. Depictions of Africans as inherently violent or authoritarian could be dismissed out of hand, as vestiges of a long-discredited scientific racism. But if harsh discipline was a cultural (or "ethnographic") trait, who was to say which culture was better? And were not *Americans* indulging in colonialism—of a cultural kind—if they presumed their own superiority? Just as they did for rote instruction, then, teachers often employed the same disciplinary practices they denounced—and constructed a new "culturalist" defense of them. "I consider quite seriously measures that are totally antithetical to innovative and progressive education and from which a few months ago I would have recoiled in horror," wrote Peace Corps volunteer Randall Barton from the Marshall Islands. "Like, what's wrong with a hickory stick??!!" After all, Barton wrote, her students came to class with an "entirely different frame of reference" from American ones. So they needed an "entirely different" disciplinary style as well.[73]

Even as Americans indicted corporal punishment as "undemocratic" or inefficient at home, they often indulged in it abroad. In Peru, Dennis Shaw put a list of improper student activities on the blackboard: copying from each other, talking out of turn, and so on. Each time a student violated part of this "Shavian law," he or she received a block of wood; and at the end of the day, whoever held the block would receive a stiff paddling. "As a result, afternoon sessions are very well behaved," Shaw wrote, "and I've discovered it does not hurt me more than it hurts them." Other teachers experienced guilt and ambivalence when they first struck children, but the feeling tended to dissipate with time. Believing that corporal punishment was "the worst thing that a teacher could do," Nepal Peace Corps teacher Phil Deutschle was despondent after slapping a boy. Once he had hit a few more students, though, he realized that "a well-timed slap could be a form of communication"; it showed children that he was "serious" about his job. Likewise, a volunteer in Africa went through "a dark night of the soul" before he hit his first pupil. After he did so, however, his students became more attentive and his Peace Corps evaluations rose from "adequate" to "excellent." Indeed, his supervisor wrote, he became "one of the best volunteers in the country."[74]

To be sure, overseas American teachers differed sharply on the issue. When Liberia's first Peace Corps group held its final conference in 1964, the most debated question was "whether 'to beat or not to beat,' " as one participant noted. The group split down the middle. So did a Nigeria end-of-service conference the following year, to the outrage of Peace Corps officials at the meeting. "The kids expect you to slap them down once in awhile," one volunteer explained, defending corporal punishment, "and if you don't they think you are weak and take further advantage of you." Teachers in Turkey cited similar concerns at their own completion-of-service conference the year after that, chaired by future historian Hugh Davis Graham. If volunteers hit students, Graham reported, "they would be succumbing to and acquiescing in an evil practice that struck them as a relic and symbol of the old authoritarian order." But if they did not, "chaos would reign in the classroom." So "most men resorted to hitting," Graham wrote, while most female volunteers engaged in "rude and demeaning shouting matches with unruly students"—or sent them to "some strapping Turkish colleague" for a "proper mauling."[75]

To Guinea-Bissau teacher Roz Wollmering, however, such utilitarian concerns were secondary to cultural ones. When she first came to Africa, Wollmering recalled, she denounced local teachers for expelling some students and threatening to whip others. Indeed, she told her students, such tactics reflected a "poisonous pedagogy." But it was *their* pedagogy, she later wrote, and she had no business interfering with it. " 'That's the right of elders in our culture,' " she approvingly quoted her students, defending the school's discipline system, " 'and we're taught in the bush to live by the established rules.' " For post–World War II American teachers, it often seemed, the only hard-and-fast rule was the ban on judging *other* teachers—or other cultures—by America's own standards.[76]

‹ AS POST–WORLD WAR II American teachers would discover, a deep tension marked their twin objectives of critical thinking and cultural tolerance. From the start of the last century, Americans went overseas to challenge rote and to foster reason in the schools of the world.

At times, they succeeded; more often, they assimilated to local norms. But in the post–World War II period, the promulgation of progressivism came into conflict with the values of cultural tolerance, equality, and democracy. If the American ideal was to "celebrate difference" and to eschew "dogma," why, exactly, *should* Americans promote their own dogmas of critical thinking, "active learning," and the like? Should they not tolerate—or even celebrate—peoples and cultures with different educational traditions and techniques?

One popular answer lay in the theory of culturally inscribed "learning styles," which argued that "active learning" was itself indigenous—not foreign—to non-Western peoples. " 'The Westerner will tend to be cerebral, whereas the African gives great play to feelings,' " wrote a pair of American missionaries in 1989, quoting the South African bishop and antiapartheid activist Desmond Tutu. " 'The Westerner emphasizes the individual person, whereas the African will give an important place to the community.' " Hence Africans learned better from group discussion and from hands-on experience than from lectures and note-taking, the missionaries claimed. Writing about India, a second missionary griped that British colonists had imposed a "formal" and "alien" learning style upon his students. "I wanted to teach through their mother culture," the missionary wrote, "rather than their second culture." Finally, on his return from a 1993 trip to South America, a third missionary condemned earlier North American attempts to spread sterile, rote teaching methods rather than "culturally relevant" ones. Like Africans and Asians, it seemed, Latinos learned better from group activities and projects than from drill, chalk, and talk.[77]

Of course, this analysis ignored the century-long history of North American teachers who had *challenged* rote methods in Third World schools. Even more, it ignored the many ways that local students, teachers, and parents had resisted these initiatives. Whatever its historical roots, the system of rote had become integrated into the lives and cultures of millions of people around the globe. By calling that system part of their "second" culture rather than their "mother" one, Americans anointed themselves the paternal arbiters of what was truly "native" to the natives. One hundred years earlier, some teachers had argued that Third World peoples lacked the inherent capabilities to learn from progressive-style methods. The theory of learning styles reversed this formulation, making the methods indigenous to these same peoples.

Of course, Americans who embraced overseas rote methods risked their own form of cultural fetishism: local cultures fostered rote, and that was that. When taken to its extreme, moreover, the cultural defense of Third World practices made it nearly impossible to promote the other goal that Americans held dear: critical thinking. Looking back on his service in Africa, TEA teacher Gene Child expressed remorse for pressing "American teaching methods" on his Kenyan students. He wanted them to probe the meanings behind their texts; but they wanted disconnected bits of information—"just the facts"—to pass their examinations. Indeed, Child concluded, his own efforts in Africa mirrored the most recent American military campaign in the Middle East. "It strikes me that what we were trying to do for education in Kenya ... was very similar to what the US is trying to do today in Iraq: impose an American way on them," Child wrote in 2004, a year after Operation Iraqi Freedom began. "It was education then, Western Political Fundamentalism now."[78]

But how could students critique the war in Iraq—or, indeed, "Western Political Fundamentalism"—*without* the so-called American techniques that Child now regrets, especially deliberation and discussion? Insofar as some peoples in some cultures resist critical thinking in their schools, Americans might well have to choose which value *they* wish to celebrate: culture *or* critique. Or they could reframe culture as a language or a toolkit—not as a "living organism," to quote Japan missionary Kathryn Taylor—and resolve to give all of their students the critical capacities they will need to understand their own cultures, not to mention the cultures of others. In a rapidly globalizing world, the preservation of culture might require precisely the analytic skills that we once feared would erode it.

2

The American Curriculum

"PRACTICAL" EDUCATION AND THE DILEMMAS OF VOCATIONALISM

In 1909, the American Industrial Mission of British East Africa held a ceremony to lay the cornerstone of a new school building. The speaker for the event was none other than Theodore Roosevelt, who had come to Africa on a big-game hunting expedition after leaving the White House. Roosevelt began with a few jokes, cautioning his hosts that the "native" might elude their pursuit—just like lions and tigers sometimes evaded him. "Missionaries have been working in England and America for hundreds of years and all the savages are not converted; not even in the U.S. Senate," Roosevelt quipped. In a more serious vein, he went on to praise the mission's noble cause. "It is the duty of all white men who occupy positions in the tropics, whether it is in the Philippines or British East Africa or any place else, to try to help the backward race," Roosevelt asserted. Africans needed more than just conversion to Christianity or the ability to read, he continued. Rather, they needed an "education for life"—and, especially, for labor. "I believe that the greatest good that can be done to the native must come thru teaching the native to work," Roosevelt began:

and I can extend that suggestion from the native to ourselves. I believe that we are on the eve of seeing a great change in the educational system throughout the world. All of us have been taught to believe that education consists in what you find inside the covers of

a book . . . *That* education had tended to educate the boy away
from the farm and the shop [when] what we need is that which will
educate him *for* the farm and the shop. That must come with us
and so it must come with the native.[1]

Six decades later, and on the other side of the continent, another
American condemned his own country for promoting precisely the type
of "bookish" education that Roosevelt bemoaned. Peace Corps evaluator David Hapgood took aim at English instruction, the most common
volunteer assignment in seven West African nations. Only two or three
out of every 100 African pupils would find that English "serves a useful
purpose" in their work or lives, Hapgood wrote. At least three-quarters
of the students dropped out of school before they completed it, he
noted, while those who did graduate received clerical jobs that rarely
required English. Americans should teach practical skills like agriculture and engineering, Hapgood wrote, even if host nations demanded
English. " 'The African governments asked for English teachers' is
true enough," Hapgood noted, "but this does not relieve Peace Corps
of passing judgment on the request." Africa deserved better, whether
Africans knew it or not.[2]

At first glance, these passages suggest a striking continuity in Americans' twentieth-century visions of schooling. At home as well as abroad,
spokespeople demanded a "practical" curriculum that more closely reflected students' day-to-day realities and probable destinies. Two years
before his Africa trip, for example, Roosevelt had sounded a similar
theme in his own State of the Union address: "Our school system is
gravely defective in so far as it puts a premium upon mere literacy training and tends therefore to train the boy away from the farm and the
workshop," Roosevelt told Congress.[3] During the next fifty years, educators would expand the American curriculum with a vast array of
nonacademic courses, from health and physical education to handicrafts
and auto repair.[4] They also linked traditional classes like English and
math to students' future job prospects, infusing the entire school sched-
ule with an applied, "vocational" spirit.[5] Meanwhile, thousands of American teachers tried to transport this vision around the world. Like
America's new public school system in the Philippines, Roosevelt hoped,
the American Industrial Mission would educate Africans for their actual
lot in life. So should Peace Corps volunteers, David Hapgood urged.

Education must prepare students for future vocations; most African vocations did not require English, so African students need not learn it.
Better to teach them technical skills that they *did* need.

But the tone, and especially the reception, of both comments also reflected crucial differences between the two speakers and their respective
eras. Roosevelt employed an explicitly racial idiom, comparing British
settlers in Kenya to white frontiersmen in the American West—and
eliciting roars of applause from the all-white English and American
teachers in his audience. "I forgot for a moment that I was not a part of
you," jibed Roosevelt, who had authored a famous history of the Western frontier. "You are, Mr. Roosevelt, you are a part of us!" the crowd
responded, not missing a beat. Roosevelt also spoke on the cusp of an
expected worldwide revolution in education, confident that the changes
underway in America would soon encircle the globe. By the 1960s,
though, this confidence had disappeared. There *was* a global revolution
occurring in education, Hapgood acknowledged, but its traditional academic focus threatened to retard—not to promote—Third World
progress. "We seem to believe that any kind of schooling is good,"
Hapgood lamented. Unless the Peace Corps shifted course, he warned,
it would educate a generation of postal clerks who could all read John
F. Kennedy's *Profiles in Courage* during their lunch hour—if they got
jobs at all.[6]

Hapgood's last comment sparked the ire of Peace Corps teachers in
the field, marking the most important difference between these volunteers and their colonial forebears. In several exchanges published in the
agency's newsletter, where Hapgood's comments first appeared, teachers admitted that most of their students would not need English in their
work. Yet they also condemned Hapgood's blithe dismissal of African
concerns, which reflected American arrogance in its extreme. "No one
really knows how development takes place," one Nigeria volunteer
wrote. "Admitting our paucity of knowledge, the wisest course would
be to accept the evaluation of the host country." Indeed, another Peace
Corps writer declared, the effort to "impose" American educational
ideas conjured the worst aspects of America's own racial past. "These
were the arguments made 50 years ago for teaching only vocational subjects to American Negroes," he noted. In an era of civil rights at home
and decolonization abroad, Theodore Roosevelt's campaign to uplift
the "backward race" had become a shameful international albatross. *Any*

critique of African educational policy risked a replay of this ugly history, even when the critique urged Africans to move in a less American or "Western" direction.[7]

Whereas teachers in Roosevelt's time rode roughshod over the global demand for so-called "bookish" education, a later generation often yielded to it. The only constant was the demand itself. From Chile and Colombia to China and India, people pleaded with American teachers to provide instruction in academic disciplines—especially math, science, and English—rather than the vocational subjects that the teachers often favored. Indeed, students embraced book-centered learning for expressly vocational reasons: as in the United States, it promised high-status, white-collar opportunities.[8] Americans had more success promoting sports and health classes, two nonacademic subjects that bore less direct connection to future job prospects. But they could never wean their students from the gospel of education, which now framed all schooling as preparation for an office job. "Education for life" had come to rule the Earth, in short, but the urban, bureaucratic life that it imagined ran counter to Americans' own agricultural and industrial vision. The world wanted to wear a white collar, whether Americans liked it or not.

Vocationalizing the Globe

In 1912, John D. DeHuff reviewed America's educational achievements during its decade-long occupation of the Philippines. The first American teachers brought with them the "academic" focus that still characterized most education in the United States, DeHuff recalled. As superintendent of schools in Manila, however, he had helped reorient Philippine schools toward the "daily life-needs" of the Filipinos themselves. Industrial and trade schools already dotted the archipelago, teaching skills that students would actually use. Even more, DeHuff emphasized, *every* student—in every type of school—took some kind of vocational course. At the elementary level, children received an hour or more of industrial training each day. Boys in the intermediate grades had to take gardening and woodworking, while girls were required to study "household arts." By 1919, another official would boast, nearly two-thirds of all Philippine pupils were taking one or more "industrial" classes. Indeed, he added, no American state could rival the Philippines' record in the arena of vocational education.[9]

He was right. Despite the millennial rhetoric that accompanied new vocational courses in the United States, students did not flock to them. Even after the passage of the 1917 Smith-Hughes Act, which provided federal aid to such programs, so-called industrial classes never rose to more than one-seventh of the total course enrollment in American high schools; as a fraction of the total, meanwhile, enrollment in agricultural courses actually dipped.[10] Presiding over far more centralized school systems, American colonial officials could implement vocational instruction on a scale that reformers back home could only imagine. In 1904, officials in Puerto Rico dedicated the island's first industrial school; the year after that, they opened its first agricultural school. Students at both institutions provided a prearranged amount of labor each day, in exchange for room and board. Under the "Cooperative Plan" in Hawaii, meanwhile, students alternated every two weeks between schools and job sites—especially sugar plantations—where they could "learn by doing," as one enthusiast wrote. Virgin Islands educators overhauled the curriculum in the 1930s, emphasizing mechanical arts for boys and home economics for girls. "We should cut loose entirely from the U.S. standards," wrote the director of schools. "Nearly every course of study is planned to fit pupils for college. Let us begin our curriculum with entire disregard for college."[11]

The most ambitious reform occurred in Haiti, where American officials unveiled a plan to replace forty "classical" or traditional schools with twelve agricultural and industrial ones. Lest these new institutions fall prey to the alleged sloth and corruption of other Haitian schools, the Americans also established a separate agency—the "Service Technique"—to administer them. Its first director was George F. Freeman, former chief of cotton breeding at the Texas Agricultural Experiment Agency. Like other officials from the American South, Freeman made no secret of his disdain for "Negro" teachers, either in the United States or in Haiti itself. So he traveled home each year to recruit white Americans, who managed his departments of printing, woodworking, and other vocational subjects. By 1929, forty Americans directed 436 Haitian teachers in the Service Technique. Haitian instructors in the new system received twice the pay of their counterparts in the remaining "classical" schools, while the Americans earned five or ten times the salary of the their local charges. Some Americans made as much as $5,000 per year, a far higher sum than they had ever earned back home.[12]

Finally, around the world American missionaries organized and staffed a broad array of industrial and agricultural schools. By 1910, Protestant missions operated twenty-nine such institutions in India alone. Most of the students came from untouchable castes, who had the greatest incentive to forsake Hinduism for Christianity—and the greatest need for paid labor. Students took a mix of academic and vocational classes, often working in the field or shop to defray their tuition. Industrial schools had much less luck luring wealthier students, who saw manual training as "something quite distinct and apart from all subject matter," as one missionary complained. Even more, he lamented, they viewed hand labor as beneath their own dignity. Missionaries looked enviously at the American experiment in the Philippines, where all students—not just disadvantaged ones—were compelled to work. As best they could, a Syria principal wrote, mission schools should try to emulate this example. "Every advanced educator admits today that the training of the hand should accompany that of the mind and heart," the principal declared. He went on to quote Samuel Armstrong, founder of the famed Hampton Institute: "Manual labor becomes a stepping-stone, a ladder of education to all higher things; to success, manhood, and character."[13]

Hampton, Tuskegee, and the World

Other Americans quoted Armstrong's best-known student, Booker T. Washington, whose Tuskegee Institute echoed Hampton's vocational emphasis. For American teachers around the world, Hampton and Tuskegee became the gold standard of "practical" education. At both institutions, the argument went, a "backwards race" learned skills, thrift, and especially hard work. American teachers would transport the same values around the globe, drawing inspiration from Armstrong and Washington. Teachers in Hawaii proudly noted that Armstrong grew up on the islands, where a mission school supposedly provided the prototype for Hampton; Armstrong's portrait hung in the principal's office in a Macedonia industrial institute, which named its carpentry shop the "Hampton Room"; and a Baptist missionary in the Philippines invoked Armstrong's legacy in a fundraising appeal, stressing that his own school's work was "comparable to that which is being done at Hampton, Virginia for the Negroes."[14] Americans in Africa more commonly invoked Booker Washington, a symbol of black achievement—not of black accommodation—across the continent.[15] One Congo missionary envisioned "a lot of little Tuskegees" sprouting throughout the colony, each staffed primarily by black teachers, just like Tuskegee was.[16]

But the best-known "Tuskegee-in-Africa" had a white principal. Begun in 1929 with a grant from the Phelps-Stokes Fund, the aptly named Booker Washington Institute was directed by James L. Sibley, a Georgia educator and adviser to Liberian president C. D. B. King. King had visited Tuskegee in the late 1920s, resolving to construct a similar institution in his own country. King hired Robert Robinson Taylor, the first black graduate of the Massachusetts Institute of Technology, to design the campus. He also appointed Sibley, who died of malaria just after the school opened. A series of white principals followed, managing a staff made of up largely of Africans and African-Americans, including several Hampton and Tuskegee alumni. Officials in the Virgin Islands also hired black Hampton graduates to direct their industrial courses, noting privately that such teachers would be cheaper than graduates from Teachers College and other schools. Finally, in Hawaii, Hampton alumna Helen James spread the "Armstrong Gospel" at a remote mission. James subscribed to the *Southern Workman,* Hampton's periodical on industrial education, which she pored over as soon as it came. "I am trying to work out the Hampton thought of training Heart, Head, and Hand," James wrote, in an appeal for books. She taught sewing, laundry, and five academic classes each day—without a single reference book. The nearest library was in Honolulu, 172 miles away.[17]

The white principal of James' school traveled 8,000 miles to see Hampton on her own, a common sojourn for American educators around the globe. The first director of schools in the Philippines, Fred W. Atkinson, visited Hampton to observe "its method of dealing with the backwards races," as the *Southern Workman* reported in 1900. Atkinson also visited Tuskegee and the Carlisle School, an institute for Native Americans modeled after Hampton. The director of education in the Virgin Islands visited Hampton, arranging for its famous singing group, the Hampton Quartet, to tour his own schools. Among missionary teachers, meanwhile, a trip to Hampton or Tuskegee became a routine feature of furloughs in the United States. Presbyterian teachers paid special attention to Hampton, especially after its longtime professor George Scott became an assistant secretary at the denominational

mission board. Visitors tripped over each other in their praise of the
institute, each vowing to promote its principles overseas. To a Korea
missionary, Hampton was "the real right thing in Industrial Education"; to a teacher in Iran, it was "a wonderful laboratory of educational
methods"; and to George Scott, summarizing the missionary visits,
Hampton was "the parent and pattern of much practical education, especially of the undeveloped races, in many parts of the world."[18]

More than anything else, Americans said, these races needed the
moral lessons of work. Back home, reformers had begun to frame economic rationales for vocational education: it would keep children in
school, improve their future earnings, and contribute to the overall
wealth of society. For racial minorities, however, the moral rationale
still predominated. Blacks, Mexicans, and Native Americans all lacked
the proper work ethos, so schools should teach it.[19] To white Americans
overseas, *all* of their students came from lesser races. Hence, the ubiquitous drive for manual and agricultural training, which would improve
students' character as much as their job prospects. "The phase of this
work that appeals to me most, is the moral effect upon the pupils," a vocational teacher in Hawaii wrote; likewise, in the Congo, a missionary
predicted that "the gospel of work" would "uplift the people morally."
In the same breath as they cited Armstrong and Washington, meanwhile, missionaries invoked an even greater Teacher on behalf of vocational training. Jesus was a "Master Carpenter" or a "Master Workman,"
teaching all of his disciples the dignity of labor; as a Syria missionary
wrote, Christ's own education occurred "more in the workshop than in
the schools." Although the Bible did not mention vocational training,
another missionary admitted, it was clearly implied in the text. Jesus
studied carpentry and Paul learned tent-making, tacitly endorsing the
American goal of "self-support" in education.[20]

Local Resistance

To Americans' chagrin, however, their students rarely shared the same
enthusiasm for vocational education. Around the world, teachers complained, children and their families regarded schooling as a way to *avoid*
manual labor, not as a means for learning it. Even in the Philippines,
where industrial training scored its greatest successes, it also faced fierce
resistance. On hearing that they would all have to work, students at the

Manila Trade School walked out on strike. "The Americans are strong in the arms, Filipinos are strong here," one striker explained, pointing to his head. Other students responded to in-school work requirements by bringing their servants, who would perform whatever hard labor the Americans demanded. Still others simply voted with their feet, eschewing special trade schools and curricula in favor of traditional "bookish" ones. By 1925, fully three-quarters of Philippine high school students were "taking academic courses leading to non-productive careers," as an American survey dejectedly reported. Although farming remained the dominant occupation in the colony, just 3 percent of students studied agriculture.[21]

In Puerto Rico, meanwhile, the territory's new legislature abolished its training schools just four years after they began. The demise of the schools also led to the dismissal of school superintendent Leonard P. Ayres, who attacked the legislature in a well-publicized address at the annual Lake Mohonk Indian Conference. "You may have noticed that I did not mention industrial schools," said Ayres, who had risen from teacher to school statistician to superintendent. "That is because we have no industrial schools. We did have them, and good ones; but what happened to them is an illustration of what is liable to happen when we try the experiment of running local self-government." The speech raised predictable hackles in the Puerto Rican House of Delegates, where one member denounced Ayres as "the Prince of the Pharisees." Ayres had returned to the mainland to pursue a now-classic study of student failure in American schools, arguing that differentiated curricula—including vocational courses—would provide a venue where these "laggards" could succeed. But vocational education was a tougher sell in Puerto Rico, Ayres warned. "It is, of course, very difficult to persuade the Spanish-American that our type of industrial education, where the boy goes in and actually works with his own hands, is what he wants for his son," Ayres told his Lake Mohonk audience.[22]

The sharpest opposition occurred in Haiti, where the separate Service Technique system of vocational schools spawned a bloody nationwide student strike. By the time it ended, five Haitians and been killed and twenty wounded in battles with American marines. Antipathy toward the Service Technique had many causes, starting with the fact that few of its American teachers spoke French or Creole. Many of them came from Southern states, where "the attitude . . . towards

Negro education is too well known to need any comment," as African-American historian and Haiti expert Rayford Logan wrote. Other critics feared that the Service Technique would siphon off students and resources from Catholic schools; still others resented the high salaries that its teachers received. Most of all, though, parents and students favored a European-style "classical" curriculum, and abhorred Americans for undermining it. Haitians "dread American influence on their educational system, fearing that if it is 'Anglo-Saxonized' it will be turned away from the French cultural tradition and given a materialist and purely utilitarian trend," wrote American pacifist Emily Balch, after visiting Haiti. "It is essentially the same issue [in] the United States as to whether in the education of the negro all emphasis should be laid on education of the Tuskegee type, or whether the education typified by Atlanta University was also important."[23]

Atlanta University was the academic home of W. E. B. Du Bois, Booker T. Washington's chief competitor for the hearts—and the soul—of black Americans. In a series of sharp articles, Du Bois condemned Washington's vision of industrial education for neglecting the so-called "Talented Tenth"—that is, black intellectual leadership—and for teaching manual skills that an industrial economy no longer demanded.[24] Not surprisingly, overseas American teachers who noticed this debate tended to side with Washington. In her 1902 Hawaii diary, for example, African-American mission teacher Helen James bemoaned the "wholesale attack" upon Washington by William Trotter in the *Boston Guardian*. James' sister had sent her Trotter's broadsides, which charged Washington with relegating African-Americans to "serfdom." Unknown to James, however, many native Hawaiians were coming to view American vocational initiatives in a similarly dour light. By 1919, a befuddled teacher noted, local critics were "beginning to wonder if the whole industrial programme is not designed by the classes for the purpose of educating the masses for 'their station' in life." Such charges were especially common among Japanese parents, who condemned the school system as a "propaganda agent for the plantations," and refused to enroll their children in its agricultural programs. Across the territory, only 6 percent of eligible high school boys took courses in agriculture.[25]

Even in Africa, Americans found, students who celebrated Booker T. Washington's achievements in the United States resisted his vocational curriculum in their own schools. Cameroonian boys refused to hoe the garden, which they regarded as "girl" work. Nor would they engage in construction and other traditional male labor, missionaries lamented. "Our aim is to raise them as children of their own soil," wrote a teacher, "but their studies, their readings, their contact with another race make them feel different. They dream of another life, despise theirs." At one mission school, students went on strike when Americans insisted they take vocational courses on top of French-language academic ones. " 'We came to [school] to learn French, to prepare ourselves to teach French, we want French and nothing else,' " the students demanded. Tired and hungry, all but two of them would soon return to beg forgiveness. The school agreed to take back the primary-level boys who had walked out, but it expelled the older strikers. Most ironically, to embittered American teachers, students at the Booker Washington Institute in Liberia rejected its namesake's vocational emphasis. The country's ruling Americo-Liberians saw manual labor as beneath their station, pleading for a Western-style "classical" education. But the school held firm to its founders' vision, eventually catering to low-status "native" tribes, which only increased the Americo-Liberians' resentment.[26]

The Americans Respond

To American teachers, the very resistance to vocational education proved the huge need for it. Acknowledging an aversion to such instruction around the world, one Korea missionary flatly concluded that Americans must "educate the people to demand industrial training." Missionaries in Burma took an economic tack, promising parents that technical courses would yield greater job opportunities than "bookish" preparation did. "We have so overdone this formal education that we have created a great horde of unemployed and unemployable men and women, qualified for no constructive work, restless almost unto revolution," one teacher warned. In neighboring India, finally, other Americans tried to link their vocational initiatives to the actual revolution against British rule. Missionaries especially pointed to Mohandas Gandhi's penchant for cottage industries like homespun cloth, which seemed to echo the missions' own program. Indeed, Gandhi aide Charles Andrews visited Tuskegee in 1929 and brought praise and good wishes from the Mahatma. But missions' historical association with colonial rule made their appeal to Gandhian principles problematic, as one American confirmed in a rare 1932 interview with Gandhi himself. Praising Americans for promoting a "practical" school curriculum, Gandhi also condemned them for seeking to convert Hindus to Christianity.[27]

Within the American empire proper, meanwhile, teachers often complained that *other* colonial powers had soured local peoples on vocational education. Filipino resistance to industrial training reflected the "Spanish belief" that "a gentleman never did manual labor," one teacher wrote, recalling his students' amazement when he began making desks for his bare classroom. In Puerto Rico, likewise, Americans attributed the slow growth of vocational training to the "Castillian idea" of "genteel idleness" that the island's former rulers had brought there. Teachers in Haiti leveled similar charges at the French, while Americans in the Virgin Islands condemned the Danes. Across the territories, meanwhile, other teachers blamed the poor reception of vocational education on the "tropical" weather. "The habits of people depend upon the climate," wrote one Philippine student in a classroom assignment, obviously mimicking her American teacher. "In warm countries like the Philippines, the people are a little bit lazy, and want more sleep and rest . . . In cold countries generally the people are more progressive and prosperous." Teachers in Puerto Rico even spoke of a "tropical temper" among their students, who lacked diligence and self-control. In circular fashion, the local climate explained both the opposition to vocational education and the necessity for it.[28]

Finally, to still other Americans, resistance to industrial training reflected Americans' own errors in implementing it. Drawing on John Dewey and other critics of domestic vocational education, teachers asserted that Americans had created an unnatural and counterproductive dichotomy between "academic" and "vocational" activities. In the Philippines, for example, female teachers at a Baptist school asked mission leaders to complement its industrial courses with a full "academic" component. In reply, the mission's male director insisted that these domains were incompatible. "Oil and water do not mix," he explained. "It would be as impossible to run them together as to serve two masters." Here he cited David Snedden, a leading vocational educator back home. Snedden hoped to create entirely separate schools for "vocational" and "liberal" studies, a goal that often proved elusive in the United States. But American missions bifurcated their schools in precisely this manner, critics said, thereby reinforcing the same antiwork prejudices that teachers frequently bemoaned. In his preface to a book by William J. McKee, a former principal of India's famed Moga School, Teachers College professor William H. Kilpatrick praised McKee for bridging "book learning" and "actual doing" at the school. "Let us have done with disparate and separating dualisms," Kilpatrick urged.[29]

In most instances, however, Americans promoted vocational education as an alternative—not as a supplement—to the book-centered kind. If a "purely academic training" taught students to depreciate manual labor, as one Philippines missionary charged, surely a uniformly industrial program did the same thing. "Under the old system of literary education it was forgotten that men had bodies to feed and clothe," wrote A. Victor Murray, a perceptive British critic of American missionary education. "Under the new it may be forgotten that they have minds to develop and spirits to kindle."[30] By promoting industrial education to the exclusion of academics, American teachers alienated a good part of their overseas audience. In sports and hygiene, by contrast, Americans would discover two "practical" curricula far more attuned to local sentiment. Like vocational education, these courses focused squarely on students' bodies rather than their brains. Bearing no direct relationship to employment, however, they proved much more popular—and more resilient—than any industrial program. Even as the prospect of physical labor drove students away from school, the pleasures of physical education were drawing them back in.

The Sporting Life

In May of 1898, just a few days after Admiral George Dewey captured Manila Bay, victorious American sailors and marines played the first recorded game of baseball in the Philippines. Within months, Philippine boys were fielding grounders and shagging pop flies at U.S. military bases. Baseball helped lure them into the new public schools, which organized teams almost as soon as they opened. On July 4, 1902, American teacher H. S. Mead led his baseball squad on a 22-mile walk to play a game; afterwards, the team turned around and walked home. By 1911, the Philippines boasted 482 uniformed baseball teams; five years after that, the total had swelled to 1,500. Many of the first American public school teachers played baseball and other sports in college. Likewise, the burgeoning missionary community often recruited athletes to staff its own schools. Perhaps the best-known teacher in the Philippines was George W. Dunlap, the "Baseball Missionary." A former minor-league catcher in the Pittsburgh Pirates' farm system, Dunlap coached his mission-school team to so many victories that Filipinos in the Cebu District pleaded with the public schools to hire him. Setting aside the usual restrictions on employing missionaries, Cebu made Dunlap its coach; Dunlap, in turn, made the "Cebu Nine" famous across the Philippines. His teams won several national titles, even defeating the local U.S. Army and Navy squads along the way.[31]

Dunlap's teams also traveled to tournaments in China and Japan, where "brown and yellow champions played the great American game," as one enthusiastic American recalled. Wherever the teachers went, indeed, they proclaimed baseball as a prime agent of American influence. A delighted Philippines teacher saw her students playing baseball with an orange and a wooden board, wrenched from the lid of an oil case. "These are the beginnings of great movements in small things," she wrote. "Those children got more real Americanism out of that corrupted ball game than they did from singing 'My Country, 'tis of Thee' every morning." Teachers said that baseball helped wean Filipinos off their less savory national pastime, cockfighting, which spawned bloodlust and gambling; it also created community spirit, forging support for the local school in particular and public education more generally. "Every spectator has come to see his own team win," one Filipino observed, "and he throws as much enthusiasm into his demonstration of partisanship as any rooter at a college meet in America." In Puerto Rico, meanwhile, teachers found that basketball, with its physical contact and constant action, provided an even better vehicle for American-style "*pep*" and "*rah-rah*," as one principal emphasized. "Athletics— I mean real, intensified athletics—is the final stamp of Americanization upon the Porto Rican high school," he declared.[32]

Binding America's colonies to their new motherland, sports would transmit many of the same values as vocational education: diligence, perseverance, physical strength, and obedience to authority. Just like industrial training, sports would also help counter the strongly "academic" bias that children brought to school. "Twenty years ago a typical Philippine student was lank, round shouldered, and wont to discuss philosophy," one American official observed in the early 1920s, "He is

now sturdy, robust, and inclined to discuss more practical matters."
Missionaries in China claimed that sports would give new physical vigor
to the so-called Sick Man of Asia, diverting students from local vices
like gambling and opium. Around the world, finally, American teachers
advertised athletics as an antidote to the worst evil of all: sexual promiscuity. "Wholesome sport seems to diminish rather than intensify the
sex feeling," wrote one Hawaii principal. "And a sum of money spent
for a well-equipped playground will perhaps do more towards eradicat-
ing the social evil than would twice the same amount expended on lectures and text-books." In Korea, an elated mission teacher noted, sports
gave students the discipline and self-control to resist Seoul's notorious
red-light district; likewise, to a Burma missionary, school sports helped
protect students from local temptations, and, especially, from their own
sinful natures.[33]

As in the United States, however, teachers also maintained that sports
would unleash their students' natural virtues and instincts. Although
Philippine children made too much noise during class, where they ha-
bitually read out loud, they were also too quiet at recess: sallow and serious, they lacked the God-given joy and spontaneity of youth. So
Americans would have to teach them to "let themselves loose," promoting sports and games that would make them act like "normal" children.
In practice, of course, that meant behaving according to *American*
norms. "It is refreshing to see them play leapfrog and marbles, with
many an argument and occasional fist fight; and dirty hands and dirty
knees bespeak the boy in every one of them," wrote a Catholic missionary in China, praising students' new interest in physical activity.
"They are typical boys, but not typical Chinese boys, for they have clear
eyes and a smile whenever a priest comes in sight—not a sickly smirk
but an honest, sturdy grin." Likewise, Baptists in Assam celebrated
when students took up badminton and croquet. "We are pleased to see
this growing impulse to play," a teacher wrote, "because the general
tendency among the children of this country is to sit around on benches
or on their heels like little old men and women." Even married female
students at a mission school in Iraq joined in the fun, their teacher exulted, becoming "girls" once more, if only for a brief recess period.[34]

Here and there, to be sure, some people assailed the American emphasis on organized athletics. Upper-class Chinese and Korean students
resisted any kind of physical exertion, sending "coolies" to play for

them at school just as these servants would hoe for them in the fields. In the Philippines, meanwhile, elites worried that outdoor sports would give their children dark complexions and rough hands, the hallmarks of a working-class physique. Others complained that athletics diverted too much public money and attention away from academic study. But such voices were a slender minority in a sports-crazed society like the Philippines, where 4,500 out of 4,702 schools provided physical training classes or sports teams by 1919. As in the case of vocational education, indeed, Philippine physical education eclipsed the provisions of most states back home. Whereas most students and their families rejected industrial training, however, they registered for physical education and sports in droves. "You have done what we have not done in the United States, made athletics an educational value," wrote Teachers College professor Paul Monroe, following his 1925 survey of Philippine schools.[35]

The Gospel of Health

Around the world, meanwhile, American teachers struggled to make overall health—not just physical activity—into an "educational value," too. In their classrooms as well as their correspondence, teachers routinely condemned the filthy conditions that they encountered abroad. "I've got a school, 32 *dirty* little Jewish girls," emphasized Belle Hawkes, a missionary in Persia. "I lecture them wildly, fiercely in splendid (so it seems to me) Persian, but they don't get cleaner." Deriding the "assorted old rags" on one student's head, Hawkes asked her mockingly if she had been "rooting in the ground like a mole." Other teachers in Persia blasted the local tradition of public baths, which exposed female students to "immodesty" as well as contagion. Elsewhere, Americans complained that their students did not bathe at all. Privately, a missionary in Colombia called her pupils "enemies of soap and water"; a teacher in Japan wrote that her students lived like animals, defecating in the fields rather than in the water closet her school constructed for them; and in India, a third teacher despaired over the "filthy habits" of her own pupils. "You can't teach these critters anything," wrote Philippines teacher Harry Cole. "They are a disgusting set from start to finish and can not be depended on in anything—except that they will go to church, & neglect everything else."[36]

In the Philippines, especially, teachers blamed poor hygiene and the spread of disease on "superstitious" Catholic beliefs. As cholera swept the territory in 1902, leaving thousands of dead in its wake, Filipinos put crosses on their doors to block the Devil from entering. Others paraded through town bearing shrines, which Protestant teachers derided as more "pagan" than Christian. "The poor, filthy, ill-fed people were dying like sheep," wrote one teacher, "and the Americans . . . besought (sic) them in vain to spend less time in prayers and religious processions, and more time in cleaning their houses and yards and boiling their drinking water." At the height of the epidemic, the territorial government closed the schools and deputized male teachers as health inspectors. Some of them strapped on Colt .45s and went door to door, enforcing sanitary precautions on pain of arrest; others set fire to the deserted homes where corpses were rotting. Since Americans rarely caught cholera themselves, however, many Filipinos concluded that they had caused it. In the epidemic of 1902 and again in 1916, villagers charged teachers with poisoning their wells. One teacher was actually brought to trial, confronting two men who produced herbs that he allegedly gave them to pollute the water supply. He lit a match to the concoction, which caused such a smoky commotion that witnesses crawled out of the room through the windows. After a laboratory confirmed that the herbs were harmless, the teacher was exonerated.[37]

Within the schools, meanwhile, American teachers tried to establish different standards of sanitation. In the Philippines, they punished children for spitting on the floor; in Hawaii, they gave students kerosene baths to remove head lice; and in China, they carefully divided a new bar of Ivory Soap—"an adjunct of civilization," in the words of one missionary—among seventeen boarding-school boys. Echoing trends back home, meanwhile, teachers also promoted "healthful habits" via games, songs, and other activities. Students at a mission school in Persia put on a health skit at commencement, "From Danger Valley to Safety Hill," featuring white-clad children dressed as fruits and vegetables, and black-frocked students playing "Coffee" and "Tea." Children at a second Persia school received an audience with "Cho-Cho the Health Clown," a standard character in hygiene campaigns back home. The clown was the brainchild of health educator Sally Lucas Jean, who visited American-run schools in China, India, the Philippines, and the Virgin Islands. Rather than warning students about dangerous behaviors,

Jean encouraged them to practice safe ones. Like industrial training, the argument went, health education should teach skills that students used in their "daily life," as a Hawaii spokesman explained.[38]

The lone exception concerned alcohol and other drugs, where teachers aimed to *prevent*, not promote, a habit. Americans reserved special ire for colleagues and students who smoked cigarettes in class, a common practice in many parts of the world. Others complained that teachers drank liquor before they came to school—or, even worse, after they arrived there. Following a holiday party at an industrial school in Guatemala, for example, one outraged American visitor found the school's Latino principal lying in a corner and clearly intoxicated. " 'This is a 'Practical' School," another Guatemalan teacher quipped, playing off the school's vocational emphasis. "And this is the Practice." Americans instinctively ascribed such habits to British and especially French influences: even as they instituted strict "academic" course requirements, European colonial educators allowed loose standards of personal conduct. As in the case of transmittable disease, meanwhile, other teachers simply blamed Catholicism. In Chile, one Protestant teacher described the local Catholic church as "the ally of the vintners and brewers"; and in the Philippines, another missionary noted, the church actually owned breweries and cigarette factories. "They also teach their people that there is no harm in smoking or in drinking," the missionary lamented. "As a result the women smoke and not a dainty cigarette but big black cigars."[39]

Of course, American teachers smoked and drank as well. Officials in the Philippines issued sharp warnings against "intemperate" behavior, occasionally dismissing teachers for public drunkenness. But many teachers used alcohol and tobacco, often in copious amounts, earning the censure of their more conservative colleagues. One teacher condemned fellow Americans for gambling and dancing as well as drinking and smoking, all "heinous sins" that his church back home had forbidden; a second Philippines teacher worried that drunken colleagues would set "poor examples" for "the natives we are trying to civilize." At a Southern Baptist school in Chile, meanwhile, the question of tobacco turned American teachers against each other. Most of them came from Kentucky and Tennessee, where the church barred smoking as well as Sunday baseball. But Baptists in Virginia allowed both activities, as one angry missionary from the Old Dominion noted. "While my people in

Virginia raise and use tobacco, and while much of the money Virginia Baptists pay to the Foreign Mission Board comes from the sale of tobacco, it makes it impossible for me to vote to turn a member out of the church who uses tobacco," the Virginia teacher argued. He even confessed to fishing and watching baseball on Sundays, accusing his austere colleagues of acting more like Jews, with their strict Sabbath rules and prohibitions, than like Christians.[40]

In schools where teetotaling teachers predominated, finally, Americans often taught the same "Scientific Temperance Instruction" (STI) curriculum that children at home received. Devised by the Woman's Christian Temperance Union (WCTU), which won mandatory STI laws in every state by 1901, the curriculum emphasized the evil effects of alcohol on the heart, lungs, eyes, and brain. Some overseas teachers also started school chapters of the WCTU or of other temperance societies, where new members pledged to eschew strong drink and tobacco; still others sponsored antialcohol speech and essay contests. After one such contest in Chile, however, the winner's mother coyly admitted that her son took wine with meals.[41] The episode provides a tidy metaphor for American health instruction abroad, which won rhetorical assent more often than it altered actual behavior.[42] Reflecting deep-seated cultural beliefs, local hygiene practices would not change with a handful of school lessons. After World War II, however, it would be American teachers, not their students, who changed their assumptions about culture. The consequences were enormous, not just for health instruction but for the entire American educational project.

From Morality to Economics

In 1955, American missionary Grace Strachan Roberts described an "evangelical" school that would open shortly in Costa Rica. The new institution would cater to Costa Rica's burgeoning Protestant population, which complained of hostility and discrimination in the public schools. Borrowing from standard educational rhetoric back home, Roberts emphasized that her school would address the "whole child." It would develop students spiritually, via chapel and Bible classes; intellectually, by maintaining "the highest scholastic standards"; morally, by instilling "proper discipline"; and physically, through "a good sports program." The school would also feature a "strong vocational department," Roberts

added, because most Protestant families could not afford higher education. Rather than preparing students for college, the new Protestant
school would "ensure them a means of earning a living."[43]

Roberts' remarks reflected a new rationale for American vocational
education in the postwar era. Around the world, teachers continued
their quest for a "practical" curriculum as well as their assault upon a
purely "academic" one. After World War II, however, American vocational education lost the heavily moral cast that had marked its birth.
To teachers in the first half of the twentieth century, vocational instruction would promote a set of ethical values—especially initiative and persistence—that host populations allegedly lacked. Post–World War II
Americans stressed *monetary* value, promoting vocational instruction
as a route to economic prosperity or "development" rather than personal transformation. Here overseas teachers followed trends in the
United States, where vocational education gradually replaced its moral
rationale—especially for racial minorities—with a utilitarian one. To
missionary Grace Strachan Roberts, indeed, almost every part of the
curriculum *except* vocational education possessed a strong moral dimension. Religious, academic, and physical instruction would yield good
minds and bodies; vocational instruction would bring good jobs.

Wherever Americans taught, then, they tried to include a vocational
component in their schools. Catholic nuns in the Marshall Islands
taught cooking and sewing to girls alongside reading and math; priests
taught navigation, carpentry, and engine studies to the boys. In Kenya,
Harvard's Volunteer Teachers for Africa (VTA) program started
courses in poultry, carpentry, bricklaying, and masonry. Across the bor-
der in Ethiopia, meanwhile, the Peace Corps supplied industrial arts,
home economics, and bookkeeping teachers for seven new "compre-
hensive" high schools, which offered "more than the traditional academic
courses," as one volunteer wrote. In 1962, Peace Corps vocational
teachers worked in twelve different countries; ten years later, the total
had risen to twenty-eight. The agency's vocational instruction would
spike again in the late 1970s, when the Peace Corps announced a new
emphasis on "Basic Human Needs." To advocates of this doctrine, cab-
inetmaking or auto repair met a basic need for employment and suste-
nance; English, math, and science did not. By 1986, fully 10 percent of
Peace Corps education volunteers taught a vocational subject. As two
Americans in Iran wrote, summarizing the vocational trend, traditional

schooling prepared students for jobs that did not exist, or that usually went to well-connected elites. Better to teach vocational skills, which would help students "earn a good living . . . independent of the favors of the rich and powerful."[44]

The Americans went on to quote Mahatma Gandhi, who also emphasized the practical role of education in ensuring a livelihood: " 'For the millions who go without two meals a day, the only form in which God dare appear is food.' " During the Indian struggle against British rule, American teachers had invoked Gandhi to underline his emphasis upon homespun cloth—and to express solidarity with the anticolonial cause. As more and more nations gained their independence, Americans linked their efforts to the vocational programs that new governments initiated on their own. In Tanzania, for example, American VTA teachers cited founding president Julius Nyerere's philosophy of *kujitegemea* or "self-reliance" in their plea for instruction in agriculture and rabbit-raising. In India, meanwhile, Americans noted parallels between their vocational curricula and the government's Junior Basic Education program, which stressed spinning, weaving, and agriculture in a Gandhian vein. Just six years after Indian independence, in fact, one provincial education department selected an American mission school as a "Pilot Project in Education," to demonstrate "better methods for rural schools," especially in the vocational realm.[45]

Most of all, Americans advocated vocational education as the key to personal mobility and prosperity. Like Booker T. Washington, Mahatma Gandhi embraced vocational instruction to promote collective moral reform as well as individual uplift: Washington aimed to teach his fellow African-Americans the virtues of work, while Gandhi wished to preserve the communal values of village India. After World War II, however, American vocationalists took a much more individualistic, economic tack. "No longer is every boy predestined to follow in his father's foot steps," wrote one mission-school principal in India, explaining his school's industrial focus. "Most of their fathers are day laborers on the land . . . Unskilled peasants are being replaced by simple forms of mechanization." So his school would give students the skills to *operate* the machinery—and to escape their economic circumstances. At the Booker Washington Institute in Liberia, Americans likewise substituted fiscal appeals for moralistic ones. Students continued to learn carpentry, brickmaking, and other construction skills, but they also started to study

African woodcarving, after Walter Wynn, the school's first African-American principal, realized that tourists would purchase it. "Their products are snapped up almost before the last chip is cut," one observer gushed, underscoring the new economic emphasis.[46]

Local Resistance, Again

As in the first half of the twentieth century, however, most students and families resisted Americans' emphasis on vocational education. A few months after India declared independence, for example, Presbyterian missionaries closed one of their leading industrial schools for lack of students. "There has been no apparent desire on the part of the youth in our Mission areas to engage in the type of technical training or trades offered in this school," one teacher explained. Instead, he continued, students sought traditional academic training for "white-collar" jobs, which most of them would never obtain. In a nation that venerated Gandhi, another missionary complained, Indians refused to enroll their children in schools or courses that followed his vocational plan. "Gandhi has stressed the spinning wheel, and we honor him for it, but it is more a matter of politics than a movement towards making people economically independent," the missionary lamented. Likewise, in Kenya and Tanzania, students who celebrated Nyerere's doctrine of "self-reliance" often pleaded for traditional classes in math and especially European languages, the ticket to an office job as well as further education. Even at the Booker Washington Institute, whose namesake made vocational education famous around the globe, Liberian students petitioned their American teachers to provide classes in French, Latin, and typing alongside standard "industrial" fare.[47]

As the combination of typing and foreign languages suggested, students shared the same utilitarian presumptions as American vocational educators: the job of school was to prepare scholars for jobs. But the students sought a different *type* of job than their American teachers envisioned for them, as Booker Washington Institute trustee Edward Robinson confirmed. "I told the boy who wanted typing that we were not trying to train white collar workers who would go sit in an office in Monrovia," Robinson wrote, following a visit to the Institute, "but agricultural and industrial graduates who would go home and use the knowledge they had gained in helping their own tribes." Responding to students' demands for Latin, meanwhile, Robinson told them that he had majored in Latin himself, and that he had never used it in his own work. Surely, then, the language "would be of no possible use in Liberia," Robinson claimed. Around the world, Americans echoed both arguments: developing nations did not need more white-collar workers, and even future white-collar workers did not need much of the academic training that schools provided. "We are educating these people for nothing," lamented a Peace Corps teacher in Ethiopia. "Our students have nowhere to go, no jobs, no hopes of any."[48]

Nevertheless, students continued to demand academic courses, in the hopes, however quixotic, of *finding* a job. The more that Americans pressed for a "practical" curriculum, in fact, the more the world pressed back. In Africa, especially, students and teachers regarded vocational education as "second best," one observer wrote, *"especially if it is claimed it is practical.* They, like us, are well aware of the prestige academic education enjoys." In the Congo, American missionaries complained, students favored Belgian "traditional" education—especially French language instruction—over agriculture, crafts, and other vocational courses. Indeed, as soon as Congo gained independence, it decreed that all state-subsidized primary schools must teach in French. Americans were quick to blame the Belgian colonists, whose racial doctrines restricted education to a tiny sliver of the African elite. To the Americans' astonishment, however, Congolese charged *them* with racism. "For stressing the practical, missionaries have often been severely censured by the Africans who interpreted this interest as *racial bias,*" stated one missionary, "and [as] disinclination to grant Africans education equal in value to that given Europeans or whites." Whereas Americans promoted vocational reform as a vehicle to social mobility, their students often regarded it as "an attempt to deprive the African of the white man's education," as a second teacher wrote.[49]

The charge placed teachers in an especially vulnerable spot. In the immediate post–World War II period, they often viewed opposition to vocational instruction as a sign of ignorance as well as a call to battle: people did not recognize their own educational needs, so Americans needed to educate them.[50] As racial conflict flared at home and anti-colonial struggles enveloped the globe, however, *any* claim about another people's "need" seemed patronizing at best, and bigoted at worst. The issue came to a head for many American teachers with the 1977 appointment of Sam Brown to head ACTION, the federal agency that oversaw the Peace Corps. A former antiwar activist and political operative for Eugene McCarthy's 1968 presidential campaign, Brown proclaimed a new focus on "Basic Human Needs" such as nutrition, health, and agriculture. He also took aim at educational programs like English instruction, which Brown condemned as a lasting vestige of "cultural imperialism." To Brown's antagonists in the Peace Corps, however, the Basic Human Needs doctrine embodied its own form of imperialist condescension. "It's offensive to me to tell another country what its needs are," declared Peace Corps director Carolyn Payton, who would resign after a year of battle with Brown.[51]

But Payton and her supporters won the war. Although the overall percentage of education volunteers dipped slightly, teachers remained by far the largest Peace Corps occupation. "The governments were always asking us for teachers, teachers, teachers," recalled a Peace Corps country director in Swaziland and Kenya. "Sam Brown just didn't understand the value of knowing English in these countries." Moreover, the vast majority of volunteers continued to instruct academic courses—especially English and math—rather than vocational or "practical" ones. The important exception was physical education, which proved immensely popular overseas. To proponents of Basic Human Needs, sports and athletics seemed like an extravagant luxury—if not a cruel joke—in countries lacking potable water or sufficient food. But as a Niger teacher explained, her students *felt* they needed physical education, and that was enough. "It was an imperialist mindset that viewed sports instruction as unnecessary," she insisted. "The Nigerians would argue, 'Why shouldn't we have as good an education as Americans?' "[52] Like vocational instruction, school sports departed from a strictly "academic" curriculum. Bearing no connection to future job prospects, however, sports engaged overseas students in ways that vocational education never would.

Sports Build a Nation

In 1966, a Senegalese principal told the local Peace Corps teacher that "all Americans are sportive." The principal had good reason to think so. Especially in the 1960s, overseas American teachers displayed an almost religious devotion to athletics and physical education. By one estimate, over half of the 12,000 Peace Corps volunteers around the globe gave part of their time to sports. About 400 volunteers taught in formal physical-education programs; others served as coaches, timers, trainers, and scoutmasters. Peace Corps trainings placed a heavy accent on sports and physical fitness, leading volunteers through a grueling regimen of calisthenics, climbing, and swimming. To complete their training at Georgetown University, for example, teachers bound for Ethiopia had to complete a 25-mile "survival hike" along the Appalachian Trail, while, to prepare for the Philippines, volunteers at a Puerto Rico train-ing site had to cross a narrow rope bridge connecting two trees 40 feet above the ground. Starting in 1963, meanwhile, the Peace Corps dis-tributed an athletic kit to all volunteers in the field. The kit contained two softballs, two bats, two soccer balls, a volleyball, a basketball, a Fris-bee, and a chess set. According to an agency memo, the equipment reflected "the universality of certain sports" as well as "the American nature of others."[53]

Like their early twentieth-century forebears in the Philippines and Puerto Rico, teachers helped spread American games—especially bas-ketball and baseball—to the rest of the world. But they promoted sports as a vehicle of indigenous nationalism rather than "Americanization," marking a key departure from the previous pattern. In Uganda, Ameri-cans organized and coached the first national basketball team; in Liberia, they prepared volleyball and basketball teams for the African Friendship Games; and in Indonesia, they helped instruct the national track squad. As in the United States, meanwhile, sports also helped promote school pride. At the Notre Dame schools in the Philippines, missionaries taught students the same fight song that Notre Dame University used back home. Jesuits wrote their own fight song for Baghdad College High School in Iraq, but they set it to a distinctly American tune: "The U.S. Field Artillery March: The Caissons Go Rolling Along." Despite their foreign origins, a Niger basketball coach explained, such rituals bound students to their own communities and countries. "When your national identity isn't stable, sports are a good way to make sure people are root-ing for the same thing," she explained. In India, a missionary proudly re-ported, weekly cricket matches united her school's fractious religious and caste groups, if only for a few glorious hours.[54]

To be sure, Americans expressed occasional frustration with the young athletes under their charge. The most common complaint was that students did not try hard enough on the field. "These people don't know what that 'die-to-win' spirit is and you don't have much success if you try to instill it in them," a Nigeria teacher and soccer coach wrote his parents. "If they win, they are happy, but if they lose they shrug their shoulders and say 'that's life,' and they can be just as happy as if they had won." Indeed, a Costa Rica teacher claimed, school sports and fitness challenged "2,000 years of complacency" in Latin America. Nigerian boys refused to train for an upcoming soccer season, Peace Corps teachers complained, because they did not care about the fortunes of the team. Around the world, students noticed that their American teachers seemed more intent upon victory than the students themselves were. "Mr. Dan like playing basketball," a Kenyan student wrote, describing her teacher. "He has a goal of winning."[55]

Reflecting on these tensions, some teachers worried that Americans were imposing their own competitive ethos on peoples who did not share it. In the Marshall Islands, for example, a Peace Corps teacher noticed that students played their own "native games" for "the sheer joy of playing"; by contrast, she wrote, Americans "play to *win*." But the concern was misplaced, reflecting Americans' anxiety over cultural imperialism rather than the actual sentiment of the peoples they taught. Despite occasional tensions, students around the world embraced American sports—and American athletic instruction—with almost constant zeal. During the colonial era, European rulers frequently barred students from playing Western sports; in the Ivory Coast, for example, Africans were admitted on tennis courts only to serve as ballboys.[56] But Americans encouraged participation by everyone, even providing opportunities for girls.[57] Most of all, team sports, unlike vocational education, tapped into the pride and spirit of young nations across the globe. When Americans pleaded for vocational instruction as a route to national vitality, students turned a deaf ear, but when their teachers touted sports in the same idiom, the students responded. Sports united students with each other *and* with their American teachers, even as other parts of the curriculum threatened to crack them apart.

Health and Culture

The first scandal in Peace Corps history began with a postcard. In 1961, Nigeria teacher Margery Michelmore sent a card to her boyfriend in the United States describing the "primitive living conditions" she had witnessed in Africa. "Everyone except us lives in the streets, sells in the streets, and even goes to the bathroom in the streets," Michelmore wrote. On her way to the post office, she dropped the postcard. It fell into the hands of university students, who distributed copies of the postcard and denounced Peace Corps volunteers as "agents of imperialism." Reported in newspapers around the world, the so-called "postcard incident" quickly became a diplomatic embarrassment for the young agency. In Washington, Nigeria's ambassador commented tartly that "no one likes to be called primitive." Peace Corps director Sargent Shriver met with his brother-in-law, President John F. Kennedy, who decided to bring Michelmore home. "Keep in touch," Kennedy would tell later volunteer groups, making light of the incident, "but not by postcard!"[58]

But the postcard incident was no joke. A *magna cum laude* graduate of Smith College, Michelmore epitomized the best-and-brightest candidate whom Shriver and Kennedy hoped to enlist in the Peace Corps. Yet her florid account of Africa forced her removal from the field, highlighting the dangers and dilemmas surrounding health in the 1960s and beyond. Just six years earlier, a missionary teacher could write with confidence—and without risk—about "primitive" hygiene in Africa. "Under these deplorable conditions, what is the attitude of the natives?" the missionary asked. "In their ignorance, they are perfectly content to continue living as they always have. Usually they do not even understand the relationship between cleanliness and health."[59] As the postcard incident showed, however, Michelmore did not perceive the relationship between *culture* and health. Health practices often reflected the most deeply held beliefs, ideas, and habits of a people, what Americans called their "culture." But in an era of decolonization, especially, calling an entire country "dirty" or "primitive" seemed to denigrate that same culture. Hence American teachers had to walk a fine line. Wherever they went, teachers would strive to change health practices without maligning the culture that surrounded them.

Few Americans taught separate courses in health, which many countries folded into their science curricula. But nearly all American teachers—not just science instructors—gave some kind of health instruction to their students. Urged on by the Peace Corps, hundreds of volunteers dug latrines for their schools and homes. The new latrines provided an object lesson in sanitation, the major concern of American teachers the world over. Privately, teachers continued to condemn their students' "complete nonchalance" regarding human waste, as one Ecuador volunteer wrote in his diary. Teachers' public comments and instruction focused on "better health habits," echoing the pre–World War II era. In Ethiopia, one volunteer started an afterschool home economics club to teach "more hygienic ways of preparing food"; shocked by her students' dirty shoes and messy desks, another teacher invited them to her house. "They can see how an American home is kept—the arrangement and cleanliness," she wrote. Most of these campaigns appeared fairly popular, generating positive remarks from local teachers and students. Nor did postwar American teachers trouble their hosts with antialcohol instruction, a hallmark of previous health efforts. In the Bahamas, indeed, missionaries took their students on a field trip to the local Bacardi rum plant, and no one seemed to complain.[60]

Instead, most health controversies surrounded issues of sex. Pre–World War II teachers had danced gingerly around the subject, providing occasional lectures in "sex hygiene," but little else.[61] Especially in the 1960s, however, American teachers began to provide more formal and in-depth sex education. Catholic missionaries in Bolivia led student dialogues on "friendship, love, and sexuality," aiming to combat the widespread "immorality" that the teachers saw around them. They also conducted a debate about whether sex education should occur at school or at home, with students favoring "school" by an overwhelming margin. But that was precisely the problem. Parents and fellow teachers objected to any instruction about sex, causing Americans to censor their own discussions of it. In Ghana, for example, colleagues warned a Peace Corps teacher never to mention the topic, even if students saw two dogs mating and asked what they were doing. "I never made a push to probe my students' feelings on such things," an Ethiopia teacher recalled. "I didn't want to tread on cultural mores . . . or make anyone feel conspicuous."[62] The last comment provided a vivid epigraph for American health instruction, which *always* risked insulting students' "cultural mores." For teachers in the post–World War II period, the basic questions remained the same: when to accommodate students' culture, when to challenge it, and why.

☞ IN 1992, Peace Corps teacher Lisa Hebl began her diary entry with a depressing title: "Doubting the Reason We're Here." Assigned to teach English in Kenya with her husband, a chemistry instructor,

Hebl wondered whether students needed them. After all, only 8 of 1,000 Kenyans passed the national university entrance examination. Even if her own pupils made it to university, meanwhile, Hebl doubted whether they could obtain a job in Kenya's corrupt, bloated state bureaucracy. "Aren't we giving the students and their families a false sense of hope?" she asked.[63]

Hebl's comments reflected a century-long anxiety among American teachers, who condemned the traditional academic training that they often provided. Pre–World War II teachers sang the moral virtues of vocational education, which would instill the persistence and drive that "lesser races" allegedly lacked. After World War II, by contrast, teachers like Hebl phrased their objections in more utilitarian terms. Academic training simply paved the way for more education, if a student was lucky, and possibly a white-collar job; more often than not, however, it led only to unemployment. Responding to American concerns, one West African educational official reportedly quipped, "We should have intelligent unemployed." But American teachers were not amused. Instead, they lamented that they were "contributing to the elitist society which educates people for jobs that do not exist," as Nigeria Peace Corps volunteers maintained. Rather than continuing down this dead-end road, two prominent agency officials concluded, Peace Corps should recruit volunteers for "vocational education and technical fields."[64]

Were they right? In an era that celebrated "culture," that was often the wrong question. Inside think tanks and development agencies, to be sure, experts debated the value of traditional and vocational education for economic development, individual mobility, public health, and more. Out in the field, however, most Americans put aside their concerns and deferred to the cultures they encountered. That meant teaching sports, which enjoyed almost uniform approval; tempering health instruction, in accord with local mores; and, most of all, providing book-centered learning in the academic disciplines. Rebutting charges of "linguistic imperialism," for example, a missionary English teacher noted in 1998 that peoples around the world *thought* they needed English instruction to succeed. Who were Americans to suggest otherwise? "The fate of students in an educational system, and their eventual ability to get and keep good jobs, may depend on how well they learn English," the missionary wrote. "The gift we offer by teaching English is thus in a very real sense a ministry of service that has powerful potential to help students in their communities meet basic physical needs."[65] To the missionary, clearly, *all* education was "vocational" insofar as it prepared students for jobs. But the students themselves were the best judges of what vocation they would pursue and how best to train for it. In their culture, it seemed all real learning was "book" learning; and in the minds of post–World War II American teachers, culture ruled.

ℐ 3

Schooling for All?

AMERICAN TEACHERS AND THE
DILEMMAS OF EQUALITY

*ℐ*ₙ 1901, British journalist W. T. Stead published a pre-
scient book with an evocative title: *The Americanization of the World*.
The United States would soon rule the globe, Stead argued, due in
large part to America's tradition of universal education. "It is to the little red school-house . . . that we must go to find the sceptre of the American dominion," Stead wrote. "In America everybody, from the richest
to the poorest, considers that education is a boon, a necessity of life, and
the more education they get the better it is for the whole country."
Even more, Stead rhapsodized, America sent girls to school alongside
boys. Thanks to its burgeoning force of missionaries, the United States
was spreading its educational traditions overseas. In Bulgaria and
Turkey, for example, dozens of American "lady teachers" scattered "the
seeds of American principles" to students of both genders—and of
many different ethnicities. "They are busy everywhere, begetting new
life in these Asiatic races," Stead wrote of the missionaries. "They stick
to their Bible and their spelling-book, but every year an increasing
number of [students] issue from the American schools familiar with the
principles of the Declaration of Independence." Over time, Stead predicted, the rest of the globe would embrace America's guiding educational philosophy: all men—and women—are created equal.[1]

Even as Americans promoted schooling for all, however, they also
embraced rigid hierarchies of race and gender. Six years before Stead's

81

book appeared, for example, an all-white American mission in West Africa rejected several black candidates for teaching jobs in its schools. The candidates would be more susceptible to sexual "immorality" with Africans, whites said, drawing on the well-worn stereotype of black promiscuity. At the same time, white missionaries feared, hiring a black American on a "white" salary would cause African teachers and other mission employees to demand equal pay for themselves. " 'He is a black man and I am a black man,' " one missionary wrote, foreseeing the African objection. " 'He is the son of an ex-slave. I was never in bondage. So, white man, why do you give him $100.00 per month and give me only $20.00?' " Like Stead, white missionaries spoke proudly of their schools' ethnic egalitarianism: all African students received equal treatment, regardless of their tribe or nationality. But no African—or black American—would be the equal of a white man, who alone understood the critical importance of universal schooling. Around the world, in fact, white Americans pointed to invidious local prejudices as proof of their *own* racial superiority.[2]

A similar irony marked early twentieth-century American campaigns for gender equality in education. Wherever Americans went, William Stead exulted, they used schools to "liberate" girls from "the darkness of ignorance and seclusion."[3] Indeed, the oppression of foreign women—and their alleged need for rescue—represented a central rationale for American overseas education, whether in the American colonies or elsewhere.[4] As in the realm of race, however, Americans promulgated their own gender biases even as they railed against the prejudices of others. Some men feared that the preponderance of American women in overseas classrooms would "feminize" boys, echoing a common anxiety in the United States. Especially in missions, others worried that women teachers wielded too much independence. Playing one prejudice off another, male mission leaders would eventually require female teachers to submit to "native" authority. "They all see quite thoroughly that the Chinese are not ready to take the work of their *own* departments," a female teacher in China wrote, condemning mission leaders for appointing a Chinese principal in her school. *"Not one of them agreed that he would be willing to thus work under the Chinese."*[5] To subjugate American women, in short, men made them subject to the same "lesser" races that allegedly oppressed *foreign* women.

After World War II, the twin developments of decolonization abroad and civil rights campaigns in the United States would bring these contradictions into sharp relief. Announcing the formation of the Peace Corps, director Sargent Shriver frankly admitted that America's ringing proclamation of human equality in the Declaration of Independence did not ring true. At home and abroad, Shriver acknowledged, racism made a mockery of the nation's professed principles. So the Peace Corps would put the principles into action, particularly in the vital realm of education. Recruiting American minorities to serve as teachers overseas, Shriver's agency would also seek to ensure that all host peoples, whatever their race, gender, or even disability, could go to school. Here it would join hands with newly independent countries around the globe, which were rapidly embracing the longtime American goal of universal education. "The new nations of the world know that to unlock their own resources and to bring their own societies into the twentieth century they must have education," Shriver told a group of American school officials in 1962. "They know that in a democratic society, as Horace Mann said, education must be open to all."[6] Amid the first stirrings of the civil rights movement, Shriver proudly noted, Americans had finally begun to apply Mann's ideal on their own shores. Now they would help do the same thing overseas, making universal schooling into a truly universal practice.

Out in the field, however, American teachers struggled in vain to realize this American dream. Freshly imbued with the doctrine of human equality, the teachers found that many peoples around the world simply did not share it. "Americans generally . . . are prone to evangelize their egalitarian values," an observer in Sierra Leone wrote. "But Sierra Leonean society is not egalitarian. Ascribed differences are regarded as natural, proper, and just. All men are *not* created equal." As in the U.S. colonial era, then, Americans often denounced their hosts for discriminating along the lines of race and, somewhat later, gender. But the very triumph of the egalitarian ideal in the United States made other teachers wary of criticizing their colleagues and students, even for deviations from egalitarianism. "Where do I draw the line between my culture and theirs?" asked a deaf Peace Corps teacher in the Philippines, noting Filipinos' prejudice against the physically handicapped. "I don't want them to adopt mine, but I do want to be comfortable in theirs."[7] The comment reflected a new American concern with cultural sensitivity, which clashed with Americans' renewed faith in human equality. Around the globe, then, teachers struggled mightily to respect all cultures equally— even when these cultures did not appear to return the favor.

Universal Education and American Exceptionalism

In 1913, Louis Lisk reflected on his dozen years of teaching in the Philippines. Across the territory, Lisk recalled, Filipinos favored their new rulers over the colonizers who preceded them. " 'The Spanish Government did not care whether the people were educated or not,' " Filipinos told Lisk, " 'while the American government not only wants the people to become educated but are [sic] always urging more people to accept the chance.' " To be sure, Lisk admitted, this difference caused a fair share of confusion during the first few months of American rule. "It was difficult to make the people understand that we wanted the children of the lowest 'tao' class in school just as much as the more advanced class," Lisk wrote. Once Filipinos grasped the American goal, however, they flocked to the public schools. By seeking to educate all sectors of society, a second American teacher wrote, the United States "departed from all precedent in Colonial administration"—and guaranteed the loyalty of its new Philippine subjects.[8]

Of course, these teachers exaggerated Philippine participation in public education as well as the overall popularity of the American occupation. Lisk himself recalled testifying against parents who withheld their children from school, suggesting somewhat less consensus than his other statements indicated. Nevertheless, he also underscored a basic truth: compared to other colonial powers, Americans placed a much greater emphasis on schooling for all. By 1923, 1.2 million Filipinos— a full 12 percent of the population—were enrolled in public schools. By contrast, just 4 percent of the population in Dutch Java and 2 percent in British India attended school. The Philippines would boast nearly two million students by the start of World War II, giving it the third largest school system under the American flag after New York and Pennsylvania. Elsewhere in the American empire, school officials had somewhat less success instituting universal education: in Puerto Rico, for example, a meager appropriation by the territorial legislature forced schools to turn away 15,000 children. But their very desire for education demonstrated both the grassroots clientele and the unique character of "The

American Idea," as one Hawaii teacher wrote. In Europe, she explained, the ruling classes kept the bulk of citizens "ignorant as well as poor." Americans sought to educate everyone, allowing each individual to rise as far as their knowledge and initiative would take them.[9]

Likewise, American missionaries proudly advertised their distinctive commitment to universal education. As early as 1902, one journalist estimated, over one million children around the world attended Protestant schools—and nearly one-half of the schools were operated by American missions. Americans played a particularly strong role in primary education, which other missions and colonial powers frequently neglected in favor of more exclusive high schools and colleges. In China alone, for example, 42,000 children attended American mission elementary schools. "To the fertile soil of the most populous country in the world, the American has transplanted the idea that education is for all the people—coolie as well as mandarin, girl as well as boy," the journalist wrote. In neighboring India, the world's next biggest population center, Americans took the lead in educating the disadvantaged. Missions from the United States financed nearly 5,000 primary schools by 1910, catering primarily to the low-caste "mass-movement" peoples who had converted to Christianity during India's periodic famines. Americans also opened schools to impoverished "hill tribes" in Assam and Burma, where missions deliberately mixed the tribes together. "They need to go to school to broaden their minds, relieve them of petty localism, and to mollify the race prejudice which increases with segregation and which is the bane of all interracial work in Burma," one missionary explained.[10]

Elsewhere, too, American missionaries took aim at the racial, religious, and class prejudices of their hosts. In the American colonies, teachers frequently blamed such discrimination on the supposed elitism of former European rulers. Missionaries more often censured the local population itself, whose biases and bigotries underscored their allegedly inferior character. In South America, missionaries blasted "Latin" snobbery for widespread restrictions on schooling for the poor; in the Middle East, they denounced Muslims for discriminating against Christians, Jews, and Bahais; and especially in South Asia they attacked Brahmans and other high castes for denigrating lower ones.[11] "Caste is the pontifical denial of the brotherhood of man," wrote one missionary in India, suggesting a parallel between Hindu and Catholic prejudices.

"It has kept permanently submerged the depressed classes." Started primarily for untouchables, mission schools would eventually attract high-caste non-Christians who sought the instruction and status that an American school afforded. "We must admit that our school here before has been made up largely of lower caste girls from the tea-garden coolie class and about half of these have been of inferior quality mentally," wrote an Assam missionary in 1932. "Now we are having a larger number of High Caste girls from the town who are doing a good grade of work and this sets a new pace."[12]

Over time, as the preceding comment illustrated, Americans often adopted the same local prejudices that they initially reviled. Even as they railed against Latin American elitism, for example, American mission schools frequently favored wealthier applicants over impoverished ones. Some missionaries tried to justify this practice on egalitarian grounds: pupils from rich families could afford to pay tuition, which in turn helped finance scholarships for the poor. Privately, however, other teachers made it clear that their hearts—not just their purses—lay with the classes rather than the masses. "These people have not the slightest conception of time or of keeping appointments," complained one teacher in Mexico, condemning so-called free scholarship families. "They want the earth and a fence around it." By contrast, she wrote, wealthier students were "more apt to stick to the rules." From China and Japan to India and Syria, meanwhile, Americans employed intelligence quotient (IQ) tests to yield a "better" clientele. The IQ pioneer Lewis Terman visited missions in China, where his tests helped teachers segment students into "academic" and "vocational" courses. "A hundred Christian merchants, lawyers, doctors and teachers are more important than a hundred Christian coolies," one Burma missionary wrote in 1924, explaining how his own school used IQ tests to identify and cultivate future leaders. In India, meanwhile, the tests allowed cash-strapped mission schools to exclude so-called dull applicants altogether.[13]

Race and American Teacher Selection

At the same time, of course, American teachers also exported prejudices from their own shores. The most vivid illustration of American bigotry lay in the skin color of the teachers themselves. Whether in missions or

in the public schools of the American empire, instructors who came
from the United States were overwhelmingly white. Of the roughly 800
American teachers in the Philippines in 1903, just seven were identified
as African-American; only three blacks served among Puerto Rico's 200
American instructors in 1912; and in 1929, the 209 high school teachers in Hawaii—most of them from the mainland—included no African-
Americans at all. Meanwhile, after sending large groups of blacks to
Africa in the 1800s, mainline American mission boards severely curtailed the numbers of African-Americans they employed—or stopped
enlisting blacks completely. In the mid-nineteenth century, for example, sixty of eighty Presbyterian missionaries in Liberia were black. But
the Presbyterians discontinued their Liberian mission in 1894, along
with any further effort to send African-Americans to the continent. By
1928, just two of eighty-eight Presbyterian missionaries in Africa were
black. Other boards restricted their black recruitment to special
"Negro" or black-dominated missions. The Congregational Church
sent two African-American families to Angola in 1919, where they
started a station for "American Negro workers." In Liberia, site of a
"Negro" project by the Methodist Church, fifteen of its eighteen missionaries were black.[14]

The paucity of black missionaries had many causes, beginning with
the policies of colonial European governments. At least three different
colonies tried to bar African-Americans, lest blacks spread the pan-
African doctrines of Marcus Garvey. Garvey was indeed a folk hero to
many people across the African continent, as a black American missionary confirmed in 1928: "They know more about Marcus Garvey than
they know about Jesus Christ, and they are anxiously awaiting the coming of the 'messianic President General of Africa,' " he wrote. "The
only thing the European powers fear is the name of Marcus Garvey." As
their private correspondence reveals, however, white missionaries also
feared that any black American would undermine *their* power. "There
is so much today of feeling on the part of the black man that he is not
getting a square deal from the white man, that it is not time for us to
be experimenting with colored missionaries!" exclaimed one white
missionary to the Cameroon in 1922. "Colored people coming out
here might very easily side with the natives." Africans would not "look
up" to American blacks as they did to whites, another missionary worried; even more, African teachers would demand the same salaries that

black Americans received. All in all, a third white missionary thought, African-Americans would "disrupt the social order" in Africa.[15]

Nor did white officials in the American colonies welcome black teachers, who expressed special interest in the so-called Negro territories of the Caribbean. Shortly after the United States acquired the Virgin Islands, school director Henry C. Blair warned against hiring African-Americans. "The American trained Negro has a sense of self importance that renders him unfit for our purposes," Blair wrote. "White teachers from the United States are, of course, the most desirable." But they were also unobtainable, he admitted, because whites would never consent to live in such an "uncivilized"—and virtually all-black—environment. So Blair suggested hiring "natives" from neighboring British islands, who spoke better English than people in the former Danish colony that America now ruled. By the following year, Blair allowed that his schools would need to hire a few instructors from America—at least to teach manual training—and that some of them might be black. "Very likely we can secure from Lincoln, Tuskegee or Hampton school, a man who would be able to teach the subjects contemplated," Blair told the territorial governor. Black teachers were hardly the ideal, in short, but they were available—and inexpensive. By the 1930s, several Hampton graduates taught in the Virgin Islands. Although they earned a smaller salary than their less-qualified white colleagues, they also had to rent a home, while white teachers received free lodging.[16]

In the Philippines, by contrast, civil service rules ensured that black teachers would receive the same pay and benefits as whites did. Future historian Carter G. Woodson joined the service in 1903 because he was attracted to its high salary of $100 per month, much more than Woodson earned teaching in segregated black schools back home. When he was insulted by a white government clerk shortly after his arrival in the Philippines, Woodson requested and received a transfer to a different district; later, he was gratified to learn that the offending clerk had been fired. Likewise, other blacks in the Philippines praised school leaders for their fair-minded race policies. To be sure, longtime black teacher John Henry Manning Butler wrote, several white colleagues tried to "arouse race feelings" by baiting him. But educational officials judged him solely by merit, providing a vivid rejoinder to the common Filipino complaint that Americans were racist. "I know that from the time I classified in the Civil Service Bureau by examinations to my last promotion every favor shown me or mine was considered by the people as an augury of good intentions towards Filipinos," wrote Butler, who remained in the archipelago for more than forty years. Had the Philippines hired more black teachers, he added, the "clamor for autonomous rule" would not be "so great nor insistent" throughout the islands.[17]

American Teachers and "Civilizational" Inequality

Yet even where Americans enforced a semblance of equality among themselves, they stood miles above their overseas counterparts—and the counterparts knew it. In 1902, for example, American teachers in the Philippines earned between five and six times as much as Filipino instructors did. Two years later, American teachers received from $900 to $2,000 per year; for Philippine teachers, the range was $240 to $600. Condemning these imbalances, Filipinos noted that 5,000 more local teachers could have been hired with the money paid to Americans. In Puerto Rico, likewise, local teachers lamented that the United States was replacing them with "continental" imports, and compensating these newcomers handsomely. Around the world, missionaries fielded similar complaints. Chinese mission school teachers earned substantially less than instructors in government schools, while missionary salaries dwarfed them both. Demanding the same pay as Americans, meanwhile, Indian and Burmese teachers invoked the anticolonial spirit sweeping the subcontinent. "The resident Missionary . . . deals with the teacher as the final authority," wrote one Burmese teacher. "He fixes their salaries, decides their promotion, and dismisses them. Too much power rests with one man." Indeed, the teacher continued, these autocratic habits violated the "spirit of democracy" at the heart of Scripture—and at the root of the Indian freedom movement.[18]

Faced with such criticism, Americans cited professional differences: most American teachers had more education, so they deserved higher salaries as well. In private, though, Americans—of every race—emphasized the inherent inadequacies of their "uncivilized" colleagues. In the Philippines and Puerto Rico, Americans wrote, local teachers were lazy, indolent, and frequently drunk; in Mexico and Colombia, corrupt and dictatorial; in Iraq, inefficient and disorganized; in Syria, violent; and in Palestine, "very excitable." All of these foreign teachers bore the various ethnic and class prejudices of their own cultures, which Americans continued to invoke as proof of *their* superiority. Most of all, American teachers said, their counterparts lacked the intellectual equipment to teach others. "The Filipinos are about as stupid as they well could be," complained one American in the Philippines, while conducting a normal school for teachers. Some of the Philippine teachers could not remember their national capital, or even the name of their own island. Another American normal instructor recalled explaining the "five races of mankind" to a Philippine teacher, who then deemed his own race "African"—a clear sign of an inept and confused mind, the American said.[19]

Unbeknownst to this white teacher, perhaps, some Filipinos did identify with African-Americans, and vice versa, during the brutal military suppression of Philippine independence fighters. But such connections faded with the end of armed hostilities in 1902, when black Americans embraced the larger "civilizational" imperative of U.S. imperialism. Whatever their outward resemblance to Filipinos, black Americans said, they were more "advanced" and "developed" than their "backwards" hosts. Likewise, outside of the American empire, black teachers assumed an inherent superiority to local counterparts. At the "Negro" mission in Angola, one African-American teacher initially tried to share authority with his African assistant. But on the advice of Henry B. McDowell, the station's director, the teacher shifted course. "I have found that a benevolent despotism is what [the African] understands and responds to," McDowell wrote. At the same time, African-Americans were not above invoking racial solidarity when it suited their purposes. Faced with a strike by African teachers for higher pay, McDowell told the teachers that "they were striking against their blood, and kinsmen." Eventually, the strikers returned to work and begged forgiveness. "The whole world is restless and longing for something better," McDowell and his wife wrote in a letter to friends at home. "It cries for higher wages and shorter hours, thinking that the toy will satisfy its fancy." Like little children, it seemed, African teachers needed strict discipline from their civilizational elders.[20]

Most of all, Americans said, overseas teachers needed the direction and control of the Americans themselves. Even skilled instructors lacked the backbone to administer their own schools, as one Korea missionary wrote; especially in "Oriental" lands, he added, only a wise white principal could keep unruly teachers and students in line. An effort by another missionary in Iran to promote "democratic decision-making" at his school unleashed "an avalanche of utterly impossible and foolish suggestions," underscoring the crucial need for American oversight. Ostensibly sent to the Philippines as "assistants" to local teachers, Americans were quietly instructed to take charge of their schools as soon as possible, but to do so with "tact" and "diplomacy," as one super-intendent wrote. "The native teachers who are in charge of the schools upon your arrival must be retained," another official wrote. "The Fil-ipino teacher will be found very easy to control and direct." Only in Puerto Rico did early twentieth-century American teachers find them-selves under the actual command of "native" principals, sparking angry letters and petitions to colonial officials. "These Principals are generally *Porto Rican* educated in the ancient method," one teacher underlined. "The methods and system prevalent is [sic] precisely the same as those which obtained in Europe, when Columbus discovered this island!" American teachers could reform education in Puerto Rico, she added confidently, but only if they first gained authority over its schools.[21]

Such statements became more controversial after World War I, which made "self-determination" a rallying cry for colonized peoples around the globe. Gradually, Americans acknowledged the need to "work ourselves out of a job" and to cede power to local leaders, as a Presbyterian in Iran wrote in 1932. By 1936, the standard Methodist missionary application asked directly, "Are you willing to work under the direction of a national?" The correct answer was clear: yes. But as women in the field quickly realized, "devolution" to local authority placed *them* under this authority before anyone else. Turning schools over to host nationals, male mission leaders retained their own power and independence. So America's largely female force of mission teach-ers became subject to the whim of "ignorant" local principals, a China teacher complained, while white men remained in control of them both. "Imagine, if you can, the conditions—Chinese with little and most likely no normal training, in charge, and with not much real knowledge even of modern education," she wrote. "Then think of for-eign women (and Chinese men have even less belief in the ability of women than most foreign men) coming to teach under them—to teach what the Chinese say to teach, when they say to teach it, and the way they say." Signaling a new challenge to racist policies, devolution—or "devilution," as skeptical female missionaries called it—would reinforce a rather different prejudice, with a very old target: women.[22]

Girls, Boys, and Schools

"Oriental parents are much more solicitous concerning the education of boys than of girls; the girls in an Oriental home are very subordinate beings, and in the past little regard has been given to their schooling." So declared a Hawaii school official in 1917, noting that three-quarters of students at the territory's largest high school were boys. But there was hope on the horizon, the official continued, thanks to the hundreds of *haole* or white instructors spreading "American ideals" in the territory. Especially at the elementary level, Hawaii's largely female teaching force made sure girls went to school, even against the wishes of their mothers. Teacher Mary Fleming received a desperate note from one such girl: "Dear Miss Fleming, Please send a policeman to take me to school. My Mother will not let me go. Your loving pupil, Annie." Fleming went to Annie's home herself, where she found the girl caring for an infant sibling while their mother relaxed in a rocking chair on the porch. Placing the baby on her mother's lap, Annie climbed into Fleming's car. But she burst into tears after they reached school, certain that her mother would "give her a licking" when she returned. At that point Fleming called the local sheriff, instructing him to visit the home and ensure that no harm came to her student.[23]

Like Mary Fleming, American teachers around the globe demonstrated a stubborn commitment to female education. By keeping girls out of school, teachers said, "Oriental" and "Latin" peoples condemned them to lives of toil and abuse. So Americans would intervene, rescuing women from "the bondage of fear and superstition," as one India missionary wrote. In many parts of the nineteenth-century world, mission schools represented the only type of formal girls' education. As late as 1885, all 13,000 female students in India attended a mission institution; until 1906, likewise, an American academy in Iran was the only school enrolling Muslim girls. In the early 1900s, government schools finally began to open their doors to children of both sexes. But girls still lagged far behind boys, American teachers noted, so mission schools would have to take up the slack. Indeed, gender enrollments at mission institutions often inverted the skew in state schools. By 1924, for example,

American Presbyterians in Cairo, Egypt, educated 1,738 girls to just 762 boys; in Alexandria, meanwhile, they operated four girls' schools to just one school for boys. Two-thirds of students at a Baptist school in South India were girls, while boys made up a similar fraction of public school pupils in the area.[24]

The Baptist school was coeducational, marking another key American initiative. Wherever local laws allowed it, missionaries sought to mix the sexes; in their own empire, meanwhile, Americans typically required it. Lest they insult age-old "Spanish" sensibilities, school officials in the Philippines initially ordered teachers to separate the sexes. But the teachers ignored the directive, setting a pattern that would hold across the century. In the American view, separate schools added an unwelcome erotic charge alongside an unnecessary expense: established to dull prurient interests and curiosities, single-sex institutions often sparked them. In Guatemala, for example, boys and girls who had never interacted with each other exhibited a dangerous "sex complex," as one missionary wrote. But Americans would bring them together, teaching the sexes to cooperate—and, even, to compete—in "natural" ways. "Boys who used to be taught that girls were inferior to themselves are beginning to harbor a higher respect for them, and scholarship is advanced through the healthy competition which leads a boy to keenly dislike being outdone by a girl," an American observer in Puerto Rico wrote. Coeducation would teach "wholesome respect" between the sexes, he added, "which strikes directly at the chief weakness of the Latin races in the tropics."[25]

Like caste and class bigotry, Americans said, sexual prejudices demonstrated the weakness of nearly all nonwhite races around the world. By corollary, of course, Americans' enlightened views on gender revealed their own natural superiority. Teachers in China took special aim at footbinding, freeing girls' feet and fitting them with larger shoes; the students would then march in parades, to show townsfolk that their feet were no longer confined. Missionaries also condemned child marriage and female infanticide, frequent practices in India as well China; they even distributed a geography textbook with fictional letters from a Chinese national living in the West, showing that none of these sins occurred in "civilized" countries. In Muslim areas, teachers reserved their greatest ire for the veils and other restrictive garments that girls wore. Like single-sex schools, Americans said, veils made it impossible for

girls and boys to "get acquainted" in a "normal" manner; more generally, such restrictions underscored the lowly status of females in Islamic
societies. As their students began to discard their *chaddaurs*, then, missionaries in Iran celebrated. "The great mass of Persian women are
awake only enough to bow their heads in submission to the will of
Allah," one teacher wrote. "But the Enlightened Few are busy and some
day the world will hear from them." American teachers might decry the
slow rate of change, in short, but they never doubted its direction—
toward "freedom" for women.[26]

In the meantime, however, they also had to carve out a place for
themselves. Primarily single women, teachers were stark anomalies in
many of the societies they entered. Thus, they faced routine insults and
indignities, which the teachers recounted with a mixture of bitterness
and mirth. After accepting a banquet invitation from a provincial official, China missionary Martha Wiley found herself seated at a table
with concubines. Wiley jumped up and announced, "I am not a con-
cubine! I am the teacher of your sons." To the shock of her hosts, she
proceeded to stroll over to a different table. In the Philippines, villagers
also frequently presumed that unattached teachers were women of
"easy" virtue. "Our 'goings out and comings in,' our entire 'walk and
conversation,' were watched most sedulously," wrote one teacher. "The
lives of American women were subjected to a more exacting scrutiny
than those of the men, for how could women go about freely as we did
and take proper care of themselves and remain good?" After an American teacher in Iran persuaded seven of her eight graduating girls to discard their veils, policemen refused to allow the group to dine in public.
They repaired to the teacher's residence for their meal, bowed but
hardly defeated.[27]

American Men versus American Women

At the same time, female teachers also suffered slights from American
men. Just as whites reviled African-Americans but denounced the "race
prejudice" of their students, so did American men demean female
colleagues while condemning locals for their "backwards" gender attitudes. Unlike blacks, of course, women represented a majority of American teachers in most overseas settings. But to anxious American school
leaders, that was precisely the problem. In Hawaii, where roughly 90

percent of elementary teachers were female, officials worried that many of them sailed to the islands on a lark, or, even worse, to find a husband. "Much is said in the islands in criticism of the 'tourist' teacher from the mainland," one official wrote, "who comes to the island merely for adventure and for sight-seeing, and who leaves after she has had her fill of both." Even in the Philippines, where 346 of the original 526 "Thomasites" were men, school officials worried that the archipelago had too many female instructors. "There is one thing that has forced itself upon us here, and that is, we don't want any more women teachers," Philippines school director Fred W. Atkinson wrote privately, after the USS *Thomas* had arrived. "In sending teachers I wish that the men would be given preference." For the first decade or two of the U.S. occupation, the American teacher force in the Philippines would retain its male majority. But by 1924, school officials complained, just one-third of the teachers were men.[28]

Explaining their zeal for male teachers—and their concerns about female ones—school officials often cited overseas sentiment: in heavily "prejudiced" societies, students and fellow teachers would not abide by women instructors. But the truth was almost exactly the reverse. Despite their occasional clashes with local authorities, female American teachers were less threatening—and more popular—than men were. During the war of 1899–1902, Filipinos specifically requested American women for their schools; if U.S. authorities sent a man, one mayor explained, children might mistake the teacher for a soldier and stay home. In the Philippines and Puerto Rico alike, meanwhile, growing female school enrollment sparked further demand for female teachers. "There is an expressed unwillingness on the part of parents . . . to place their adolescent daughters under the tutelage of young men," reported one Puerto Rico school official, "such relations being so contrary to their general ideas of propriety." On his first day teaching in the Philippines, Benjamin Neal was surprised to find over 100 boys and just one girl. The rest of the villagers had withheld their daughters "because there was no lady teacher," as Neal later learned.[29]

Against this backdrop, school officials' animus against female teachers had less to do with local attitudes than with *American* ones, especially regarding gender and power. As in the United States, American female teachers rarely rose to positions of authority within overseas schools. Plum jobs almost always went to men, causing recriminations and jealousies on all sides. Given the small pool of men in the teaching force, one male veteran of the Hawaii schools admitted, "some very mediocre people" became principals and superintendents, and assumed command over women with more talent and experience. "The deputy superintendent knows rather less about teaching than an infant," lamented Philippines teacher Philinda Rand, a trained teacher and a magna cum laude graduate of Radcliffe. "He is supposed to visit the schools and report on the teachers. As a matter of fact he has not been in my school for five minutes." Even worse were the supervisors who visited frequently to flex their dictatorial muscles, making snap judgments about matters beyond their wisdom. One Hawaii teacher received an unsatisfactory grade from her supervisor, who simply asserted that she lacked any "aptitude" for instruction; nor was she likely to improve, he added gratuitously, even with training. "The school is a very discouraging one," the teacher wrote, condemning her supervisor, "and the teacher needs no additional depression, who has the listlessness of half-fed, overworked children to contend with."[30]

For their own part, male administrators regarded their female charges with a blend of condescension and scorn. Superintendents lectured new women teachers in the Philippines about "proper deportment," offering to chaperone these "dear girls" if they went out in the evening. (" 'Dear girls' was touching in the extreme,' " recalled one bemused teacher, "as most of us were on the wrong side of 25, and a large majority of 30.") When women openly challenged them, however, officials' chivalry could turn quickly into contempt. One outraged Hawaii superintendent reported that a teacher had veered from the official course of study, against his explicit order to follow it; meanwhile, she had the gall to criticize *him* for placing 39 students in her classroom. But the teacher was simply dissatisfied because she could not afford new furniture and a cook, the superintendent said, invoking the common stereotype of female envy and materialism. In Puerto Rico, one supervisor became so frustrated by his American women teachers that he requested "native" instructors instead. "They are inclined to feel independent of the rules of the department of education," the supervisor wrote, castigating the American women, "and to assume unwarranted authority over the native teachers."[31]

Only in missions did women routinely exert *actual* authority over schools and teachers, setting the stage for the sharpest gender conflict among overseas Americans. Most female teachers in the early twentieth-century went abroad under the auspices of women's missionary societies, which operated independently from their denominational mission boards. In many missions, so-called single ladies vastly outnumbered men; they also assumed sole responsibility for the schools, where they created separate beachheads of authority. In Burma, for example, Baptist mission official Edward Stevens complained that his own station actually had "four heads": three "single lady school 'Superintendents' " plus himself. All three women remained "independent of the male missionary in charge of the station"—that is, of Stevens—and seemed unwilling to consider his advice. "What relation should the male missionary sustain to the school under the care of the lady missionary?" another Burma station director asked. His answer was simple: Men should direct women. "Schools should be under the direct care of the missionary in charge of the station," a third station chief wrote, "who should have control of the payment of all teachers, thus controlling their employment." The mission, it seemed, was a house divided by gender; and without a clear line of male authority, it could not stand.[32]

Beneath this dispute lay not just a struggle for power, but also competing ideas about education itself. Noting that the Burma mission possessed more "single ladies" than men, another mission leader worried that these women would sway the mission too far toward their special bailiwick—schools—and too far from its original purpose. "School work will encroach upon direct evangelistic work or become out of proportion to it," he wrote. "The trouble is not that the school work is not good, but that preaching is better." Other mission spokesmen took special aim at girls' education, which could never generate the indigenous Christian leaders that the world needed. In Guatemala, for example, an angry Presbyterian official censured the mission for establishing several girls' schools, but ignoring boys. "The girls' schools are good but they are not cardinal," he wrote. "If we don't get a pastor factory started soon the day is not distant when the entire enterprise . . . will crumble like Guatemala in the earthquake." Even as it denounced prejudice overseas, then, the entire enterprise of American education rested upon its own gender and racial bigotries. Only after midcentury would these biases begin to wither, creating a new set of challenges and dilemmas for American teachers.[33]

Civil Rights and the New Global Equality

In 1964, Queens College senior Nancy Scheper attended two memorable talks by volunteer recruiters on her campus. The first appeal came from Peace Corps director Sargent Shriver, who asked the students to join in the worldwide struggle for freedom. Then came a young man clad in overalls, representing "Mississippi Freedom Summer," who implored his listeners to fight "racial apartheid" at home. Scheper applied to both projects, but only the Peace Corps offered her a position. She accepted it.

Scheper was packing for her Peace Corps training when she heard about the death of Andrew Goodman, a fellow student at Queens College. Goodman had applied to Mississippi Freedom Summer, too, but he was accepted. Now Scheper learned that he had been murdered, along with two co-workers, and buried in a swamp. Nancy Scheper made the sign of the cross to bless Andy Goodman, with whom she had once taken a creative writing class. Then, "struck by the guilt of the survivor," she resolved to campaign for racial equality in the United States after she completed her Peace Corps assignment in Brazil. Upon her return, Scheper would travel to Selma, Alabama, and do exactly that.[34]

Scheper's story highlights a profound shift in the sensibilities of many post–World War II Americans who chose to teach overseas. Previous generations of American teachers had condemned the "prejudice" they encountered abroad, but they largely ignored bias and discrimination at home. Amid the searing heat of the civil rights struggle in the United States, however, post–World War II teachers linked their overseas efforts to that same struggle. "Have you been arrested five times in the last five months for sitting in?" a Peace Corps advertisement asked in 1965, tongue only slightly in cheek. "Do you think we should ban the bomb, integrate Mississippi into the United States, abolish the State Department and turn the Met over to folksingers? The Peace Corps is just your cup of espresso." To be sure, many Peace Corps teachers did not fit this radical caricature; nor did most missionaries, who continued to outnumber Peace Corps volunteers in some parts of the world. Clearly, though, post–World War II American teachers drew much of their inspiration from the civil rights movement. By one estimate, 5 percent of Freedom Summer participants went on to join the Peace

Corps. In Guinea, volunteers met with Fannie Lou Hamer and other visiting delegates from the Student Non-Violent Coordinating Committee; in Ghana and Ethiopia, they had audiences with Malcolm X; and upon their return, many volunteers joined Nancy Scheper in renewed civil rights protest.[35]

Here they received encouragement from top Peace Corps officials, who frequently drew their own parallels between social justice campaigns at home and volunteer efforts overseas. Starting with Sargent Shriver, whose civil rights advocacy earned him the nickname of "house communist" in John F. Kennedy's White House, Peace Corps leaders came overwhelmingly from the left flank of the Democratic Party. They peppered their rhetoric with praise for black freedom fighters like Martin Luther King, Jr., whom they briefly considered for an appointment in Africa. They even tried to hire radical student leader Tom Hayden, who had once mocked the Peace Corps as "a group of 4-H graduates." Most of all, Peace Corps leaders sought to link the agency to the youthful energy, idealism, and egalitarianism of the civil rights movement itself. To one official, Peace Corps was an "international sit-in"; to another, it symbolized the liberation of "oppressed peoples" at home and abroad. "No one who travels in the outside world—among the two-thirds of the world's people who are colored—can underestimate the importance of ending all forms of racial discrimination in all parts of our national life," wrote Harris Wofford, who had left his White House civil rights post to join the agency. "But the Peace Corps is working on the larger, perhaps more difficult form of this problem: the integration of our less-colored Western minority into a newly developing world community."[36]

Out in the field, teachers echoed many of these themes. For white volunteers, especially, the overseas experience heightened their awareness of racism in the United States. "If we joined the Peace Corps out of a conviction for human rights we rejoin American society with an even greater conviction," wrote one returned volunteer. "We will personally participate, even intervene, in the effort to secure equal rights for all people." Like Nancy Scheper, some volunteers felt guilty for exempting themselves from the violent struggles back home; to others, particularly African-Americans, the Peace Corps provided a welcome respite from beatings, water hoses, and other consequences of civil rights protest. But nearly all of the teachers embraced the egalitarian *ideology* of the civil rights movement, as many observers noted. In Colombia, a survey of Peace Corps volunteers found that they emphasized "all men are equal" more than any other value. In a skeptical vein, meanwhile, anthropologist David Szanton described the "primitive egalitarianism" that Peace Corps teachers brought to the Philippines. "All things Philippine were to be admired and respected," he wrote, summarizing the volunteer ethos, "and Filipinos were regarded as being only superficially different from Americans."[37]

Yet many Americans found that they could *not* respect certain local habits and practices. American teachers especially resented colleagues who ignored, neglected, or abused their own students. Others issued more blanket condemnations of host peoples, privately deriding them as dishonest, dirty, lazy, and corrupt. "The majority of Peace Corps Volunteers in Iran despise Iranians," admitted one American. "But this majority knows that Christians do not say such things in public or for the record." For volunteers imbued with the new gospel of egalitarianism, indeed, even *thinking* such things proved extraordinarily painful. "[T]hey could not deny their own tired anti-Filipino reactions—reactions that inescapably implied a sense of superiority to their hosts," wrote David Szanton, analyzing Peace Corps teachers in the Philippines. "This quandary often produced powerful feelings of guilt for not living up to one's own professed ideals—one hated oneself for hating the Filipinos." In Kenya, likewise, teachers often discovered—to their chagrin—that they disliked their counterparts, despite Americans' repeated insistence that "Africans are just as good as we are." To the Americans, "good" meant being honest, punctual, and persistent. Many African teachers simply did not fit the bill, which in turn appeared to contradict the Americans' ringing proclamations of equality.[38]

Race and Ethnicity: Equality Upheld

Most of all, the teachers found, many of their hosts enforced vicious forms of discrimination against each other. Despite their covert distaste for some of the cultures they encountered, the Americans never wavered from the *principle* of equality; indeed, they disparaged their own negative reactions precisely because these feelings violated the egalitarian ideal. Around the world, however, American teachers would come into contact with peoples who viewed themselves as inherently superior—or inferior—to others. In many societies, wealthier families simply did not believe that the poor needed or deserved an education. *"The root problem in Guatemala* is the vast socio-economic gap between the few rich and the masses of oppressed, poverty-stricken people," Catholic Maryknoll missioners emphasized in 1963. Maryknolls started three schools in remote mountain regions, to serve the nation's poor, while in more affluent areas, they devised curricula to make rich Guatemalans "conscious of their social responsibility," as one teacher wrote. At their high school, Maryknolls asked students to imagine living in a poor *barrio* or going to bed on an empty stomach. They also formed a student club of "Christian Militants," who held evening discussions about social injustice in Latin America.[39]

Not surprisingly, local elites resisted such efforts. Bolivian military authorities arrested Catholic missioners for allegedly indoctrinating poor students with "the theology of liberation and communism," interrogating the Americans for hours before they were finally released. At the same time in Nicaragua, missioners' own students at a well-to-do Managua school condemned them for teaching poorer children in the countryside. Class prejudice was compounded by ethnic bigotry, teachers found, because many impoverished students were also Native American. "Often the public school teachers are Latinos who do not wish to see the Indian educated," wrote one Guatemala missioner. When Native American children did attend school, meanwhile, teachers openly exploited them for menial labor. "The Indian pupil spends the greater part of the school day running errands, hauling water and planting a garden for the teacher," the missioner continued. "After two years of such routine he barely signs his name. Then they say that the Indian is uneducable." In Ecuador, similarly, Peace Corps teacher David Matthes blasted the majority "white" population for denigrating Native Americans. Across the country, whites used "Indian" as a term of insult: choice phrases included "dirtier than an Indian" or "drunk like an Indian." They also forced Native Americans to ride in the back of busses, like blacks in the American South. So Matthes went out of his way to make friends with Indians, which offended his Latino colleagues.[40]

The sharpest conflicts over ethnicity occurred in Africa, where appalled American teachers encountered a wide range of tribal divisions and discrimination. In Nigeria, for example, a university-educated Hausa told one teacher that all of the Ibo people—even children—should simply be killed. Arriving on the continent with visions of racial unity, African-Americans were especially shocked and troubled by the ethnic prejudice they witnessed. Occasionally, such bigotries placed American blacks at physical risk. A Hausa soldier at a Nigerian roadblock mistook Peace Corps volunteer Charles Gray for an Ibo, refusing to believe that Gray was an American because, the soldier said, "Americans are white." So Gray said he was Japanese, which mollified the soldier enough to let Gray pass. In Ethiopia, meanwhile, a Tigrinean hotel clerk asked African-American William Seraile if he was a member of the rival Amharic tribe. Seraile replied simply that he was "American"; had Seraile answered "Amharic," the clerk said, he might have been murdered. Finally, in neighboring Somalia, a beggar told Leander Jones that his "hard" or "nappy" hair marked him as a member of the nation's lowest order. "Soft" or curly-headed clans dominated Somalia, brutalizing other peoples with impunity.[41]

More commonly, Africans grouped black Americans with the dominant tribe or ethnicity in their respective countries. For teachers who themselves faced harsh racial discrimination back home, such identification proved even more problematic. In Liberia, for example, Carl Meacham found that the ruling Americo-Liberians blocked indigenous tribes from political power and abused them "in the same sexual way" as white planters had exploited slave women in America. So Meacham cringed when Americo-Liberians tried to claim him as their own. "They were as 'racist' as many whites I had encountered in the South," Meacham wrote. "The discriminatory system in Liberia reminded me of racism and segregation in Alabama." Yet when he challenged his colleagues' ethnic prejudice, they used the same parallel to argue that Meacham should fight racism back home, not abroad. "Why don't you do this in your country?" asked Americo-Liberian students, after Meacham condemned the unequal funding of indigenous tribes' schools. "You're not as free in your country as you are here." Likewise, Ghanaian students blasted black teacher Ed Smith as a "meddler" after he denounced their tribal biases. Smith came to Ghana only to "escape from the police dogs of America," the students said, underscoring prejudice in America as well as Smith's lowly status there.[42]

This retort placed American teachers—of every race—in a difficult spot. None of them wished to deny prejudice or discrimination in the United States; indeed, the Peace Corps' frequent nods to the civil rights movement reflected a consensus on the existence, and the evil, of racism back home. Moreover, the continued paucity of blacks among America's overseas teachers provided a vivid reminder of racial inequality in the so-called land of freedom.[43] To Americans, though, the very presence of black teachers, even in small numbers, reflected the enormous strides that African-Americans had made. "People ask me why I'm discriminated against, why the white man in America doesn't like the black man, and how they would be treated if they went to America," lamented an annoyed black teacher in Senegal. "Every time they find a new picture of the hoses or the dogs in Mississippi or something, they bring it over to the house to show me." Likewise, a black volunteer in India bridled when local villagers harped on racial discrimination back home. Yes, he told them, blacks in America suffered from racism. But they had also begun to overcome it, thanks to a rising egalitarian spirit that was sweeping the country and, Americans hoped, the world.[44]

They were wrong. Like the United States, the societies they visited were wracked by ethnic and racial prejudice. Although American teachers regarded these biases as invented and invidious, their hosts often saw them as natural and normal. Here lay a true philosophical Rubicon, which most Americans refused to cross. On many other matters, ranging from dress and diet to instructional methods and discipline, the teachers proudly asserted their "cultural sensitivity"; unlike previous generations of Americans as well as present-day European expatriates, they accepted local mores without trying to change them.[45] "A people could be equally human, could be equally entitled to consideration, while at the same time they were significantly *different* in their values," wrote anthropologist David Szanton, underlining this tolerant and open-minded ethos. "Difference, in short, no longer implied inferiority. Differences, indeed, were to be respected." Yet post–World War II American teachers simply could not respect people who did not regard *other* humans as equal. Hardly a universal doctrine, the civil rights–era doctrine of egalitarianism was the most distinctive feature of the teachers' own "Americanness," as several observers noted.[46] It also marked the far end of their cultural tolerance, which would not extend to people who openly discriminated for reasons of race or ethnicity.

Gender: Equality Deferred

Gender, as always, was a different story. Back home, the civil rights spirit of "brotherhood" took little note of women; by some accounts, indeed, America's feminist movement would emerge from the tension between racial egalitarianism and the subordinate status of women.[47] Officials at the top of avowedly liberal agencies like the Peace Corps largely ignored issues of gender. Sponsored by Hubert Humphrey of Minnesota, the original Peace Corps bill in the Senate excluded women altogether; although 40 percent of volunteers in the 1960s were female, the agency took few steps to attract, integrate, or understand them. Here they stood in sharp contrast to African-Americans, whom the Peace Corps recruited with zeal, albeit with little success. As in the pre–World War II period, missionary and Christian lay groups reported higher percentages of women. But male leaders paid them little mind, except as targets of pop psychology or sexist humor. Reporting on several new members of the Papal Volunteers for Latin America, training director Ivan Illich described the women as selfish, sex-starved, or in need of "psychotherapeutic treatment"; when men had problems, he suggested pastoral counseling. In Protestant missions, meanwhile, officials took special glee in mocking "spinster" teachers. "Half of the women on the field are there because of disappointing love lives," joked one official. Another listened to a woman describe her problems overseas, then concluded, flatly, "She needs a husband."[48]

Out in the field, meanwhile, Peace Corps officials worried that American women were trying to *find* a husband, or, even worse, simply a sex partner. "Impressionable, previously lonely, emotionally immature females fall prey to the male attention," wrote one evaluator in the Philippines, "and are believed sometimes to mistake physical attraction for love." While turning a blind eye to sexual promiscuity by male volunteers, the Peace Corps frequently sent home women for the same offense. In Liberia, for example, a male volunteer who contracted venereal disease from an African woman merely received a lecture on "sexual responsibility"; by contrast, the Peace Corps dismissed several women for "multiple sexual relationships" with Africans. Likewise, during its first two years in the Philippines, the agency fired ten women "for misbehavior connected with romance and sex." Over the same span, not a single man was dismissed for a similar infraction. Peace Corps officials pictured female volunteers as fickle sexual creatures, blinded by lust in a faraway land.[49]

In fact, love affairs between American women and local men were fraught with tensions and acrimony. Echoing a common scenario in the United States, some Africans invoked Americans' civil rights ethos to pressure white women into sex. If they *really* believed in human equality, whites would take a black lover; and if they said no, they risked being called a bigot. One local magazine even ran an article explaining "how to make out with American Peace Corps volunteers," explicitly prescribing such appeals to racial guilt. Other women described constant physical harassment—lewd remarks, exhibitionism, and so on—plus the most serious threat of all: sexual assault. But Peace Corps officials did not take it seriously. "It seems as if Hugh Hefner got there first, peddling his Playboy Philosophy," quipped two staff members in Senegal, responding to female complaints about sexually aggressive African men. "Could it really be that bad?" It was. Despite officials' dismissive tone, rape was a fairly common experience for female American teachers. In Kenya, Peace Corps women tried—in vain—to create counseling sessions for volunteers who had been sexually assaulted by fellow teachers or headmasters. After a volunteer in Micronesia was nearly raped by an intruder, Peace Corps officials told her group that the victim was partially at fault. She had slept in a room by herself and without a blanket to cover her, which left her prey to male intruders.[50]

In the schools, meanwhile, American teachers rarely launched direct challenges against the harsh gender discrimination they encountered. The same male volunteers who condemned African ethnic prejudice ignored sexism, which simply did not rise to the same level of evil in their minds. To be sure, one Somalia volunteer built a library at a girls' school against the wishes of village elders; in Uganda, a teacher used his classroom to denounce domestic violence; and in Senegal, another instructor asked his students why only girls swept the floors. The students laughed and he dropped the subject, providing an apt metaphor for male American efforts in this realm. For women volunteers, meanwhile, their mere presence in many foreign societies represented a huge challenge to gender norms. Somalian passersby spit at female American teachers; in Afghanistan, boys threw rocks at them; and in Iran, men bumped up against them and hissed obscenities. Especially in Islamic nations, some single American women could not even talk with their male colleagues for fear of being labeled a tramp or a prostitute. Indeed, one female teacher in Iran ruefully concluded, Americans should stop sending unmarried women to the country. "I didn't expect it to be easy," she wrote. "But I didn't understand what it means to be a second-class human—a female."[51]

Meanwhile, some American men seemed willing to accept or even to justify gender discrimination overseas. Women abided by local norms for practical reasons, not for principled ones: in some situations, talking with a man could literally get you killed. But American males sometimes defended the sexist norms on their own merit, invoking relativist arguments that were rarely applied to racial or ethnic prejudice. In Iran, for example, one teacher acknowledged that restrictive laws against women seemed "Victorian" to Americans. But the rules were a "very comfortable set of behavioral codes—built up over the ages," he continued, so volunteers should be wary of interfering with them. Such messages were reinforced by Peace Corps officials, who warned teachers against "judging" local gender ideas or "imposing" their own. At a training for Nigeria teachers, one speaker explained how polygamy made sense within West African culture; trainers in Micronesia warned against blaming local peoples for rape, which was "a concept from our own culture"; and in Iran, a Peace Corps consultant urged volunteers to accept local gender values even if the Americans could not approve them. Iranian ideas about gender were surely "debatable," the consultant acknowledged, but they stemmed from centuries of tradition. Americans might find good reasons to dislike the tradition, but they should not try to change it.[52]

Disability: Equality Introduced

When it came to the physically disabled, by contrast, American teachers openly questioned local prejudices. Like minority ethnicities and women, deaf and blind people faced discrimination, hostility, and ridicule in many of their respective societies. But they were also largely invisible, so Americans could defend them without incurring serious risks. American missions started schools for the deaf and other disabled people around the world, insisting, against local wisdom, that these groups could and should be educated. In Korea, for example, five Protestant denominations helped start and operate a school for blind children; in Taiwan, Catholic missioners ran a school for the mentally handicapped; and in Bolivia, they started the country's first institute for deaf students. The missions received frequent visits from Helen Keller, whose global tours sparked new awareness about the true abilities of "disabled" persons. "Everyone who heard Miss Keller was much impressed by her achievements in spite of her handicap, and deeply moved by her courage," wrote one Lebanon missionary in 1952, after Keller came to her school. A pacifist and frequent critic of American foreign policy, Keller was nevertheless embraced by overseas missions—and by the U.S. State Department—as an embodiment of key American virtues: initiative, determination, persistence, and self-reliance.[53]

During its first few years, the Peace Corps showed little interest in the disabled. It sent its first deaf volunteer in 1967 to Kenya, where she taught science at a "regular" boys school; two years later, a second deaf volunteer went to Ghana to teach in a state institute for the deaf. The Peace Corps did not establish its first official program in deaf education until 1974, when Gallaudet University professor Frances Parsons persuaded the agency to send three of her students to teach at a deaf school in the Philippines. Unable to hear since birth, Parsons traveled to over a dozen countries in the late 1960s and found "widespread prejudice against the deaf," as she told an interviewer. In Catholic cultures, families often saw deaf children as a punishment from God; Hindu cultures viewed them as a product of "bad karma," or wrongdoing in a previous life. They were also frequent targets of abuse: in one classroom, for example, Parsons watched in horror as a teacher put metal tongs on a deaf child's tongue to "correct" her speech. By 1980, fifteen Peace Corps volunteers worked in deaf education in the Philippines alone. Around the world, forty-five others taught in schools for the blind, deaf, or mentally handicapped. "We want the children here at the school to be like us and never feel ashamed," explained Guy Vollmar, a deaf protégé of Parsons in the Philippines. "Many children had an inferiority complex when they came, but they are changing."[54]

At the same time, of course, Vollmar's frankly transformative goal—to remake deaf Filipinos in his own image—implied that Americans were *superior* to other peoples, at least in the way they regarded the disabled. Indeed, as a second volunteer confirmed, the Peace Corps' programs for the handicapped inevitably bore a "revolutionary touch." Americans aimed not simply to provide services to disabled groups but to "empower" them, that is, to promote a new spirit of pride, confidence, and determination. Just as important, Americans aimed at rebutting the profound social bias against the disabled. "I try to educate the public that deaf people can do almost everything a hearing person does," wrote Marie Greenstone, a deaf teacher in Malaysia. "And deaf people themselves need to see successful deaf persons so they can build up their image and try to follow our examples." Some hearing volunteers even found themselves identifying with the deaf, because both of them lay outside of the social mainstream. Communicating in sign language with her students in Nepal, Patricia Ross often heard onlookers call her the *lati Americani*, or "dumb American." Ross usually ignored such remarks, but now and again her temper would flare. "I'm not dumb, my friends are not dumb!" she shouted. Working with two local artists, Ross authored the first dictionary of the sign language that deaf Nepalis had developed. A Peace Corps teacher did the same in Mongolia, helping to standardize its indigenous system of signs.[55]

Yet deaf-education volunteers fought bitterly among themselves over the relative value of sign language and oral communication, extending a debate that had raged in the United States for years. Teachers who were deaf themselves tended to favor sign language, which would promote independence and pride within a formerly stigmatized group. Hearing teachers supported oral instruction, arguing that deaf children needed it in order to communicate with other members of society. "There have been terrific clashes between the deaf and hearing PCVs about how soon and how much a deaf child should be trained to speak," observed Frances Parsons in the Philippines, "and they have parents bewildered and confused." Swayed by former colonial rulers, who required oralism in deaf schools, most parents and teachers in the Third World preferred speech instruction to sign language. So deaf Americans resolved to fight this "oralist prejudice," just as they challenged the bias against deaf people in general. Parsons advocated a philosophy called "Total Communication," which endorsed any system that deaf people chose on their own. Like most other deaf leaders in America, however, she had little doubt that manual instruction was the better choice. Freed from the "benevolent paternalism" and "mental cruelty" of misguided oralists, deaf people would take their place as full citizens of the nation—and of the world.[56]

Yet the deaf teachers' emphasis on manual instruction was itself paternalistic, as their own rhetoric revealed. "Many educators still believe in Oralism," lamented Marie Greenstone, criticizing Asian ideas about the deaf. "Malaysia is slow and backwards . . . and we, as deaf PCVs, can show them the way to upgrade the standards of deaf education and the deaf community." From a different perspective, indeed, the entire American effort on behalf of the handicapped was paternalistic. "As a Peace Corps Volunteer, you cannot just impose ideas on host country people," warned one teacher in Paraguay. "Rather, you must teach through their value systems and ideals." In the Philippines, likewise, a Peace Corps official urged deaf volunteers to change local attitudes "in the context of Filipino culture." Here and elsewhere, paeans to local culture revealed post–World War II Americans' almost instinctual reluctance to "impose values" on others. But sometimes, they could not help themselves. Changing local attitudes about the deaf "in the context" of local culture was simply impossible, if that same culture tended to deny the humanity of deaf people. As in the case of ethnicity and gender, then, American teachers faced a difficult but inescapable choice: defer to local sentiment *or* expand human rights. Try as they might, they could not have it both ways.[57]

⌁ IN THE 1980s AND 1990s, American teachers became bolder about challenging gender bias around the world. Many host nations passed antidiscrimination laws and established special programs for women, signaling a new global consciousness about the issues. Not surprisingly, more overseas American teachers were women themselves. Females made up nearly 60 percent of Peace Corps volunteers by 2004, a 20 percent increase since the founding of the agency. Most American mission school teachers were women, as before, but they also displayed a new willingness to fight for female rights overseas. In 1988, for example, a teacher in the Grail movement of Catholic lay workers took her Ugandan female students to an army base for a freewheeling debate about gender discrimination. To the teacher's delight, the girls bravely challenged military officers on the subject of bridal dowries. They also launched a wider critique of sexism in Africa, condemning "the status of a wife as a chattel valued only as child-bearer, house-keeper, and field worker," the teacher proudly recalled. No longer would African girls simply accept their second-class citizenship, she exulted. Instead, with the help of the Grail teachers, the girls would shape a new destiny of freedom and equality.[58]

Here, Grail women frequently invoked Brazilian author and activist Paolo Freire, whose *Pedagogy of the Oppressed* became something of a second Bible within the organization. "Either the educator is domesticating the students, training them to accept the status quo, or liberating them to take control of their lives," wrote Grail veteran Janet Kalven, summarizing Freire's argument and influence. "As Grail, we were definitely on the side of liberation." Begun as a lay mission, the Grail would eventually drop the term "mission" in favor of "overseas service" and, finally, "international exchange." For too much of history, "missionaries saw themselves as having important truths to impart to the ignorant heathen, whom they visualized as 'sitting in darkness and the shadow of death,' " Kalven explained. "They were givers rather than receivers, doing good to the other according to their own definition of good." In a new era of equality across peoples and cultures, however, American teachers took a much more open-minded approach. They instructed, but they did not impose; they spoke, but also listened; and they learned.[59]

On questions of human rights, however, even the most culturally sensitive American teachers sometimes assumed the same missionary stance that they detested. Their hosts might no longer be ignorant heathen, suffering in darkness, but they still needed the enlightenment that only the West could bring. In a 2001 handbook about "empowering girls," for example, the Peace Corps warned against imposing new gender ideas from outside of the local culture. Under the heading "Things to Consider as You Read," the manual asked, "What are my community's priorities? Does the idea correspond with what community members want to do, or is it something that just I want to do?" But the handbook went on to praise the ways that Peace Corps teachers were *changing* community sentiment, precisely *because* it was so biased against women. In Kenya, teachers screened textbooks for gender stereotypes; in Burkina Faso, they presented awards to the best female student in each class; and in Niger, they produced skits about why families should send girls to school. Around the world, they also held "discussions" with colleagues about gender inequality and discrimination. Inevitably, however, these dialogues were designed to yield a single conclusion: women must be free and equal. Americans had the right answer, which they would urge—and, if need be, impose—upon people who did not share it.[60]

To be sure, post–World War II teachers worked diligently to dress this dynamic in the gentle rhetoric of cultural tolerance. Americans were not really trying to convert a foreign culture to their own way of thinking; instead, the teachers were simply working for "progress" or "development" in a "culturally appropriate" manner. On occasion, however, the true missionary roots of the process shone through. In 1993, Kenya Peace Corps teacher Lisa Hebl became enraged when her male students tried to evict girls from the volleyball field. She ordered the boys off the field, allowing the girls to play until their scheduled hour had elapsed. At the end of the day, she gave the boys a lecture. "I reminded them of how they tell about their grandparents who lived in the bush and were so uncivilized," Hebl wrote. "I then told them that what they had just done was also uncivilized."[61] As the imperial-era language of "civilization" underscored, Americans still saw other cultures as inferior—at least when it came to gender roles and rights. And to the degree that discrimination did inflect these cultures, the Americans were probably correct.

Certainly gay teachers thought so. By the 1990s, female equality had gained enough traction overseas that women like Lisa Hebl felt safe enough to fight for it. Gay Peace Corps teachers were not so fortunate. The agency itself welcomed homosexual volunteers, establishing a strict nondiscrimination policy in the 1990s and providing special counseling for gay applicants.[62] But it also warned gay volunteers against discussing or demonstrating their identity overseas, where the mere intimation of homosexuality would alienate them from their counterparts. Even worse, it could place them at severe physical risk. In Mauritania, homosexuality was a capital crime; and in Mongolia, one appalled gay volunteer wrote, students reported that the police had shot a local teacher because he was gay. To be sure, some Third World cities had active and relatively open gay communities. When they got to the village, however, most gay volunteers also had to return to the closet. "Other countries and cultures are not as accepting as the more progressive places in America, Europe, Australia and New Zealand," warned one gay Peace Corps veteran. "There are not many gay-friendly countries in the developing world."[63]

As the volunteer's language acknowledged, the Western world had its own fair share of homophobia: only in its "more progressive places" could gay people find safety and equality. But his comments also left little doubt that the West, even with its myriad flaws, was itself more progressive than the "developing world." When it came to rights for gays—or for ethnic minorities, or for women, or for the disabled—American teachers were not simply "different" from the cultures where they worked. They were also better, or so they thought. The very idea provoked waves of anxiety in post–World War II teachers, who were conditioned to "tolerate" and "accept" other cultures. How could post-war teachers uphold egalitarianism and cultural sensitivity, when so many host cultures seemed insensitive to women and minorities? Did not Americans' pleas for ethnic and racial equality reflect their own form of missionary-style ethnocentrism?

Part of the problem lay in their concept of culture itself: viewing foreign cultures as organic wholes, teachers could easily dismiss entire populations as sexist, racist, or homophobic. Insofar as some foreign peoples *did* oppress women and minorities, however, Americans need not have worried about "imposing" egalitarian ideas upon them. "Don't apologize," quipped one historian in the 1980s, comforting an embarrassed former missionary. "All Americans are missionaries."[64] All *teachers* are missionaries, too, inasmuch as they try to get students to behave or believe in new ways. Better to proselytize for a shared humanity than to surrender to invidious inequalities, all in the name of "cultures" that are themselves more complex, and more diverse, than any of us can divine.

⁓ II

American Critiques

$\mathcal{I}_{\text{N}}$ 1904, St. Louis hosted the World's Fair to commemorate the one hundredth anniversary of the Louisiana Purchase. It devoted no fewer than 130 buildings to the Philippine Islands, including a model classroom with dozens of "real Filipino children" who were transported to America for the event. President Theodore Roosevelt attended one of the classroom lessons, praising American educators for bringing "civilization" to the tropics. Elsewhere at the fair, however, America's leading cultural anthropologist warned against presuming that American education—or, indeed, American culture—was inherently superior. Addressing an audience of international scholars, Franz Boas argued that the "anthropological method" would demonstrate "the relative value of all forms of culture." It would also "serve as a check to an exaggerated valuation of the standpoint of our own period," Boas declared, "which we are only too liable to consider the ultimate goal of human evolution." Cataloguing the dizzying array of human differences, cultural anthropology would cast a new and trenchant light upon America's own cultural assumptions.[1]

Boas' remarks highlight the strong element of self-critique at the heart of the twentieth-century culture concept. The concept endowed every people with a basic unity and integrity, making American teachers hesitant to impose their distinct values and practices upon "another culture." But it also made the teachers critique *American* culture, which

113

looked very different from afar than from up close. Working in societies that accorded high respect to educators, Americans began to assail the relatively low status of teachers back home. At the same time, and especially among missionaries, church–state admixtures in the Third World spawned a new critique of America's own "separationist" tradition. If African and Asian children could pray in public schools and receive government subsidies at private ones, the teachers asked, why should American children be any different? Finally, the overseas experience made teachers of every type question America's growing cultural power and influence around the globe. Even as its formal empire faded, the teachers said, America foisted a new imperialism—of Cokes, cars, and consumerism—upon peoples who did not need them.

To be sure, the idea of using foreign practices to critique one's own predated the modern concept of culture. Three centuries before Franz Boas, for example, the French essayist Michel Montaigne noted that "each man calls barbarism whatever is not his own practice . . . for we have no other criterion of reason than the example and idea of the opinions and customs of the country we live in." By uniting these "opinions and customs" into an integrated whole, however, the culture concept provided a fresh theoretical apparatus for understanding "the foreigner"—and, most of all, for critiquing the familiar. The concept seeped gradually into American public discourse in the 1920s and 1930s, thanks in part to popular texts by Boas protégés Ruth Benedict and Margaret Mead. But it exploded in the post–World War II period, when "cultural relativism" became the semiofficial dogma of American teachers everywhere. "Values expressed in any culture are to be understood and themselves valued only according to the way the people who carry that culture see things," wrote anthropologist Robert Redfield, in a passage read by Peace Corps trainees for a deaf-education program in 1980. "In looking at a polygamous society and a monogamous society, we have no valid way to assert that the one is better than the other."[2]

But there was a tension between cultural relativism and cultural critique, as the quotes from Redfield and Montaigne both suggest. For if all cultures were truly relative, how could the concept help critique *any* society, including America? As it turned out, most teachers who called themselves "cultural relativists" were anything but. Instead, like most of us, they used the culture concept to defend certain practices and to indict others. Insofar as the concept made Americans look anew at their own values and assumptions, it was all for the good. But it could also en-gender a noble-savage romanticization of other peoples as well as a re-flexive rejection of American culture, which was neither as unified nor as insidious as many teachers feared. Indeed, their very critique of America—as insular, arrogant, and ethnocentric—proved its opposite. A nation that was so closed-minded could never have opened so many hearts to its own defects.

4

The Protective Garb of the "Job"

TEACHER PROFESSIONALISM
AND ITS CRITICS

$\mathcal{I}$n 1904, Helen P. Beattie wrote an article describing her fellow American teachers in the Philippines. "There were fresh young college graduates seeking adventure or a sight of the Orient, or money with which to resume study," she began. "Earnest men and women signed for the work whose only qualification was missionary zeal, and with them came the kickers whose only object in life seemed to be criticism of the rest." A few Americans had taught for long periods in the United States, Beattie added, but this background became irrelevant when they went abroad. "The experienced teachers who came with firmly established ideals and methods had probably more to discard and forget than the inexperienced college graduate had to learn," she observed. "Energy and the ability to organize and manage counted for more than pedagogy and methods of instruction, for the teaching done in the Philippines is of the simplest character." Whether they came for profit or for principles, Beattie concluded, teachers could learn everything they needed on the job.[1]

Sixty years later, a second American teacher in the Philippines echoed Beattie's sentiment, but added a strong dose of skepticism. "The main prerequisites for a successful Peace Corps volunteer are: a love of people, courage to try anything once, and a sense of humor," she wrote. "He must be an expert an organizing libraries, curing snake bites, setting up summer camps, teaching swimming . . . Besides these extracurricular

117

skills he is most certainly an expert teacher, although he has just graduated from college and taught only one class in his life before entering
his own *barrio* school. He of course understands completely all the principles and methods of teaching English the second language way, as
well as being a 'whiz' in demonstrating elementary science, though his
last science course was high school biology." As this passage suggests,
most of the American teachers in the Philippines were men; few had
any formal training in education, or even in their subjects of instruction;
but the Peace Corps pretended they could do the job anyway, as long as
they possessed the proper character. Personal attributes trumped professional ones, at least when American teachers left their own shores.[2]

Together, these two passages encapsulate the consistently antiprofessional spirit of America's overseas teachers. Sociologists have described teachers in the United States as a "semiprofession," possessing
several hallmarks of the so-called classic professions, especially an orientation toward service, but very little of their cultural or social authority. Historians debate the origins, costs, and benefits of professionalism
for America's increasingly female teaching force, which occasionally eschewed but eventually embraced the concept.[3] Overseas, however,
teachers often rejected it. Even as more and more countries around the
world increased their requirements for teacher preparation, Americans
continued to insist that anyone of the proper intellect and spirit could
succeed in the classroom. At the same time, they often neglected or ignored the classroom itself in pursuit of other goals. For many teachers
in the American colonies, as in the United States, teaching represented
a stepping stone to other careers; for missionaries, it was a secondary
task to the real business of winning souls; and for post–World War II
volunteers in the Peace Corps and elsewhere, classroom instruction
took a back seat to health, athletics, and other extracurricular projects.
"Teaching . . . is often just an excuse for being there," admitted a 1968
Peace Corps pamphlet, describing volunteers' myriad activities outside
of class.[4]

To be sure, American teachers differed from each other across time,
space, and especially gender. Given the preponderance of women among
instructors back home, females who went abroad were more likely to
value teaching experience than their male counterparts. But they were
also more likely to find themselves in teaching roles for which they had
no experience, particularly in mission schools between World Wars I

and II. Forced to conduct five or even six different subjects in a non-English language, women bore the blame for flawed religious-school instruction around the globe. After World War II, teachers of both sexes began to question the received American dogma of antiprofessionalism. Teaching, it turned out, was difficult work; and teachers resented both their lack of preparation for the job and officials' blithe dismissal of it. Indeed, Peace Corps officer Daniel Fulmer complained, many volunteers had developed a professional identity as an explicit challenge to the agency. "Tanzania VII never got around to joining the Peace Corps," Fulmer observed, describing a departing group of teachers in 1967. "As secondary school teachers they succeeded in a highly professional manner, but they resisted the idea of Peace Corps all the way." Instead of devising construction and health projects, as the Peace Corps urged, the Tanzania group "proceeded to wrap itself in the protective garb of the 'job.' "[5]

By bracketing the "job" in quotation marks, Fulmer punctuated his own lowly estimation of it. He also underscored the odd, contrapuntal rhythm of American dialogues about teacher professionalism across the twentieth century. In the early 1900s, school officials in the new American colonies recruited "credentialed" teachers while the teachers themselves—even those with credentials—mocked the value of this pedigree. After World War II, the two groups switched sides: American officials downplayed the demands of "the job," as Daniel Fulmer dismissively called it, while the teachers demanded more preparation for it. "Peace Corps training fitted me very well for the climate, politics, living, and culture . . . but I am sadly lacking in teaching method and technique," one teacher wrote from Africa in the early 1960s, in a typical passage. "In short I was prepared for everything except my job."[6] Across the developing world, many Americans developed a new appreciation for the rigors and the prerequisites of teaching. Leaving America with a profound skepticism of teacher credentialism, they would often return home as staunch advocates for it.

Recruiting the "Island Teacher": Dreams and Realities

In 1896, a high school principal in Springfield, Massachusetts, published an anguished essay on the abject status of the typical American teacher. "Were his case to be tried before a jury of foreign educational

experts," wrote Fred W. Atkinson, "he would be found guilty on the
three following counts: 1) lack of general culture, 2) lack of scholarship,
and 3) lack of professional preparation." Most teachers ignored the
"social side of life," Atkinson complained, presenting themselves in
the slovenly garb of the "old-fashioned scholar." They also neglected
intellectual cultivation, often acquiring just enough knowledge to stay
one step ahead of their students. Too many men regarded teaching
simply as a "stepping stone to other callings," Atkinson added, while
women saw it as a waystation to matrimony. "Often an American girl,
after she leaves school, 'keeps school' until she has the opportunity to
keep house," Atkinson quipped. Only when schools demanded a higher
"standard of scholarship"—and demonstrable "professional skill"—
would the status of teaching rise. It would also attract and retain more
men, the sine qua non of a respected profession.[7]

Five years later, as America's first superintendent of schools in the
Philippines, Atkinson would receive the rare chance to shape a teaching
force in his own image. In a widely circulated 1901 announcement, he
called for 1,000 teachers to sail for the islands. Applicants needed college or normal school degrees plus "several years' successful teaching
experience," Atkinson wrote. He also authorized thirty university pres-
idents and every state department of education to appoint three to six
teachers each, subject to his approval. Of the 526 teachers who sailed
aboard the *Thomas* in July 1901, all but 31 had attended college or a
normal school, while all except 107 had some teaching experience.
They included recent graduates of Amherst, Bowdoin, and Cornell; the
largest single contingent came from the University of Michigan, whose
thirty-five boisterous alumna entertained the boat with school songs
and cheers. Older passengers included a former principal of the
Choctaw Female School in Indian Territory, a manual training supervisor from Oakland, and a veteran of a mission school in Singapore.
"The crowd is hardly what I supposed it would be," wrote Blaine Free
Moore, who had recently graduated from the University of Kansas.
"The majority are not fresh from college or normal schools . . . but are
people who have had quite considerable teaching experience."[8]

The majority were also men, belying the norm back home. In 1900,
nearly three-quarters of American teachers were female; on the USS
Thomas, by contrast, two-thirds were male. On the average, the female
teachers were older and more experienced than the men. As one

California reporter wrote, before the *Thomas* set sail, Atkinson had specifically requested veteran female instructors rather than novices. "He wanted none of the young and giddy kind, and good looks were considered a drawback," the reporter wrote, "which made it necessary for such applicants to be above average in other qualifications." For several months thereafter, Atkinson told an associate, he hired only male teachers. But then they began to complain about "loneliness," so he authorized the appointment of their wives, fiancees, and sisters—but no other women. This policy would continue after Atkinson's departure and the 1903 establishment of civil service examinations, which were open to all prospective teachers regardless of gender or marital status. Behind the scenes, however, Philippines officials continued to favor men. "Personally, I do not believe that it is desirable to appoint many women to this service," wrote an American official, in private. "However, it seems necessary to permit women generally to enter the next teacher examination." By 1908, the service would include 535 men and only 187 women—almost the exact opposite of the typical imbalance in the United States.[9]

At first glance, then, Americans in the Philippines achieved Fred Atkinson's vision: a largely male teaching force, bearing strong educational credentials as well as instructional experience. But a closer look reveals a very different picture. The 722 teachers in 1908 included just 253 college-degree holders and 108 graduates of normal schools, marking a sharp decline in credentials since the days of the *Thomas*. By 1925, only 13 percent of American teachers in the Philippines had a degree in the subject they taught. The service would also relax its demands for teaching experience, allowing more and more novices into the classroom. Seeking domestic science teachers, officials eventually allowed unmarried women back into the Philippines if they were over 30 years old. But the age restriction eliminated three-quarters of qualified applicants, a recruiter lamented, leaving only "failures" and "women of doubtful characteristics." Meanwhile, teacher shortages in America increased stateside salaries and made it difficult to lure capable men, either. By the end of World War I, teachers in the Philippines had assumed many of the same traits that Atkinson had bemoaned back home: inexperienced, academically marginal, and mostly female. "I myself have not been satisfied with the quality of all the American teachers sent to the Philippine Islands," one school official told the territorial governor in 1922.[10]

With only a few minor variations, a similar pattern of disappoint-
ment marked teacher recruitment in other American territories.
Puerto Rico school officials sought skilled female instructors, rather
than males, fearing that parents on the heavily Catholic island would
object to men teaching their daughters. Given the low pay and cost of
transport, however, the cream of the crop did not come to Puerto
Rico. "We are compelled to employ only the inexperienced, the rov-
ing, or the rejected teachers from the States," one official complained.
True, he continued, small handfuls of qualified teachers had ventured
to the island to restore their health in its tropical climate—or, even
better, to help with "the Americanizing of the people of Puerto Rico."
("These," he added, "are the true patriots.") For the most part, however, schools had to make do with tired castoffs or "raw college graduates," who "waste a year . . . in finding themselves." At first, Puerto
Rico required teachers to possess a four-year degree or a state teaching
certificate. Failing to attract enough candidates with either credential,
however, school officials eventually created a third pay category for
teachers who had neither.[11]

All of these problems proved especially acute in Hawaii, which relied
on mainland teachers more than the other territories did. By 1911, fully
one-third of the teachers in Hawaii came from the continental United
States; ten years later, their proportion rose to 40 percent. Over half
were young women who stayed for less than two years, earning the so-
briquet "tourist teachers" from embittered school officials. Even worse,
a local newspaper noted, most of them had done very little teaching before they reached the islands. "No mainland school system would
dream of loading up exclusively with inexperienced teachers," the paper
argued. "There, young teachers are introduced in small numbers, to be
absorbed by more experienced ones." Nor could Hawaii lure women
from elite northeastern colleges such as Vassar and Wellesley, which
sent handfuls of teachers to the Philippines and Puerto Rico. The Philippines offered higher pay, plus a U.S. Civil Service pedigree; Puerto
Rico was relatively close to the Eastern seaboard; but Hawaii was a
world away. Its cost of living was steep, while its teacher salaries often
fell below the wages of unskilled plantation laborers. "This astonish-
ing and deplorable disparity . . . not only depletes the teacher-supply,"
admitted one school official, "but spreads dissatisfaction among the
teachers at present in service."[12] Across the American empire, indeed,

teachers would condemn the roles and conditions that educational officials designed for them. Some teachers would renounce education altogether.

Teacher Antiprofessionalism I: Attacking the System

"Who can analyze his own motives, not to say the motives of others?" So asked Henry Townsend, looking back on his voyage aboard the *Thomas*.[13] Like Townsend, who spent many years teaching in Hawaii before coming to the Philippines, some of America's overseas instructors were career teachers who hopped from state to state, and, sometimes, from territory to territory, seeking better opportunities.[14] Others were self-proclaimed "adventurers" in pursuit of new experiences, or, sometimes, a chance to strike it rich. Significantly, both types of teachers rejected the vision of professionalism that American officials propounded. Like classroom instructors in the United States, experienced overseas teachers mocked the pretensions of educational supervisors who knew little about education themselves; others saw professionalism as a ruse to subject teachers even more tightly to administrative whim.[15] In a more cynical vein, meanwhile, some younger instructors dismissed the very goal of schooling in the tropics. Mostly male and untrained, they viewed their work as a springboard to other professions rather than as a contribution to education per se.

Consider Edgar L. Morphet, a vivid example of the first type of antiprofessionalism. A normal-school graduate and a former high school principal in his native Indiana, Morphet epitomized exactly the type of instructor that overseas officials sought: male, trained, and experienced. Upon his arrival in the Philippines, however, Morphet became a bitter critic of the school system. In the name of professionalism, he argued, officials placed an undue emphasis upon academic pedigree and neglected the actual practice of teachers in the classroom. "What we want is pedagogues with a Russian alphabet to their names, a P. D. Podunk Center College of a B.S. from the University of Dogrib," Morphet wrote, satirizing officials' quest for credentials. "The erudite professions need erudite personnel, and there is nothing that will so impress the surrounding low-brow nations than 76 assorted letters behind the cognomen. Degrees and more degrees even ten degrees below zero." Morphet himself had two letters next to his name, an A.B. from Indiana

State Normal School. But his sojourn abroad had underscored the relative importance of experience, and the ultimate irrelevance of credentials, in professional life.[16]

Even more, Morphet claimed, school authorities used their *own* professional power to muzzle teachers. The Philippines had established a "Prussian system" rather than an American one, he wrote, which "wants to know where you eat breakfast, if you are a Dimmycraat, if your hat and shoes fit you, if you read the Manila Times." Most of all, Morphet continued, school officials monitored "pedagog pilgrims" for any "disparaging word" against the schools themselves. "Line up for inspection," Morphet wrote, mocking the authorities' tyrannical tone. "Anybody can hire you, but we can fire you." Morphet published his remarks in a Philippine weekly, under an obvious pseudonym—"Omar Khayam"—and beneath a revealing headline: "American Writer Lets Himself Loose." In a culture of censorship and intimidation, clearly, the mere expression of a teacher complaint—even an unsigned one— was big news.[17]

Finally, Morphet lamented elsewhere, the Philippines did not compensate teachers in a manner that signaled professional status or respect. Teachers' salaries barely covered living expenses, he claimed, while teachers who became ill—a common enough event in the tropics—received nothing at all for the school days they missed. "An American is hired to come over here and help enlighten the Filipinos," Morphet wrote. "If his health holds out . . . well and good. But if he should get sick he can go to the dogs!" Teachers who recovered often had to remain in the Philippines beyond the dates of their contracts, to save enough money to pay for their passage home. Worst of all, if a teacher died, school officials contributed nothing to the burial; instead, teachers would sponsor a "charity funeral" from their own meager paychecks. "And under penalty of being fired teachers are frightened out of writing such truths to friends back in the States," Morphet wrote privately. "Nice State of affairs! Nice example of injustices!"[18]

Across the American territories, Morphet's three themes—credentials, civil liberties, and compensation—dominated teachers' critiques of school policies. In early twentieth-century parlance, "credentials" connoted prior teaching experience as well as academic degrees. Like Morphet, even instructors who possessed both types of preparation came to question their value overseas. Looking back on her voyage aboard the *Thomas*, one teacher recalled meeting two sisters who showed her their "two drawers-full of credentials and letters." Yet they were miserable failures in the field, so fearful of "the natives" that the sisters took turns sleeping and standing on guard every evening. After a few brief months, they went home. Indeed, the *Thomas* veteran continued, her own experiences as an instructor on an Indian reservation proved irrelevant in the Philippines. On the reservation, she wrote, students sat quietly until she called on them. But Philippine children shouted everything they heard at the top of their lungs, as she learned on her first harrowing day with them. "I retired precipitately from the scene," she remembered, "and proceeded to reconstruct my theories of teaching non-English speaking children."[19]

In his recollections of the Philippines, Carter G. Woodson also mocked Americans' emphasis upon academic pedigree as well as teaching experience. "Men trained at institutions like Harvard, Yale, Columbia and Chicago could not reach these people," wrote Woodson, who would later receive his own Ph.D. from Harvard. The best teacher he met overseas was a former insurance agent who "had never taught at all" and "had never studied authorities like Bagley, Judd, and Thorndike," Woodson added, naming three prominent educational theorists in the United States. Puerto Rico teacher Leonard Ayres, who would himself become a leading educational expert upon his return to the States, urged his sister to take a "short rush-em-through course" in manual training back home, which would increase her chances of receiving an appointment on the island. "This is not for the sake of learning anything you understand," Ayres wrote, "but to put on your name as a title of qualification." In Hawaii, meanwhile, a new vocational instructor dispensed with qualifications altogether. "Almost any bright young lady could teach cooking and sewing or even gardening," he wrote, seeking new teachers from the mainland, "while a man who is at all handy with tools can . . . give a very creditable course in wood work."[20]

At the same time, American teachers did not hesitate to invoke their own professional authority when school officials sought to reform, bully, or silence them. In the Philippines, one instructor complained, her supervisor knew "less about teaching than an infant"—and based his judgment of her upon a single five-minute visit. A Puerto Rico teacher wrote home to condemn the island's school director, whose training lay in medicine rather than in education. Most of all, instructors resented restrictions upon their freedom to issue such complaints in public. School officials fired a Philippines teacher for criticizing her principal

and superintendent, even though the teacher was "very bright" and effective in the classroom. "For many years I have believed that 'an ounce
of loyalty is worth a pound of brains,' " a Bureau of Education official
wrote, defending the decision. "I would rather have a man or woman
who will do just as I ask him [and] will always speak well of the Bureau
than to have an exceedingly able man who is not loyal." Getting the
message, most teachers confined their attacks to private correspondence. In 1903, for example, Herbert Priestley told his mother to ignore the much-ballyhooed St. Louis Exposition of Philippine culture,
industry, and education. Priestley had prepared student "show papers"
for the exposition, he admitted, "very interesting deceptions" that no
teacher would dare to expose as fraudulent, at least not in public.[21]

Another instructor complained that he had to pay for postage of student essays to St. Louis out of his own pocket, reflecting the most common teacher jeremiad: low salary and benefits. Denied access to the
cheaper, high-quality goods at the American commissary in Manila,
teachers sent a cable of objection to President William McKinley a few
days before he was assassinated.[22] Other teachers reported that that
their salary came late; that they received it in the depreciated local currency, rather than in gold; that the Bureau did not pay for extra teaching during vacation, as originally promised; that teachers had to stay
three years to receive free passage home; and so on. Handfuls of teachers resigned in protest.[23] Instructors in Puerto Rico formed an "American Teacher's Association" to condemn their pay, which remained
lower than "the most incompetent native teachers in the same schools."
To school officials, however, the very demand for higher salaries reflected a *lack* of professional spirit. In the Philippines, they noted, the
average teacher salary was 50 percent higher than back home. Hence
"those who have resigned . . . may be set down as of that class of men of
insincere purpose, who from the deck of the steamer departing for the
field . . . assured their friends on shore that they would be with them
again within a year." In fact, such teachers were hardly rare in the islands, and most were men.[24]

Teacher Antiprofessionalism II: Working the System

In October 1901, Harry Cole wrote a despondent letter to his brother
in the United States. Two months earlier, Cole and his wife had arrived

on the *Thomas* with hopes of making a fortune in the Philippines. "As far as being an expansionist is concerned, I am perfectly willing to let the next man do the expanding," Cole wrote. "It was mainly with the thought that perhaps we could earn enough in three years to make it easier for us all . . . that we came." Thanks to the depreciated local currency, however, the Coles had barely saved a cent. Nor did other job opportunities emerge upon their arrival, as the couple had hoped. Schools in the Philippines were a "huge political deal," Harry Cole wrote, designed only to burnish America's local and international image. As soon as he and his wife managed to save $1,000, he wrote, they would jump on the first boat home.[25]

Cole's letter encapsulates a second, more cynical form of teacher antiprofessionalism in the American territories. Other teachers sought personal wealth and advancement, to be sure, but they merged this impulse with a wish to educate or "Americanize" their students; indeed, they critiqued school officials' vision of professionalism because it failed to deliver on its own educational promise. Cole and his ilk aimed only to enrich themselves, mocking the very premise of their presence overseas. "The teachers were a regiment of carpet-baggers, come to exploit the country in their small way," wrote one embittered American instructor, assailing his avaricious colleagues, "and then, after a few years, would sail happily home without a regret to spare." Like the Coles, some of them failed in the effort; others were more successful. But no one could miss their strong "commercial proclivities," as one journalist wrote. "The expression, 'There ought to be money in this, or that,' . . . was on many tongues," he observed, after interviewing several dozen American instructors in the Philippines.[26]

The chatter began aboard the *Thomas* itself, where passengers ruminated about the best ways to strike it rich on the other shore. "There are a great many people on this boat who will not remain there any length of time as teachers," Herbert Priestley wrote his mother. One man implored Priestley to join him in plans to purchase a pushcart and peddle water filters, Catholic figurines of saints, or "anything to gather coin." He also urged Priestley and his wife to request teaching posts in Manila, site of the best business possibilities. Confident that they would save a sufficient sum from their salaries, the Priestleys initially resisted such entreaties. Once they reached the Philippines, however, they began to reconsider. Manila lacked a high-quality dry-goods store, Herbert

Priestley wrote his sister, so the first person to open one would make a killing. "Please send us $10,000 by next cable," Priestley wrote, in a half-serious mood. "If we had a stake here, we would lay in a supply of American goods, and be rich in five years." Sent to Luzon province, the Priestleys would supplement their regular income by teaching night school and writing columns for several American newspapers. They would never become wealthy, Herbert Priestley concluded, but they earned and saved more money than they would have done in their native California—and that was enough.[27]

To many other teachers, however, the allure of wider riches was too great to ignore. In 1903, fifty American teachers in the Philippines resigned to "go into business" and twenty-one others took better-paying jobs in other new government agencies. More commonly, teachers pursued both types of opportunities while retaining their classroom positions. Several Americans drew salaries as postmasters as well as teachers, despite rules that barred such dual roles. One teacher brought a collection of eyeglass lenses and frames to the Philippines, setting up a successful optical business; another taught himself dentistry, which proved equally profitable. "If a Chinaman wanted several teeth extracted, [he] would pull them out for a peso each," recalled one bemused observer. "He always carried his extracting forceps in his pocket, and woe to the child who happened to smile at him and disclose any decayed teeth." Such schemes were less prevalent in Puerto Rico and Hawaii, but teachers embraced them when they could. Some Puerto Rico instructors gave private English lessons to wealthy clients—and to the neglect of their regular classroom duties, supervisors charged—while others established a lucrative side business exporting Caribbean cigars to the mainland.[28]

Still other teachers came mainly to relax and luxuriate in the tropics, a point that was not lost on their territorial hosts. "Their interest is more for enjoyment, not for the welfare of the kids," remembered one Hawaiian student. "These *Haole* (white) teachers had rah-rah times." Whenever a new crop of instructors was expected from the mainland, a teacher recalled, local white bachelors would line up along the wharf to "give the girls the 'once over' "; on occasion, she added, "romances and even marriages were started from this first exhibition." Teachers who remained single kept up a steady pace of dating, dancing, and even drinking, scandalizing school officials. In Puerto Rico, likewise, women instructors basked in the attention of soldiers and fellow teachers who "act as though they have never seen a girl before," as teacher Helen French told her parents. "I have discovered the conditions under which we can be belles—when there are no other girls," French added, earning a warning from her mother about her suitors' ill intentions. To be sure, teachers could and did combine active social lives with professional commitments. Yet over time, as French admitted, the former tended to erode the latter. "I am getting fat, lazy, and *good natured*," French wrote, adding the emphasis. "It even affects my discipline at school." On hot afternoons, she commandeered the coolest spot in the classroom and told her pupils to "keep still" and study. "More often than not they do neither," French wrote, "but I don't seem to care much."[29]

Yet host populations—students, parents, and teachers—*did* care. In the Philippines, especially, critics took note of the slovenly dress, blithe manner, and poor preparation of many American teachers. Condemning a 1913 group of teachers as "lobsters" and "bloodsuckers" on the state treasury, one Filipino suggested that the United States had sent its worst educational specimens overseas. By 1930, the territorial House of Representatives debated a bill to bar American teachers altogether. Some of the Americans were simply lazy, the bill's authors claimed; others had insulted pupils with bigoted remarks, sparking strikes and other "student troubles"; and almost none of teachers bore adequate credentials for the job. "Most of the American teachers imported to teach in our schools are not academically prepared to be mentors of the youth of the land," legislators charged. "Most of them . . . while posing as specialists in English and literature are in fact 'mere nobodies.' "[30] While Americans were doubting the value of an academic pedigree—and, sometimes, of all overseas schooling—their hosts were demanding both. The problem would prove even more acute in European empires, where American teachers faced much higher standards than they had ever encountered at home.

Preparing the Mission Teacher

In 1916, representatives from 43 American foreign mission boards met in New York City to discuss the preparation of "educational missionaries." One after another, speakers demanded higher levels of academic training and of instructional experience for America's overseas mission teachers. Of 1,100 educational missionaries in China, one official reported, only 200 could be fairly described as "professionally trained." Most missions made overseas evangelists take a "full theological course," noted Teachers College professor T. H. P. Sailer, while medical missionaries needed a four-year course and one or two years of internship before they went abroad. By contrast, American missions seldom required future teachers to receive any additional preparation. Most teachers were college or theological school graduates who never studied education, or normal-school degree-holders without any teaching experience. "We must simply make up our minds to recommend more thorough professional training," Sailer stated. As the first professor of missions at Teachers College, Sailer taught classes on "Educational Development in Oriental Countries," as well as "Problems in Missionary Education." More institutions needed to offer such courses, and more missionaries needed to take them.[31]

But one speaker at the conference struck a note of dissent. While praising the efforts of Sailer and others to improve mission education, Lutheran official George Drach questioned their "secular" spirit. "Our Lord Jesus Christ did not teach men through an industrial mission," Drach quipped, satirizing missions' growing emphasis upon vocational training. "Paul did not go into industrial work to teach other people how to make good tents. He labored in order to set people a good example in being free from earthly, physical entanglement." Early Christians sought only to prepare for life everlasting, Drach added, whereas modern missions stressed the here and now: sports, hygiene, vocation, and even academic preparation for national examinations. "There is where our educationalists in the foreign field are wrong, absolutely wrong," Drach intoned. The more that schools tried to meet every educational goal, the less they could emphasize Christ's original one.[32]

Caught in the middle of this debate lay America's overseas mission teachers, who shared both the yearning for more preparation and the skepticism about their overall purpose. Unlike teachers in the American colonies, who typically taught English or vocational subjects, mission instructors had to cover everything from chemistry and physics to Bible history and homiletics—in a foreign language, no less. No matter what their background, then, most mission teachers felt dramatically *unprepared* for their overseas jobs. At the same time, they also reflected the larger ambivalence about schooling itself. Overwhelmingly female, many mission instructors went overseas in an effort to *avoid* teaching.

But they found themselves shunted into educational roles anyway, where they wondered how, and whether, their efforts furthered the ultimate Christian cause. "I haven't read anywhere that Paul spent his time teaching school," wrote one teacher from Africa, in an almost exact echo of George Drach. "God called us to give [Africans] the Gospel and there our duty begins and ends."[33] Saddled with school subjects that taxed their knowledge, mission teachers faced the added burden of justifying them. For some teachers, it was more than they could bear.

To be sure, many missionaries taught at home before they went abroad. In China, by one estimate, over two-thirds of mission women at the turn of the twentieth century had been teachers in the United States. The typical female missionary grew up as the eldest child in a rural household, attended a small, church-affiliated college, and taught school after that. She had much more education than the average teacher in America, where only 5 percent of classroom instructors in 1910 studied beyond high school. But she still lacked adequate training for the job, mission leaders argued, for two reasons. First, many mission teachers served as school principals as well as classroom instructors; while a B.A. degree might qualify them to work with children, as T. H. P. Sailer wrote, the supervision of adults required a different set of skills. In addition, foreign governments had begun to raise their own teacher standard—and to reject Americans' lowly one. In Rhodesia, British educators accused Americans of sending "illiterate workers" into the schools; Angolan officials required new mission teachers to obtain a Portuguese teaching diploma, which included courses in pedagogy; and in Iran, Americans turned away a candidate who taught in the United States, but lacked the credentials for Persian schools. "I myself am bored by all this advanced degree business," admitted one mission official, "but our workers are under educational and governmental systems on the foreign field which they cannot control, and sometimes they have to have these degrees."[34]

Increasingly, the same official noted, overseas governments wanted mission teachers to possess an M.A. in education. By the 1920s, then, some denominational boards began to urge or require postgraduate training for teachers as well as for ministers and physicians. After completing her B.A. at Nebraska Wesleyan, Katherine B. Ward applied to the Methodist Board of Missions as a teacher for China. The board replied that she needed "professional experience," including teaching practice and an advanced degree. So Ward taught for two years in Midwestern public schools and obtained a one-year master's from Teachers College, which qualified her to go to China in 1925. Teachers College also awarded several annual scholarships for missionaries on furlough, making it the lodestar in the small field of mission education. Other prominent institutions offering courses or degrees in the field included Yale, the University of Chicago, Peabody College of Education, and the Hartford Seminary. The best-known professor of the subject was Mabel Carney, who taught "Methods of Approach to Primitive Peoples," later renamed "Methods of Education in Foreign Lands," at Teachers College and Hartford for two decades. Students read descriptive works about education in Africa, Asia, and Latin America along with theoretical treatises by William Kilpatrick and other pedagogical luminaries in the United States.[35]

Yet as late as 1942, Carney complained, the vast majority of mission teachers remained "utterly innocent of real professional training in education." Despite pressures from foreign governments to hire teachers with advanced degrees, mission boards continued to hire "B.A.-only" teachers under the "fallacious idea" that "a man who has studied a subject must be therefore able to teach it," as a Japan missionary admitted. An advertisement for new mission teachers in Chile provided a perfect illustration of the problem: "As to academic qualifications, the teacher should be a graduate of College or University, or if he has not completed this undergraduate work, should have progressed so far as to be able to teach any subject in the High School curriculum." A normal-school degree would be a "great asset," the advertisement added, but it was not necessary.[36]

Several factors limited the amount of professional preparation that teachers received. First of all, it was expensive: for cash-starved missionaries and the denominational boards that hired them, a year or more of postgraduate training was often more than they could afford. Second, as Teacher College's T. H. P. Sailer noted, mission boards retained the same prejudices against educational study that infected the American public at large. "The tendency of many of our colleges and universities has been to consider almost exclusively the claims of subject matter rather than those of methods of instruction—the what of education rather than the how," Sailer wrote. "Normal schools and teacher training colleges are looked down upon as narrow in their aims and culture, and the whole science of education falls under the same condemnation." Finally, mission boards simply needed warm bodies to staff and direct their burgeoning school systems. In Japan, for example, Quaker missionary Esther Rhoads, whose background lay in science, pleaded with her home board to send another teacher. "I hope the next person who comes will be musical and literary but anybody will do," Rhoads wrote. "We just need somebody."[37]

The Mission Teacher's Lament I: In the Classroom

As Rhoads' own case demonstrates, however, no teacher could have prepared for the enormously diverse tasks that awaited her in overseas missions. Born into a wealthy Philadelphia family, Rhoads graduated from the prestigious Westtown Boarding School and then received a teacher's certificate in home economics from Drexel Institute. She taught the subject at an Episcopal girls' school for a year before going to Japan, where she gave courses in "foreign cooking" and sewing at the Friends Girls School in Tokyo. To Rhoads' chagrin, however, she also had to teach Bible and English. "My Bible Class does most horribly reveal my ignorance," she confided to a cousin back home. Rhoads spent two hours each night reading an American religion textbook in Japanese translation, "and longer on thinking what to say and how to say it." To teach English, meanwhile, Rhoads relied upon a single methods book. Later, on furloughs, Rhoads would receive a B.S. degree from Earlham College and a joint master's in religious education from Teachers College and Union Theological Seminary. But she continued to feel inadequate in the classroom, as she admitted in private. "I still wonder a great deal of the time whether teaching is my line!" Rhoads wrote her sister. Indeed, she found the work so difficult, and so demoralizing, that she was considering going home, to "raise flowers or something."[38]

Even her home economics background proved insufficient when she went abroad, as Rhoads discovered. "Tomorrow I have to teach the 5th year how to make trousers," she wrote her mother, in a despondent mood. "I doubt if I know how my self. Will have to try tonight." Other teachers with significant training and experience in the United States received overseas assignments that drew upon neither, as many missionaries complained. In Palestine, a nine-year veteran of the Connecticut Institute for the Adult Blind found herself teaching English grammar to teenagers and fielding questions she could not answer; a former normal-school instructor who taught elementary-level children in Mexico lamented that her "training and real interests lie with high school or college people"; and in Burma, a longtime high school English teacher became editor of a Burmese-language magazine for primary-school instructors. "I feel eminently well qualified!" she wrote, facetiously. "I think I could almost qualify to teach a vernacular jungle school myself in time." A mission principal in Iran feared that a new teacher with an M.S. degree in Domestic Science might be *too* qualified—or too pampered—to teach English, general science, and the rest of the curriculum. "What we need is a very keen *missionary* who has had enough college chemistry to teach it, and is willing and eager to undertake any of the many other tasks which need to be done," the principal wrote.[39]

Just as high school experience did not translate to success among primary-level pupils, however, a few courses in any given subject did not give teachers enough information to instruct it. More than anything else, missionaries around the globe complained that they lacked adequate understanding of the courses they taught. Teaching science in Sierra Leone, Muriel Nichols became flustered when a student asked her how electricity flowed through wires. "Believe me it's awful hard to teach this when you only learned definitions when you had it [in college]," she wrote her family, "and now to really make it clear to a black one who has no idea." Other teachers marveled at the academic abilities of their foreign pupils, which merely underscored the missionaries' own lack of knowledge. Forced to teach geography, algebra, and other classes for which he was "equally ignorant and unprepared," Iran principal Edwin Wright routinely apologized to his students for his errors at the blackboard. To receive a permit from the Persian government, Wright's school had to offer an enormous variety of academic subjects; rather than saddling other teachers with difficult technical courses, Wright assigned them to himself. He even taught physics and chemistry, which he had not studied in nearly 20 years.[40]

To be sure, some missionaries taught themselves enough material to succeed in the classroom. Fresh out of college, and lacking any teaching experience, Palestine missionary Nancy Parker was assigned eight different subjects, including Medieval history, European geography, biology, hygiene, and baseball. ("Imagine me—baseball!" an anguished

Parker wrote her mother.) Within a few months, however, Parker felt "more confident" about teaching such a wide range of courses. "I am not so strong in history, studied very little of that in college, but I manage to keep ahead," she wrote in her diary. But Parker conducted class in English, she went on to note, which made it much easier to stay a step in front of her Arabic-speaking students. Other teachers were not as fortunate. A missionary to Colombia had to teach five different subjects in Spanish, ranging from history and geography to physics and physiology; a teacher in China taught science and geography in Chinese, taxing her "inadequate knowledge" of the course matter as well as the language. Even subjects that did not rely so heavily on the written word proved difficult for teachers who lacked preparation in them. "Having had no training for teaching music it seemed like a colossal task," wrote a female missionary in Chile. "How is one to train a chorus of some 200 boys with a husky weak voice. The only answer is God. So God and I ventured forth."[41]

The Mission Teacher's Lament II: "Just Teaching School"

Yet many women ventured into mission teaching against their own will, as their private correspondence reveals. Indeed, they often joined overseas missions to *escape* the classroom. After teaching for three years in the United States, for example, Esther Bartlett resigned. "I decided that I did not want to spend the rest of my life teaching school," she wrote. So Bartlett enrolled in a theological seminary, envisioning a new career in the ministry. Appointed to the Cameroon as an evangelist rather than an educator, she was nevertheless assigned to supervise and teach schools when she got there. Her Presbyterian mission board ran dozens of schools in the Cameroon; she had a teaching degree and experience; so who better to do the job? "My efforts to escape school teaching all seem to have been in vain," a dejected Bartlett wrote in 1937. "For where I had one class to teach, I now have 107 schools to supervise and many classes to teach. Where I had 30 pupils, I now have 1922 under my supervision." Around the world, women repeated Bartlett's experience. Of the 1,305 Americans serving as overseas Presbyterian missionaries in 1936, for example, 409 were teachers; 267 of these teachers were female to just 142 males; and a sizable fraction of the women probably wanted to do something else.[42]

Like Esther Bartlett, many women imagined themselves as ministers or "missionary evangelists," the catchall term for religious workers. Missionaries of every denomination were seized by the romance of itinerant rural evangelists in China, whose heroic exploits made headlines back home. "In general we did not want to be teachers," recalled two Catholic instructors in Bolivia, "but to be like our Sisters in China who went out into small communities without structures." Inside China itself, meanwhile, Jesuit teachers bemoaned Americans' prejudice against "the less romantic side of missionary life," namely, education. "To deny the title of 'Missionary' to anyone who does not spend his days on a Chinese donkey would be to cut off from the missionary list many of the greatest names that there are," wrote one priest. Clearly, however, many teachers, particularly women, viewed their work as a lesser form of mission. "During the past year I have done nothing spectacular," wrote a Chile teacher, in a typical passage. "On the contrary, I have worked away at the same tasks in the daily routine." Another Chile missionary reported that she was " 'Just teaching school,' " and left it at that. To teachers who belittled their efforts in the classroom, there was little else to say.[43]

Other female missionaries went through the motions of teaching, but kept looking for other opportunities. As soon as teachers learned the local language, a China mission school principal complained, they sought to "preach the Gospel in Chinese" rather than "just teaching English." Indeed, a second China principal pleaded with her board to send a "young lady" who would be satisfied with "regular teaching work," not one aiming at "some other missionary career," particularly evangelism. As mission schools multiplied and host nations increased their professional standards, officials noted, missions needed qualified teachers more than they needed preachers. Others argued that local populations would not countenance female evangelists; still others noted that male *missionaries* would not accept them. "You can no more expect women to do your preaching or train your preachers in Burma than you can in America," declared one Baptist official, in 1893. Schools provided "the most appropriate and hopeful fields of labor for our single young lady missionaries—even for those who burn to be evangelists and preachers," added another Baptist leader.[44]

Throughout the ensuing half-century, then, "single young lady missionaries" would be urged or forced into teaching.[45] Especially in Latin America, however, mission officials also worried that some single women lacked the moral rectitude to resist the allegedly hot-blooded men of the tropics. "These young men are as beautiful as Greek Gods," warned Eunice Blackburn, a principal at a Mexico mission school, "and as vile as it is possible to imagine anything." Rejecting a 20-year-old teacher candidate who had just graduated high school, Blackburn suggested that she obtain a normal degree in domestic science and come down when she was 23 or 24. By then, Blackburn wrote, "there would be no danger that she would let them prove too attractive to her." In Colombia, meanwhile, another female principal fired a teacher for unchaperoned dancing and tennis with local men. "We have remonstrated her but to no avail," the principal wrote. "She says the churches at home are not opposed to such things so why should she not do them." Actually, the principal continued, American Protestants were sharply divided on such activities, but Colombians were united—against them. "Customs of the country . . . must be observed for the good of our work," she explained. From now on, an official in New York promised, the mission board would screen single candidates more carefully to ensure that they would follow "accepted standards" overseas.[46]

One solution was to select "spinsters" or "old maids," women who had advanced beyond the usual age of marriage. Another was to hire couples, assigning the husband to evangelistic or administrative work and the wife to teaching. Such arrangements represented the "surer investment," one African mission leader argued, because single women were always liable to get married and go home. But the preacher–teacher tandem also put an inordinate onus on the female side of the equation, as many wives testified. Women were expected to teach their own classes, serve as "housemothers" to boarders, supervise cooks and other staff—*and* care for their own families. "It was no small task," wrote one such teacher from Chile. "30 girls must be kept clean and neat for their classes, and must be kept at their lessons and work." Her own baby served as a object lesson for the students, who helped bathe and dress the infant. Many other teachers lost their children to illness or accidents, adding unspeakable grief to their other burdens. One couple in Mexico watched all five of their children die of scarlet fever over a span of a single week; later that year, the wife would suffer a miscarriage and then a nervous breakdown. In Angola, Bessie McDowell gave birth to a baby girl prematurely, which onlookers attributed to overwork; shortly thereafter, the child died. "Mrs. McDowell has not quite been herself since we lost our little girl," her husband told an associate, a year later. "She does a tremendous amount of work but it is telling on her." From the outside, however, no one could tell. McDowell continued her tireless routine, including teaching five classes, supervising other instructors, and helping her own son learn to read and write.[47]

Nevertheless, married and single teachers alike tended to denigrate their enormous contribution to American missions. On the one hand, the teachers felt their efforts were not worthy of the job, and on the other hand, that the job itself was not worthy of their efforts. "This year, more than ever, it seems I have been going to school, Christ's school," wrote Kathryn Dutton, a teacher, housemother, and parent in Chile. "The main text book has been the Book of Experience. Needless to say, I have not stood at the head of the class." A second Chile housemother introduced herself as the school's "Extra Hand," while a third one compared her work to "The Old Woman Who Lived in a Shoe"— with apologies to Mother Goose:

> She kept them all busy from morning till night,
> Playing, studying, learning to write . . .
> Confidence and character we tried to train
> But felt many efforts were alas! in vain.[48]

Both types of anxiety infected single women, as well: some doubted they had the necessary skills for teaching, while others doubted whether teaching itself was necessary. "I still get spells of wondering if the school wouldn't be better off without foreigners like me," wrote Quaker teacher Esther Rhoads from Japan, in 1930. "I felt unable to give any justification for being here other than that it is fun." In Nigeria, meanwhile, the more theologically conservative Susan Anderson suggested that her own school had lost sight of its larger goal. "We have failed in putting the kingdom first," lamented Anderson, a Southern Baptist. "Here in the school we have grown and grown and grown . . . but I have the feeling, the conviction, that we have prospered materially far more than spiritually."[49] After World War II, a new generation of secular and mission teachers would raise fresh questions about their purpose overseas. They would also demand more training and status for themselves, countering the same gospel of antiprofessionalism that Americans carried around the globe.

A New Kind of Teacher?

In 1968, a new book about the Peace Corps featured a picture of Marylee Meyers. An English and biology teacher in Belize, Meyers held an undergraduate liberal arts degree from the University of Washington. According to the caption adjoining her photo, Meyers also epitomized the global educational revolution that the Peace Corps had unleashed. "A new kind of teacher has appeared in the schools of the developing world," the caption declared, "a college graduate with an A.B. in science or the humanities and who, before Peace Corps training, had never taught a class or thought of spending two years of his or her life teaching." Americans like Marylee Meyers were challenging the entire conception of what it meant to be a teacher, both within the United States and outside of it.[50]

But there was nothing new about inexperienced, "B.A.-only" Americans traveling abroad to work as teachers. In the first half of the twentieth century, many territorial and mission teachers bore a background quite similar to Marylee Meyers'. What *was* new was the enormous number of such teachers who traversed the globe in the post–World War II period, and especially the new rationale that accompanied their journey. The architects of America's colonial and missionary education systems were professionalizers in spirit if not in deed, seeking to develop a skilled and credentialed teaching force that would transmit its expertise to the rest of the world. They were stymied by a wide variety of structural constraints as well as by the teachers themselves, who frequently resisted the professional identities that officials tried to attach to them. The post–World War II era witnessed a stark inversion of this pattern. In the Peace Corps and other volunteer agencies—including short-term missions—officials sent out teachers as a *challenge* to so-called modern or even Western professionalism. But the teachers altered this formula when they arrived overseas, embracing some of the same professional values that their leaders eschewed. In the Peace Corps, especially, antiprofessional ideologues spawned a new, grass-roots respect for professionalism in education.

The raw volume of Americans who taught abroad in the post–World War II period dwarfed earlier eras. At its peak in 1902, the American teaching force in the Philippines numbered 928; by 1941, roughly 4,000 Americans had taught there. Perhaps 3,000 mainlanders taught in

Hawaii and 1,000 in Puerto Rico over the same span. By comparison, the Peace Corps alone sent 2,674 teachers abroad in its first two years. By its twentieth anniversary, in 1981, over 31,000 Americans had taught for the agency. Missionary teachers also increased in number steadily, if not as sharply, in this same postwar era. Nearly 30,000 American Protestant and Catholic missionaries served around the globe in 1958, three times their number in 1903 and 50 percent more than in 1936. Roughly a third of missionaries worked as teachers, a fraction that seems to have held steady across the century. The number of religiously affiliated instructors spiked in the 1960s, when American missions, imitating the Peace Corps, engaged more "short-term" teachers. So did a vast array of lay organizations from different denominations. By 1971, a clearinghouse for short-term Protestant workers would advertise over 2,000 available positions, with "education" as the largest category. Twelve years after that, thirteen different Catholic organizations offered teaching opportunities to lay volunteers.[51]

Only one of these thirteen agencies required experience or formal preparation for the job. The rest advertised for "B.A. generalists," the hallmark of post–World War II overseas American teachers. In previous eras, to be sure, plenty of instructors went abroad with only a B.A. degree, or less. But the Peace Corps and its missionary rivals actively *sought* such candidates, rejecting the entire principle of teacher credentialism—indeed, of teacher professionalism—in the United States. "What is most important about these Volunteers is that they are liberal arts educated, not teacher trained," wrote a sympathetic observer in 1968. "Most people coming out of teachers' colleges are not as well-prepared as those coming out of liberal arts colleges. Volunteers have a good education. In the Peace Corps, a math teacher most likely was a math major, not an education major who had a few math courses." Indeed, a Ghana volunteer confirmed, the entire Peace Corps effort represented "an indictment of American teacher-training programs." To be sure, education professors complained that the agency did not require experience or preparation. Rather than caving to this objection, however, the Peace Corps wore it as a badge of pride. "Our disdain for these things enabled us, like the good private schools, to make teachers out of bright graduates from the best colleges who wouldn't have taken an education course if they had been paid to," a Peace Corps official recalled.[52]

To identify such individuals, the Peace Corps administered an hour-long "placement" examination in thirteen different subjects. It also required an arduous battery of personality tests, reflecting the larger post–World War II faith in psychological forms of wisdom and measurement. To the Peace Corps and missionary organizations alike, successful teachers would be marked not just by subject-matter knowledge but also by ego strength, emotional stability, and the other accepted barometers of mental health. As early as 1943, Southern Baptists administered psychological tests to mission candidates; by 1962, over half of all American mission boards did the same. The Presbyterian mission in Egypt hired C. R. Thayer, Ph.D., "Psychological Examiner of Missionaries," to screen all of its applicants from 1949 on. "My 'business' is picking up rather heavily," Thayer wrote privately in 1955, requesting more "Sentence Completion blanks" for one of his tests. Thayer's evaluations of mission candidates illustrate the subtle blend of individuality and social adaptation that marked midcentury conceptions of psychological well-being. "Relatively free from nervous symptoms," wrote Thayer, in a typical assessment. "Better than average self confidence but not too high. Reasonably aggressive, but rather dependent upon the opinion and advice of others." As Thayer's other notes reveal, missions sought people who were thoughtful, but not too "philosophical"; independent, but not "lone-wolfish"; socially adept, but not overly "extroverted."[53]

In the Peace Corps, meanwhile, officials placed such a strong accent on psychological tests that they spawned minirevolts by the volunteers themselves. Unlike mission boards, which typically administered the tests before applicants entered the service, the Peace Corps gave the tests as part of preservice training and "deselected" volunteers who failed. At Peace Corps training sites, then, the staff psychologist became the most feared and reviled figure in the agency. "I've grown more wary of the headshrinkers on the University of California campus where I'm training, than in Africa (where they're supposed to have the genuine articles)," quipped Arnold Zeitlin, on his way to Ghana. At Zeitlin's training, volunteers received eleven hours of "psychological inspection" to just an hour of physical examination. Like C. R. Thayer's "sentence completion" exercise, many of the Peace Corps tests aimed at identifying "abnormal" volunteers; for all of the agency's talk about rugged individuals and new frontiers, critics noted, its mental-health tests prized conformity above all else. At Alan Weiss' training for Nigeria, one male volunteer was deselected for his allegedly high "femininity quotient"; knowing better, Weiss kept his own homosexual thoughts to himself. But he could not hide his high intelligence, which marked him as a "high-risk" Peace Corps candidate. "What do you do, Mr. Weiss, besides think?" one suspicious agency psychologist asked.[54]

Significantly, Peace Corps trainings provided only the most cursory forms of teacher preparation. Echoing John F. Kennedy's emphasis on "vigor" (or "vigah," as skeptics called it), trainings stressed physical conditioning and endurance. At their 1961 training at Pennsylvania State University, for example, the first contingent of female teachers for the Philippines camped atop a nearby mountain—nicknamed "New Frontier Ridge"—to learn "survival techniques" for the Orient. Later, the same group practice taught for several weeks at sugar-plantation schools in Hawaii. But they were the exceptions. Another Philippines group taught for just two hours before reaching their posts; volunteers bound for Thailand taught for a single hour; and one Somalia volunteer taught a group of children at his own training for just five minutes. The Peace Corps did provide lectures on educational theory, but they went over the heads of most listeners. "We had to go it alone," recalled another Somalia teacher, looking back on his service, "and it was like having lost your flashlight in a coal mine." Just as the Peace Corps' psychological tests would spawn volunteer outrage during trainings, so would its antiprofessional bias spark resistance overseas. Indeed, teachers would develop professional identities to counter the image that the Peace Corps had manufactured for them.[55]

The Kiddie Crusade

Predictably enough, the first groups of volunteer teachers, like their mission counterparts, were overwhelmingly young, inexperienced, and untrained. Dubbed the "Kiddie Crusade," Peace Corps volunteers averaged 24 years of age in the 1960s; for teachers, the average was probably even lower. One Ethiopia district hosted fourteen Peace Corps teachers in 1962, all between 21 and 23 years old, who possessed just two years of prior teaching experience between them. In neighboring Somalia, meanwhile, only six of fifty-six Peace Corps instructors in 1966 had taught in the United States. Elsewhere, the proportion of experienced teachers was slightly higher. By 1968, roughly one-third of all Peace Corps teachers had some kind of instructional experience before going overseas. Despite agency rhetoric about recruiting from the "best" schools, however, most volunteers hailed from state universities and small colleges rather than from elite private institutions. Nor did they typically excel in their studies, as a Peace Corps trainer noted. "The majority of these people were in the upper half of their class at college. But there aren't many Phi Beta Kappas," he said. "They aren't Ivy League, or beatnik. They come mostly from small schools and small communities." A volunteer from an upper-crust Eastern college offered a similar—and snobbish—assessment: "They aren't the intellectual cream of America. But they're sincere, friendly, and stable."[56]

Small handfuls of middle-aged and even senior citizens joined the Peace Corps, to be sure, including public school teachers on sabbatical or in retirement. By contrast, short-term mission and lay religious groups specifically restricted their membership to the young. The Methodists' "A-3" program, which sent over 800 volunteers abroad for three-year terms from 1948 to 1963, capped their maximum age at thirty. So did the Lutheran and Baptist churches, although both made exceptions in "special" cases. Of seven lay Catholic groups that sent teachers abroad in 1960, five barred applicants older than thirty-six. As in the case of the Peace Corps, most of these people went overseas fresh out of college—with no prior teaching background. "While I do not want to spend my life teaching, I would like to spend a year or two at it," wrote an applicant to a Quaker mission. "Since I do not have a teaching credential, the only teaching I could do would be in private schools or with some program like VISTA or the Peace Corps." Like secular volunteer agencies, missions offered young, untested Americans the chance to get their feet wet in the classroom, and to do "something meaningful and helpful to others," as the Quaker applicant added.[57]

When they arrived overseas, however, Americans frequently found that they lacked the skills or knowledge to help anybody. Lesson planning, lecturing, homework assignments, and student discipline all proved enormous hurdles for Americans who had never experienced them from the teacher's side of the blackboard. "I felt like the 'great impostor' at times," recalled one Catholic missionary to Bolivia, describing her difficulties in the classroom. Another Catholic teacher in Mexico blamed herself for her "lack of competence professionally," acknowledging that she should have read more about pedagogy on her own. More commonly, teachers blamed the agency that hired them to do a job without

preparing them for it. "To send PCVs over with as few hours of super-
vised teaching as I've had is unthinkable," a Liberia Peace Corps volunteer fumed. At her training, an Ethiopia teacher complained, Peace
Corps officials told her "there would be very few discipline problems to
handle" in Africa. "A great number of us, like numbskulls, believed
this," she continued, so the teachers arrived at their schools without any
strategies for addressing their students' frequent insolence and disobedience. Assigned to teach English to three classes of seventy girls each
in Korea, one missionary worried that her students were not learning
enough to justify their tuition. She had received no training in classroom methods, the missionary admitted, and it showed in her work.[58]

Other teachers realized how little they knew about the subjects they
were asked to instruct. Contrary to official Peace Corps claims, volunteers frequently taught courses that they had barely studied in college.
In a 1964 survey of Peace Corps teachers in Cameroon, over 60 percent
said they were "unfamiliar" with the subjects they taught; a full 85 percent instructed music, which almost none of them had studied at home.
One volunteer was even assigned to teach a course he had "flunked in
college," as embarrassed Peace Corps officials admitted. Whereas the
official Mennonite handbook said missionaries needed a major in their
"teaching field," teachers in the real field found themselves instructing
everything *except* their specialty. Ironically, some liberal-arts graduates
even taught courses in education. "The first month I would wake up
about four o'clock in the morning and just lie there in the darkness and
dread the day ahead, mostly the classes for which I had no training, particularly something called 'Pedagogy,' which was to teach the students
how to teach," one Mennonite recalled. "And African sociology, the ab-
surdity of which my trying to teach it bordered on madness, for what
did I know of Africa and her peoples to teach a year's course?" Other
Americans envied expatriate teachers from European countries, who
generally possessed both degrees and experience in the subjects that
they taught.[59]

Local Critics

Especially in Africa, Americans entered school systems that were still
dominated by European teachers and administrators. In 1959, nearly
20,000 expatriates from England and 10,000 from France taught in

African schools; Congo alone contained over 5,000 European instructors. Well after winning their freedom, many African nations continued to rely upon expatriate teachers. Two years after independence, 97 percent of high school teachers in Nigeria came from Europe; likewise, in Senegal, all of the school principals and the vast majority of teachers came from France or from a French colony. Meanwhile, new European volunteer agencies began to flood the globe with their own teachers. Fifty-two other nations sent a total of 38,000 people overseas by 1967, matching America's volunteer force; as in the Peace Corps, probably half of the European enlistees were teachers. Around the world, then, American teachers often shared schools, offices, and even living quarters with other foreigners. One school in Botswana hired teachers from seven different volunteer agencies—including Danes, Swedes, Germans, and Americans—plus some "very British" expatriates, as one observer quipped. An American missionary described his own African school as "a miniature United Nations," boasting teachers from England and Scotland, the United States and Canada, and Australia and New Zealand.[60]

Yet these international communities were hardly as peaceful as the missionary's metaphor implied. European expatriates blasted American teachers as slovenly and ill-prepared, while Americans condemned the Europeans as supercilious prigs. Especially in Africa, Peace Corps volunteers denounced their expatriate counterparts for racist comments about black students and teachers.[61] To European headmasters, meanwhile, American teachers violated basic standards of professional training and decorum. "The trouble with your Volunteers is their lack of experience, their impetuousness, their lack of a broad-based education," one British principal in Sierra Leone told a Peace Corps official. In Nigeria, another British official mocked Americans' liberal-arts background; in Morocco, likewise, French *lycee* teachers "took a dim view generally of American degrees and qualifications"; and in Senegal, French principals refused to let Americans teach any subject other than English. Across the continent, meanwhile, expatriates berated American teachers for their unkempt beards, bedraggled clothing, and informal manner. Europeans in Malawi called Peace Corps volunteers the "Tacky Brigade," after the sneakers ("tackys," in British parlance) that the volunteers wore to school, to formal restaurants, and even to official government ceremonies.[62]

To Americans' chagrin, many indigenous peoples came to view them in an even harsher light. In India and several African countries, anti-American pamphleteers pointed to the teachers' lack of training as evidence of their real purpose: espionage. Elsewhere, local teachers condemned the Peace Corps for sending instructors with even less preparation than they had. In the Philippines, where Americans were assigned to "assist" local instructors, Filipinos took offense that "someone without a degree was supposed to be telling them how to teach." Nor could Americans mollify teachers with gifts of educational materials and equipment, as one Morocco volunteer warned. "These goodies seem to be our peace offerings," he observed, "sent to compensate for lack of teaching skills." To local educational officials, meanwhile, the very presence of untrained instructors represented a standing rebuke. "It is an insult to be sent inexperienced teachers!" one African administrator told a Peace Corps representative in 1964. By the late 1960s, several African nations required all foreign teachers to possess at least two years of experience or a teacher's certificate. Such policies favored European teachers—the "truly skilled and qualified," as one American admitted—and discouraged volunteers from the United States, who moved to other African countries or left the continent altogether.[63]

Most of all, local critics denounced the Americans' disheveled appearance. "The teacher is a highly revered person in the community and in the Ethiopian social structure," one Peace Corps volunteer explained. "My Ethiopian colleagues are proud of their Western dress, and are rarely to be seen without a white shirt, tie, and coat." When volunteers wore Bermuda shorts and ankle-length socks to class, then, local teachers complained that the Americans were "undercutting their status as highly trained professionals," as another American observer wrote. Several Ethiopian principals ordered their Peace Corps teachers to wear neckties and to stop sitting on desks, a common American habit. Elsewhere, critics attacked Americans' impoverished lifestyle as well as their sloppy attire. Noting that Peace Corps teachers rarely drove cars or hired servants, like other expatriates did, one Nigerian newspaper suggested that the volunteers were "second-rate American citizens" sent to Africa as punishment for a crime, or were graduates of "substandard" colleges who could not find jobs. Predictably, then, most students did not accord them the same esteem as they did European teachers. To win Africans' respect, an American observer wrote, teachers would have to look and act more like "professional people."[64]

Professionalism from the Bottom Up

To become professionals, however, Peace Corps teachers would have to fight the Peace Corps itself. Upon completing their service in 1963, Ghana's first group of teachers bitterly denounced the agency's "Mud Huts and Dale Carnegie" conception of their proper role. On the one hand, teachers were supposed to lead an ascetic lifestyle that ran counter to African and expatriate notions of professional decorum. On the other hand, they were urged to start a wide variety of so-called "secondary projects," especially in health, nutrition, or school construction, that seemed to diminish their classroom work. "There was unanimous resentment in the group over what they believed to be a basic tenet in Peace Corps Washington philosophy," an agency official in Ghana wrote, "that the truly important job of a Volunteer is the community development projects he initiates—not the students he educates." Indeed, the Peace Corps' overweening emphasis upon secondary projects made *teaching* into a secondary activity. "If I just teach, I feel like a crumb," one volunteer lamented.[65]

Across Africa, teachers echoed these complaints. If they did not build dormitories or raise chickens, they were not seen as "real" Peace Corps volunteers; but when they did engage in such activities, they became less than "real" teachers.[66] Volunteers particularly bridled at pressure to dig latrines, which became a pungent symbol for the Peace Corps' denigration of classroom instruction. Indeed, one Nigeria volunteer complained, the agency devoted more of its in-service workshops to latrines than it did to teachers' day-to-day work. "Peace Corps should be helping us organize ourselves, act more professionally," he argued. "We should be collecting examinations, syllabi, books, etc.—use them to establish research centers to help share educational experience." But his pleas fell on deaf ears. "Instead of helping us, Peace Corps staff exerts negative pressure," the volunteer continued. "Rep [Peace Corps Representative] says: 'If you're just teaching, maybe you should think about it.' You begin to feel guilty about correcting papers on Saturday morning instead of helping someone build a latrine." The fetish for secondary projects further confused teachers' African hosts, who had invited the Peace Corps "to do a job in the schools, and not to dig latrines," an Ethiopia volunteer added. Indeed, a truly dedicated teacher would not have much room in the day for anything else. "Teaching, particularly at a boarding school, is a full-time job," a Uganda volunteer wrote. "The people seemed capable of digging their own latrines."[67]

Rejecting the Peace Corps' rhetoric, then, thousands of teachers threw themselves into "the job." To be sure, some volunteers devoted more energy and attention to extracurricular activities than to the classroom.[68] Others neglected both, relaxing by the pool during the day and drowning in drink or drugs at night.[69] Around the world, however, many Americans discovered, and embraced, the real rigors of teaching. "Things are going fine here, but I never thought I'd be so swamped with work when I joined the Peace Corps," Sierra Leone volunteer Nathan Lindgren wrote his parents. Lindgren taught twenty-two hours a week to classes as large as fifty-one, which created an enormous stack of homework papers to correct. Teaching for thirty-two hours a week, Nigeria volunteer Robert Randall also found time to coach tennis and basketball, direct the school library and health dispensary, and drive an ambulance. In Liberia, Sally Ruffino taught from 7:30 AM to 4 PM every day, then monitored a study hall from 7 PM to 9 PM at night; she also started a school choir and edited the student newspaper. Dedication to the mundane tasks of teaching represented a direct challenge to the reigning Peace Corps philosophy, as volunteers correctly sensed. "I don't agree with the mud-hut image," a Cameroon teacher told a Peace Corps official, after describing his arduous daily routine. "Professionalism is more important."[70]

The Peace Corps official dismissed such sentiments as "parochial" and "limited," reflecting the typical agency response to teachers' nascent professionalism. As two Peace Corps spokespersons in Uganda lamented, too many teachers had embraced the Peace Corps' third goal—providing technical assistance—while neglecting its first and second ones: to inform the rest of the world about the United States, and vice versa. Indeed, the officials continued, many teachers identified more with their colleagues at school—both African and European— than with the country as a whole. "Most of this group of volunteers seems to have missed the rewards of being a PCV," the Uganda officials wrote. "They were almost entirely job-oriented." Indeed, most teachers saw themselves "*as teachers*" rather than as Peace Corps volunteers, as an outraged Kenya official emphasized. Yet perhaps their new identity contained a silver lining, a Cameroon official argued, because many of them now planned to teach back home. "The job professionalism of the group dominated," the official began, dejectedly. "But the Volunteers were not interested in 'suburbia' teaching. They wanted the tough teaching jobs in the slums, among the underprivileged." Indeed, he predicted, the Peace Corps might one day provide "a better and more continuing source of supply for 'socially conscious teachers' " than the domestic Teacher Corps, which was already recruiting "better people" for America's poorer schools. Inadvertently, it seemed, the Peace Corps' antiprofessionalism was spawning a new generation of educational professionals.[71]

᠅ IN THE 1960S AND 1970S, at least half of the Americans who taught in the Peace Corps became elementary, secondary, or university-level teachers in the United States.[72] Many of them worked in urban districts like Philadelphia, where a severe teacher shortage led the city to hire 175 volunteers through the mail—sight unseen—before they even came home. By 1968, sixteen states gave teachers credit for their Peace Corps work; a small handful awarded full certification to any returned volunteer, while others provided an emergency certificate that allowed volunteers to teach while they completed required education courses. Scarred by their sink-or-swim experience overseas, many Peace Corps volunteers, like their mission counterparts, came home with a new interest in these classes. "I considered education courses as a waste of time in college," recalled one Peace Corps teacher in Ethiopia. "I was naive to think that my own methods could work out better than those of people who had years of experience." Similarly, to a mission teacher in Honduras, her overseas difficulties highlighted her need for formal preparation. Upon her return to America, then, she enrolled in a master's program to study educational theory, philosophy, and methodology.[73]

America, however, continued to send teachers overseas who possessed little real preparation for the job. The problem was especially acute among English instructors, whom the Peace Corps selected on "the myth that any native speaker of English can be converted into an adequate English teacher," as one skeptic wrote in 1969. In the 1970s, the Peace Corps began to make stronger efforts to recruit skilled professionals. But the agency exempted education volunteers, who remained the only people who could enter the Peace Corps without either experience or a postgraduate degree in their field. Writing in 1971, one observer hailed the Peace Corps' first deaf volunteer, who taught sign language in Ghana, as an example of the agency's new emphasis upon "specific qualifications" for its recruits. Yet most of the early deaf Peace Corps volunteers lacked any background in *instructing* sign language; like nondeaf English speakers, their only "skill" was facility in the language itself. "I wanted some teaching experience," recalled a deaf volunteer in the Philippines, explaining her decision to join the agency. In Sierra Leone, an overworked deaf teacher implored the Peace Corps to send another one, no matter what the person's background. "I don't care if he/she has a degree in education as long as he/she has a strong psychological mind," the volunteer wrote. "I need some helping hands and I can train them with minimum difficulty."[74]

In contrast, some post–World War II missions required their teachers to have experience or credentials before they went abroad. The trend was particularly stark among so-called independent or fundamentalist sects, who increasingly dominated the mission field. In 1947, only 12 of 58 surveyed missionaries, mostly from independent churches, said that an American teacher's certificate would give an "advantage" to their members; by 1964, 17 of 46 independent mission boards specifically mandated the certificate for classroom instructors. "Because the educational standards are rising all over the world, the missionary teacher must raise his educational level to keep in step," one scholar observed. As the worldwide demand for English boomed, however, more and more missions, like the Peace Corps, hired teachers whose only real qualification lay in their ability to speak it. By 2001, one mission official observed, the "substantial majority" of American missionaries taught English as their "overt and official profession"; yet too many missions still maintained the "widespread and pernicious belief that anyone who can speak a language can teach it," as a second official wrote. Although teachers might list education as their "profession," in short, they typically lacked the training and experience to justify the label.[75]

As always, the teachers knew it. In 1990, shortly after the fall of the Berlin Wall, the Peace Corps sent its first group of Peace Corps volunteers to Poland and Hungary. Assigned to teach English, the 121 new recruits represented "the best America has to offer," Peace Corps director Paul Coverdell said at a White House ceremony in their honor. Upon reaching Eastern Europe, however, the volunteers themselves told a different story. "Polish education is quite rigorous," one teacher worried, "and I have a feeling that the Peace Corps' standards may be lower than Polish standards as far as teachers go." Indeed, twenty of the first sixty American teachers in Poland had just graduated from college and had majored in subjects other than English. During the teachers' first weeks in the country, Polish students routinely corrected the Americans' grammar and spelling errors. "The Peace Corps said we'd be great teachers when we were done with training, but many were *not* prepared," a second volunteer underlined. "How could you claim you're sending all these 'points of light' and 'the brightest and best'?"[76] Between the presidencies of John F. Kennedy ("brightest and best") and George H. W. Bush ("points of light"), it seemed, little had changed. Despite their rhetorical paeans to education, Americans still did not regard teaching as a true profession. But much of the globe did. America's overseas teachers stood in the middle, sandwiched between a nation that maligned their profession and a world that embraced it.

5

Going Global, or Going It Alone?

AMERICAN TEACHERS AND CHURCH–STATE RELATIONS

IN OCTOBER 1902, an American Presbyterian in India condemned his mission for accepting state funds for its schools. Across the British Empire, Edgar M. Wilson noted, colonial governments offered grants-in-aid to religious schools that maintained minimum standards in facilities, curriculum, and inspection. But when Americans accepted such aid, Wilson argued, they violated "the fundamental principle" of their own nation: the separation of church and state. Just ten years earlier, he recalled, Presbyterians in the United States had denounced federal assistance to denominational schools for American Indians, but now the church accepted such aid on behalf of *Asian* Indians, dismissing the same precepts it defended at home. These principles were true in every case, Wilson added, or they were not true at all. "Church and State should be entirely separate—the majority of mankind to the contrary notwithstanding," he intoned.[1]

As Wilson's final comment implied, nearly every Western imperial power provided some type of direct public aid to religious schools. The United States was the exception.[2] The previous year, for example, American officials had barred the use of government funds for parochial education in the Philippines. But they also prohibited public school teachers from preaching their religion, even outside of class, prompting a different set of objections from American missionaries. School authorities censured several teachers for holding Bible classes in their own homes, others were barred from teaching Sunday school, while still others refrained from any acts of public worship, lest they incur the suspicions of their supervisors. At the same time, missionaries complained, Catholic public school teachers freely participated in processions, feasts, and other religious rites. "Church and state are not separate in the Philippines," one missionary flatly declared, condemning the restrictions on Protestant teachers. A second missionary took a more nuanced approach. "The principle of separation of Church and State may be used to do violence to the companion principle of liberty of individual religious belief and worship," he wrote. "There must be something wrong when, in order that a governmental department may guarantee individual religious liberty, to those to whom it ministers, its own agents must thereby have their own individual liberty curtailed."[3]

The missionary's remarks spoke to an erstwhile tension in American church–state doctrine, which bars the government from establishing religion even as it guarantees each citizen's "free exercise" of it.[4] In their own colonies, Americans would limit the second principle on behalf of the first one: lest the heavily Catholic population of the Philippines mistake public schools for "Protestant" ones, officials said, teachers needed to restrain their religious activities. Outside of the U.S. empire, meanwhile, Protestant missionaries frequently embraced the same types of church–state arrangements that the American establishment clause prohibited. From India and Burma to Kenya and the Congo, Americans sought and secured government aid for their budding mission schools. They also accepted a wide range of state regulations, including—in some instances—a ban on religious instruction itself. Facing a new Chinese prohibition upon proselytizing, for example, missionary principal Sophie Lanneau scoffed at suggestions that she should close her school in protest. "A protest in behalf of religious liberty?" a skeptical Lanneau asked. "It is too late now." Better to accept the odious restrictions of the government than to send her students to state schools, where they would be lost to God forever.[5]

Such concessions sparked the ire of more conservative missionaries like Joseph Wilson of India, who insisted that Americans hold fast to their founding traditions of church–state separation. Indeed, the entire issue exposed massive fault lines between liberals and conservatives—or, sometimes, between "modernists" and "fundamentalists"—in American Protestantism. Most historical accounts have examined the fiery

domestic theater of this conflict, focusing especially upon evolution instruction. But the battle also had an explosive foreign dimension, which
pit "social-gospel" missions against self-described "evangelical" ones.
Like their counterparts in the United States, social-gospel missionaries
aimed to improve public conditions—in housing, labor, and education—as well as to convert individuals; evangelicals clung to an older
creed, asserting that personal faith held the sole key to salvation. Hardly
the exclusive province of "faith" or "independent" missions, as scholars
once supposed, the evangelical view dominated mainline denominations until World War II.[6] Liberal voices were a distinct minority,
pressing missions to develop a more open-minded, cosmopolitan stance
toward other faiths, customs, and cultures.[7]

For the first half of the twentieth century, then, liberals were also
more likely to adopt the different church–state traditions that they encountered overseas. Replying to Wilson, for example, another Presbyterian urged his mission to accept the "British" norm—that is, state aid
to parochial schools—rather than imposing "American" ideals. "The
conditions prevailing in India differ so much from those which exist in
the USA that I fail to see how you can expect or wish to apply the same
policy here," he wrote.[8] Like Sophie Lanneau, liberals also urged compromise when governments slapped restrictions on their own religious
activities. To conservatives, meanwhile, both types of concessions reflected an unholy surrender of bedrock American principles. As the
Founding Fathers understood, religious liberty required strict neutrality on the part of the state. So Americans must eschew government aid
and government regulation, they argued, no matter what their foreign
hosts might believe.

After World War II, by contrast, conservatives would take the cosmopolitan tack. Indeed, they took their liberal brethren one better:
rather than simply upholding foreign traditions in foreign locales, they
used their overseas experience to critique church–state relations at home.
As court decisions slowly removed overt spiritual rituals from public
schools in the United States, missionaries pointed approvingly to state-
sponsored religious instruction in European colonies and newly independent nations. Joining hands with their erstwhile Catholic enemies,
some Protestants even suggested that America mimic the European system of direct public aid to private schools. Most recent scholarship
about American cosmopolitanism has linked the concept to liberals,

who borrowed heavily from European models of economic regulation and public welfare. Likewise, on questions of race and civil rights, liberals frequently looked to Africa and Asia for inspiration and examples.[9] But American conservatives developed their own brand of cosmopolitanism, focused less on "social politics" than on church–state relations. As the missionary experience demonstrates, the post–World War II Right—more than the Left—assumed an explicitly global perspective on religion, education, and the state.

Church and State in the American Colonies I: Policy

In March of 1902, Harry and Mary Cole wrote a long, angry letter to Harry's family in the United States. The Coles had come to the Philippines aboard the USS *Thomas*, just seven months earlier, but they were already counting the days until they could go home. They disliked the climate, the food, and the lack of entertainment; most of all, though, the Coles disliked the Filipinos. Whatever their age, it seemed, Filipinos were lazy, dirty, and superstitious; and so they would remain, Mary Cole wrote, as long as they stayed in the Catholic Church. "Harrie gets *so* disgusted with so much tomfoolery in their religion," Mary wrote,

> and I have to keep my thumb on him considerable to keep him from saying too much. As you say, it is best to keep the good will of the people, but so long as this religion has such a hold on them, I fear they cannot be uplifted to any great extent. Our instructions were not to interfere with their religion; but are they always to spend the greater part of their time in conforming to the rule of such a belief?[10]

Mary Cole's comments neatly captured the twin themes in American religious policy for the new United States empire. By law, public schools maintained a strict neutrality on matters of faith. Officials in Hawaii, Puerto Rico, and the Virgin Islands all issued bans on "sectarian" instruction in the schools; in the Philippines, meanwhile, the 1901 School Act threatened dismissal for any instructor who taught "the doctrines of any Church" or who tried to influence students "for or against any Church." But America's largely Protestant teachers also hoped to undermine the faith of their pupils, as the teachers' private correspondence

clearly reveals. In Puerto Rico and the Philippines, where over 90 percent of the population was Catholic, Americans complained that their
students would never learn to work, listen, or reason if they remained
caught in the clutches of "Romanism." Teachers in Hawaii faced a
bewildering array of religious groups, which allegedly inhibited the
progress and "civilization" that Americans had come to bestow. "Protestantism has been depleted," worried one school official, noting the large
numbers of Buddhists, Confucians, and Catholics in the public schools.
"Hawaii can not be American until she truly Christianizes her population, and makes dominant *the Christian home*." To most American teachers, indeed, Catholicism hardly qualified as "Christian" at all.[11]

In optimistic moments, teachers predicted that public schools—with
their emphasis upon free will, logic, and responsibility—would wean
students away from the Catholic Church, which allegedly promoted ir-
rationality and duplicity. "You asked if we were trying to teach these
people the true religion," Mary Cole wrote, in another letter home.
"Well, yes and no. We are not allowed to say anything about religion
but we do try to teach the school children to be honest and not lie."
Other teachers were more sanguine, noting the ongoing power and influence of local priests. Across the American empire, Catholic clergy
threatened to excommunicate families who patronized public schools.
Other priests started their own schools, sparking a spirited competition
for students as well as for souls. In the Virgin Islands, priests complained that the new public schools were "stealing" Catholic children;
in the Philippines, meanwhile, American teachers leveled the same
charge at the priests. After one Philippine padre opened a new school
and lured almost all of the local children away from the public school,
their American teacher appeared at his door with a heavy cane. Threatening to beat the priest, he ordered the children back into his own classroom. In another town, where a large church bell summoned children
to the Catholic school, Americans mounted an even louder bell atop
the public one.[12]

Reports of this sort sent shock waves through the Catholic press in
the United States, which launched an angry letter-writing campaign
against public schools in the Philippines. Hardly "public" at all, the
schools were simply Protestant agencies "masquerading in the name
of Americanism," as one critic told president Theodore Roosevelt. A
year after the *Thomas* arrived, the critic added, just eighteen of 1,000
American teachers were Catholic. Other Catholics claimed that several

leading school officials were Protestant clerics, that Catholic teachers earned less money than their counterparts, and that the Catholics were assigned to remote, less desirable posts. All the while, new laws barred the Filipinos from teaching *their* own religion in public schools. "What right have we to send a herd of anti-Catholic, half-educated Bible bangers to run the Schools of a Catholic people," asked one Rhode Island critic, "and say that we cannot allow the taxpayers . . . to teach their own religion in them? Where does the Constitution come in?" Other Americans wondered whether that document could or should apply to America's new Catholic possessions. "The clause of the Constitution which requires the absolute separation of Church and State was intended . . . to meet the conditions in the United States of America," declared an Ohio bishop, in a petition signed by 60,000 Catholics, "and not those which obtain in the Orient and among a people unanimously of one form of belief."[13]

Church and State in the American Colonies II: Practice

Amid this chorus of opposition from Philippine as well as American Catholics, officials made several concessions. First, they began a semi-clandestine effort to recruit more Catholic teachers from the United States. In public, American officials continued to insist that they hired teachers "without respect to religion"; behind the scenes, however, they worked closely with bishops in the United States to identify and attract qualified Catholics. "I am quietly but energetically looking up candidates for the position of teachers in the Philippines," wrote St. Paul bishop John Ireland, who recommended 200 Catholics to school officials. "I have friends co-operating with me all thorough the country, but we are operating very quietly so as not to awaken any talk or opposition." By 1904, 122 of roughly 800 American teachers in the Philippines were Catholic. The figure fell below the 20 percent target set by territorial governor William H. Taft, but it seems to have mollified some of the Catholic criticism. More importantly, perhaps, Roosevelt and Taft elevated the Catholic ex-general James F. Smith to education secretary—and, later, governor—in the Philippines.[14]

Second, school officials moved to ban all proselytizing by public school teachers, even outside of schools. In 1901, school officials assured Presbyterian mission leader Arthur J. Brown that teachers would remain "as free in their private lives . . . as teachers in the United

States." The following year, however, they censured teacher G. M. Palmer for hosting children at his house to read the Bible. Palmer described the meeting in a letter to a friend back home, who—unbeknownst to Palmer—published his letter in a local newspaper. The article quickly found its way into the Catholic press, which called for Palmer's dismissal. "If this is not proselytism in a public official, if this is not using his office to interfere with the religion of his pupils, then we do not know what proselytism is," wrote one Catholic spokesman in California, in a note to Governor Taft. "Palmer and his like have caused the lack of confidence which exists in this country towards the School Department of the Philippines." Wary of any further criticism from Catholics, Taft recommended that Palmer be fired. "It is easy to say that this is a suppression of free speech," Taft cautioned. "But as long as he is a teacher he does give up the right of free speech." No less than religious instruction in the classroom, Taft wrote, teacher evangelism outside of school would feed Catholic fears—and undermine the entire American educational project. So teachers should refrain from saying "anything upon the subject," he cautioned, at least when Filipinos were within earshot.[15]

For the most part, the teachers appear to have abided by this policy. But they also resented it, enlisting the Philippines' growing missionary community to fight the religious restrictions. "Many of the best teachers . . . feel that this is an invasion of their rights," wrote one Methodist official. "When the government follows a man over the threshold of his own door . . . it is exceeding the bounds set for it by the constitution under which we live." Large numbers of teachers had taught in Sunday Schools back home, so they were surprised and dejected to discover that they could not do the same overseas. Others refrained from religious activity altogether, fearful that a mere appearance in church would arouse the ire of snooping school officials. Without the anchor of organized faith, missionaries reported, still other teachers turned to "tropical" vices: sex, gambling, and especially strong drink. "Would it not be better if the government ordered its employees to abstain from alcohol than from religion?" asked one Presbyterian minister.[16]

Finally, Protestants charged, school officials did not impose the same religious restrictions upon the Catholic minority in the American teaching force. Catholic teachers routinely attended Mass, went to confessional, or led processions in their respective towns. As American

bishops began to arrive in the Philippines, meanwhile, teachers accompanied them on itinerating trips around the islands. But school officials
turned a blind eye to such breaches, causing Protestant missionaries and
teachers alike to conclude that the American government had forsaken
its avowed religious neutrality. "Our Government has repeatedly insisted that in the Philippine Islands there is the same separation of
Church and State that there is in other parts of American territory,"
wrote Presbyterian leader Arthur J. Brown. Yet the school system's official order barring teacher proselytizing referred to the Philippines as
a "Catholic country," Brown noted, suggesting that Americans had altered their church–state principles for overseas consumption. "We have
a right to ask," Brown concluded, "that the Government shall not be
practically anti-Protestant and pro-Roman Catholic."[17]

Widely repeated by Protestant teachers and clerics, such claims seem
absurd at first glance. After all, the vast majority of school officials and
instructors were themselves Protestant; even more, they made no secret
of their deep hostility toward the Catholic faith. But the "pro-Catholic"
charge spoke to an important truth about the U.S. empire, where Americans imposed restrictions on teachers that would have been unusual—
and, possibly, unconstitutional—back home. Most states allowed Bible
reading within schools and several actually required it; in the Philippines, by contrast, officials barred teachers from any scriptural allusions
whatsoever. In 1908, indeed, two American teachers were censured for
reading from the Bible as part of their "literary and historical" study of
Evangeline, the Henry W. Longfellow poem. Nor did public school
teachers in America face pressures or penalties against outside religious
activities, as Protestants in the Philippines routinely noted. "The principle of religious liberty is very little understood in this Province," complained a Presbyterian missionary, "and Americans at home ought to
know what is happening under the American flag."[18] As they moved
across other nations and empires, meanwhile, Americans would themselves alter their ideas of "religious liberty" to suit the new conditions
that they confronted.

In Other Empires: The Question of State Aid

American missionaries around the world closely followed events in the
Philippines and other U.S. territories, focusing especially upon efforts

at compulsory attendance, industrial training, and coeducation.[19] In British colonies, however, missionaries also encountered a dilemma that was absent from the American empire: state funding for mission schools. At different points in the twentieth century, nearly every imperial power provided government funds to parochial institutions. Prior to World War II, Belgian and Portuguese colonies limited their grants to Catholic schools; French practices fluctuated according to religious politics back home, but they generally barred foreign missionaries from receiving state aid. Hence, America's largely Protestant missionary corps usually encountered the issue in British territories, where almost all religious organizations were eligible for state aid. In 1911, for example, British officials in Kenya decreed that the government would provide £5 for each student who could pass an examination in "Industrial Work"; in 1919, they would alter the system to grant funds to any school that agreed to a yearly inspection. In South Africa, by contrast, schools received aid based on annual attendance as well as inspections. In 1914, the American Congregational mission in Natal, South Africa, accepted over $4,000 each year in state assistance to fifty-eight different schools.[20]

As the largest colony in the empire, meanwhile, British India also provided the greatest number of school grants. In 1854, its Education Despatch promised public monies for any school—municipal, private, or religious—that provided some secular instruction and allowed government inspection. The colony's Educational Council of 1884 formalized this process, recommending grants-in-aid to schools that maintained minimum standards in staff, facilities, and curriculum. By 1930, missionaries to India received over $1 million for their schools. At least half of this sum probably went to two American missions, the Baptists and Presbyterians, who dotted the colony with a diverse array of schools. In 1932, for example, American Baptists in Burma—a subdistrict of British India—took in over $300,000 in state funds. Presbyterians operated a comparable number of schools across India, so they most likely received a similar amount of aid. During these same years, British officials stepped up the construction of government schools. But they continued to favor mission institutions, for clear economic reasons. As one official confided to a Baptist teacher in Burma, it cost the state over twice as much to educate a child in its own schools as it did in an "aided" one.[21]

Even as American schools reaped government support, however, they would also sow a bitter controversy among American missionaries.

A magazine captured the nub of the issue in a 1916 editorial: "Do Baptists believe one thing in the United States and practice its opposite in India?" Back home, Catholics demanded public aid to parochial schools, while Protestants joined hands to block it: by 1915, indeed, all but three American states had amended their constitutions to prohibit such funding. But Protestants took government money when they went overseas, critics complained, echoing their erstwhile "Romish" enemies in the United States. "If our taxes were used to support Catholic schools in America we Baptists would be the first to cut their grants if power came into our hands," admitted one Burma missionary. "It cannot be questioned that we are perpetuating a system . . . which as Baptists we would not tolerate in America."[22]

But the missionaries were *not* in America, other Protestants responded—and that was the whole point. The United States had a long tradition of universal public education, another Baptist noted, which it had recently bestowed on the eight million people in the Philippines. But over 300 million souls lived in British India, where the state could not possibly provide for their education. Given that fact, the government needed to assist parochial schools; even more, taxpaying citizens deserved the assistance. "The people are taxed for educational purposes," wrote a third Baptist, in an ironic mimicry of Catholics back home, "so their participation in these funds is but just." Most of all, missionaries argued, American church–state concepts were simply inappropriate in a foreign context. "There is a possibility of our institutions becoming too much American for India," a Presbyterian warned, in support of government grants. Rather than foisting America's different ethos upon other nations, he explained, his mission should adapt its ethos in accord with national differences.[23]

The debate would come to a head with the 1922 passage of a so-called "Conscience Clause" in India's United Provinces, which required schools to let students exempt themselves from religious instruction; schools that refused to comply would forsake their government grants. The measure reflected the growing influence of Hindu nationalists, who feared that mission schools were forcing Christianity upon their young charges. Back in New York, the Presbyterian Board of Foreign Missions—America's largest missionary body—ordered schools to reject the Conscience Clause, because it violated missionaries' freedom to spread God's word. In India, however, most mission teachers seemed willing to abide by it. Many of them already allowed students to excuse themselves from chapel; and without government aid, the missionaries argued, most schools would have to close their doors. At least one teacher told Board secretary Robert E. Speer that she planned to ignore his order, which violated *her* freedom to conduct school as she wished. "What can I ask—to be allowed to disobey?" wrote Emily L. Peterson. "I suppose it is foolish to send this letter—but I have written it [and] I will send it."[24]

Liberals, Conservatives, and the Conscience Clause

Beneath this dispute lay a sharp rift between liberal and conservative Protestants, affecting missionary efforts as well as churches back home. Liberals placed their central emphasis on social services such as medicine and education, which would make people more "Christ-like" even if they failed to embrace Christ. But to conservatives, the sole purpose of *any* missionary effort, including schools, was to win souls for the Lord; everything else was mere "institutionalism," diverting money and energy into mundane, worldly concerns. Whereas liberals could accept the Conscience Clause, conservatives despised it. To the avowedly "orthodox" Woman's Union Missionary Society, which sent hundreds of single females to India, the clause inhibited their essential goal: "to bring the knowledge of Jesus Christ to non-Christian women and children." By contrast, India's mostly liberal Lutheran and Methodist missions insisted that Christ's example required them to respect the rights of unbelievers—and to abide by the new regulation. "No student should be compelled to sit under religious instruction to which he is conscientiously opposed," a group of Methodist bishops declared. After all, they added, Jesus never used force to transmit His message. Nor should His messengers in India.[25]

The issue also exposed divisions within the largest American mission, the Presbyterians. The split was partially geographical, pitting officials in America against teachers in the field. But it was ideological, as well, reflecting a growing liberal–conservative tension that would tear the mission apart in the 1930s. Conservatives in India corresponded regularly with board secretary Speer, a theological traditionalist who insisted that Christ's resurrection was literal—and that missions should seek to displace other religions, lest non-Christians suffer eternal doom.

"I am with you *in toto*," India missionary W. T. Mitchell wrote to Speer, thanking him for opposing the Conscience Clause. At several local meetings, Mitchell continued, India Presbyterians had alleged that Speer stood "with the liberal Modernists" in supporting the clause. But as a self-described "old timer and conservative," Mitchell knew better. "Your statement . . . should do much to assure our Presbyterian Church that Union Seminary and leaders of very liberal beliefs do not make up our Board of Foreign Missions," he wrote. Here Mitchell took aim at the Union Theological Seminary of Columbia University, where professors supposedly denied "the divinity of our Lord."[26]

Shrewdly, meanwhile, Speer tried to invoke Teachers College— another liberal bastion at Columbia—in his missives against the Conscience Clause. If mission schools abided by the clause, Speer told his allies in India, they would forsake the best new technique of modern, "progressive" education: the "project method." Associated most closely with William H. Kilpatrick, a colleague of John Dewey at Teachers College, the project method integrated different subjects into practical, hands-on activities instead of presenting them as separate, desiccated bodies of knowledge. Kilpatrick himself would travel to India in 1919, urging missionaries as well as native educators to develop a "unified head-hand-heart program" for their schools. To Speer, however, any school that embraced this method could not possibly countenance the Conscience Clause. The clause would require missions to isolate religious instruction into a single class period, from which non-Christians could be exempted; yet under the project system, religion, like any other course, would suffuse the curriculum. "How are we to teach ethics and history and English literature without expressing our Christian conviction?" Speer asked. "By the project method . . . Christian teaching ought to be permeating and interwoven with all the life and work of the school."[27]

Out in the field, however, missionaries invoked other aspects of the project method to argue *in favor* of the Conscience Clause. First, as one teacher told Speer, the method required "enlistment of the child's active and willing cooperation"; anyone who valued such cooperation "would certainly not object to the Conscience Clause," which simply barred schools from imposing religious doctrine upon dissenting minds. Second, the project method placed an enormous emphasis upon experience: schools should reflect the real world, not the musty abstractions of books. But the lived experience of mission schools showed that most teachers wanted schools to accept the Conscience Clause—and to continue receiving government grants. Even without compulsion, moreover, the vast majority of students continued to opt for religious instruction. By rejecting the clause and forcing schools to close, missions would be "sacrificing everything to Abstract theory," and perpetuating the same error that the project method sought to prevent.[28]

Eventually, Robert E. Speer would come to agree. Despite his own conservative theological bent, Speer was also a pragmatist: opposed to ironclad creeds of any kind, he argued that Christians should seize every opportunity to preach God's Word. Once he became convinced that the Conscience Clause did not inhibit schools from proselytizing, he dropped his opposition to it. "I am finding it very hard here to be faithful to my own convictions on the one hand, yet to be a fair and sympathetic representative of the India Missions on the other," Speer wrote from New York in 1934. Reversing its own position, the Board of Foreign Missions resolved that the Conscience Clause could only enhance the "Christian character" of schools in India. Around the world, however, other American missionaries were facing much harsher constraints upon their educational work, including outright bans on religious instruction itself. More than state aid, even, these restrictions would unleash divisive passions at the heart—and in the soul—of America's missionary endeavor.[29]

The Struggle for "Liberty"

In January 1932, a missionary council met in New York City to discuss "infringements of religious liberty" against American teachers overseas. Even in U.S. colonies like the Philippines, the group noted, public school teachers could not openly preach or practice their faith; meanwhile, civil service rules blocked missionaries from obtaining jobs in the public schools. But the worst problems occurred in other empires and, especially, in independent countries. From Egypt, Persia, and Turkey to Peru, Mexico, and Chile, revived nationalist movements placed severe restrictions on religious instruction in mission schools, or banned it altogether. "The very terms of the phrase 'religious liberty' are no longer fixed," wrote a Presbyterian observer, summarizing the chaotic global scene. "Does it mean freedom to believe, or freedom to propagate belief or freedom both to believe and to propagate belief and also to use any means of propagation desired?" Around the world, he wrote, nations were recognizing education as "an agency of power"; in different ways, meanwhile, all of them sought to make it "compatible with state interests." Wherever they went, then, Americans would need to decide when to yield to the state—and why.[30]

As in the battle over government grants, the issue drove a wedge between liberal and conservative missionaries. Yet the stakes were higher, affecting not just the budgets of mission schools but also their most basic purpose. In China, for example, conservatives in the Southern Baptist mission closed their schools rather than comply with a state mandate that barred evangelism in the classroom. "We are here to teach and preach the old time sin saving Gospel, Jesus our God, our Lord, our Savior," wrote one mission principal in 1933. "We are not here to run schools . . . with God and his Word left out." But other Southern Baptists accepted the new regulations, sparking a bitter internecine battle. "WHAT GOOD WILL IT DO THE CAUSE OF CHRIST in China or America to close WEI LING and YATES ACADEMY?" asked Sophie Lanneau, referring to two schools where she taught. "What loyalty to Christ or to the Bible would require us to send these 800 boys and girls away from the Christian opportunities which we missionary and Chinese teachers offer them here?" Despite the removal of religious worship and instruction from official curricula, Lanneau stressed, mission schools continued to conduct prayer services at student assemblies and other informal gatherings. If the schools closed their doors to Chinese pupils, they would also close many Chinese hearts to God.[31]

Like Protestant teachers at government schools in the Philippines, meanwhile, other liberal missionaries in China insisted that *any* education—even of a purely "secular" type—would help lead students to the "true" Christian faith. "They got Christian teaching indirectly although there was no religious teaching in the school," recalled Alice Reed, a Congregationalist missionary. "Any Christian teaching really holds that you must make up your own mind about things, wouldn't you say?" Likewise, Episcopalian missionary Netta Allen insisted that she taught "implicit Christian ethics" via literature—including books by Charles Dickens and Guy de Maupassant—even though "explicit Christian teaching" was prohibited. Both teachers added jabs at missionary conservatives, whether in mainline denominations or in burgeoning "independent" sects. "The great certainties!" Reed scoffed, condemning conservatives for their theological inflexibility. "You see, they never have any doubts about anything, they are always sure of everything . . . The strange things people do believe!"[32]

Likewise, in the Muslim-majority countries of the Middle East, liberal missionaries called for compromise with new restrictions while conservatives held fast to old verities—especially Christ's injunction to preach His word. After Persian officials barred schools from teaching the Bible to Muslim children, for example, Presbyterian teachers won permission to substitute a nominally ecumenical "ethics" class. Since Muslims regarded Christ as a prophet, one principal reported, she could include His teachings in the course; other missionaries taught ethics by staging student plays from the Old Testament, such as the Prodigal Son and the "Story of Joseph." Like teachers in China, still other Persia missionaries argued that the entire curriculum—not just the ethics class—would imbue students with "a larger vision of Christian service," even if they did not accept Christ. But any such concession offended conservative Presbyterians, who blasted schools for trying to " 'sneak in' their Bible teaching" via ethics courses. "If our mission schools produce merely a character formed from Christian ethics, built upon a foundation of Islam or infidelity, it will be like a house built upon sand," wrote one outraged missionary. "It is the old question of Amaziah, what shall we do for the hundred talents of silver? What shall we do for the money spent on educational institutions and equipment and educational missionaries in Persia?"[33]

The same question hounded mission teachers in Latin America, finally, where state restrictions upon religious instruction reflected a widespread animus against the Catholic Church. In some places, indeed, Protestant missionaries applauded new regulations for reining in "Romish" influence. "Things may not be as hard for us," wrote Presbyterian teacher Eunice Blackburn, after the Mexican government barred mention of "God" in all schools. "Some of the propaganda is strictly against the Catholic Clergy and things we consider as really heathen idolatry and of course would like to teach against." When it became clear that the state intended to constrain Protestants, as well, Blackburn argued for abiding by the regulation—and keeping her school open. "To starving people a half a loaf is better than none," she wrote. "If you cannot feed your baby certified milk is no reason for giving him rat poison." Here she was echoed by Southern Baptist teachers, who insisted that "hindered and handicapped" mission education was superior to the "atheistic" schooling that students would otherwise receive. When she joined her mission in 1920, Blackburn recalled, Mexico already barred religious instruction; so mission officials charged her with improving its "intellectual standards," a precondition for the advance of Protestantism. Fifteen years later, though, a new generation of mission leaders took a more old-fashioned tack. "If school work does not ooze with definite Bible teaching from the Bible the school is no longer of use," Blackburn quipped, paraphrasing the conservative critique.[34]

Here she took aim at the Presbyterian Board of Foreign Missions (BFM) in New York, where Robert E. Speer's retirement did nothing to diminish the theologically conservative instincts of mission officials. In Colombia, which required all schools to teach "Catholic doctrine," a BFM visitor complained that education occupied over half of the mission's staff and budget—with very little "evangelism" to show for it. "The best results, i.e., direct results in the salvation of souls, comes thro' the *preaching of the work*," he wrote, adding emphasis. "I do not say that no results are obtained thro' education work, but I do say that if the same effort, the same number of workers, the same costly plant were dedicated to the direct preaching of the Gospel greater results would be seen today." In a like manner, after visiting Mexico, BFM official L. K. Anderson moved to close Eunice Blackburn's school. True, Anderson acknowledged, Blackburn had sometimes managed to provide religious instruction while Mexican authorities "winked at our disobedience." But this very subterfuge violated Christian teachings, he argued, creating an "intolerable situation" for the mission. To console Blackburn, meanwhile, Anderson emphasized that she was hardly alone. "It may be of interest to you to know that many such heartaches are taking place all over the world as schools are being closed," he wrote.[35]

To Bow or Not to Bow?

Anderson went on to bemoan the situation in Korea, where American missionary teachers faced their toughest dilemma of all. Boasting one of the world's fastest-growing Christian populations, Korea was also a leader in missionary education: between 1885 and 1910, missions established over 700 schools for roughly 20,000 students. As many observers noted, this explosion owed a great deal to the Japanese occupation of Korea in the 1890s. Within nations colonized by the West, conversion to Christianity often signified support for an imperial regime; in Korea, by contrast, the faith symbolized antipathy toward a non-Christian one. Upon annexing Korea in 1910, then, the Japanese moved quickly to bring mission schools under their control. Imposing a standard curriculum, including the Japanese language in every grade, colonial authorities also banned religious instruction during school hours. These measures spawned predictable debates between liberal and conservative missionaries: one side counseled compromise with the restrictions, while the other urged resistance to them. Japanese authorities relaxed their rules in 1920 to let schools teach religion, provided that the schools met other standards and allowed periodic inspections. Missionaries initially celebrated this concession, but soon came to regard it as a "Pyrrhic victory," as one American recalled.[36] For by winning government approval, the schools would also become subject to the most contentious mandate of all: worship at state shrines.[37]

The shrine controversy began with the Japanese invasion of Manchuria in 1931, which sparked jolts of "high-voltage patriotism" across the empire, as one missionary reported. In Korea, officials ordered school children to salute the Japanese flag, conduct military drills, and visit railroad stations to cheer departing soldiers—sometimes as often as twelve times per day. Starting in 1935, officials also required school personnel to attend periodic ceremonies at more than fifty *jinja* or state shrines across Korea. Participants typically bowed to the east—that is, toward Japan—and also to the shrine, which contained pictures or relics of the Imperial Family. Japanese authorities justified the new mandates in the language of national cohesion: especially during wartime, they argued, schools needed to bind disparate peoples into a united whole. For missionaries, meanwhile, the new rules posed an agonizing quandary—and, eventually, a bitter quarrel. In Korea and elsewhere, most state regulations had merely barred missionaries' Christian rituals; by contrast, the shrine mandate required active participation in a non-Christian one. The problem was neatly captured in the title of one mission school's annual report for 1937: "To Bow or Not to Bow?" For American teachers across Korea, that was the question.[38]

As in prior disputes, answers on every side invoked religious liberty: opponents said that mandatory shrine attendance violated their free-

dom, while supporters insisted that each individual should be free to attend. The large Methodist contingent favored compliance with the *jinja*
mandate, fearing that Korea would drift toward Catholicism if Protestants began to close their schools. For their own part, Catholics received a Vatican order to visit the shrines instead of shutting down
schools; but several missionary and Korean priests objected, filing
an appeal with the Pope. The most bitter controversies occurred within
the Presbyterian camp, which was dominated by doctrinal conservatives. The mission had voted overwhelmingly to condemn *Re-Thinking
Missions*, the renowned 1932 report by liberal American clerics urging
social service over proselytism. "Against the 'Contribution to the uplift
of the Orient' idea, we would say that that was mere philanthropy, not
missions," Korea Presbyterians responded. "The [Report] has not been
able to appreciate that old line Christian faith and zeal are still alive in
the homeland and on the Mission field." The first duty of the missionary was to "proclaim the Gospel" and to "teach the Bible as a revelation
from God," the Presbyterians added. Everything else came second.[39]

To this conservative majority, the new shrine requirements were
simply anathema. After all, God's first commandment instructed Christians to worship Him, and Him alone; but the Japanese required them
to bow before a pagan idol, just like the ancient cults of Greece and
Rome. Pressing for compliance with the *jinja* order, meanwhile, liberal
Presbyterians insisted that the ritual was a "patriotic" rather than a religious one. Indeed, they noted, the very same Americans who condemned *jinja* in Korea often pressed for similar school exercises back
home. Conservatives showed little sympathy for the Jehovah's Witnesses, for example, after members of the sect refused to salute the flag
in American schools. Like critics of Japanese *jinja*, the Witnesses regarded flag ceremonies as worship of a "graven image"—in other
words, as idolatry. Yet when the Supreme Court upheld mandatory flag
salutes in June 1940, conservatives applauded; and they shed few tears
for the Witnesses in the succeeding summer, when vigilantes brutalized
more than 1,000 sect members in 236 separate incidents. Why, liberals
asked, did conservatives endorse mandatory patriotism in the United
States—including the Pledge of Allegiance, the National Anthem, and
the flag salute—but demur when the Japanese demanded the same?[40]

Of course, liberals evinced the opposite contradiction: skeptical of
patriotic requirements in the United States, they acceded to these
laws in Korea. Just after the Supreme Court upheld compulsory flag

salutes, for example, one missionary approvingly cited an editorial in
the *Christian Century*—the leading voice of liberal Protestantism—that
condemned the Court's decision for harming "religious liberty" and
"freedom of conscience." But the missionary brushed aside the editorial's attack upon states that required "an arbitrary piece of ritual," focusing instead on the consciences of those who wished to *participate* in it.
"The individual performing an act should have a right to define the
meaning and import of that act," declared Horace H. Underwood,
scion of a leading missionary family and a liberal standard-bearer in
Kora. His wife went further, linking the mission's antishrine majority to
an intolerant Scriptural literalism. "This is not easy to think—harder
to write," she began, in a letter to a confidant:

> As a whole . . . missionaries have put any degree of drinking or to-
> bacco using or card playing; any deviation from the straightest,
> narrowest, "Fundamentalist" view of theology upon the same hor-
> rible "dung heap" as fornication, murder, hate, ancestor worship,
> and all unrighteousness. I do not disagree with any of their theo-
> logical views except that they are the *only* ones right. I do not ap-
> prove of drink, I regret that Horace smokes . . . Nevertheless they
> have cultivated an uncompromising attitude that demands not
> only the substance but the whole outward form to agree with their
> own ideas.[41]

In a similar vein, Methodist James B. Moore condemned "cut and
dried fundamentalists" for their inflexible opposition to *jinja*. "They have
got to be a little liberal, and not so ungodly dogmatic and stubborn," he
wrote, "always arguing about the form, and ever forgetting the spirit."
Moore added a jab at the alleged paternalism of the antishrine camp,
which ignored Koreans' clear wish to attend the *jinja* ceremonies. "Most
of the missionaries have not discarded the idea of the 'white man's burden' and the 'white man's boss,' " Moore complained, quoting prominent Korean Christians who supported shrine visits.[42] To be sure,
Koreans were far more divided on the issue than Moore allowed: some
of them openly disdained *jinja*, while others complied simply to save
their schools—or even their lives.[43] By invoking Korean public opinion,
however, liberal missionaries underscored the sharp divergence between
their views of religious freedom at home and abroad. On the flag-salute

question in America, liberals argued that individual rights trumped majoritarian ones: no matter how many people favored the ritual, the state could not require it. But in Korea, liberals cited popular attitudes as a reason to *support* coercive rituals. The only coercion they condemned was that of their conservative or "fundamentalist" counterparts, who blocked Christians from deciding on their own: to bow or not to bow?

The issue would come to a head in 1938, when the Presbyterian Board of Foreign Missions approved the transfer of its schools to "responsible" Korean Christians. Here the BFM overruled its own Executive Committee in Korea, which had ordered schools to close their doors rather than allowing them to participate in *jinja*. Widely reported in the American religious press, the decision sparked angry protests among conservative Presbyterians across the United States. "There are many of us plain laypeople who would give more freely to mission support if the Board changed from an 'inclusive' and middle of the road policy to one definitely and wholly evangelical," cautioned one Indiana correspondent. A Minnesota woman urged the BFM to "keep Modernism out of Korea," condemning the Board for "compromising with the world." Indeed, critics feared, this small conflict in Asia anticipated a much larger battle—between God and the Devil—for control of the world. "It all shows the work of Satan, because he knows Christ is coming soon," an Ohio critic warned. "I am a presbyterian and a fundamentalist [and] will have nothing whatever to do with a missionary society that will dishonor their Lord."[44]

Such critics often drifted toward the Independent Board of Presbyterian Foreign Missions—a group of fundamentalist dissidents, dismayed by the BFM's allegedly "apostate" policies—or into the mushrooming network of nondenominational "faith" missions, which downplayed schools and other institutions in favor of simple, soul-to-soul evangelism. As the shrine controversy seemed to illustrate, institutions enmeshed missions in the machinery of the state; and the state, in turn, drained missions of their passion as well as their principles. By the 1930s, roughly one of every seven North American missionaries came from a "faith" or fundamentalist mission. After World War II, however, even these missions proved unable to avoid the perils of "institutionalism," as its critics called it. Around the world, faith missions were forced to establish their own schools, and, inevitably, to engage with the modern state.[45]

A New Consensus

In 1950, the American Baptist mission in the Congo conducted a survey on state subsidies to religious schools. The vote was unanimous: of eighteen respondents, all eighteen wished to accept state aid. Although such assistance was clearly unconstitutional back home, several missionaries admitted, Americans needed to "look at the European picture." Before World War II, Belgian colonial authorities limited grants-in-aid to Catholic schools. Now that Protestants were eligible for the grants, the missionaries said, Baptists must take advantage of them; without such aid, indeed, they would cede the entire school field to the Catholics. In the Cameroon, meanwhile, American Presbyterians held a similar poll—with a similar result. Like Belgians in the Congo, the Presbyterians noted, French authorities were offering new school aid to Protestants as well as Catholics. But these same opportunities also extended to the burgeoning "faith" and independent sects, they added, creating a new threat to mainline denominations, and a new argument for accepting state funds. Both colonies had expanded their network of government schools, finally, presenting yet another challenge to mainline missions. "Let us clearly understand the forces now at work: politics, catholicism, adventism, Jehovah's Witnesses, etc. vie for schools," warned one mission leader. "Education opens the doors." Only by accepting state aid could Presbyterians keep up with their erstwhile Catholic foes, with upstart faith missions, and with the state itself.[46]

Together, these surveys illustrate the fresh overseas American consensus on church–state relations in the post–World War II period. Wracked by internal conflict during the first half of the century, most mainline denominations embraced state aid to mission schools with a renewed zeal. As in the Congo and the Cameroon, the shift reflected new funding opportunities for Protestant churches. But it also reflected a strong and sudden challenge from so-called faith or "evangelical" missions, which entered the educational arena for the first time. Around the world, mainline denominations found themselves competing for students—and for souls—with a wide array of independent sects. They also continued to struggle against the Catholic Church, which stepped up its own educational efforts. Last, the expansion of government schools in colonies and newly independent nations posed yet another peril. "Comparing our schools to the ascending rockets of the Roman

Catholics and the public schools brings only discouragement and de-
spair," one Presbyterian in the Cameroon lamented. To win the battle
against these foes and the so-called emotional sects—especially Pente-
costals and Seventh-Day Adventists—mainline educators would need a
new arsenal of weapons, a second Presbyterian warned.[47]

The first and most critical step was obtaining state assistance to their
schools. By 1951, for example, Presbyterians would take in over $100,000
each year in grants-in-aid from French authorities in the Cameroon.
The church also received funds from governments in Thailand and
Japan, as well as from the newly independent regimes in India and Pak-
istan, which continued the school aid policies of their British ex-rulers.
Three years after winning their freedom, the two countries awarded
grants to thirty-eight different Presbyterian educational institutions.
The same trend appeared across the new nations of Africa, which were
especially dependent on mission schools, and on expatriate teachers.
Five years after independence, for example, the Cameroon awarded
grants-in-aid to sixteen of its sixty Baptist missionaries from the United
States. As in the pre–World War II period, to be sure, some missionaries criticized state aid for violating "the historic American tradition of
separation of Church and State." But such voices were faint amid the
chorus of hosannas, as a Cameroon Presbyterian observed. "The majority feels that in a primitive country of this kind, where [the] Government simply has not the facilities available but does have the money to
help, we should be *stupid not to carry on until the government is ready to do
so*," he emphasized.[48]

As colonial and independent governments opened their own schools,
meanwhile, missionaries availed themselves of yet another new opportunity: teaching religion in state classrooms. Most African governments
allowed students to choose Protestant, Catholic, or "neutral" moral instruction; a few countries provided public subsidies to teachers of religion, in any faith that students selected; and at least one nation, Liberia,
required Bible reading in all of its schools. Even as Americans purged
religious instruction from government classrooms back home, one
Presbyterian in the Cameroon urged them to seize on the prospect that
new African public schools afforded. By 1957, Presbyterians taught
Bible to over 1,000 Cameroonian public school children each week.
Other mainline denominations taught these classes, too, as did Catholic
churches and the newest challengers: faith missions. In neighboring

Nigeria, a single teacher from the fundamentalist Sudan Interior Mission taught forty-two classes per week in Religious Knowledge, a mandatory course in the national curriculum. "Scripture classes in government schools have now become a major tactic of mission strategy," one SIM spokesman wrote. Like education in general, the Bible classes would also become a major venue for mission competition—between mainline and independent churches.[49]

Faith Missions Enter the Fray

Before World War II, nobody could have predicted the sudden entrance of faith missions into educational work. Indeed, faith missions frequently defined themselves by their *refusal* to build or operate schools: such enterprises would require missions to save money as a hedge against future needs, whereas the Bible enjoined them to trust in God for all things. As fundamentalists peeled off from mainline missions, they often cited "institutionalism" as a central cause for the schism. Announcing the formation of their "Independent Board" in 1935, for example, Presbyterian dissidents noted that only twenty of 130 Protestant missionaries in India were engaged in full-time evangelism; most of the rest did "philanthropic work," in education or medicine. By contrast, the Independent Board noted proudly, it had not appointed a single doctor, nurse, or "professional teacher" for overseas service.[50]

Starting in the late 1940s, however, these burgeoning missions would embrace exactly the type of institution-building that they had long eschewed. By 1952, roughly one thousand independent missionaries taught in mission schools; perhaps 500 more teachers came from conservative denominational boards that had left the Division of Foreign Missions in the National Council of Churches (NCC), the union of mainline Protestantism. In 1953, just three years after withdrawing from the NCC, the Southern Baptist Convention operated 350 elementary schools and eighteen high schools around the world, serving nearly 50,000 children.[51] The trend toward formal education within evangelical churches was especially stark in Africa, where the continent's largest faith mission declared a new faith in formal schooling. Since its founding at the turn of the twentieth century, the African Inland Mission (AIM) had largely eschewed education.[52] But the new zeal for schooling among Africans—and the renewed competition from other churches—caused the AIM to shift course. Some mainline schools allowed teachers to introduce the theory of evolution, AIM critics noted; a few schools even let their students smoke. Catholics also accelerated their educational activities, a worried faith missionary wrote, substituting "charms and crosses" for traditional African "spirits" and "fetishes." Finally, new secular government schools foretold the worst of both worlds. They not only taught evolution and other "modern" doctrines, but they also preserved "heathen" folk beliefs.[53]

Like its mainline competitors, then, the AIM plunged into educational work. In Tanganyika alone, the number of AIM primary schools skyrocketed from three to forty-nine between 1950 and 1955. For the most part, African teachers staffed these so-called bush schools; the AIM reserved its own personnel for its four middle schools, which employed nine full- or part-time missionaries. The most frenzied growth occurred in the Congo, where a renewed Catholic effort to establish schools—and to recruit students—sparked similar campaigns by the AIM. As one alarmed AIM spokesperson noted in 1950, a recently opened Catholic school had already lured 600 young acolytes. To keep pace with this competition, he continued, the AIM would need several dozen new schools, and at least twenty-five new missionaries.[54]

A Faith Mission and State Aid

Most of all, it would need government grants. Like other faith missionaries, AIM members had previously raised only enough money to sustain their personal evangelistic activities. Yet the construction and operation of schools required a much more consistent source of income than the old faith system could possibly generate. Starting in the early 1940s, then, AIM missions in Kenya and Tanganyika began an active effort to win government grants-in-aid from British colonial officials; Congo missions had to wait until 1945, when Belgian authorities finally cleared the way for Protestants to obtain state funds. In all three colonies, mission schools also received student fees. But even when the fees were collected in full, they only covered a small fraction of a school's expenses. "We must cooperate with the Government if we are going to keep our schools," wrote one AIM official in 1953, "in spite of the risk we have to take."[55]

The risk was obvious. Government money meant government oversight, which threatened to erode the religious mission of a mission
school. From the start, then, the solicitation of state funds caused
considerable debate inside the AIM. One Tanganyika missionary worried that, as in India, any government assistance would require schools
to accept the British colonial authority's Conscience Clause, that is, a
pledge to exempt any student from religious instruction on the request
of a parent. Others feared that state monies would bring new state regulation of facilities, which would in turn require more funds. Most of
all, critics claimed that any such grant would violate a bedrock principle of their entire enterprise: the separation of religion from government. "As a Faith Mission we do not believe in an alliance of Church
and State," one AIM dissenter flatly declared, capitalizing both phrases
for good measure.[56]

In response, grant advocates instinctively cited the Catholic threat:
as a practical matter, the AIM could never keep up with its "Romish" rivals in Africa unless it received public funds. Philosophically, meanwhile, its rationale for state aid almost exactly echoed the rhetoric of
Catholics in the United States. "We are heartily in favor of accepting
Government grants for our Mission's schools because this money is
paid in by our own people through their taxes," one Kenya AIM member argued. True, missionaries allowed, there was a "discrepancy" between their rejection of grants-in-aid at home and their support for
such grants in Africa. But Africans' distinct spiritual traditions justified
the double standard. "The British concept of the relatedness of religion
to all of life . . . may be more closely related to the African concept of
the wholeness and interrelatedness of life than is the American concept
of separation of church and state," one missionary declared. While in-
tegral to U.S. principles, church–state separation was irrelevant—and
unnecessary—in Africa.[57]

The first few years of government assistance to AIM schools seemed
to confirm this sunny assessment. "This grant aided system was entered
into with fear and trembling and even opposition," recalled Tanganyika
AIM education director Allan G. Marsh in 1958, reviewing a decade of
activity. "None of these fears have materialized." Government grants
covered the salaries of all 122 African teachers at the AIM's seventy
primary schools; grants also subsidized three missionaries who served
as middle school instructors. When one of these teachers went on

furlough the following year, however, Marsh could not locate a replacement for her. As a condition for supplying state aid, Tanganyika required teachers to possess a minimal amount of experience and training; indeed, colonial authorities had rejected the most recent AIM recruit for lack of qualifications. Unless the mission found certified instructors, then, it risked losing its grants—and, eventually, its schools—in Tanganyika. "We face a very acute need in our entire Education program," Marsh warned in 1959, pleading with AIM officials at home to scour teacher training institutions for candidates.[58]

Likewise, in the Congo, an initial burst of enthusiasm for AIM schools gave way to a sober reconsideration. In 1948, the Congo mission voted to accept grants-in-aid from the Belgian government. To qualify for these funds, however, mission teachers had to spend a full year in Brussels, possibly Europe's most expensive capital, receiving instruction in French, methods of pedagogy, and "General Colonial" affairs. Remarkably, three AIM teachers were able to finance their Brussels trip and to earn Congolese certification. But they were the exceptions. Like mission schools themselves, Belgian training required much more money than individual missionaries normally possessed. Many AIM members were reluctant to solicit large-scale donations for the training, which, like state aid, seemed to contradict the "faith" premises of their mission. As early as 1950, then, AIM leaders in the Congo complained that their schools lacked sufficient personnel to receive state grants. A decade later, many of them regretted soliciting the grants in the first place. "What was looked upon as a blessing—the windfall of government subsidies—became in many respects a burden," one observer wrote in 1964.[59]

Two years later, even Allan Marsh would come to agree with this assessment. Formerly Africa's most zealous advocate of government grants, Marsh reported that state-aided AIM schools in the newly independent Tanzania were losing their Christian character. At the high school where he and his wife taught, state regulations required the school to accept students of every faith—and barred it from requiring religious instruction. "We base our educational philosophy on the Gospel," Allan and Elizabeth Marsh wrote in 1966. "There are others, however, who, while coveting the quality of education which is given, want it on their own terms." Unless the school reclaimed its religious mission, the Marshes warned, they would refuse to teach there. But the school beat them to the punch. In 1969, citing the need to comply with new government rules, a new African principal fired the couple. Founded by the Marshes with state aid, their school had sacrificed its original purpose upon the altar of state control.[60]

⁊ In 1958, Tanganyika AIM missionary Edward Arnesen bemoaned the steady secularization of public education in the United States. In its 1948 decision, *McCollum v. Board of Education*, the Supreme Court had removed church-sponsored instruction from school premises. Now even "nondenominational" prayer and Bible reading were under fire, foreshadowing the final ejection of God from the nation's classrooms. The United States should borrow a page from Tanganyika, Arnesen urged, where "Christian teachers" provided "systematic Bible teaching" alongside their other lessons. "In America there is not freedom enough to read God's Word and pray within the confines of the little red schoolhouse," Arnesen wrote. "While Africa's keynote had been suppression and slavery, the school systems are now wide open to the propagation of religious knowledge." On the question of religion in schools, at least, America was falling behind the global curve.[61]

The gap would grow still greater in 1962, when, as missionaries had long feared, the Supreme Court struck down school prayer back home. Condemning the Court's decision, evangelical missionary Carol Carlson boasted that she taught a "Bible elective" to forty-five students in a Kenyan government high school. As in other school subjects in the British colonies, students took a "Cambridge Certificate" examination in Bible upon finishing her course. "Since the exams are very thorough," Carlson wrote, "they give the teacher opportunities to present the full plan of salvation." Best of all, missionaries noted, teachers retained "complete freedom" to interpret Scripture in the manner they chose. "No Supreme Court 'Ruling' in Kenya," blared a headline atop Carlson's remarks in a missionary magazine.[62]

Together, these comments reflected conservatives' newly cosmopolitan attack on American church–state doctrine in the post–World War II era. Earlier in the twentieth century, conservatives had attacked missions for deviating from basic American principles. In India, Robert Speer and his allies urged mission schools to reject government funds and preserve America's separatist tradition; in Korea, meanwhile, a burgeoning fundamentalist movement resisted mandatory shrine visits in the name of the rights and freedoms enshrined in the Declaration of Independence. As courts removed religious ritual from public schools back home, however, missionaries increasingly cited other countries' religious practices as a critique of America's "secular" ways. Indeed, conservatives claimed, international examples could help the United States reclaim its elapsed spiritual tradition. "Like the founding Pilgrim Fathers in America who wanted their children to be taught the Christian truths with the three Rs, so the Kenya government *wants* a Christian education for its young people," wrote one AIM missionary, praising Kenya's state aid to religious schools.[63]

In truth, of course, America had rarely provided direct aid to parochial schools. For more than a century, Catholics had pressed for state assistance and Protestants had balked, citing the "wall of separation" between church and state. As American public schools lost their explicitly Protestant character, however, more and more missionaries began to question their long-standing position on private school funding. "As an American . . . I admire the efforts of the Congolese government [in] allowing students and parents to choose," one missionary admitted in 1962, praising state aid to mission schools. "I have often felt that the Congo government had something to teach other nations in regard to this." Likewise, following a conference with several European missions, an AIM educator in Tanganyika praised their national traditions of school finance. In Holland, he wrote enviously, students could select from several types of state-aided schools, including "schools with the Bible."[64]

Here conservative Protestants echoed their longtime Catholic foes in America, who had often cited international precedent in their pleas for state aid to private schools.[65] Starting in the late 1950s, indeed, domestic Protestant opinion on the issue underwent a dramatic shift. As early as 1962, the National Union of Christian Schools demanded government funds for American parochial schools; by the end of the decade, the Lutheran and Christian Reformed churches would do the same. By the early 1990s, almost half of American evangelical Protestants—and a strong majority of Catholics—favored direct assistance to parochial schools.[66] As these voters realized, nearly every other democracy provided some form of public aid for religious educational institutions. Why not America? Conservatives, who were typically the most vocal advocates of American exceptionalism and superiority, looked to other countries as models for church–state relations at home.[67]

Meanwhile, Protestant liberals freely admitted that their mission policies were "inconsistent with the American pattern of church–state 'separation,' " as one spokesman wrote in 1961. But they held fast to the separationist tradition in the United States, drawing a sharp line between national and international practices. In the NCC, America's largest umbrella organization of mainline denominations, officials continued to oppose state aid to American parochial schools while accepting government grants to mission institutions. Likewise, they supported the U.S. Supreme Court ban on school prayer at home, but backed mission-sponsored prayer in public schools overseas. Even as they defended strict church–state separation in America, one NCC leader summarized, Protestants should accommodate the distinct cultures and customs that they encountered abroad. "We must not forget that there are other traditions of church-state relations than the American," he warned.[68]

By conceding the equal worth of church–state patterns in other countries, however, liberals might have ceded too much to their foes at home. Into the present, conservatives invoke international comparisons to denounce America's pattern of church–state separation, especially its historic ban on direct state aid to parochial schools.[69] Departing from this tradition, several states have recently established court-approved, European-style "voucher" programs that subsidize private school tuition with public funds.[70] Meanwhile, Christian conservatives have continued to press for state-sponsored school prayer—noting, correctly, that many other democracies permit or even encourage it.[71] Yet just as conservatives cite global examples to support these initiatives, so could liberals cite Americans' own global *experience* to rebut them. During the pre–World War II period, shrine worship and other concessions to the state made missions into accomplices of despotism; government aid after the war saddled them with expensive regulations, which eventually cost the schools their distinct spiritual purpose. While missionaries adapted to other systems of religious education, in short, their frustrations also underscored the prudence of what Africans called "The American Plan": a strict separation between church and state.[72] Whatever the fate of this tradition around the globe, we might still find some good reasons to retain it on our own shores.

ᴈ 6

Ambivalent Imperialists

AMERICAN TEACHERS AND THE
PROBLEM OF EMPIRE

$\mathcal{I}_\mathrm{N}$ 1908, the American journalist Edgar Allen Forbes published an article about American teachers around the world. In bold block letters, a lengthy headline announced his theme: "The Vast Intellectual Empire of Government Teachers and Protestant Missionaries Working Under Many Flags." To Forbes and his editors, clearly, Jesuits and other American Catholics did not form a part of this "empire." Even more, the empire was intellectual—an empire of ideas—rather than one of force. Forbes contrasted it to the British empire, which combined education *with* force. To underline the point, he quoted England's most famous imperial poet:

> They terribly carpet the earth with dead, and before
>   their cannon cool
> They walk unarmed by twos and threes to call the
>   living to school

The passage came from "Kitchener's School," where Rudyard Kipling paid tribute to the British conquest of Egypt. But as Forbes emphasized, Lord Kitchener marched past 100 American mission schools on his way to founding a single college. "When an American poet comes whose soul shall be moved by great achievements," Forbes wrote, "the American teacher as an educational empire-builder will be one of his themes." The English empire had Kipling, but America's unique pedagogical kingdom awaited its own imperial muse.[1]

Aboard the transport ship USS *Thomas*, it had already found one. In the summer of 1901, en route for the Philippines, teacher Bradford K. Daniels addressed his 500 compatriots in verse:

> First with the scourge of the sword
> We went to the dusky race
> Broke with one blow the chains
> That fettered; now in their place
> Bring we the bonds of peace
> Invisible, lighter than air
> Stronger than engines of war
> Blinding the near and the far
> Aliens of aim and of blood
> In a mighty brotherhood.[2]

Like the British masters at Kitchener's school, American teachers came to the Philippines in the wake of a brutal war against a defiant local population. Just two years earlier, indeed, Kipling had dedicated his most famous poem of all, "The White Man's Burden," to "The United States in the Philippine Islands." Kipling warned Americans to expect resistance and recrimination in their new imperial adventure:

> The blame of those ye better
> The hate of those ye guard[3]

But to Bradford Daniels and his fellow teachers, education would bind Filipinos and Americans in ways that belied the experience of England and other colonial powers.[4] Indeed, Daniels insisted, it made little sense to speak of America as "colonial" at all. Even within the newly acquired territories of the United States, America's "educational empire" promised to make actual empire melt away.

Out in the schools themselves, however, a far less harmonious story unfolded. In the Philippines and Puerto Rico, students resisted American efforts to foster English; and in other empires, where Americans promoted vernacular languages, they found that students preferred European ones. Most of all, teachers started to wonder whether host populations could change at all. In the American Empire proper, some teachers concluded that local peoples lacked the racial fortitude to become "real" Americans; others worried that tropical climates and mores were undermining whites' own eugenic strength. In European colonies, meanwhile, American missionaries defended indigenous "national" cultures against the alleged assaults of the West. But when these cultures took an expressly political form—that is, when they became *nationalist*, not simply national—American teachers often turned away. Rejecting the "disorder" that accompanied anticolonial revolutions, the Americans frequently sided with the same imperial powers that their exceptionalist rhetoric indicted.[5]

After World War II, as its formal empire faded, the United States resolved to remake the entire "free world" in its own image: a confederation of stable democracies, allied to vanquish an encroaching Communist foe.[6] But many overseas teachers dissented from this vision, condemning America for foisting a new form of "cultural imperialism" on a defenseless globe.[7] The charge brought together teachers' various anxieties about the imposition of American values—in instruction, curriculum, and so on—but added a stronger element of political critique: by discounting or diminishing local cultures, the argument went, Americans had developed a new strategy for dominating the earth. In this analysis, teachers were not merely depriving foreign peoples of "rights"; instead, the teachers were promoting a far more insidious form of American global hegemony.[8] "Am I simply offering a useful service to a truly emerging nation, or taking advantage of an induced weakness to further sap the vitality of a culture in order to impose an American import in its place?" Peace Corps teacher Alfred T. Giannini wrote in 1972, from his post in Senegal. "I can still remember when the good guys wore white hats."[9]

But as Giannini acknowledged, several weeks later, the attack on cultural imperialism could contain its own imperialist assumptions. "Resolved political difficulties—The ultimate choice rests with the Africans," he wrote in his diary. "To 'protect' them from western influence is both paternalistic & unrealistic. I'm still Catholic enough—both kinds—to let each man make his own choice."[10] Here was an "educational empire-builder" that Edgar Allen Forbes could not have pictured a half-century before: Catholic rather than Protestant, deeply wary of American power, but dedicated to the ideal, however quixotic, of

individual freedom. Writing in an earlier era, men like Edgar Allen
Forbes and Bradford Daniels never asked whether America *should*
spread "civilization" around the globe; the only issue was whether it
could do so, and how. Post–World War II teachers inverted this formula, questioning the entire moral status of America in the world. Sent
abroad as tribunes of American benevolence, teachers would launch
their own critique of American influence, and of their own role in perpetuating it.

"Civilizing" New Americans

In 1905, Frederick Behner collected a set of papers for a speech contest
at his school in the Philippines. One student chose to write about
"Laffayatte" (sic), the French general who defended the "rights and liberties" of the American colonies in their war against England; in a similar fashion, the student expounded, American soldiers helped secure
Philippine freedom from Spain. But unlike the United States, another
student added, the Philippines were not yet ready to go out on their
own. "Many people of the Philippine Islands desire to get Independence," he wrote, "but . . . we should wait until we have reached a more
general civilization." Specifically, a third student added, schools must
teach Filipinos a common language—that is, English—and a shared set
of skills for self-government: industry, thrift, and honesty. Without
such education, he warned, "we would remain disorderly, and there
would be no civil right (sic) at all." Filipinos would stay gripped in a
state of "uncivilization," a fourth student worried, and "uncivilization is
the worst thing that a person could be."[11]

Together, these essays captured the central themes in the American
gospel of civilization in the new American colonies.[12] From the Philippines and Hawaii to Puerto Rico and the Virgin Islands, teachers proclaimed the republican virtues of the United States via textbooks, stories,
verse, and song. During her first week in the Philippines, Philinda Rand
taught her students the melody, "I Love the Name of Washington"; to
drill them in English, meanwhile, she used patriotic poems. "I lub the
pfleg, the dear old pfleg," Rand recalled her students chanting, "Wit its
rrred and whi te and bloo." Detailed to a school after 12 months of
army duty, another instructor taught his pupils "Marching Through
Georgia"; two weeks later, children in a distant barrio were singing it.

Other teachers led their students in "rollicking college songs" and "bright catchy tunes" like "A Hot Time in the Old Town Tonight," which one instructor jokingly described as the Philippine "National Air." Fittingly, though, the real national anthem was written by an American school teacher. Calling it "Philippines, My Philippines," he adapted the anthem from "Maryland, My Maryland"—his own state song.[13]

Even more, the anthem was in English. Given the diversity of dialects in the archipelago, the argument went, Filipinos needed a single tongue to bind them together; and to imitate the American political tradition, they had to learn the language that gave birth to it. Upon her arrival at her post, Alice M. Kelly resolved to speak English to everyone she encountered. Grabbing an old man by the shoulders, she repeated "Good morning, Mrs. Kelly" until he did the same. By the next week, townspeople were greeting all the Americans they encountered—judges, soldiers, and other teachers—with the same salutation: "Good Morning, Mrs. Kelly." Teachers had somewhat more success in schools, where they could draw upon traditional methods of coercion and punishment. Conducting all of their classes in English, many Americans also forbade students from speaking other languages anywhere on school property. Some violators received fines, suspensions, and lowered grades; others were forced to kneel on sand or on piles of small beans.[14]

Similarly, in Puerto Rico, teachers claimed that English would unite the territory and teach principles of republican government. "You ought to see me stand up in front of 60 little grinning white black and brown children and teach them American patriotic songs!" Leonard Ayres told his brother. "They can now sing 'America' in a way to curdle your blood." Unlike the multilingual Filipinos, Puerto Ricans already possessed a single, shared tongue: Spanish. But they spoke a "patois" rather than "pure Spanish," as an American school superintendent argued, so teachers could easily replace it with English. "There does not seem to be among the masses the same devotion to their native tongue," the superintendent declared. "It possesses no literature and little value as an intellectual medium." Lacking enough Anglophone teachers to make English the sole medium of instruction, American school officials later allowed the primary grades to study in Spanish. Yet they evinced little doubt that English would—and should—come to dominate the island. As one official noted, in both Pennsylvania and New Mexico, "it required generations to put English, and English only, into the schools." Just as those states eventually converted their German- and Spanish-speaking populations to the American national idiom, so would Puerto Rico.[15]

Most of all, as Frederick Behner's students wrote in their speeches, schools would teach "civilization" to the new American territories. Like any classroom exercise, these speeches tell us more about what the teacher wanted—that is, the "right" or expected answer—than about what the pupils actually believed. Whether or not the students shared the American gospel of "civilization," it is clear that teachers like Behner worked hard to spread it. Americans subsumed an enormous variety of virtues under this term, ranging from cleanliness and punctuality to hard work and fair play.[16] But they agreed that these qualities should be *taught*, and, most of all, that schools were the place to teach them. "Civilization can not be decreed," a Hawaii teacher wrote in the first page of her 1903 diary. "It must be acquired by the slow process of development." At the helm of this project sat American teachers, a Philippines observer added, "evangels of a better civilization" who would prepare others to govern themselves.[17]

Comparing Empires

But was the civilization uniquely *American?* As concepts of eugenic hierarchy spread across the United States and Europe, some teachers described their mission in racial terms rather than national ones. One Hawaii educator urged teachers to transmit "Anglo-Saxon knowledge and manners and customs," which would slowly—but surely—bring "inferior races" up to speed. "The Oriental student is rarely lacking in ambition and willingness to learn," he noted, "but he has hundreds—yea thousands—of years of traditions and tendencies to undo." In a similar vein, a teacher in the Philippines contrasted her students' "Malay cunning"—that is, their endemic dissembling and dishonesty—with "Anglo-Saxon" integrity. Other teachers connected their civilizing efforts to England, the lodestar of Anglo-Saxonism and America's own colonial ex-ruler. "British people claim that Americans have an exaggerated idea of the value of universal compulsory education," wrote mission educator Edward Capen, surveying American overseas instruction. "It is probably true, but we are the true children of the mother country and all English-speaking people tend to do this."[18]

Like Capen's British informants, however, most American teachers believed that their commitment to universal schooling *differentiated* them from the English empire—indeed, from all empires. "Never in the history of colonization has such an effort been made," Philippines teacher George M. Briggs flatly declared. Indeed, the American faith in schools was itself the most distinctive lesson that the United States could teach the world. "Education is the real religion of America," another Philippines school official intoned. "We believe . . . in its efficiency to solve all the problems of society and we assert its necessity as a basis of political stability." Other colonial powers educated only a small fraction of their conquered populations, fearing challenges to imperial rule. But to Americans, free and universal schools held the key to *maintaining* imperial rule—and "political stability"—around the globe. "Effective colonization must come through the schools, even at great pecuniary cost," wrote an observer in Puerto Rico. "It is far cheaper than by means of military force."[19]

The United States *did* use military force, of course, especially in the Philippines. Roughly 250,000 Filipinos died during the war of 1899–1902, while countless others were injured or tortured. Reports of atrocities made headlines across the United States, sowing the first seeds of domestic anti-imperialism. Within the Philippines themselves, meanwhile, teachers often condemned army abuses. "It is a matter of common knowledge that the military do not like the teachers," wrote Harry Cole, "because they are too much like *Americans* and they are liable to write the truth." Cole sent a letter of protest to military authorities after witnessing the notorious "water-cure," whereby soldiers poured water down a prisoner's throat and then made him throw up. "I had heard of the terrible water-cure, but had supposed it mostly soldiers' fabrications," Cole wrote his family at home. "At your end you may believe you are reading about the Spanish Inquisition. I can assure you however it is of more recent date, and—can it be possible?—under American rule!" To Cole and his wife Mary, a fellow teacher who also protested the water-cure, military torture vitiated American exceptionalism in imperial affairs. The United States was no better than any other colonial power; in some ways, it was worse.[20]

At the same time, however, Cole's query about American torture—*can it be possible?*—reinforced the exceptionalist narrative. The United States *should* behave better than other imperial nations, the story went, because it possessed a unique and providential destiny. Even if Americans had renounced this mission in their conduct of the war, schools would help them rediscover it. "The schoolma'am and the schoolmaster have captured the Philippines," wrote one hopeful American official in 1904, "and the scratch of the slate-pencil has become mightier than the slash of the sword."[21] Out in the schools themselves, though, more and more teachers started to dissent from the imperialist vision. Joining hands with local protesters, a small handful condemned the United States for imposing its educational system, and, especially, its language, on conquered populations. More often, though, they rejected empire for racial reasons. Elevating inferior peoples beyond their proper station, the imperial project threatened to submerge white Americans below their own.

Teachers and Anti-Imperialism I: The Argument for Reform

From the very inception of the American empire, its education system drew fire from its new colonial wards. Filipinos took aim at imported history textbooks, especially one that described an independent Philippines as "impossible." Others condemned America's English-only policy, deeming it a "menace to the Filipino soul." The battle over language proved especially sharp in Puerto Rico, where a 1903 newspaper blasted English instruction as a "yoke" upon the island. "The despotism weighing over Puerto Rico manifests itself in different ways," the paper blared, "but in none more horrible than the inconsiderate forcing upon us of the English language." In 1915, authorities would expel a student for collecting signatures in support of a bill to require Spanish instruction in all schools. The year after that, a spokesperson urged other youth to enter the struggle. "To all young Puerto Rican students who keep within your hearts the rebelliousness against the illegitimate owner of our patriotic soil," he began. "To you, who through imposition receive instruction in a foreign language and who by your own will preserve your native tongue." Between 1911 and 1949, native Puerto Rican teachers passed an annual resolution demanding the elimination of English as a medium of instruction. But the territory clung to a dual-language system, teaching elementary grades in Spanish and secondary students in English.[22]

Despite their status as English instructors, many American teachers sympathized with the attacks on school language policies. Here they echoed critics back home, where English instruction had already become a lightning rod for anti-imperial protest. "We will erect schoolhouses," quipped Mr. Dooley, the ubiquitous voice of satirist Finley Peter Dunne, "an' we'll larn ye our language, because 'tis easier to larn ye our thin to larn oursilves ye'ers." But teachers' skepticism also reflected their own experience with English-only instruction. "The child gets a few sounds and definitions in his head during the years he is *neglecting his own language*," emphasized one teacher in the Philippines, "and grows up to know nothing at all, not being able to write a sentence correctly in any language." The teacher sent the letter to Martin G. Brumbaugh, a former education commissioner in Puerto Rico, who in turn forwarded it to Philippines ex-governor William Howard Taft. "The faithful teachers who are actually face to face with the problem find it necessary to dissent from the work," Brumbaugh told Taft, in an accompanying note. Indeed, Brumbaugh added, the teacher's letter reflected the "wide-spread judgment" of instructors across "the Islands"— that is, throughout America's new overseas possessions.[23]

Like Brumbaugh's correspondent, some teachers worried about stunting students' development in their native tongues. Others underscored pupils' distaste for English, which virtually guaranteed its failure. "We cannot educate a people against their will, nay, without their earnest and whole-hearted cooperation," wrote Philippines teacher Theodore Laguna, who would rise to prominence as a philosophy professor on his return. "You cannot make people the present of a new language." Laguna urged Americans to mimic colonial India, where British rulers had abandoned a futile English-only policy in favor of a much more popular dual-language system. Indeed, an American school superintendent argued, all colonial educators had the greatest success when they spoke in the local idiom—not in an "alien" one. "If the American teacher in the Philippines is to have in the least the attributes of the missionary and exercise a general uplifting influence upon the Filipinos, he must certainly gain a working knowledge of the native speech," the superintendent wrote, "and no possible harm could come from the use of the native languages . . . as one of the mediums of school instruction." To reform the natives, in short, Americans would need to reform themselves.[24]

Teachers and Anti-Imperialism II:
The Argument from Race

Out in the field, however, more and more teachers began to question the very possibility of "uplift"—or of reform—outside of the United States. The problem lay in the racial inferiority of its new imperial population, which would upset even the best-laid plans of the right-minded American. At home and abroad, teachers complained, reformers pretended that nonwhites could benefit and improve under watchful "Anglo-Saxon" tutelage. But that was a myth, borne of ignorance as much as wishful thinking. "It is difficult for people in the states to get a just idea of these people," wrote one teacher from the Philippines, in a typical jeremiad. "They are masters of deceit and are the most consummate liars that the Orient produces." Hawaiians, teachers said, were indolent and dirty; Puerto Ricans, impulsive and hypersensitive; Samoans, sly and dishonest, and Virgin Islanders, lazy and irresponsible. "Whether from habit or congenital shiftlessness, the average Virgin Islander finds it extremely difficult to work steadily at a regular job," one American complained. "It is impossible to build up a self-disciplined people from children whose homes are of the character prevailing in the Virgin Islands." Even if these poor qualities stemmed from environment rather than from "race," they were so indelibly stamped upon nonwhite peoples that teachers could never overcome them.[25]

Instead, the poor qualities threatened to overwhelm the teachers. Across the American empire, teachers worried that the less savory aspects of "tropical" life would erode their own moral—or, even, racial—constitutions. "The natives will never assimilate anything American," Philippines teacher Herbert Priestley told his mother. "The inevitable result must be a *lowering* of the American ideals, more than the *raising* of the native tone." Without the social constraints of home, teachers said, too many Americans fell victim to gambling, drink, and especially sex. Some teachers made light of these temptations, as in this poetic tribute to "El Mujer":

> Who, on Manila's narrow streets
> Our weary vision often greets
> And makes us practice base deceits?
> El Mujer

> When driven by a fluffy dress
> From off the paths of righteousness
> Who makes us pay for all the mess?
> El Mujer

But to most Americans, such debauchery was no laughing matter. Outraged teachers complained about colleagues who took mistresses, gambled away their salaries, or drank wine with their nonwhite hosts. "It is much easier to get down to their level," one teacher warned, "than to bring them up to ours." In Hawaii, even female instructors were seen drinking and consorting with local men. The worst offenders lived in the beachfront village of Waikiki, where a dense community of single—and morally suspect—young teachers in the 1920s earned the nickname of "Flappers' Acre." If Americans let down their guard, critics said, there was no telling how far they could fall.[26]

Finally, in isolated cases, teachers faced a much more immediate and tangible danger: armed insurgency. Roughly a dozen American teachers were killed in the Philippines by so-called *ladrones* or bandits, some of whom had links to the Philippine resistance. Dubbed the "Fighting Maestro," one teacher actually took up arms against the *ladrones;* another instructor slept with a revolver under his pillow. A third teacher was so certain of an attack that he nailed shut his doors and windows, then sat in a dark corner with a sword, pistol, and 30 rounds of ammunition. Hearing men in an adjacent room, he jumped to his feet and fired several rounds in their direction. A subsequent police investigation turned up nothing, leading one authority to conclude that the teacher had imagined the entire episode. But in Samar, site of some of the most vicious military action, teachers remained in enough danger that the government removed them from "unprotected"—that is, ungarrisoned—towns after the war ended. "The patient had become so violent that it was impossible to apply the remedy," explained a school official. "Nothing but the straight-jacket remained."[27]

To many teachers, *ladrone* attacks proved that the entire Philippines *needed* a "straight-jacket"—and that the educational remedy was futile. "The only way to accomplish anything with these people is through *force*," wrote Harry Cole, adding emphasis, in an angry 1902 letter home. Several months earlier, Cole had complained about soldiers' use of the "water-cure." But now he understood the need for it, in limited doses. "I guess it is a good thing I am not a soldier, for I am afraid I should shoot every 'dirty nigger' I should come across," Cole blared. "Too many American lives have already been sacrificed to the treachery of these people." Three years later, another teacher mocked Taft and other civilian officials for their faith in educational solutions. "I wish such people had to live among [Filipinos] the way we teachers are forced to do," he wrote. "The anti-imperialists are right when they maintain that it was foolish policy for our country to take the islands. But they err greatly when they claim the Filipino is capable of self-government."[28]

Here, then, was anti-imperial racism with a vengeance. The American imperial project placed an enormous burden on education, which would simultaneously "civilize" colonial wards, prepare them for self-government, and distinguish America's own empire from less benevolent ones. But if these new peoples lacked the capacity to change their minds—if they were not *educable*, as Americans saw it—there was nothing left to do but coerce their bodies. "I only wish we were under military employ," Harry Cole wrote his family in 1902. "The present mixture is what a druggist calls incompatible."[29] Meanwhile, outside the American empire, teachers would indict other imperial powers for imposing their cultures upon unwilling peoples. Even as Americans tried to assimilate newly conquered peoples—or abandoned the effort, deeming these peoples unassimilable—they condemned the rest of the world for attempting much the same.

Missionaries and Empire: The "Cultural" Critique

In 1930, African-American missionary Bessie McDowell came home on furlough from Angola to obtain a Master's degree in religious education. In her thesis, McDowell drew a sharp distinction between American and colonial educational initiatives in Africa. Across the continent, McDowell wrote, American missionaries tried to educate as many Africans as possible; by contrast, European colonial officials restricted schooling to the chosen few. More than that, though, Americans emphasized the "conservation of native culture." Especially in French and Portuguese territories, McDowell wrote, colonial officials were "ruthlessly denouncing native customs and systems"—including art, games, and languages. At the same time, they allowed commercial enterprises to insert the most sinful aspects of Western culture—greed, alcohol, and pornography—in place of wholesome African traditions. American missionary schooling, on the other hand, rested firmly upon indigenous heritage. Celebrating what was best about local cultures, Americans would block the worst features of the West.[30]

Across the world—and across the first half of the twentieth century—American missionaries put forth a similar critique of European colonial education. In some respects, the critique echoed American teachers in the American empire: whereas other powers educated only a small handful of people, the United States tried to educate everybody.[31] Like teachers in the Philippines and Puerto Rico, moreover, missionaries occasionally identified their "Anglo-Saxon" project with the British Empire.[32] For the most part, however, American missionaries condemned England, like other imperial powers, for denigrating native cultures. To highlight the point, Catholic mission leader John Considine quoted Lord Macaulay's infamous Minute of 1835: " 'A single shelf of a good European library is worth the whole native literature of India and Arabia.' " Since then, Considine allowed, British colonists had "modified" Macaulay's "extreme position." Nevertheless, he concluded, "education in India today has a strong European bias and relatively little of the rich Indian background."[33]

By contrast, American missionaries said, their own educational efforts paid close attention to local culture. As early as 1916, missions professor T. H. P. Sailer urged all overseas teachers to study the history of schooling around the world—and to acknowledge that "our ways of educating the young are not the only effective ways." By 1935, another American would condemn the "unfortunate *missionary complex*" of "thinking that our culture, customs, arts and crafts are superior and the natives' inferior." The essay earned him an offer to direct the Booker Washington Institute, the so-called "Tuskegee of Liberia," where he vowed to "train the native African to express himself in his own hand crafts." The institute was the brainchild of the Phelps-Stokes Fund and the Methodist Episcopal Church, whose own standard missionary application bore tribute to the new solicitude for indigenous traditions. "What are some of the cultural values in the country of your preference which you think the missionary should help to conserve?" the application asked. Significantly, it did not inquire *whether* the applicant should protect these values; it only asked *which* values were most worthy of protection.[34]

To teachers in the field, the answer often lay in the realm of visual culture: clothing, art, and interior design. Missionaries in Iran decorated their new school addition with locally made furniture and carpets, resolving to "make everything as Persian as possible"; in Syria, they built girls' hostels "according to the prevailing type of . . . home architecture," with a kitchen opening onto a central court; in India, they required students to cover their heads and remove their shoes during prayer, echoing Hindu and Muslim norms; and in Burma, they despaired that girl students were jettisoning traditional garb in favor of "English dress." Teachers reserved special distaste for imported fashion catalogues, which decreased the demand for the "native" shoes and garments that mission industrial schools produced. Worst of all, they said, Western magazines and books threatened to corrupt students' ethics along with their aesthetics. In Natal, for example, African-American missionary Fred Bunker worried that "lewd pictures of white women"— as well as "new forms of brewing drink"—were leading Africans astray. "The old heathen darkness has come to assume a character of respectability in comparison with the Egyptian darkness of the civilized heathenism which is sweeping over the land," wrote Bunker, blasting pornography and strong drink. "All these and other forms of 'education' of like nature are creating a 'Black Peril.' "[35]

The Problem of Language

Fittingly, missionaries said, most of these degenerate publications appeared in European languages rather than in local ones. No aspect of colonial education drew more hostility from Americans than did language policies, which banned or severely restricted vernacular instruction. Most British colonies allowed local tongues in lower grades, but limited secondary grades to English. In Angola, by contrast, Portuguese authorities barred all schools from teaching in any non-Portuguese language; after France acquired the Cameroon from Germany, it instituted a similar rule. "We cannot tolerate the teaching of foreign idioms, European or others, giving to the native manner of thinking a form different from France," explained Cameroon's French governor. "Between the natives and ourselves no solid tie can exist except by the initiation of natives into our tongue." The territory even required foreign teachers to obtain a colonial teaching certificate, which typically required six months of study in France.[36]

In part, American opposition to such policies stemmed from the enormous fiscal burden they entailed. But missionaries also objected in the idiom of pluralism, invoking the new rhetorical authority of anthropology. "The whole tendency in our modern days is for the stronger nations, such as Britain, France, and the United States, to overwhelm the weaker—to annihilate their culture, to swamp their language," wrote Albert D. Helser, a Nigeria missionary who studied with Franz Boas, the father of American cultural anthropology. "This makes not for the enrichment but for the impoverishment of humanity."[37] Presciently, Helser linked European language restrictions to the United States' English-only mandates in the Philippines and elsewhere.[38] But most Americans failed to see the connection, indicting European powers for precisely the same policies that America pursued. "All peoples have an inherent right to their own languages," declared Thomas Jesse Jones, in a 1925 survey of colonial African education. "It is a means of giving expression to their own personality." Across European empires, Jones observed, independence movements sought to reinscribe vernacular study in the schools. The same went for anti-imperialists in Puerto Rico and other American colonies, of course, although Jones did not acknowledge it. Instead, he praised native language campaigns in French and Portuguese territories. "The longing for their own language is natural and justifiable," Jones wrote.[39]

To Americans' chagrin, however, students seemed more interested in learning imported tongues than indigenous ones. After all, they already "knew" their home language; European idioms would provide a portal to prosperity, while studying the vernacular would simply keep them in their place. "How is it that you denounce our religion, our drums and dances, our whole system of life and then become so concerned about our language?" an Angolan teacher asked American missionaries. "Our language was once as vile as anything else in our system but you chose to use it." European authorities quickly pounced on this argument, indicting Americans for inhibiting students' progress. In Natal, for example, an appalled British inspector discovered one American school where just three of 104 pupils were studying English. "This appears to me to be regrettable," he wrote in his 1909 report. "The native as a rule is eager to learn English, and its value, even in light of a purely commercial asset to him, is great." By comparison, critics said, vernacular training provided almost no practical benefit. Business and professional life rarely required written facility in the local language; moreover,

Americans sometimes taught vernaculars that their students did not even *speak*. Missionaries in the Ngoumba region of the Cameroon required their students to learn Bulu, one African complained, a language that was just as "foreign" as French or English.[40]

Faced with these objections, and with competition from other schools, some Americans capitulated. In Burma, reluctant Protestants taught English to all grades lest they lose students to a nearby Catholic mission; and in China, they reinstated the language after wealthier pupils threatened to take their tuition money elsewhere. But other Americans held their ground, teaching in the vernacular even where colonial law barred it. After Portuguese officials prohibited Angola missions from teaching any subject—including religion—in the local Umbundu dialect, for example, Henry C. McDowell told his mission board that he would ignore the order. "If they close the school down, I shall not reopen it," McDowell wrote. "If our schools are to be mere language schools to teach Portuguese with no evangelistic bend (sic) or Biblical instruction in the language the people understand, I am in favor of closing them all." In Syria, meanwhile, American mission schools hired French teachers to meet demands for the new "language of commerce." But the schools also required Arabic, which provided a further lure to students who opposed French rule. "The fact that we encourage the study of the Arabic language has drawn toward us the nationalistic party," wrote one missionary, "even though of course we take no direct part in politics." Around the world, however, missionaries would themselves be drawn into colonial politics—whether they liked it or not.[41]

Missionaries, Decolonization, and "Disorder"

The flames and fallout of World War I placed missionaries in an "embarrassing position," as Korea missionary James E. Fisher explained in his 1928 doctoral dissertation. Dedicated to William Kilpatrick, Fisher's mentor at Teachers College, the dissertation echoed Kilpatrick's emphasis on "education for community." It also paid tribute to Woodrow Wilson's credo of "self-determination," as articulated in his postwar Fourteen Points. But in Korea, a Japanese colony, the two principles clashed. Japanese authorities had instituted many features of Kilpatrick's communal vision, meeting "real life needs" via industrial training and Korean language instruction. Nevertheless, large parts of the Korean community obviously objected to Japanese rule. What, then, were American missionaries to do? Fisher's answer quoted Scripture: render unto Caesar what was Caesar's. Americans were guests of the Japanese government, which, like the Americans themselves, claimed to work for the common good; moreover, Korean rebels used tactics that missionaries could not endorse. "The principles of both Christianity and democracy forbid the use of violence or coercion in bringing about social and political changes," Fisher wrote. Even as missions embraced an education for community in Korea, they could not support the communal movement for independence from Japan.[42]

Fisher's comments highlighted the major dilemmas and contradictions of American missionaries during the anti-imperial struggles that swept the interwar globe. Wherever they went, Americans claimed to protect indigenous peoples from cultural subjection; yet when these same peoples sought freedom from *political* subjection, Americans proclaimed their neutrality. Fear of revolutionary violence caused some missionaries to find new virtues in the colonial education schemes they had formerly detested. Others invoked Christian pacifism to reject violent means of every sort, no matter what the ends. Missionaries in Iran sponsored the "world hero" contest of the New York-based National Council for the Prevention of War, which taught students to value philanthropists over militarists; in India, they celebrated when a class of seventh graders declared themselves pacifists; and in British Palestine, they sent a cable of congratulations to Neville Chamberlain upon his 1938 treaty with Adolf Hitler. Whatever the rationale, missions made it clear that members must eschew all political conflict, local as well as international. The same Methodist application that asked which "cultural values" to conserve also asked how missionaries should address "nationalistic aspirations." Leaving the first question blank, a 1936 applicant gave the expected answer to the second one: "I think the Christian missionary should be neutral along all political lines."[43]

Yet in education, especially, missionary neutrality proved elusive. To protest colonial regimes, students staged frequent school strikes, and by their very nature, strikes required teachers to take sides. Most Americans framed the strikes around "discipline" rather than politics, punishing students for transgressions against school order. After one strike in Korea, for example, the American principal suspended the entire upper school for a full year; at another school, the principal suspended forty alleged strikers and refused to readmit them until they could prove their innocence. "Strikes were instigated by various malcontents," wrote a third principal in Korea. "The strike fever is contagious in the Orient." But the fever spread to the Asian subcontinent, too, where Americans responded with a similar mix of outrage and retribution. Condemning school protests by the anti-imperial Congress Party, one India teacher argued that "the Congress people rather than the Government . . . interfered with our liberty"; in Assam, another American denounced Congress operatives for inciting student riots; and in Burma, a third missionary blamed pupil unrest upon a "small, radical, nationalistic minority that makes the majority of the noise."[44]

To be sure, some Americans expressed private support for independence movements. In India, for example, one missionary compared the Congress Party's Salt Act protests to the Boston Tea Party; another linked Mahatma Gandhi's emphasis upon village industries to her own efforts in the "project method" of education. Especially in places where mission educators received government grants-in-aid, however, they could not openly endorse anticolonial campaigns without risking the loss of these funds. In 1930, for example, British authorities threatened to cancel one mission's grant unless it disciplined Ralph Keithahn, a notable critic of colonial rule. Keithahn eventually severed his connection with the mission and moved into "a small native hut," an American newspaper reported, where he "dressed in Indian clothes, ate Indian food . . . and became associated with the student movement." In other words, Keithahn embraced nationalist politics alongside national culture. Among Americans, however, he represented the exception rather than the rule. Keithahn was expelled by the government in 1944, an action that showed the boundary of acceptable missionary dissent. Only with the end of World War II, and the dissolution of formal empires, would American teachers embrace political as well as cultural freedom for colonized peoples. After that, ironically, Americans would stand accused of colonizing their minds.[45]

Cold Warriors for the Classroom

In 1958, Elvessa Ann Stewart retired after forty-five years in the Philippines. One of five remaining American teachers in its public schools, Stewart had started as a classroom instructor in 1912. Seven years after that, she became the director of a new educational bureau that evolved into the Home Economics Division. During World War II, when the Philippines came under Japanese occupation, Stewart was imprisoned with other American teachers at Manila's notorious Santo Tomas internment camp; her weight dropped from 145 to 80 pounds, but she survived. After the war, the United States faced a new challenge—global Communism—which in turn required a new generation of teachers. "Our national capacity for winning acceptance [of] the democratic values we profess will depend largely upon the number of such Americans who are prepared to come here and serve with a dedication comparable to hers," wrote Albert Ravenholt, a Philippines correspondent and former World War II reporter, in a glowing profile of Elvessa Stewart. Back in 1912, Stewart aimed to prepare a young colony for democratic self-government. Ravenholt hoped the next wave of teachers would assist and protect an expanding roster of new nations, repelling the Red menace that imperiled them all.[46]

Here Ravenholt added his voice to a swelling Cold War chorus of Americans, all seeking a fresh contingent of teachers to defend the so-called "free world." Their dream would come true with the 1961 birth of the Peace Corps, which sent thousands of Americans, over half of them teachers, to newly independent countries around the globe. Peace Corps volunteers joined a burgeoning contingent of American missionaries, who continued to place a heavy accent upon education. This expansion was already evident in 1958 at the time Elvessa Stewart retired, when more than 29,000 North Americans served as overseas missionaries—a 50 percent increase since 1936—and at least a quarter of them taught in schools. In the Philippines, for example, the American Oblate Fathers opened their first "Notre Dame" school in 1945. Nine years later, 9,000 Filipinos attended 19 different Notre Dame institutions—all of them wearing uniforms of green and white, mirroring their namesake in the United States. Although Albert Ravenholt did not seem to notice them, Protestant and Catholic educators saw their work in much the same light as the Peace Corps. "A few of those men could do much . . . in the fight against Communism," wrote one Catholic missionary, welcoming Peace Corps teachers to the Philippines in 1961. "We would be happy to have some of them at our sides in our schools." Volunteers could teach English or science, he continued, or give "courses on Communism."[47]

To be sure, tensions sometimes wracked this diverse American coalition. In the Philippines, for example, another Catholic priest worried that Peace Corps teachers—like Elvessa Stewart and her pre–World War II generation—would press Protestantism on unwary public school students; within the Peace Corps, meanwhile, some volunteers resisted assignments at religious institutions. Protestant and Catholic missions competed with each other, of course, as did so-called "mainline" and "evangelical" schools. Nevertheless, all of these organizations aimed to spread American-style democracy, and to counter an omnipresent Communist enemy. In 1954, the National Council of Churches (NCC) devoted much of its six-week missionary training course to "Red intrigue and propaganda" around the world. "What you will be running into is a new religion, the most powerful since the advent of Christianity," one lecturer warned the 110 recruits, destined for twenty-seven "tension spots" in Asia and Africa. Similarly, Methodists gave new missionaries a special training course to prepare them for "coping with Communists." An instructor would present Soviet-style propaganda for several days at a time, until he had converted a large fraction of the group. Then he would expose his own logical errors, eliciting guffaws of embarrassment along with sighs of relief. "If you miss the last half, you're headed for Moscow," quipped one young missionary, on her way to Rhodesia.[48]

Finally, Peace Corps teachers also received extensive preparation to combat the Communist foe. Every new volunteer received a pamphlet called *What You Must Know About Communism*, while some trainings staged role-play debates between Peace Corps workers and an imaginary "Red" critic. Schools would play a critical part in this long twilight struggle, as officials consistently emphasized. "Our educational system is the touchstone of our freedom," declared Peace Corps director Sargent Shriver in 1961, upon his return from a worldwide tour to promote the new agency. "With our help, perhaps the educational systems of the lesser developed nations will be their touchstones of freedom, too." By the following year, Shriver boasted, 444 Peace Corps teachers had gone overseas, and host countries had requested 1,200 more. To Shriver deputy Harris Wofford, this effort reflected the same spirit as America's own struggle for independence. Like Thomas Jefferson, he wrote, America's overseas teachers would help "overthrow historical traditions" of tyranny, and pave a new path of liberty.[49]

In the Philippines, meanwhile, observers compared Peace Corps teachers to a more recent and local precedent: the so-called Thomasite generation of Elvessa Stewart. Newspapers greeted the Peace Corps' arrival with features about turn-of-the-century American teachers, who were inevitably labeled "America's First PCVs." Volunteers heard stories about the early teachers at their training as well as in the Philippines, where the Thomasites' ex-students included several prominent politicians. In Washington, meanwhile, seventy-eight-year-old Peace Corps staffer John Noffsinger spanned both cohorts. Hailed by Shriver as a "Peace Corps pioneer," Noffsinger had taught in the Philippines from 1909 to 1912; after World War II, he also helped found International Voluntary Services (IVS). As commentators correctly noted, the two generations shared youthful energy and a spirit of service. But the post–World War II teachers also developed a new language for discussing human difference, which in turn embodied an entirely different way of looking at the world—and, most of all, at the role of Americans within it.[50]

Indicting "the West"

Nowhere was this shift clearer than in the new meanings that teachers attached to the term "missionary." During the pre–World War II era, educators in the American colonies spoke proudly of their "missionary spirit" and earnest efforts at "uplift."[51] Yet to post–World War II teachers, often including missionaries themselves, these terms assumed an almost demonic connotation. "We've just about abolished the word 'missionary,' " declared a Presbyterian official in 1959. "We have a strong conviction that the era of the white man's burden in religious work is over." The following year, Pentecostal churches advised their members to remove the term from their passports. In 1964, a Methodist educator warned short-term missionaries—ambiguously renamed "A-3"s— against use of the word and its ideological cousins, *pagan* and *heathen.* "The very word *missionary* calls up notions of superiority," wrote a member of the Grails, explaining the Catholic group's decision to jettison the term in favor of "overseas service." For Peace Corps teachers around the world, the term also became the deepest insult that one could fling at a fellow volunteer, or at anyone else.[52]

The attack on missionaries—by the missions and by others—reflected an egregious caricature of earlier religious workers, who displayed much more concern for local culture than post–World War II critics realized.[53] But it also revealed a profound ambivalence about

Western culture, as sociologist Gerald Ditz observed in 1969. Reviewing a report on mission education by the NCC, Ditz was struck by the dour, pessimistic tone of the entire enterprise. "Your organizational doubts are less about your manifest operational effectiveness, the tangible results of your foreign missionary activities," Ditz told an NCC official. *"Rather you have doubts about your ideology, the moral validity of your activity; whether you are supporting the right causes, fighting on the right side, whether the 'right side' can win and what victory would mean."* (emphasis added). An education professor, commenting on the same document, underscored the crucial issue. "The big term in international education has for a decade been 'development,' " he began. "Yet whether this means developing others in our likeness or whether there are fundamental ethical problems in carrying Western, and Christian (in some sense) ideas into other lands remains too far frequently unexamined."[54] Amid so much doubt and confusion about their own values, missionaries were reluctant—or, sometimes, unwilling—to visit them upon anybody else.

Whereas earlier Americans had condemned fashion catalogues and other specific Western imports, post–World War II teachers of every type increasingly indicted "the West" as a whole. Teachers especially reviled the alleged avarice and materialism of the United States, which threatened to drown human spontaneity and hospitality in a sea of cheap plastic products. Indeed, one Peace Corps teacher in Liberia feared American commercial influence would erode the "generous spirit" that still prevailed in Africa. "When did you last meet a generous American?" she asked. Others worried about replacing Third World "communal" values with the "tradition of independent action" in America and Europe. " 'While you in the West have developed your fierce individualism, we in Africa have always said that, 'I am, because we are,' " wrote one American Catholic, quoting approvingly from a critic at a 1968 missions conference. Meanwhile, at the height of the Vietnam War, an IVS English teacher in Danang was apalled to discover that his textbook showed a "typical American boy" waking up to an electric alarm clock, eating toast from an electric toaster, and watching television. "The book made us Apostles of the American Dream," the IVS teacher complained. "I began to feel like a Green Beret on temporary detail for hearts and minds work." Like the war itself, he concluded, the effort to "educate" Vietnamese was really a project to impose American culture—and American power—on the rest of the world.[55]

Indeed, many teachers came to conclude, they were part of the problem and not of the solution. An earlier generation of missionary educators had condemned the cruder side of foreign influence, resolving to "conserve" indigenous culture from its ravages. Post–World War II teachers launched a more generic indictment of America and the West, so they quite naturally came to include themselves in the accusation. After planning a school program for Native Americans in Mexico, for example, two Catholic missionaries called the entire effort into doubt. "We questioned what right we have to intervene (sic) in the education of people of another culture, and what our motives are in desiring to intervine," they wrote. "Do we want to 'domesticate' the people in one way or another (make them like us, convince them to adopt our culture)?"[56] The missioners' parenthetical question contained its own answer. Across a wide range of nations, American teachers would express guilt and regret for foisting their values on others. They even adopted a new name for this ignoble effort: cultural imperialism.

A New American Empire?

By 1966, the term cultural imperialism already possessed enough currency that the Peace Corps took pains to deny it. "Cultural imperialism, the imposition of values, is as bad as the military kind," deputy director Warren Wiggins told an American college audience. Out in the field, however, volunteers were more likely to plead guilty than innocent. Teachers proved particularly vulnerable to the accusation of cultural imperialism, because their work dealt directly with the transfer—or, critics said, the intrusion—of ideas and beliefs. Engineers or foresters might plausibly claim that they provided a value-free, technical skill to nations that needed it. But education was inherently *value-laden*, so teachers could not escape questions about their own values, or about the value of sharing them. English instructors, in particular, viewed their role as "imperialistic," Peace Corps officials reported. Like their forebears in the period between the World Wars, the teachers wished to preserve the indigenous vernacular of their students. But they added a jab at the United States—and, of course, at themselves—for encouraging its own language over local ones. "We realize our jobs are meaningless," wrote three English teachers in Turkey, announcing their resignations in 1969. They resolved to work for real peace—via protests against the war in Vietnam—rather than serving as a "clean, smiling commercial of American militarism, imperialism, materialism, and racism."[57]

As the last remark indicated, the charge of cultural domination went hand in glove with a critique of U.S. armed intervention around the world: although soldiers used guns and teachers used blackboards, the argument went, their purposes were the same. This analysis inverted the claims of pre–World War II teachers in colonies like the Philippines, who often saw their own efforts as countering—or, at least, tempering—the American military. By contrast, Vietnam-era teachers connected them. "Once abroad, we discovered that we were part of the U.S. worldwide pacification program . . . to build an Empire for the U.S.," a group of returned Peace Corps members declared during a 1970 protest at agency headquarters. "As volunteers we were part of that strategy; we were the Marines in velvet gloves." One volunteer from this period captured its spirit in the title of his Peace Corps memoir: "Confessions of an Imperialist Lackey." The same terms dominated the discourse of missionary educators, especially in Latin America. Quoting a local activist, a Presbyterian report called Protestant missions "the prime vehicle of cultural imperialism" in the region; maverick priest Ivan Illich denounced the typical Catholic missionary—along with the Peace Corps and Papal Volunteers for Latin America (PAVLA)—as a "lackey chaplain" for "colonial power"; and PAVLA's own director called the organization "an act of imperialism," laden with the bigotry and "messianic rhetoric" of "19th-century missiology."[58]

Here teachers could draw on a rising tide of anti-American rhetoric around the world, which frequently tarred U.S. military and educational efforts with a single incriminating brush. Eleven different countries expelled the Peace Corps by 1971, mainly to protest the war in Vietnam; while, around the world, Peace Corps teachers stood accused of spying for the Central Intelligence Agency. (Most of the American teachers lacked "proper qualifications," one Indian critic wrote, so "it is logical to suppose that their main purpose here may be rather different.") Even if the teachers were not engaged in actual espionage, detractors said, they nevertheless served as agents of imperialism. "Dear Brothers: You know only too well the 'civilizing mission' of the former European colonisers," declared one pamphleteer, denouncing the "Pest Corps" in Africa. "See that the American neo-colonialists do not succeed in double-crossing [us] a second time!" In Ghana, president Kwame Nkrumah, who would later author a book on neocolonialism, barred Peace Corps volunteers from teaching history or English, lest they spread the "microbes" of imperial doctrine; Tunisian critics charged teachers with transmitting "pro-imperialist propaganda," to discredit Arab nationalism; and in the Philippines, students revived memories of military atrocities like the water-cure, and blasted the Peace Corps as a "neo-colonial tool of American imperialism."[59]

In rare instances, meanwhile, teachers faced threats of physical violence from anti-American activists. Charging a Peace Corps sports instructor with espionage and "imperialism," an Indonesian mob dragged him from his home to the governor's office for expulsion; shortly thereafter, the Peace Corps decided to withdraw from the country. In Ethiopia harassment from student radicals became so severe that ninety-two of 235 Peace Corps teachers decided to quit.[60] But such episodes were rare, for a number of reasons. Despite their anti-imperial rhetoric, young nations needed Americans to staff their burgeoning school systems.[61] Second, as we have seen, the Americans themselves often shared the so-called Third World critique of their own supposed imperialism. Many of the teachers strongly identified with Nkrumah and other nationalist leaders, reviling earlier generations of Americans for embracing—or, at least, for tolerating—European colonial rule. Even as they celebrated the political independence of new nations, however, teachers worried that indigenous peoples were themselves collaborating with the wiles of Western cultural imperialism. Indeed, it sometimes seemed, their hosts were more "Western" than the teachers themselves.

Imperial Anti-Imperialism, Again

For overseas teachers, like educators at home, the problem often began with new forms of popular music. As early as 1947, missionaries in Syria complained that students preferred "raucous" jazz records—with highly sexual overtones—from the West. By the early 1960s, Peace Corps volunteers in the Philippines worried about a newer American craze: rock and roll. To these teachers, the problem with the music lay not in sex per se, but in culture: like other imports, rock and roll made their students more Western than they should be. "The Filipinos want so much to be like Americans," one teacher wrote in 1962, "but they take the superficial things from our society." Along with music, teachers complained, students adopted American slang, clothing, hair style, movie idols—even America's iconic soda pop, Coca-Cola. Around the world, "Coke" became an ideological shorthand for the destructive global embrace of American popular and material culture. "We don't believe those stupid advertisements that suggest lasting good breath and bright teeth will come with one flick of the toothbrush or that deodorant is an automatic assurance of popularity but these people do," another Philippines teacher wailed. "They drink coca-cola almost as a cult ritual—every swallow makes one more American." Filipinos should be "proud to be what they are," she added, but their consumer habits suggested otherwise. Indeed, a third Philippines teacher said, their zest for American products reflected a "colonial mentality."[62]

Around the world, teachers complained, newly independent nations made a devil's bargain with imported commercial culture. The tension was especially apparent in Africa, where a new generation of leaders promised political as well as cultural freedom from the "neocolonial" West. But out in the schools, teachers found, students wanted everything that the West could sell them, especially if it came from the United States. " 'America' is a John Wayne with six-guns flaming in technicolor, an Elvis with 'geetah' twanging, a tanned Kennedy with hair blowing in the wind," wrote a Peace Corps teacher who served in Nigeria. "The Americans command powerful technicolored Pontiacs, kissable blondes, yes, and egg-splattered Negroes—though even Nigerians wonder just how racism can fit into such an otherwise glorious picture." Indeed, teachers found, no account of American misdeeds—at home or abroad—could tame Africans' quest for American popular culture, despite what their "anti-imperialist" rhetoric might suggest. In Sierra Leone, members of a school band even insisted that their Peace Corps teacher lead them through "The Stars and Stripes Forever." The teacher had hoped to show them musical notation, so the Africans could record and transmit their own folk melodies. But they preferred to play an American patriotic jingle that came in over their radios, "the most detestable sound" that the teacher had ever heard.[63]

In many ways, these tensions stemmed from the built-in biases of Americans who chose to work overseas. As one Mennonite teacher wrote, he went to Africa "to get away from the seemingly inevitable 'rat race' of Western civilization." When he finally crossed the ocean, however, he found that he had romanticized the other shore. "The materialism which I thought I'd left in North America seems somehow to have come along," he noted. "This thing about keeping up with the Joneses—well there are quite a few Joneses here." Other teachers chose a specific destination because of their interest in its culture and traditions, suffering regret and disillusionment after their hosts proved markedly less interested than Americans were. When an African-American in Liberia attempted to promote traditional wood carving at his school, he discovered, to his chagrin, that "Liberians preferred Woolworth products to the carved animals and gods of their ancestors." Likewise, Catholic missionaries encountered local resistance when they tried to teach so-called "local crafts" in Uganda. "You just don't want us to have sewing machines," one student protested.[64]

As the last comment suggests, denunciations of Western cultural imperialism could contain their own imperialistic assumptions. By denying their students sewing machines, Americans took it upon themselves to determine what was "authentically" African. Their conceptions lay firmly in the noble-savage tradition, as several Peace Corps teachers admitted. In Togo, Americans arrived with "Rousseau-like notions of the Africans as people whose faults were due only to outside sources"; similarly, in Nigeria, teachers brought "visions of a native society quite pure, free, and open—the glorious 'state of nature.'" Even more, the very wish to preserve this allegedly pristine condition prevented Africans from choosing their own path, as one missionary warned. "We must be careful that we do not allow our policy of making everything adaptable to African culture rob our African friends of the opportunity to borrow what they want from other cultures," he wrote.[65]

Most of all, the neglect of actual preferences in other lands echoed a long tradition of imperial anti-imperialism in overseas American education. Denouncing turn-of-the-century schools in the colonial Philippines, teachers argued that students there lacked the capacity to learn; others feared that these same racial weaknesses would rub off on white instructors; still others worried that the entire imperial project would corrupt America's republican virtue. Such arguments were themselves imperialist, as historian Matthew Jacobson has written, because they "took but little account of Filipino lives." The post–World War II analysis of cultural imperialism reversed the moral sides of the equation, casting America as the culprit and other nations as victims. Like the earlier campaign against empire, however, it too took little interest in the actual perceptions and wishes of foreign peoples. In 1975, an English teacher wrote a long screed against her own efforts in the Central African Republic: Africans did not need English, which reinforced "colonial" presumptions of linguistic superiority, and so on. Then she caught herself. "It should be noted, however, that the criticisms I have just made are arrogant, culturally closed, and even imperialistic," she admitted. "It's an easy trap to fall into." Try as they might, many American teachers could not avoid it.[66]

⌁ IN 1994, a leading professor of "missions and anthropology" reviewed the history of American missionaries and cultural difference. During the "colonial" era of mission development, Paul G. Hiebert wrote, Americans equated Western civilization with Christianity and assumed the superiority of both. Then came the "anticolonial" period, when missionaries renounced their bigoted past and embraced the validity—indeed, the equality—of other cultures and religions. "No society had the right to judge another by its own values," Hiebert wrote. "Ethnocentrism became the cardinal sin and cultural relativism the acknowledged good." Sometimes, the new analysis simply inverted the moral judgments of the old one: instead of West-as-good, missions embraced a doctrine of West-as-bad. Worst of all, though, the anticolonial position simply did not allow missionaries to preach Ultimate Truth. In the forthcoming "global Era" of "Hard Love," Hiebert hoped, missionaries would retain the baby of cultural sensitivity without throwing out the bathwater of Biblical certainty.[67]

In other words, they needed to be more explicit imperialists. *All* educators are to some degree imperialists—just as all educators are missionaries—because they seek to bring a new idea, belief, or skill to students who might not share it. Why else would they bother? "If the American people are superior to the Filipinos in the matter of civilization they should spread that civilization," wrote a teacher in the Philippines in 1917, during the heart of Hiebert's "colonial" period. "If our so-called civilized ways are not good, we would better abandon them ourselves." During the ensuing anticolonial era, Americans would indeed question their own civilization, and, especially, whether they had a right to spread it elsewhere. But the very act of rejecting corrupt

Western values—or of defending allegedly "indigenous" ones—could embody its own imperialism, insofar as it ignored or discounted the expressed desires of the people it purported to protect. "Africans who have been exposed to some of the Western way of life . . . reject their own culture and adopt the White-collar aspirations they see around them," wrote a teacher in Ethiopia in 1970. "I feel very strongly (although perhaps I have no right to make this judgment, as I am a white collar) that this [is] personally injurious." Only the teacher's offhand, parenthetical remark—"perhaps I have no right to make this judgment"—betrayed any hint that it *was* a judgment, every bit as certain and severe as anything uttered by a colonial-era teacher.[68]

So the only real question becomes *which* values Americans will try to transmit. Hiebert and his fellow "mission anthropologists" make no bones about their ultimate goal: to convert the world to Christianity. Indeed, their entire embrace of multicultural idioms, like their renunciation of "colonial" ones, is directed, quite explicitly, at this very end.[69] Peace Corps volunteers and other secular teachers more commonly invoke cultural self-determination as an end in itself, helping other countries discover, develop, and defend their "real" heritage. But we should not pretend that this objective is any less imperial, even if it comes dressed up in the arch garb of anti-imperialism. In 2003, for example, a returned Peace Corps teacher from Bulgaria bemoaned his students' embrace of American commercial products like McDonald's and, yes, Coca-Cola. "The love for American culture is indiscriminate," he complained, "a rather empty worship that will not serve this developing country."[70] But how did he know that the love was indiscriminate, or the worship empty? And how could he divine whether the love and the worship would serve Bulgarians?

Whether they admitted it or not, American teachers have always wanted the world to worship *their* gods. Pre–World War II teachers said that Americans alone possessed "civilization," which they would share with the natives; post–World War II teachers claimed that every people had a "culture," so Americans needed to resist the imperial impulse to impose their own values and ideas on others. In each case, however, teachers assumed a basic, essential difference between their students and themselves. Whether Americans wished to erase or preserve this difference, they believed first and foremost in its existence— across continents, and across centuries. But the world was changing in

ways that escaped the narrow confines of culture, as the teachers defined it. In a global era, especially, peoples around the world had more
in common than Americans sometimes acknowledged. Without a
recognition of this common humanity, moreover, Americans will never
learn to appreciate the irreducible diversity of the global cultures that
surround them.

Epilogue

AMERICAN TEACHERS IN
A GLOBAL AGE

O<small>N THE MORNING OF</small> S<small>EPTEMBER</small> 11, 2001, I was walking to work through Washington Square Park when a homeless man asked me for money. I shook my head, no, and trudged on.

"World Trade Center's on fire," he called after me. I ignored him, without even looking up at the Twin Towers.

World Trade Center's on fire. When I reached my office, I found out that he was right. A few hours later, both towers crumbled into smoke, dust, and death. I spent the next week contacting friends and students, to make sure they were safe—and to assure them that I was. Then, on September 20, I watched our president address a special session of Congress in a nationally televised speech:

> As long as the United States of America is determined and strong, this will not be an age of terror; this will be an age of liberty, here and across the world. (Applause) . . . The advance of human freedom—the great achievement of our time, and the great hope of every time—now depends on us. Our nation—this generation—will lift a dark threat of violence from our people and our future. We will rally the world to this cause by our courage. We will not tire, we will not falter, and we will not fail. (Applause).[1]

Widely quoted by historians, George W. Bush's words reflect a perennial national narrative about American strength, benevolence, and innocence.[2] Uniquely among the countries of the Earth, the narrative asserts, the United States has the right—and the might—to remake the world in accord with its allegedly universal values. "What internationalism have we Americans to offer?" asked Henry Luce in 1941. "It must be a sharing with all peoples of our Bill of Rights, our Declaration of Independence, our Constitution." The principles embodied in America's founding documents were not America's alone; they applied to all peoples, everywhere. As the progenitor and ultimate symbol of these universal principles, however, the United States bore a special duty to promulgate them around the globe. America must "exert upon the world the full impact of our influence," Luce insisted, "for such purposes as we see fit and by such means as we see fit."[3] Anything less would betray the American birthright, along with the shared human values that were inscribed within it.

It followed that human beings around the world should mimic Americans; and if they did not, we should make them do so. As the British philosopher John Gray has quipped, we like to think that everyone is born American—but that certain people become something else, due to a bad upbringing.[4] Historians have spun this insight into a strong counternarrative, stressing the many ways that America denigrated, suppressed, or simply eliminated people who did not share its supposedly universal character. On the Western frontier and in new colonial possessions like the Philippines, Americans warned, "lesser" races must learn to live like whites or face extinction. After World War II, the story goes, culture replaced race as the central trope of America's assault on difference. Although most white Americans no longer maligned other races as biologically inferior, they increasingly viewed foreigners as *culturally* inadequate. So the job of America remained the same: to raise other peoples out of the primeval muck, to spread liberty and democracy, and to stamp out atavistic cultures that were not ready, or willing, to take their seats at the table of humanity.[5]

This book suggests far more nuance, complexity, and change than either of these narratives allows. Despite their apparent divergence, the story of American innocence and the story of American iniquity assume a basic consensus among Americans themselves. Both sides maintain that Americans promoted a single set of values—or, sometimes, a single culture—across space and time. But America's overseas teachers did not. At the outset of the American Century, admittedly, most teachers did aim to transmit their "civilization" to people who seemed to lack it. Even in this era of confidence, however, there was also ambivalence: think of American teachers in the Philippines who denounced English-language instruction, or missionaries in Africa seeking to preserve vernacular tongues. After midcentury, such concerns would explode into an all-encompassing critique of America's role and purpose in the world. Hardly the tribunes of universal values that Henry Luce imagined, American teachers began to doubt whether American values *were* universal, and, most of all, whether Americans should impose them upon the rest of the universe.

To be fair, historians have carefully described the various minorities who dissented from Luce's vision of American purity and power: female pacifists, black civil rights activists, left-leaning intellectuals, and so on.[6] But these studies focus almost entirely on domestic politics, omitting Americans who actually went abroad. The United States' overseas project remains a united and static affair, challenged only by a handful of brave radicals back home (including, conveniently, radical historians).[7] This view exaggerates the degree of consensus among overseas Americans and probably among stateside Americans, as well. Remember that the vast majority of teachers who went abroad in the twentieth century were white, from small towns and small colleges, "sincere, friendly, and stable"—as one Peace Corps volunteer observed in 1961—and resolutely middle-class.[8] As educators, moreover, they inevitably transmitted a set of values: *all* education involves the transmission of values, whether educators acknowledge it or not.[9] But the values that American teachers proclaimed often deviated from the so-called hegemonic message of American diplomats, businessmen, or journalists. In short, Americans were neither as concerted nor as conceited as many historical portraits of the American Century would suggest.

Nor do most recent studies of "globalization" address the extraordinary variety and vicissitudes of American influence overseas. Most authors use this term to describe the accelerated interchange—of peoples, products, and ideas—across nations and regions, especially since the 1980s.[10] As the lone superpower for most of these years, the United States clearly casts the longest shadow in a globalized world. To some scholars, American economic and cultural supremacy has spawned a bland, homogeneous cultural wasteland of McDonald's and MTV; others emphasize the many ways that local societies alter and reinterpret these American imports, spawning new hybrid forms. Even as they devote admirable attention to local agency and accommodation, however, most students of globalization assume a relatively undifferentiated view of America itself. Surely, though, America is also a hybrid—quite possibly, the *most* hybrid nation in human history. The present-day anxiety about the pervasiveness of "American culture" grants this culture more integrity, consistency, and cohesion than it probably deserves.[11]

Post–World War II American teachers experienced the same anxiety, of course. Wherever they went, teachers worried about imposing "their" culture on peoples who did not share it; even more, they feared that people who *did* share American culture were abandoning "real" or indigenous traditions. But the very nature and frequency of this concern belied the idea of a singular, unified American project overseas. Whereas Henry Luce and his latter-day imitators declared the universality of American values, post–World War II teachers saw mostly difference and particularity; whereas Luce underscored American benevolence and superiority, the teachers perceived hubris and inconsistency; and whereas many Americans assumed a license to alter or eliminate "lesser" cultures, the teachers struggled to defend and preserve them. As countless scholars have correctly reminded us, Americans demonstrated a profound arrogance and ethnocentrism across the twentieth-century world. But that was never the whole story, or even the half of it, because Americans also evinced a welcome capacity to critique their own ways.

Culture and Critique

The key element of this critique, as this book has shown, was the concept of culture itself. In most historical interpretations, Americans readily adapted this concept, as they did earlier ideas of race, to their erstwhile assumptions of innocence, benevolence, and superiority. "Turning toward culture and stressing the essential malleability of the 'traditionals,' American modernizers, like the more optimistic advocates of Indian assimilation and overseas imperialism, carved out another kind of redemptive mission for themselves," writes Michael E. Latham, in his superb study of post–World War II social science and international relations. "The foreign would not fade away, but, under American influence, their deficient cultures would."[12] To be sure, early twentieth-century teachers echoed many of these presumptions. But post–World War II teachers assumed a very different perspective, focused less on "modernizing" other cultures than on preserving them. In this view, each culture possessed a special unity, beauty, and integrity. So the proper role of the American teacher was to respect different cultures, not to press America's own culture-bound ideas upon them. "Here is Western culture, harming an aspect of another culture more healthy than itself," wrote a teacher in Fiji, in a typical 1971 remark. "The day of the duodenal ulcer is not far off."[13]

This culture concept made Americans less eager to remake the world, not more so. As the quip about ulcers illustrates, it also helped Americans reflect on their own culture in a new and critical light. Here they often echoed the midcentury jeremiads of domestic critics like William Whyte and David Riesman, himself a close observer, and frequent speaker, at Peace Corps trainings. Transmuting the idea of culture into "national character," these best-selling authors described an America that was soft, conformist, addled by consumerism, and unfit to lead the free world. In the hands of policymakers back home, such critiques became fodder for a renewed global outreach: by projecting their power into other frontiers, the argument went, Americans could rediscover the pioneer virtues of their own past.[14] Out in the field, however, the culture concept made teachers question whether these "American" qualities were appropriate for other societies, and whether Americans should transport them there. As one post–World War II missionary to the Philippines mused, in a quip that began this book, Daniel Boone would have made a poor Filipino. So it made little sense—and even less justice—for Americans to try to make Filipinos into Daniel Boone.

But how could Americans identify a "real" Filipino when they saw one? Even as the culture concept discouraged Americans from imposing their ideals upon others, it also led them to caricature the very nature of The Other. Like the concept of civilization that preceded it, "culture" placed every member of a given society into the same characterological box. The problem returns us to anthropologist Clifford Geertz, who vividly described the influence of this concept during his graduate training in the 1950s. "Everyone knew," recalls Geertz,

> that the Kwakiutl were megalomanic, the Dobu paranoid, the Zuni poised, the Germans authoritarian, the Russians violent, the Americans practical and optimistic, the Samoans laid-back, the Navaho

prudential, the Tepotzlanos either unshakably unified or hope-
lessly divided (there were two anthropologists who studied them,
one the student of the other), and the Japanese shame-driven; and
everyone knew they were that way because their culture (each one
had one, and none had more than one) made them so.

More than any other scholar, Geertz helped shatter this all-encompassing
conception of culture in American scholarship. Today, another anthropologist reports, the discipline has "largely abandoned traditional assumptions about bounded autonomous cultural systems."[15] For American
teachers overseas, however, the assumptions remained. People behaved,
thought, and believed in the manner they did because of their culture;
and everyone in a given culture behaved, thought, and believed in
roughly the same manner.

So the teachers faced only two choices: impose their own culture, or
capitulate to the local one. But the very terms of this dilemma blinded
them to diversity *within* the cultures they encountered and—especially—to values they might have shared with their hosts. Consider the
teachers' oft-repeated complaint that other cultures denigrated or oppressed women. By Western standards, to be sure, many host societies
did exactly that. Third World women faced, and still face, substandard
education, limited job opportunities, honor killings, genital mutila-
tion . . . the list could go on and on. But these societies also contained
educated, professional women who had managed to overcome such
handicaps. Dismissing an entire culture as sexist actually denigrated the
achievements of these women, all in the guise of defending them. Even
more, it framed a battle of different local cultures—that is, between a
sector of women and their opponents—as a clash between a progressive,
cosmopolitan "American" culture and a traditional, conservative "foreign" one. The anxiety about imposing America's egalitarian ethos reflected a degree of self-caricature, because Americans were never quite
as equal as they liked to think. And it caricatured host cultures, which
themselves embodied more variety than Americans often allowed.[16]

Worst of all, the culture concept sometimes made teachers reluctant
to promote their own values in situations where they *should* have done
so. Here, too, the example of women is instructive. In the Peace Corps,
some teachers openly challenged the gender inequities and iniquities
that they encountered overseas. But this position "was more didactic

than many volunteers were comfortable with," as historian Fritz Fischer has noted. Female volunteers, especially, believed that "trying to change local attitudes about women overstepped the bounds of their role." Even when teachers did denounce local gender practices, they suffered guilt and torment for doing so. "You don't force your cultural things on people," recalled one Uganda volunteer, who condemned his male students' belief that women should be beaten. "But I thought some of my ideas were universal."[17]

Diversity and Universality

Some ideas *are* universal, or, at least, they should be. Without shared values, indeed, human beings cannot communicate (literally: "to make common") across their innumerable cultural differences. Nor can they value the differences themselves. In a very real sense, then, the "cultural defense" for invidious discrimination—along the lines of gender, race, disability, or sexual orientation—is self-defeating: in pretending to respect other cultures, it makes them inaccessible to outsiders. "The pursuit of universality does not involve the smothering of cultural polyvalence or the pressure to reach cultural consensus," explains the sociologist Zygmunt Bauman, in a recent plea for a renewed humanism. "Universality means no more, yet no less either, than the across-the-species ability to communicate and reach mutual understanding."[18] Insofar as some people in some places denied other human beings a place in the human family, then, it was perfectly reasonable for American teachers to challenge them; indeed, the Americans' own gospel of cultural diversity *required* precisely such a challenge. We simply cannot learn to appreciate human difference if some of us remain less than human.

Nor can we learn to navigate the increased diversity and complexity of a globalized world without an education of inquiry, deliberation, and the free exchange of ideas.[19] Here, too, American teachers sometimes balked at promoting such methods for fear of violating local cultures. As always, the concern reflected a bland and undifferentiated conception of culture itself: surely every society contained its fair share of individualists and conformists, of freethinkers and fundamentalists. Moreover, like the "culturalist" defense of sexism, the defense of rote learning and memorization actually threatens the same cultures it purports to protect. As the pace of human interchange quickens around the globe, students in every society—and in every culture—will require the capacity to ask questions, to frame arguments, and to separate fact from cant. To deny any people these cognitive skills returns us to the world of early twentieth-century imperialism, when American teachers often maintained that nonwhite students could do little else than bleat and repeat. In a global era, especially, *all* peoples—of every culture—need an education for critical thinking. Indeed, the very survival of their cultures might depend on it.

Of course, this is not to suggest that the United States provides such an education to all or even to most of its own people. In fact, teachers often came home with a new awareness of America's educational inadequacies. "Many of the limitations of the Ghanaian educational system exist in the United States," a Peace Corps teacher told an interviewer in 1964. "Rote learning is an eternal problem, as are crowded classrooms and apathetic pupils and teachers." Most of all, Americans came to recognize, and to deplore, the low status that their own society assigned to teaching itself. Largely novices to the craft, many Americans found that their counterparts possessed more experience and skill than they did. Meanwhile, students displayed an energy and drive that was often missing at home. "Polish children study two foreign languages, algebra, and chemistry while in elementary school!" a Peace Corps volunteer exclaimed in the early 1990s. "School is a priority in most children's lives, and parents encourage their children to excel." Likewise, an African-American instructor in Kenya discovered that his students worked harder than most black children at home, because British teachers set higher expectations. "What I witnessed," he recalled, "was the day-to-day achievement of students whose teachers believed in them."[20]

In mission communities, meanwhile, teachers began to question America's longstanding tradition of church–state separation. Whereas America barred religious schools from receiving public funds and public schools from practicing religion, teachers found, most other nations did not. Just as secular teachers used their overseas experience to critique low standards in schools back home, mission teachers started to attack "creeping secularism" in American classrooms. "For me, this whole doctrine, important to the history of our government, needs to be reexamined in these times," wrote a mission teacher from the Congo in 1963, in an exchange about church–state separation. "Most non-

Americans expect a religious faith to permeate *all* living; they do not comprehend the idea of ruling religion out of education."[21] Why, then, should America be different? It is a good question, borne of the critical insight that cross-cultural experience can bring. American liberals like to think that they hold exclusive possession of such insight, casting their right-wing opponents as hidebound nationalists who ignore global opinion.[22] They might want to think again.

Exceptionals Abroad?

Most of all, liberals and conservatives alike might wish to rethink which values are "American," which ones are "global," and why. Observing American tourists shortly after the Civil War, Mark Twain never doubted that they possessed a unique set of national characteristics. "We always took care to make it understood that we were Americans—Americans!" Twain exclaimed, upon returning from his journey to Europe and the Middle East. "Many and many a simple community in the Eastern Hemisphere will remember for years the incursion of the strange horde in the year of our Lord 1867 that called themselves American and seemed to imagine in some unaccountable way that they had a right to be proud of it."[23] Twain, too, took pride in Americans' energy, ingenuity, and boisterous enthusiasms; at the same time, he was embarrassed by their boorish manners and their craven mimicry of Europeans. Yet he insisted that all of these traits—whether positive or negative—were distinctively "American." Indeed, Twain's *Innocents Abroad* served mainly to underscore them.

And surely, as this book has demonstrated, Americans often *did* exhibit a shared set of qualities when they went overseas. The first one was a commitment to universal education, which Twain also highlighted in his own travelogue. Shocked at the level of illiteracy he encountered in Italy, he imagined a "modern Roman" visiting America. " 'I saw common men and common women who could read,' " the Roman wrote. " 'There are hundreds and thousands of schools, and anybody may go and learn to be wise, like a priest.' " As his final jab suggested, Twain thought that the Catholic Church kept Italians shrouded in ignorance; elsewhere in his book, he denounced "Jesuit humbuggery" and deemed Protestantism the only "true religion."[24] American teachers would export this prejudice, and many others, alongside their faith in universal education; indeed, teachers often argued, local populations needed schooling precisely *because* of their inherent deficiencies. "There was a great desire to improve the conditions of these poverty-stricken ignorant people," recalled Philippines colonial teacher Philinda Rand Anglemyer, in a typical remark, "and the Americans' first prescription for any trouble is education." As the German historian Jurgen Osterhammel has confirmed, no other imperial power devoted more resources or attention to overseas public schools than the United States.[25]

Second, Americans displayed an easy-going informality that distinguished them from host populations and from European expatriates alike. Twain underlined this quality, as well, contrasting the informal affability in the United States to the stuffed-shirt decorum of the "Old World." The difference was even sharper for American teachers, who encountered much more strict, standardized school systems than they had experienced at home. From the 1901 docking of the USS *Thomas* in Manila to the arrival of Peace Corps Volunteers in Eastern Europe in the 1990s, observers of every stripe noted the teachers' casual style of speech, dress, and manners. Especially in Africa, indigenous instructors worried that the Americans' tendency to "befriend" students would erode school discipline; meanwhile, other white expatriates feared that the Americans would prove more popular than they were. "Headmaster said long experience had led British to shy away from fraternizing, being too friendly, having boys to tea and the like," wrote one evaluator in 1961, after visiting an American teacher—and his English principal—in Kenya. In the eyes of the headmaster, the teacher "was trying too hard to be friendly *in order to show up* the British as especially priggish and austere."[26]

Finally, American teachers across the twentieth century shared the same belief in their own unique qualities—that is, in American exceptionalism—that Twain evinced in the 1800s. Of course, every people or nation assumes that it is different in certain ways from every other one. As a score of scholars have confirmed, however, the ideology of exceptionalism has operated with a special force—perhaps, even, with an *exceptional* force—among Americans.[27] Overseas, teachers spoke knowingly of the "American Method" of teaching, the "American Curriculum" of vocational instruction, the "American System" of coeducation, the "American Plan" of church–state separation, and so on. It mattered little that other expatriate and indigenous teachers sometimes shared or even pioneered these ideas, particularly in pedagogy and curriculum.[28] "Regardless of whether or not the United States is actually exceptional," as one British historian recently emphasized, "the *belief* in American exceptionalism persists."[29] Especially when they went abroad, Americans insisted that they differed in basic ways from everyone around them.

But as this book has shown, the logic and implications of American exceptionalism changed dramatically over time. Like Henry Luce, early twentieth-century teachers came to view "American" ideas as universal ones; indeed, American exceptionalism lay less in the content of these principles than in America's unique role in promoting them. When he first came to the Congo in 1905, missionary Seymour Moon recalled, he erroneously viewed the "Hampton and Tuskegee Plan" of vocational education as "peculiarly adapted" to black Americans and Africans. "But lo!" Moon exclaimed in 1933, "these two schools . . . have become models for all education everywhere in the world." Indeed, "the emphasis on 'Education for Life,' 'Manual Training,' 'Industrial Training' . . . is commonplace in all educational work," Moon concluded, with perhaps more anticipation than accuracy.[30] As it matured into a world power, America would help ensure that its universal principles became truly universal in practice.

After World War II, the teachers' exceptionalism took a very different form. Eschewing confident bromides from the likes of Luce, teachers worried that American values, beliefs, and practices were distinct in kind rather than simply in degree; indeed, these values were *so* distinct that Americans should not transport them elsewhere. Most historical accounts of American exceptionalism associate the idea with national chauvinism and superiority, whereby America's alleged uniqueness becomes a rationale for ignoring other countries, or, even worse, for invading them.[31] Married to the modern concept of culture, however, exceptionalism could just as easily buttress a strong respect for local cultures, and an even stronger reluctance to interfere with them. For if every society or nation was endowed with a distinct culture, and if all cultures were equally worthy of respect, how could Americans justifiably impose "their" culture on others? Indeed, the more that any quality or belief became identified as uniquely American, the less comfortable Americans felt in exporting it abroad.

The problem brings us back to Mark Twain, whose final travel book anticipated this belief. *Following the Equator* appeared in 1897, nearly three decades after *Innocents Abroad*. Focused largely on British colonies, the book lacked the boyish optimism of its more popular predecessor. Instead, Twain worried that Western styles, habits, and beliefs were eroding "native" ones. In Ceylon, where Twain praised the "stunning colors" of "Oriental costumes," he was appalled to encounter a group of church school students in full Western uniform. "Out of a missionary school came marching, two and two, sixteen prim and pious little Christian black girls, Europeanly clothed—dressed, to the last detail, as they would have been dressed on a summer Sunday in an English or American village," Twain wrote. "Those clothes—oh, they were unspeakably ugly! Ugly, barbarous, destitute of taste, destitute of grace, repulsive as a shroud." Glancing at the American women who accompanied him, Twain saw that their clothes were simply "full-grown duplicates" of the garments worn by the "poor little abused creatures" from the mission school. "I . . . was ashamed to be seen on the street with them," he admitted, turning away from his American companions. "Then I looked at my own clothes, and was ashamed to be seen on the street with myself."[32]

In the ensuing century, to be sure, Americans have done many things around the world for which they *should* be ashamed. *Following the Equator* appeared on the eve of America's own imperial war in the Philippines, which Twain would condemn for its duplicity and brutality.[33] Hardly innocent bystanders in the quest for empire, American teachers often served as its advance guard: in America's colonies and elsewhere, they denigrated local languages, religions, and cultures in a misguided effort to substitute their own. After midcentury, though, the very language of culture sometimes discouraged them from making *any* purposeful changes or interventions in other people's lives. The anxiety was already evident in the dour 1897 narrative of Mark Twain, who worried that drab Western clothes were replacing bright local ones. By the 1960s, it burst into a full-throated critique of the West itself. American teachers looked around the world and envisioned millions of schoolchildren, marching lockstep in Western dress: a nightmare of cultural domination and manipulation. Even in Algeria, one teacher wrote, girls wore slacks and "an occasional 'love' T-shirt" underneath their heavy dark veils. "All of them seem to be chewing gum," the teacher added, "the very symbol of Western imperialism." Some teachers went on to wonder if the entire concept of female education was also a foreign import, another way to bleach colorful local cultures into a pale white hue.[34]

Yet this anxiety made Americans into the all-purpose umpire of what was "local" or "indigenous," and what was not. It denied other societies' freedom in deciding whether to change, presuming that The Other should remain the same. Worst of all, the idea of culture sometimes caused Americans to conflate outward differences of language, style, and ritual with the human universals inside each of us. Even as he railed against schoolgirls' pallid dress, Twain never paused to ask whether the girls should attend school. Nor should we. The ideal of equality—across gender, race, disability, and sexual orientation—is *not* unique to our own culture, like a style of clothing or speech. It is the birthright of every people, everywhere. Whether we march separately or together, in a great many outfits or a single uniform, we must not exclude the least among us. We can and should respect human differences, but never at the cost of human dignity.

Indeed, we do an enormous harm to this universal ideal when we call it "American." At its best, the post–World War II concept of culture encouraged teachers to critique their inherited beliefs, assumptions, and biases; at the same time, it brought a welcome respect and attention to the mores and lifeways of other peoples. At its worst, though, the culture concept made Americans label certain universal concepts—especially the basic equality of all human beings—as distinctly or even uniquely American. We mock and constrict this common human identity by linking it to our own narrow national aspirations. In an age of globalization, especially, we can no longer pretend that a single nation holds a monopoly on the human universals that should bind us all.

Notes

Introduction

1. Amparo Santamaria Lardizabal, *Pioneer American Teachers and Philippine Education* (Quezon City: Phoenix Press, 1991), 7; Mary Cole to Dear Folks at Home, 24 July 1901, "July 1901" folder, box 1, Harry N. Cole Papers, Bentley Historical Library, Ann Arbor, Mich.; Benjamin E. Neal, "Introductory. Object. Condition in the Philippines. Expenses" (ms, 1901), p. 2, "Corres. 1901–1904" folder, Benjamin E. Neal Papers, George Arents Research Library, Syracuse University, Syracuse, N.Y.; *The Log of the 'Thomas': July 23 to August 21, 1901*, ed. Ronald P. Gleason (n.p., 1901), 49, 11. Every published account of the *Thomas* provides a different statistic for the total number of teachers on board, ranging from 503 to 560. I have relied on the unpublished remarks of teacher Mary Cole, who counted the passengers carefully and reported the results in a letter that she wrote shortly after the boat left San Francisco.

2. Diary entry, 23 July 1901, "Diaries (Transcripts) 1901" folder, p. 3, Frederick G. Behner Papers, Bentley Historical Library; diary entries, 26 and 27 July 1901, "Syracuse-Manila" diary, "Diaries and Account Books 1901–1902" folder, box 1, Neal Papers; diary entry, 27 July 1901, "Diary 1/4" folder, box 1, Blaine Free Moore Papers, Library of Congress, Washington, D.C.

3. Mary Cole to "Dear Bro. and Sister," 15 October 1901, "October–November 1901" folder, box 1, Cole Papers; George N. Briggs to Frank Crone, 21 August 1913, p. 222; Anna M. Donaldson, "Account of First Two Years of Work in the Philippines" (ms, 1914), p. 246, both in "Bureau of Education. Activities 1914. Early Experiences of American Teachers" binder, box 6, Walter W. Marquardt Papers, Bentley Historical Library; diary entry, 2 August 1901, "Diary 1/4" folder, box 1, Moore Papers.

4. Blaine Free Moore to "Dear Pa and Ma," 23 August 1901, "Correspondence 1901" folder, box 1, Moore Papers; Herbert I. Priestley to "Dear Sister Ethel," 29 August 1901, "Transcriptions of letters, July–August 1901" folder, box 1, Herbert

I. Priestley Papers, Bancroft Library, University of California–Berkeley; Neal, "Introductory," p. 2.

5. Henry R. Luce, "The American Century" [1941], in *The Ambiguous Legacy: United States Foreign Relations in the "American Century,"* ed. Michael J. Hogan (New York: Cambridge University Press, 1999), 28.

6. Ann and Terry Marshall, "Curriculum Writing," *Peace Corps Volunteer* 5 (May 1967): 16; "This Is the Peace Corps, Miss Jones!" *Sunday News* [University Park, Penn.], 20 August 1961, folder 61, box 195, National Catholic Welfare Conference/United States Catholic Conference Collection [hereafter "NCWC/USCC"], American Catholic History Research Center, Catholic University, Washington, D.C.; Kenneth O. Gangel, "Using Filipino Culture to Enhance Christian Education," *Evangelical Missions Quarterly* 9 (Summer 1973): 223–224, 228.

7. P. David Searles, *The Peace Corps Experience: Challenge and Change, 1969–1976* (Lexington: University Press of Kentucky, 1997), 61.

8. A. L. Kroeber and Clyde Kluckhohn, *Culture: A Critical Review of Concepts and Definitions* (New York: Vintage, 1952), 291, 3, 68.

9. Ibid., v; Clifford Geertz, *Available Light: Anthropological Reflections on Philosophical Topics* (Princeton: Princeton University Press, 2000), 12, 15; William Appleman Williams, *The Tragedy of American Diplomacy*, rev. ed. (New York: Dell, 1962 [1959]), 9.

10. Susan Hegeman, *Patterns for America: Modernism and the Concept of Culture* (Princeton: Princeton University Press, 1999), 6; Warren Susman, "The Culture of the Thirties," in Susman, *Culture as History: The Transformation of American Society in the Twentieth Century* (New York: Pantheon, 1984), 153–154; Philip Gleason, *Speaking of Diversity: Language and Ethnicity in Twentieth-Century America* (Baltimore: Johns Hopkins University Press, 1992), 136–137, 195; John Fousek, *To Lead the Free World: American Nationalism and the Cultural Roots of the Cold War* (Chapel Hill: University of North Carolina Press, 2000), 7, 10.

11. Penny von Eschen, *Race against Empire* (Ithaca, N.Y.: Cornell University Press, 1997); Azza Salama Layton, *International Politics and Civil Rights Policies in the United States, 1941–1960* (New York: Cambridge University Press, 2000); Mary L. Dudziak, *Cold War Civil Rights: Race and the Image of American Democracy* (Princeton: Princeton University Press, 2000); Thomas Borstelmann, *The Cold War and the Color Line: American Race Relations in the Global Arena* (Cambridge, Mass.: Harvard University Press, 2001).

12. Gary Gerstle, *American Crucible: Race and Nation in the Twentieth Century* (Princeton: Princeton University Press, 2001), 268–310; David Hollinger, *Postethnic America: Beyond Multiculturalism* (New York: Basic Books, 1995), 51–77; John Higham, "Multiculturalism and Universalism: A History and Critique," *American Quarterly* 45 (June 1993): 195–219; Charles Taylor, *Multiculturalism: Examining the Politics of Recognition*, ed. Amy Gutmann (Princeton: Princeton University Press, 1994). Whereas many historians view these ideals as sequential in time—from civil rights universalism and integration to cultural particularism and "identity politics"—I see them as simultaneous. From its inception, the American civil rights movement reflected a strong ideal of "cultural rights" *and* of human rights. See Jonathan Zimmerman, "*Brown*-ing the American Textbook: History, Psychology, and the Origins of Modern Multiculturalism," *History of Education Quarterly* 44 (Spring 2004): 45–69.

13. Clifford Geertz, *The Interpretation of Cultures*, rev. ed. (New York: Basic Books, 2000 [1973]), 5; Warren Susman, "Culture and Commitment," in *Culture as History*, 186.

14. As Susan Hegeman and others have argued, the very idea of midcentury culture contained a strong inherent component of critique: by studying other ways of life, proponents of the concept argued, Americans could gain new perspective and insight on their own. Hegeman, *Patterns for America*, 31, 126–127; Susman, "Culture and Commitment," 191; Terry Eagleton, *The Idea of Culture* (Malden, Mass.: Blackwell, 2000), 27; George E. Marcus and Michael M. J. Fischer, *Anthropology as Cultural Critique: An Experimental Moment in the Human Sciences* (Chicago: University of Chicago Press, 1986), 130.

15. See, for example, H. W. Brands, *What America Owes the World: The Struggle for the Soul of Foreign Policy* (Cambridge: Cambridge University Press, 1998); Trevor B. McCrisken, *American Exceptionalism and the Legacy of Vietnam: United States Foreign Policy since 1974* (New York: Palgrave Macmillan, 2003); Walter A. McDougall, *Promised Land, Crusader State: The American Encounter with the World since 1776* (Boston: Houghton Mifflin, 1997); Frank Ninkovich, *The Wilsonian Century: United States Foreign Policy since 1900* (Chicago: University of Chicago Press, 1999); Anders Stephanson, *Manifest Destiny: American Expansion and the Empire of Right* (New York: Hill and Wang, 1995).

16. See, for example, Michael H. Hunt, *Ideology and U.S. Foreign Policy* (New Haven: Yale University Press, 1987), 190; Elizabeth Cobbs Hoffman, *All You Need Is Love: The Peace Corps and the Spirit of the 1960s* (Cambridge, Mass.: Harvard University Press, 1998), 6, 257.

17. Daniel Rodgers, *Atlantic Crossings: Social Politics in a Progressive Age* (Cambridge, Mass.: Harvard University Press, 1998); von Eschen, *Race against Empire*; Layton, *International Politics and Civil Rights Policies*.

18. See, for example, Michael Lienesch, *Redeeming America: Piety and Politics in the New Christian Right* (Chapel Hill: University of North Carolina Press, 1993), 139–194; Maurice Isserman and Michael Kazin, *America Divided: The Civil War of the 1960s* (New York: Oxford University Press, 2000), 205–220; Robert Wuthnow, "Divided We Fall: America's Two Civil Religions," *Christian Century* 105 (20 April 1988): 395–399.

19. William A. Smalley, "Christian Education and Christian Preaching," *Practical Anthropology* 4 (September–October 1957): 202.

20. Following the classic formulation of the concept by Edward Said, most scholars use "Orientalism" to describe the negative attributes that Europeans attributed to non-Western peoples in the first half of the twentieth century—or that Americans assigned to the "Third World" in the post–World War II period. During this same postwar era, however, American teachers often engaged in a positive or even celebratory Orientalism: rather than rendering The Other as inferior to Americans, teachers often insisted that foreign customs and habits were *more* "civilized" than their own. But The Other remained *different*, marked by a set of "cultures" that were every bit as powerful and permanent as the negative portraits of the pre–World War II era. Edward W. Said, *Orientalism* (New York: Random House, 1978); Said, *Culture and Imperialism* (New York: Random House, 1993); Andrew J. Rotter, "Saidism without Said: *Orientalism* and United States Diplomatic History," *American Historical Review* 105 (October 2000): 1205–1217.

21. George W. Carpenter, *A Study of the School Work of Evangelical Missions in the Bas-Congo* (Leopoldville: ABFMS Press, January 1940), p. 14, folder 11, box 13, National Council of Churches Papers, Division of Overseas Ministries [hereafter "NCC-DOM"], Record Group 8, Presbyterian Historical Society, Philadelphia, Pa.

22. Jonathan Zimmerman, "Religious Bigotry," *Atlanta Constitution*, 16 November 1999.

23. For various perspectives on the perils of writing "personal" history, see the essays collected in "Round Table: Self and Subject," *Journal of American History* 89 (June 2002): 17–53.

24. Helen L. French to "My dear Mamma," 12 April 1901, "March–April 1901" folder, box 1, Wood Family Papers, Rare Books and Manuscripts Division, Cornell University Libraries, Ithaca, N.Y.; diary entry, 11 March 1904, 1903 diary, folder 7, box 14, Frank P. and Helen Chisholm Papers, Special Collections, Emory University, Atlanta, Ga.; Esther B. Rhoads to Carolyn Frank, 26 January 1951, "Letters from Rhoads. January–July 1951" folder, box 21, Esther B. Rhoads Papers, Quaker Collection, Haverford College, Haverford, Penn.; "In Memory of Mickey Fedor, a Very Special Peace Corps Volunteer," *Congressional Record* 129, pt. 20, 98th Cong., lst sess. (20 October 1983), 28828–28829; Jacqueline Goggin, *Carter G. Woodson: A Life in Black History* (Baton Rouge: Louisiana State University Press, 1993), 16–18; Leonard P. Ayres to "Dear Papa," 31 October 1907, "1902–1930" folder, box 2, Leonard P. Ayres Papers, Library of Congress; Edgar Tom Williams to "Dear friends," 25 November 1962, "Ethiopia—Volunteer Information" folder, Collection 31, Peace Corps Volunteers Collection, National Anthropology Archives, Museum Support Center, Smithsonian Institution, Suitland, Md.

25. Thomas B. Vance, "Jobs, Job Opportunities and Job Attitudes in Hawaii," *Hawaii Educational Review* 17 (November 1928): 62.

26. Donald S. Stroetzel, "The Other 49 Peace Corps," *Christian Herald*, n.d. [1967], folder 57, box 11, Short Terms Abroad Papers, Billy Graham Center Archives, Wheaton College, Wheaton, Ill.; Hoffman, *All You Need Is Love*, 73–120.

27. "AAI—A Brief History" (ms, n.d. [1968]), fiche 000.123–1, Schomburg Clipping File, Schomburg Center for Research in Black Culture, New York Public Libraries; Raymond J. Smyke, "Teaching in West Africa," *Africa Special Report* 3 (November 1958): 12; Susanne Nanka-Bruce, "Teachers College Projects in East Africa: A History of Educational Cooperation, 1961–1971," (Ph.D. diss., Teachers College, Columbia University, 1988), 116; *Volunteer Teachers for Africa* (n.p., n.d. [1970]), folder 18, box 17, NCC-DOM; *The IVS Experience: From Algeria to Vietnam*, ed. Stuart Rawlings (Washington, D.C.: International Voluntary Services, 1992), 1–2.

28. Raymond Prigodich, "Wanted: Missionaries, Two Weeks to Five Years," *Eternity* (March 1969), folder 16, box 12, Short Terms Abroad Papers; "A Look at Lay Missionary Groups" (ms, 16 January 1960), folder 58, box 194, NCWC/USCC; Gerald M. Costello, *Mission to Latin America: The Successes and Failures of a Twentieth Century Crusade* (Maryknoll, N.Y.: Orbis, 1979), 48, 90.

29. Jeffrey Alan Melton, *Mark Twain, Travel Books, and Tourism: The Tide of a Great Popular Movement* (Tuscaloosa: University of Alabama Press, 2002), 2; Mark Twain, *The Innocents Abroad* (New York: Signet, 1966 [1869]).

Part I: American Dilemmas

1. Gunnar Myrdal, *An American Dilemma: The Negro Problem and Modern Democracy*, rev. ed. (New York: Harper and Row, 1962 [1944]), lxxi, 928.

2. David W. Southern, *Gunnar Myrdal and Black-White Relations: The Use and Abuse of* An American Dilemma, *1944–1969* (Baton Rouge: Louisiana State University Press, 1987), 261–292; John Higham, "Another American Dilemma" [1974], in Higham, *Send These to Me: Immigrants in Urban America*, rev. ed. (Baltimore: Johns Hopkins University Press, 1984 [1975]), 234.

3. Marjorie Pfankuch to Family, 29 April 1962, microfilm reel 1, Marjorie Pfankuch Papers, Wisconsin Historical Society, Madison, Wis.

4. Katherine B. Tatman to Sarah Swan, 1 January 1970, folder 2-A, box 23, Philadelphia Yearly Meeting—Japan Committee, Quaker Collection, Haverford College, Haverford, Pa.

1. The American Method

1. Harry Cole to "Dear Folks at Home," 5 November 1901; Cole to "My dear Mother," 18 November 1901, both in "October–November 1901" folder, box 1, Harry N. Cole Papers, Bentley Historical Library, Ann Arbor, Mich.

2. Velma Adams, *The Peace Corps in Action* (Chicago: Follett, 1964), 167.

3. David Tyack, *The One Best System: A History of American Urban Education* (Cambridge, Mass.: Harvard University Press, 1974), 197; John L. Rury, *Education and Social Change: Themes in the History of American Schooling* (Mahwah, N.J.: Lawrence Erlbaum, 2002), 142–148; David F. Labaree, *The Trouble with Ed Schools* (New Haven: Yale University Press, 2004), 144–145.

4. On the gap between progressive ideals and classroom practice in the United States, the classic text is Larry Cuban, *How Teachers Taught: Constancy and Change in American Classrooms, 1890–1990*, 2nd ed. (New York: Teachers College Press, 1993). See also David K. Cohen, "Practice and Policy: Notes on the History of Instruction," in *American Teachers: Histories of a Profession at Work*, ed. Donald Warren (New York: Macmillan, 1989), 393–407; Wayne E. Fuller, *The Old Country School: The Story of Rural Education in the Middle West* (Chicago: University of Chicago Press, 1982), 201–207; Kathleen Weiler, *Country Schoolwomen: Teaching in Rural California, 1850–1950* (Stanford: Stanford University Press, 1998), 199–201; Jonathan Zimmerman, *Distilling Democracy: Alcohol Education in American Public Schools, 1880–1925* (Lawrence: University of Kansas Press, 1999), 85–87.

5. Ronald E. Butchart, "Punishments, Penalties, Prizes, and Procedures," in *Classroom Discipline in American Schools: Problems and Possibilities for Democratic Education*, ed. Ronald E. Butchart & Barbara McEwan (Albany: State University Press of New York, 1998), 21–22; Fuller, *Old Country School*, 8–9; Kate Rousmaniere, *City Teachers: Teaching and School Reform in Historical Perspective* (New York: Teachers College Press, 1997), 121–126; Weiler, *Country Schoolwomen*, 189.

6. Joseph S. Murphy and Paul Cromwell, "Close of Service Conference. Nigeria VII. Ibandan, April 19–21, 1965" (ms), p. 5, "Nigeria VII" folder, box 5, Close of Service Conference Reports, Peace Corps Records [hereafter "PC-COS"], National Archives II, College Park, Md.; *Making a Difference: The Peace Corps at Twenty-Five*, ed. Milton Viorst (New York: Weidenfeld and Nicolson, 1986), 65–66.

7. On racial and ethnic learning styles, see, for example, Geneva Gay, *Culturally Responsive Teaching: Theory, Research, and Practice* (New York: Teachers College Press, 2000); for a withering critique, see Rob Reich, *Bridging Liberalism and Multiculturalism in American Education* (Chicago: University of Chicago Press, 2002), 179–184.

8. T. H. P. Sailer, "Bi-Monthly Letter to Educational Missionaries" (ms, 15 February 1911), folder 22, box 1, Arthur Leroy Carson Papers, Record Group 59, Presbyterian Historical Society, Philadelphia, Penn.

9. George C. Kindley to Frank L. Crone, 4 July 1913, p. 314; Bedford B. Hunter to Director of Education, 7 July 1913, p. 295, both in "Bureau of Education Activities 1914. Early Experiences of American Teachers" binder, box 6, Walter W. Marquardt Papers, Bentley Historical Library; Roland P. Falkner, "A Few Notable Changes," *Porto Rico School Record* 1 (May 1905), 5, "General File: Puerto Rico—1901–1912—Printed" folder, box 189, Samuel McCune Lindsay Papers, Manuscript Collections, Columbia University Libraries, New York; "Report of the Boys' Academy of the General Educational Work of Taiku Station for the year 1913–1914" (ms), folder 31, box 7, Board of Foreign Missions—Korea Missions Papers, Record Group 140, Presbyterian Historical Society.

10. William Axling to Helen Montgomery, 31 March 1921, folder 4, box 42, Ernest DeWitt Burton Papers, Joseph Regenstein Memorial Library, University of Chicago, Chicago, Ill.

11. Mary H. Fee, *A Woman's Impressions of the Philippines* (Chicago: A. C. McClurg, 1910), 80–81; George C. Kindley to Frank L. Crone, 4 July 1913, p. 312, "Bureau of Education Activities 1914. Early Experiences of American Teachers" binder, box 6, Marquardt Papers; Katherine M. Burke to T. H. Gibson, 13 October 1913, folder 5, box 61, Records of the Department of Education, Series 261 [hereafter "RDE-HA"], Hawaii State Archives, Honolulu, Hawaii; Helen L. French to "Dear Grandpa and Grandma," 26 December 1899, "November-December 1899" folder, box 1, Wood Family Papers, Rare Books and Manuscripts Division, Cornell University Libraries, Ithaca, N.Y.; Lois Harned Jordan, *Ramallah Teacher: The Life of Mildred White, Quaker Missionary* (n.p., 1995), 79.

12. See, for example, Edmund B. Butterfield, "An Account of Lieutenant Governor Mason Stone's Service in Organizing Schools in the Philippines" (ms, n.d.), p. 18, Manuscript Miscellaneous File No. 160, Vermont History Center, Barre, Vt.; Helen Pratt, "Silent Reading," *Hawaii Educational Review* 5 (January 1924): 76.

13. Ann Catherine Ryan, M.M., et al., "Our Lady of Mount Carmel Primary School—Riberalta, Beni, Bolivia" (ms, n.d. [1945?]), 1; "History of the Mission Riberalta, Beni, Bolivia, San Jose Convent" (ms, 1958), 7, both in Finding Aid 8a, Maryknoll Fathers and Brothers Archives, Ossining, N.Y.

14. Samuel Guy Inman, "Problems of an Educational Missionary in Latin America," in *Report of a Conference on the Preparation of Educational Missionaries*, ed. Frank K. Sanders (New York: Board of Missionary Preparation, n.d. [1917]), 96.

15. See, for example, Oliver George Wolcott, untitled manuscript, n.d. (1929), p. 9, "My Philippines Experiences, 1904–1907 and 1908–1909" folder, box 1, Oliver George Wolcott Papers, Bancroft Library, University of California-Berkeley; Butterfield, "An Account of Lieutenant Governor Mason Stone's Service," 49; *Report of the Commissioner of Education for Porto Rico to the Secretary of the Interior, USA* (Washington, D.C.: Government Printing Office, 1902), p. 64, "General File:

Puerto-Rico—Publications on Puerto Rican Education" folder, box 193, Lindsay Papers.

16. Alice B. Van Doren, *Christian High Schools in India: Being the Report of a Survey Conducted on Behalf of the National Christian Council of India, Burma, and Ceylon* (Calcutta: YMCA Publishing House, 1936), 17; Maza R. Evans to Minnie Sandberg, 15 January 1933, "Assam: Golaghat Girls High School" folder, Board of International Missions Subject Files [hereafter "BIMSF"], American Baptist Archives Center, Valley Forge, Penn. For similar complaints about the effects of examinations in French colonies, see, for example, George Schwab, "Report of the Superintendent of Schools" (ms, n.d. [1927?]), p. 2, folder 22, box 9, Board of Foreign Missions—West Africa Mission [hereafter "BFM-West Africa"], Record Group 142, Presbyterian Historical Society.

17. Henry S. Townsend, "Recollections and Reflections of a Writer" (ms, n.d. [1935?]), vol. 2, ch. 42, p. 3, 14; vol. 1, chap. 13, pp. 4–10; Townsend, "Hawaii in the 'Nineties,' " (ms, n.d. [1937?]), ed. Benjamin O. Wist, p. 31, 81, both in Hamilton Hawaiian Collection, University of Hawaii-Manoa Libraries, Honolulu, Hawaii.

18. Robert L. Wharton, *On the March with Cuba: The Story of La Progresiva* (New York: Board of National Missions, 1942), folder 43, box 21, Board of National Missions: Educational and Medical Work Papers, Record Group 301.8, Presbyterian Historical Society.

19. G. W. Carpenter to "Dear Friends of the C.I.M.," 5 October 1939, folder 11, box 13, National Council of Churches Papers, Division of Overseas Ministries [hereafter "NCC-DOM"], Record Group 8, Presbyterian Historical Society.

20. For examples of American paeans to "learning by doing" overseas, see William B. Freer, *The Philippine Experiences of An American Teacher: A Narrative of Work and Travel in the Philippine Islands* (New York: Scribner, 1906), 106; Alice Van Doren, *Projects in Indian Education: Experiments in the Project Method in Indian Schools* (Calcutta: Association Press, 1930), 151. On learning-by-doing as a progressive watchword in the United States, see, for example, Arthur Zilversmit, *Changing Schools: Progressive Education Theory and Practice, 1930–1960* (Chicago: University of Chicago Press, 1993), 10, 46; Diane Ravitch, *Left Back: A Century of Failed School Reforms* (New York: Simon and Schuster, 2000), 200.

21. *The Torch* (March 1939), p. 7, folder 4, box 20, Board of Foreign Missions—Iran Mission [hereafter "BFM-Iran"], Record Group 91, Presbyterian Historical Society. For other overseas testimonies to "experience" in education, see Irene Mason Harper, "Moga and the Better Village," *Women and Missions* (n.d. [1932]), folder 20, box 33, Board of Foreign Missions—India Mission [hereafter "BFM-India"], Record Group 83, Presbyterian Historical Society; Mary E. Fleming, "The Changing Functions of Hawaii's Schools," *Hawaii Educational Review* 16 (April 1928): 214; Benjamin O. Wist, *A Century of Public Education in Hawaii* (Honolulu: Hawaii Educational Review, 1940), 139. On "experience" and progressive education in the interwar United States, see, for example, Herbert M. Kliebard, *The Struggle for the American Curriculum*, 3rd ed. (New York: Routledge, 2004), 143–44; John Dewey, *Experience and Education* (New York: Macmillan, 1938).

22. Diary entry, 10 August 1901, "Diaries (Transcripts) 1901" folder, box 1, Frederick G. Behner Papers, Bentley Historical Library; Lewis S. Thomas to Director of Education, 2 August 1913, p. 348, "Bureau of Education. Activities 1914. Early Experiences of American Teachers" binder, box 6; "Recollections of a

Teacher in the Philippines after 20 Years," *Philippine Education* 18 (August 1921): p. 2, "Articles Correspondence Philippines 1922" binder, box 7, both in Marquardt Papers; Marius John, *Philippine Saga* (New York: House of Field, n.d. [1941]), 90; Andrew W. Cain, "What do you think of the Philippine Public School System?" *School and Home* 12 (October 1920), "Articles 19–22" binder, box 7, Marquardt Papers; Amparo Santamaria Lardizabal, *Pioneer American Teachers and Philippine Education* (Quezon City: Phoenix Press, 1991), 76. On the genealogy and implementation of the "object method" in the United States, see Cuban, *How Teachers Taught*, 39; Kim Tolley, *The Science Education of American Girls: A Historical Perspective* (New York: Routledge Falmer, 2003), 32, 132.

23. Van Doren, *Projects in Indian Education*, title page; Irene Mason Harper, *Modern Miracles at Moga* (n.p., February 1932), 84–85; Van Doren, *Fourteen Experiments in Rural Education* (Calcutta: Association Press, 1928), 5; Moga Training School, *Making Men at Moga* (Board of Foreign Missions, 1930), 2; William J. McKee, *New Schools for Young India: A Survey of the Educational, Economic, and Social Conditions in India with Special Reference to More Effective Education* (Chapel Hill: University of North Carolina Press, 1930), vii. For examples of Americans using the project method outside of India, see, for example, Felix M. Keesing, *Education in Pacific Countries* (Shanghai: Kelly and Walsh, 1937), 99; William G. MacLean, "Annual Report, 1934, Colegio Americano para Varones, Bogota, Colombia, November 30, 1934" (ms), folder 15, box 10, Board of Foreign Missions—Colombia Mission Papers, Record Group 88, Presbyterian Historical Society. Describing a fifth grade pen-pal exchange with students in the continental United States, a Hawaii teacher quoted Kilpatrick's definition of a "project": " 'A Wholehearted Purposeful Act Brought to Completion in a Social Environment.' " "News Notes," *Hawaii Educational Review* 12 (March 1924): 129.

24. Van Doren, *Christian High Schools In India* (1936), 71, 96 (1936); Thelma Ragsdale, "Teaching Problems of the Foreign Missionary: A Questionnaire Study" (M.A. thesis, Wheaton College, Wheaton, Ill., 1947), 41; J. W. Prentice, "Syllabus for Scripture Teaching" (ms, 9 September 1953), folder 4, box 20; "Audio-Visual Review," *Audio-Visual News* 10 (October 1956), pp. 5–7, folder 13, box 22; Frank Remple, "Can Christian Truth Be Visualized?" *Audio-Visual News* 12 (October 1958), p. 3, folder 12, box 22, all in BFM-India.

25. George W. Carpenter, *A Study of the School Work of Evangelical Missions in the Bas-Congo* (Leopoldville: ABFMS Press, January 1940), pp. 3, 6, folder 11, box 13, NCC-DOM.

26. "In an African Nutshell," *Inland Africa* 25 (November–December 1941): 16; Ruth E. Dickey, "Missionary News Letter Van. 49" (ms, 27 March 1943), fiche 003.084-1, Schomburg Clipping File, Schomburg Center for Research in Black Culture, New York Public Libraries; diary entry, 16 October 1902, September 1901–July 30 1902 diary, "Diaries and Account Books 1901–1902" folder, box 1, Benjamin E. Neal Papers, George Arents Research Library, Syracuse University; Leonard P. Ayres to "Dear Mayblossom," 23 December 1902, "1902–1930" folder, box 2, Leonard P. Ayres Papers, Library of Congress, Washington, D.C.

27. "Congo Mission: Modern Missionaries Combine Faith with Medicine and Education," *Life*, 2 June 1947, fiche 003.086-4, Schomburg Clipping File; *Fiftieth Anniversary of our Bahama Missions. Under the Patronage of Mary Immaculate 1889–1939* (Mount St. Vincent-on-Hudson, N.Y.: Mother House of the Sisters of

Charity, n.d. [1939]), folder 4, box 3, Sisters of Charity Archives, Mount St. Vincent College, Bronx, N.Y.

28. Horace H. Underwood, *Modern Education in Korea* (New York: International Press, 1926), 237; E. Grace Bullard to Miss McVeigh, 1 July 1927, "South India: Kavali station and Middle School" folder, BIMSF; Christina Jones, *The Untempered Wind: Forty Years in Palestine* (London: Longman, 1975), 138.

29. Freer, *The Philippine Experiences*, 152, 279; Geronima T. Pecson and Maria Racelis, *Tales of the American Teachers in the Philippines* (Manila: Carmelo and Bauermann, 1959), 124.

30. See, for example, Elsie Weeks to Irene Sheppard, 6 January 1930, folder 11, box 5, Board of Foreign Missions—Chile Mission Papers, Record Group 160; James W. Willoughby, "The United Mission in Iraq, 1924–1962. A Brief Historical Survey (ms, 20 September 1962), p. 18, folder 27, box 2, United Mission in Iraq Papers, Record Group 89, both at Presbyterian Historical Society; Mansur Dabiri Shamlu, "Where is the Source of Evils? A Glimpse of our Present Education," *Kanun*, 16 November 1941, enclosed with Wallace Murray to J. L. Dodds, 31 January 1942, folder 19, box 22, BFM-Iran.

31. James H. Nicol to Lois C. Wilson, 4 June 1929; Wilson to Nicol, 6 June 1929, both in folder 17, box 17; Frances Irwin to Nicol, 2 March 1927; Ottora M. Horne to Nicol, 10 June 1929, both in folder 2, box 3; Margaret Doolittle to S. M. Jessup, 10 May 1926, folder 7, box 19, all in Syria Mission Archives [hereafter "SMA"], Record Group 115, Presbyterian Historical Society.

32. See, for example, E. M. Wright, "Resht Boys' School Annual Report. 1931–1932" (ms, 1932), folder 3, box 20, BFM-Iran; Lardizabal, *Pioneer American Teachers*, 103.

33. *Report of the Philippine Commission to the Secretary of War*, pt. 2 (Washington, D.C.: Government Printing Office, 1901), 540; Louis H. Lisk to Director of Education, 27 September 1913, p. 329, "Bureau of Education Activities 1914. Early Experiences of American Teachers" binder, box 6, Marquardt Papers; T. H. Gibson to Sarah Cliffe, 20 October 1913, folder 14, box 62, RDE-HA.

34. See, for example, Henrietta J. Inglis, "Mary Wanamaker High School, Katra, Allahabad, U.P. India" (ms, June 1935), folder 3, box 33, BFM-India; Willard E. Givens, "Department of Public Instruction," *Hawaii Educational Review* 12 (October 1923): 26.

35. Frank L. Crone to H. S. Martin, 11 March 1916, pp. 490–491, "Inspection Reports" binder, box 6, Marquardt Papers; *Report of the Commissioner of Education for Porto Rico to the Secretary of the Interior, USA* (1902), 57–58; Bertha B. Taylor to W. T. Pope, 9 December 1911, folder 6, box 73, RDE-HA; H. J. Benedict to Director of Education, 15 March 1928, folder 46–1927–8, Virgin Islands Records, Record Group 55, National Archives II. On corporal-punishment regulations in the urban United States, see Butchart, "Punishments, Penalties, Prizes, and Procedures," 21; Rousmaniere, *City Teachers*, 122–123.

36. "Seeks Teachers for the Philippines," clipping, n.t., 15 March 1917, file 3725A, box 512, Bureau of Insular Affairs Records, Record Group 350, National Archives II.

37. Eileen H. Tamura, *Americanization, Acculturation, and Ethnic Identity: The Nisei Generation in Hawaii* (Urbana: University of Illinois Press, 1994), 94; Mary Cole to "Dear Folks at Home," 9 February 1902, "January–March 1902" folder,

box 1, Cole Papers; Aida Negron de Montilla, *Americanization in Puerto Rico and the Public School System, 1900–1930* (Rio Piedras: Editorial Edil, 1971), 84.

38. James H. Brayton to W. T. Pope, 27 January 1912; T. H. Gibson to Brayton, 6 February 1912; Brayton to Gibson, 10 February 1912; Brayton to Department of Public Instruction, 12 June 1912, all in folder 20, box 60; Lillian Mesick to Willis T. Pope, 10 November 1911, folder 6, box 73, all in RDE-HA. Several years later, ironically, Bertha Taylor would charge James Brayton—the former Honokaa principal—with abusing his own students. Brayton replied that he never hit misbehaving children; he instead made them put their heads on their chairs, with their legs bent over the back of the seat. "I humiliate the children instead of [physically] punishing them," Brayton declared, drawing a sharp distinction between beatings and other types of corporal discipline. He also claimed that the charges against him were racially motivated. "The Hawaiians . . . expected an Hawaiian principal here this year," Brayton wrote, "and have shown their resentment against me and the teaching force of 'whites' here, ever since our arrival." Brayton to Bertha B. Taylor, 10 January 1915, folder 10, box 73, RDE-HA.

39. Ruth Parker to "Dear Home Folks," 27 August 1925, folder 2, box 1, Parker Family Papers, Record Group 278, Presbyterian Historical Society; E. Marie Holmes, *Sowing Seed in Assam: Missionary Life and Labours in Northeast India* (New York: Fleming H. Revell, 1925), 85; Sister Marie Dolores Van Rensselaer, "The Children of Providence," *Children of Providence* 1 (December 1894), p. 5, bound volume, box 3, Sisters of Charity Archives. For other examples of parents demanding corporal punishment for their children, see Henry C. Brown to Willis T. Pope, 6 December 1912, folder 2, box 61, RDE-HA; Townsend, "Hawaii in the 'Nineties,' " 77.

40. Muriel Murray Nichols to "Dear Mother," 21 August 1923; illustration by Albert Nichols, n.d., enclosed with Muriel Murray Nichols to "Dear Mother," 13 July 1923, both in folder 7, box 1, Albert Sylvanus Nichols Papers, Billy Graham Center Archives, Wheaton College, Wheaton, Ill.

41. *An Encouraging Letter from the McDowells to the Friends at Home* (n.p., n.d. [1924]), folder 3/5/3/2, "TC/Afr." box, Archives of Talladega College; Samuel B. Coles to Henry C. McDowell, "HCM/Ang.2/9/1" folder, box 2, Henry C. McDowell Papers, both in Savery Library, Talladega College, Talladega, Ala.; "Minutes of the Meeting of the Board of Trustees of the Booker Washington Agricultural and Industrial Institute of Liberia" (ms, 11 April 1945), p. 8, folder 7, box 325, Claude A. Barnett Papers, Chicago Historical Society, Chicago, Ill.

42. See, for example, Georges Anker, "Report of the Superintendent of Schools for the year 1937" (ms), folder 24, box 9, BFM-West Africa; Mary Cole to "Dear Folks at Home," 9 February 1902, "January-March 1902" folder, box 1, Cole Papers.

43. Interview with Hubert V. Everly by Michiko Kodama-Nishimoto and Warren Nishimoto, 19 April 1991, *Public Education in Hawaii: Oral Histories* 1 (Honolulu: Center for Oral History, Social Science Research Institute, University of Hawaii at Manoa, September 1991): 279; Townsend, "Hawaii in the 'Nineties,' " 77–78; diary entry, 16 April 1903, "1902. Honolulu High School" diary, folder 6, box 14, Frank and Helen Chisholm Papers, Special Collections, Emory University, Atlanta, Ga.

44. George Packer, *The Village of Waiting* (New York: Random House, 1984), 57–58, 68, 52.

45. Adams, *The Peace Corps in Action*, 142; "Teaching in West Africa: Volunteers Sum up Progress, Problems," *The Volunteer* 1 (September 1962): 9.

46. F. L. White, "Annual Report of Gerard Institute 1954–1955" (ms), p. 4, folder 15, box 17; M. Claire Bailey, "American School for Girls. 1946–1947" (ms), pp. 1–2, folder 1, box 3, both in SMA; Theodore A. Braun, "Report on Trip to Africa, April 5–May 17, 1964" (ms, 18 June 1964), pp. 4–5, "TEA" folder, box 192, R. Freeman Butts Papers, Hoover Institution Archives, Stanford University, Palo Alto, Calif.

47. Murphy and Cromwell, "Close of Service Conference. Nigeria VII. Ibandan," 3; Louisa Beck to "Dear People Who Made it Possible for Me to Be Here," 20 September 1970, folder 5c, box 1, Records of the Philadelphia Yearly Meeting—Japan Committee [hereafter "YM-Japan"], Quaker Collection, Haverford College, Haverford, Penn.; Packer, *Village of Waiting*, 68; Sister Constance Mary to ?, Palm Sunday 1956, folder 1, box 6, Sisters of Charity Archives; Garrison Keillor, *Lake Wobegon Days* (New York: Viking, 1985).

48. R. Freeman Butts, "Confidential Notes by R. Freeman Butts," p. 2, "First impressions of TEAers in Africa" folder, box 193, Butts Papers; Arnold Zeiltin, *To the Peace Corps, With Love* (Garden City, N.Y.: Doubleday, 1965), 104; diary entry, 23 May 1963, microfilm reel 1, George Lewerenz Papers, Wisconsin Historical Society, Madison, Wis.; Sister Mary Rose Kohn to "Dear Family, Relatives, and Sisters," Feast of All Saints, 1985, "Madagascar. Correspondence, Newsclips, etc." folder, collection 12–10–8/12, Daughters of Charity of the Northeast Province Archives, Albany, N.Y.

49. See, for example, "Volunteer Teachers for Africa. 1960 to 1970" (ms, n.d. [1970]), pp. 3, 6, folder 18, box 17, NCC-DOM; Milton Carr and Harry Freeman, "COS Conference Ivory Coast IV" (ms, 27 April 1966), p. 5, appendix, "Ivory Coast" folder, box 8, PC-COS.

50. Composition notebook, 20 May 1970 and 23 June 1970, Linda J. Muller Papers, Collection No. 3, Peace Corps Volunteers Collection, National Anthropology Archives [hereafter "PC-NAA"], Museum Support Center, Smithsonian Institution, Suitland, Md.; "For Eastern Europe, U.S. Teachers," *New York Times*, 4 July 1990, p. 60; Omar Eby, *How Full the River* (Scottsdale, Pa.: Herald Press, 1972), 60.

51. Eby, *How Full the River*, 61; *Peace Corps—Information and Commentary, Volunteer Teaching Series* (n.p., n.d. [1969]), p. 3, "Peace Corps—Teaching" file, Vertical Files, Peace Corps Library, Washington, D.C.; Linda Bergthold, "View from the Classroom," *Peace Corps Volunteer* 1 (March 1963): 18; Raymond L. Gold, *A Teaching Safari: A Study of American Teachers in East Africa* (Baltimore: Publish America, 2004), 160.

52. Braun, "Report on a Trip to Africa," 4–5; Gold, *A Teaching Safari*, 191; Karl W. Bigelow to "CLG & Co.," 24 April 1963, "TEA" folder, box 192, Butts Papers; Bela C. Baker, "COS Conference. Nepal IV" (ms, 22 August 1966), p. 5, "Nepal IV" folder, box 8, PC-COS.

53. See, for example, "The Upper Primary School in Tanzania" (ms, n.d. [1970]), p. 22, "Tanzania—Education" file, Vertical Files, Peace Corps Library; John Rex, "Why Stay? A Point of View" (ms, 12 March 1964), "Ethiopia—Volunteer Information" folder, Collection No. 31, PC-NAA.

54. See, for example, Richard Lipez, "Culture and the Classroom," in *The Evaluation Reader: Selections from Evaluation Reports Published 1961–66 Describing and*

Attempting to Illuminate the Main Problems of the Peace Corps, ed. Ann Anderson (Washington, D.C.: Peace Corps Office of Evaluation and Research, 1967), 93.

55. Ruth Irwin to Beth Irwin, 17 October 1950, folder 1, box 3, Irwin Family Papers, Record Group 205, Presbyterian Historical Society.

56. "Upper Primary School in Tanzania," 22; Dick Lipez, "To friends I'll see soon" (ms, 24 April 1964), "Ethiopia—Volunteer Information" folder, Collection No. 31, PC-NAA.

57. William M. Baxter, "COS Conference. Nigeria XIV. Secondary Education" (ms, 23 February 1967), pp. 8–9, 18, "Nigeria XIV" folder, box 9, PC-COS.

58. Harry Freeman, "COS Conference. Turkey VIII. Parts I, II, V" (ms, 2 October 1967), p. 4, "Turkey VIII" folder, box 15, PC-COS; Phil Deutschle, *The Two Year Mountain: A Nepal Journey* (Chalfont St. Peter, U.K.: Brandt Publications, 1986), 83; Judy Cowan Chaimson, untitled reminiscence in *The TEA Experience*, ed. Judith Lindfors (n.p., 2002, in possession of Brooks Goddard, Needham, Mass.); Roz Wollmering, "My Side vs. Their Side," in *Peace Corps: The Great Adventure* (Washington, D.C.: Peace Corps, 1997), 76.

59. Gold, *A Teaching Safari*, 220. For examples of teachers who refused to compromise with local methods, see Gold, *A Teaching Safari*, 148; Judith Bloch, *Diary of a Peace Corps Volunteer* (n.p.: Miracle Printers, 1985), 4; Packer, *Village of Waiting*, 54; Gary May, "Passing the Torch and Lighting Fires: The Peace Corps," in *Kennedy's Quest for Victory: American Foreign Policy, 1961–1963*, ed. Thomas G. Paterson (New York: Oxford University Press, 1989), 299–300.

60. Paul Cromwell, "COS Conference. Nigeria VII" (ms, 9 January 1966), "Nigeria VII" folder, box 5, PC-COS.

61. See, for example, Freeman, "COS Conference. Turkey VIII. Parts I, II, V," 3; Randall Barton to "Dear All," n.d. [1974], pp. 13–14, Randall Barton Papers, Collection No. 25, PC-NAA.

62. Cynthia Courtney et al., "COS Service Conference. Nigeria VII. Nsukka, Eastern Region. April 25–27, 1965" (ms), p. 2, "Nigeria VII" folder, box 5, PC-COS; Murphy and Cromwell, "COS Service Conference. Nigeria VII," 3; Barry Ulanov, "Missionary Educators," in *Beyond All Horizons: Jesuits and the Missions*, ed. Thomas J. M. Burke, S.J. (Garden City, N.Y.: Hanover House, 1957), 212.

63. Beulah Barrett and Blythe Monroe to ?, n.d. [March 1963], "Ethiopia—Volunteer Information" folder, Collection No. 31, PC-NAA.

64. Gold, *A Teaching Safari*, 139, 163–64; Kathryn Taylor to Sarah Swan, 10 April 1970, folder 4A, box 24, YM-Japan.

65. Lawrence W. Howard, "Chapter Two: The Launching of the Peace Corps" (ms, n.d. [1964]), p. 57, folder 1, box 35, James H. Robinson Papers, Amistad Research Center, Tulane University, New Orleans, La.

66. "My Failure—the First Year. By a PC English Teacher," *Peace Corps–Ethiopia News*, n.d. [1963], p. 6, "Ethiopia—Volunteer Information" folder, Collection No. 31, PC-NAA.

67. Carol A. Trachtenberg, "Alumni Profile Questionnaire" (ms, n.d. [1976?]), "Peace Corps—Volunteer Questionnaire and Alumni Profile Questionnaire" folder, box 30, International Center on Deafness Collection, Gallaudet University Archives, Washington, D.C.; Kathryn Taylor to "Dear Friends," 9 December 1968, folder 4A, box 23, YM-Japan; "Syllabuses and Ghosts," *Peace Corps Volunteer* 1 (April 1963): 13; "Personal Report of Margaret S. C. Thomson" (ms, June 1958),

folder 21, box 5, Korea Mission Papers, Presbyterian Church of the USA, Record Group 197, Presbyterian Historical Society.

68. James and Marie Kenney, "Progress Report of Volunteer Activities" (ms, 1 June 1968), p. 3; application by Warren Perkins (ms, n.d. [1969]), both in folder 19, box 17, NCC-DOM; Agnes Miyo Moriuchi to Sarah Swan, 24 January 1971; Moriuchi to Swan, 2 June 1971, both in folder 2B, box 16, YM-Japan.

69. Jane Rittenhouse to Agnes Moriuchi, 28 February 1971, folder 2B, box 16, YM-Japan; "History of the Work of the Maryknoll Sisters at Holy Rosary School, Likiep, Marshall Islands" (ms, 1958), Finding Aid 11, Maryknoll Fathers and Brothers Archives; Marjorie Pfankuch to family, 29 April 1962, microfilm reel 1, Marjorie Pfankuch Papers, Wisconsin Historical Society.

70. Kathryn Taylor to Sarah Swan, 24 May 1970, folder 2-A, box 23, YM-Japan; Lipez, "Culture and the Classroom," 101, 98–99.

71. Bill Shurtleff, *Peace Corps Year with Nigerians*, ed. Hans Brinkmann (Frankfurt: Verlag Moritz Diesterweg, 1966), 25; Adams, *Peace Corps in Action*, 82; Martin Ford, "Stepping into the Same River Twice," in *Anthropology and the Peace Corps: Case Studies in Career Preparation*, eds. Brian E. Schwimmer and D. Michael Warren (Ames: Iowa State University Press, 1993), 213; Paul Gesell, untitled report from Teacher Training School (ms, December 1963), pp. 2–3, "Ethiopia—Volunteer Information" folder, Collection No. 31, PC-NAA; Sister Martha Murphy, "Mission News Service" (ms, May 1968), folder 9, box 1, Mexico Collection, Maryknoll Fathers and Brothers Archives; Mark Harris, *Twentyone Twice: A Journal* (Boston: Little, Brown, 1966), 218–219.

72. Zeitlin, *To the Peace Corps, with Love*, 108; Packer, *Village of Waiting*, 57, 60.

73. Randall Barton to "Dear All," 17 September 1972, Barton Papers.

74. Dennis F. Shaw, "A Puppeteer Gives Teaching Tips," *Peace Corps Volunteer* 5 (November 1966): 21; Deutschle, *Two Year Mountain*, 68, 167–168; David Pearson, "The Peace Corps Volunteer Returns," *SR*, 17 October 1964, fiche 005.462–1, Schomburg Clipping File.

75. Warren Graham Fuller to Cynthia A. Courtney, 11 February 1966, "Liberia I" folder, box 8, PC-COS; Murphy and Cromwell, "Close of Service Conference. Nigeria VII," 4; Hugh Davis Graham, "COS Conference. Turkey IV" (ms, 21 April 1966), p. 7, "Turkey IV" folder, box 10, PC-COS.

76. Wollmering, "My Side vs. Their Side," 89, 96.

77. Earle and Dorothy Bowen, "Contextualizing Teaching Methods in Africa," *Evangelical Missions Quarterly* 25 (July 1989): 270–275; Ray Badgero, "Teaching Tips and Tools," ibid. 22 (April 1986): 187–189; Kevin Lawson, "Educating Youth in South America," ibid. 32 (January 1996): 35, 41.

78. Gene Child, "Reactions to Raymond Gold's *A Teaching Safari: A Study of American Teachers in East Africa*," *Teachers for East Africa Alumni Newsletter*, No. 10 (July 2004): 18.

2. The American Curriculum

1. Theodore Roosevelt, *African Game Trails: An Account of the African Wanderings of an American Hunter-Naturalist* (New York: Syndicate Publishing House, 1909), 174; "Address of Colonel Roosevelt Made at the Laying of Corner Stone of School Building, Kijabe, B. E. Africa. August 4, 1909" (ms), 2; "Roosevelt Snap

Shots" (ms, 1909); "Address of Colonel Roosevelt, Kijabe, B. E. A., June 4, 1909" (ms), 2–3, all in folder 32, box 15, Africa Inland Mission Papers, Billy Graham Center Archives, Wheaton College, Wheaton, Ill.

2. David Hapgood, "The Case Against TEFL," *Peace Corps Volunteer* 5 (January 1967): 2–3.

3. Quoted in Edward A. Krug, *The Shaping of the American High School, 1880–1920* (Madison: University of Wisconsin Press, 1969), 225.

4. For varied accounts of this trend, see David L. Angus and Jeffrey E. Mirel, *The Failed Promise of the American High School, 1890–1995* (New York: Teachers College Press, 1995); Herbert M. Kliebard, *The Struggle for the American Curriculum, 1893–1958*, 3rd ed. (New York: Routledge Falmer, 2004); Arthur G. Powell, Eleanor Farrar, and David K. Cohen, *The Shopping Mall High School: Winners and Losers in the Educational Marketplace* (Boston: Houghton Mifflin, 1985); Diane Ravitch, *Left Back: A Century of Failed School Reforms* (New York: Simon and Schuster, 2000), esp. chaps. 5, 7, 9.

5. W. Norton Grubb and Marvin Lazerson, *The Education Gospel: The Economic Power of Schooling* (Cambridge, Mass.: Harvard University Press, 2004); Herbert M. Kliebard, *Schooled to Work: Vocationalism and the American Curriculum 1876–1946* (New York: Teachers College Press, 1999).

6. "Roosevelt Snap Shots"; "Address of Colonel Roosevelt, Kijabe, B. E. A.," 2; Hapgood, "The Case against TEFL," 3.

7. Richard H. Beaupre, "Iran," *Peace Corps Volunteer* 5 (April 1967): 18–19; Stephen D. Krasner, "A smug Peace Corps," ibid. 5 (March 1967): 24; Roger Kuhn, "Washington," ibid. 5 (April 1967): 19.

8. John L. Rury, *Education and Social Change: Themes in the History of American Schooling* (Mahwah, N.J.: Lawrence Erlbaum, 2002), 210–216.

9. John D. DeHuff, "The Trend of Educational Thought," *The Philippine Craftsman* 1 (November 1912): 428–431; Walter W. Marquardt, "The Philippine Schools" (ms, 1922), p. 145, "Scrap book. Talks and Papers. 1922–30," box 6, Walter W. Marquardt Papers, Bentley Historical Library, Ann Arbor, Mich.

10. Kliebard, *Schooled to Work*, 150; Angus and Mirel, *Failed Promise*, 53.

11. "Speech of Dr. Lindsay, Commissioner of Education, at the dedication of the Roosevelt Industrial School in Ponce, February 22nd 1904" (ms), "General File: Puerto-Rico—Photographs and Artwork by Puerto Rican Students, Scrapbooks" folder, box 192, Samuel McCune Lindsay Papers, Manuscript Division, Columbia University Libraries, New York; Jose-Manuel Navarro, *Creating Tropical Yankees: Social Science Textbooks and United States Ideological Control in Puerto Rico, 1898–1908* (New York: Routledge, 2002), 87; Frank E. Midkiff, "The Cooperative Plan of Education as Employed at Kamehameha Schools," *Hawaii Educational Review* 16 (June 1928): 267–269; Emanuel Hurwitz, Julius Menacker, and Ward Weldon, *Educational Imperialism: American School Policy and The U.S. Virgin Islands* (Lanham, Md.: University Press of America, 1987), 56; George H. Ivins to Paul M. Pearson, 9 May 1932, file 46–1931–32, box 19, Virgin Islands Records, Record Group 55, National Archives II, College Park, Md.

12. Leon D. Pamphile, "America's Policy-Making in Haitian Education, 1915–1934," *Journal of Negro Education* 54 (1985): 102, 104; Emily Balch, *Occupied Haiti* (New York: Garland, 1972 [1927]), 93–94; Rayford Logan, "Education in Haiti," *Journal of Negro History* 15 (October 1930): 443, 447; Arthur Lindborg to Waldo Evans, 31 July 1928, file 46–1928–29, box 18, Virgin Islands Records.

13. Sushil Madhava Pathak, *American Missionaries and Hinduism: A Study of Their Contacts from 1813 to 1910* (Delhi: Munshiram Manoharlal, 1967), 166; M. C. Lehman, "Experiments in Rural Education at Dhamatari, C.P.," in *Fourteen Experiments in Rural Education*, ed. Alice B. Van Doren (Calcutta: Association Press, 1928), 38; T. H. P. Sailer, "Proposed Draft for Discussion" (ms, n.d. [1916]), pp. 6–7, enclosed with Sailer to E. D. Burton, 11 November 1916, folder 1, box 44, Ernest DeWitt Burton Papers, Joseph Regenstein Memorial Library, University of Chicago; George A. Ford, *Industrial Work in the Syria Mission* (n.p., 1904), p. 1, folder 13, box 17, Syria Mission Archives [hereafter "SMA"], Record Group 115, Presbyterian Historical Society.

14. Jay O. Warner, "Teaching Citizenship to Boys of Fifteen Nationalities," *Survey* 32 (16 May 1914): 197; John Henry House to James E. Gregg, 30 December 1925, "1922–1929" folder, box 50; *The Thessalonica Agricultural and Industrial Institute for the Christian Industrial Training of Macedonian Boys, Annual Report, 1907* (Salonica, Turkey: n.p., 1908), p. 11, "Annual Reports" folder, box 49, both in Hampton Collection, Hampton University Archives, Hampton, Va.; James H. Franklin, "The Jaro Industrial School Republic" (ms, n.d. [1917]), p. 3, "Philippines: Jaro Industrial School 1914–1917" folder, Board of International Missions Subject Files [hereafter "BIMSF"], American Baptist Archives Center, Valley Forge, Penn.

15. On this point, see Kenneth James King, *Pan-Africanism and Education* (Oxford: Clarendon Press, 1971), 17–18; George M. Fredrickson, *Black Liberation: A Comparative History of Black Ideologies in the United States and South Africa* (New York: Oxford University Press, 1995), 119–120.

16. Seymour E. Moon, "Rural Education for Congo," *Congo Mission News* No. 106 (April 1939), p. 18, folder 11, box 13, National Council of Churches Papers, Division of Overseas Ministries [hereafter "NCC-DOM"], Record Group 8, Presbyterian Historical Society.

17. "The Booker T. Washington Industrial and Agricultural Institute of Liberia. Plans for the Development of a Tuskegee-in-Africa" (ms, n.d. [1929]), p. 1, folder 1, box 114, Phelps-Stokes Collection, Schomburg Center for Research in Black Culture, New York Public Libraries; "An Army of Educators Saves a Liberian College," *New York Times*, 1 September 2003, p. A4; Fred G. Leasure to Thomas Jesse Jones, 18 January 1934, folder 6, box 119, Phelps-Stokes Collection; Pearl L. Byrd to Arthur Howe, 4 August 1933, "Virgin Islands—1933" folder, box 38, Arthur Howe Papers, Hampton University Archives; Paul M. Pearson to George H. Ivins, 17 May 1932, file 46–1931–32, box 19, Virgin Islands Records; diary entry, 20 March 1902, "1902. Honolulu HS" diary, folder 6, box 14; "Hawaii's Young Ones. Hartford Woman's Work in Sandwich Islands," *Hartford Courant*, January ? 1903, folder 6, box 22, both in Frank P. and Helen Chisholm Papers, Special Collections, Emory University, Atlanta, Ga.

18. Alice F. Beard to Helen James, 26 May 1903, folder 6, box 2, Chisholm Papers; "The Training of Teachers," *Southern Workman* 29 (July 1900): 390; Mary Bonzo Suzuki, "American Education in the Philippines, the Early Years: American Pioneer Teachers and the Filipino Response, 1900–1935" (Ph.D. diss., University of California-Berkeley, 1991), 83; Paul M. Pearson to George Foster Peabody, 11 July 1932, "Virgin Islands—1932" folder, box 38, Howe Papers; George Scott to William H. Scoville, 6 April 1914; Scott to Scoville, 14 April 1914; Scott to H. B. Frissell and H. B Turner, 7 September 1916; Scott to Frissell, 31 March 1916;

George T. Scott, "Education For Life" (ms, 1918), all in folder 14, box 4, Board of Foreign Missions Secretaries' Files, Presbyterian Church of the USA [hereafter "BFM-PCUSA"], Record Group 81, Presbyterian Historical Society.

19. On this point, see esp. Kliebard, *Schooled to Work*, 21; James D. Anderson, "The Historical Development of Black Vocational Education," in *Work, Youth, and Schooling*, eds. Harvey A. Kantor and David B. Tyack (Stanford, Calif.: Stanford University Press, 1982), 186–187; Jane Bernard Powers, *The 'Girl Question' in Education: Vocational Education for Young Women in the Progressive Era* (London: Falmer, 1992), 87–89.

20. Sarah A. Cliffe, "Convention at Kapaa, Kauai, January 1915" (ms), folder 14, box 62, Records of the Department of Education, Series 261 [hereafter "RDE-HA"], Hawaii State Archives, Honolulu, Hawaii; J. H. Franklin to A. H. Halsey, 6 October 1919, folder 11, box 1, Board of Foreign Missions—West Africa Mission [hereafter "BFM-West Africa"], Record Group 142, Presbyterian Historical Society; L. B. Hughes to Members of the Burma Reference Committee, 17 January 1918, "Burma—Scheme for Tenasserim School" folder, BIMSF; Abby R. Jacobs, *Overalls in Silliman* (New York: Board of Foreign Missions of the Presbyterian Church, 1938), p. 10, folder 39, box 1, Arthur Leroy Carson Papers [hereafter "Carson-PHS"], Record Group 59, Presbyterian Historical Society; Ford, *Industrial Work in the Syria Mission*, 2; Arthur Judson Brown, "Industrial Training in Asia," *Southern Workman* 32 (August 1903): 376.

21. Jo Anne Barker Maniago, "The First Peace Corps: The Work of the American Teachers in the Philippines, 1900–1910" (Ph.D. diss., Boston University, 1971), 147; Marquardt, "The Philippine Schools," 149; Walter Robb, "Philippine Schools Assailed in Survey," *Daily News* [Chicago], 5 May 1925, file 3725A, box 512, Bureau of Insular Affairs Records [hereafter "BIA"], Record Group 350, National Archives II.

22. "House of Delegates Asks Superintendent Ayres' Dismissal," *San Juan Times*, 25 January 1908, folder 1908-A, box 18, Smiley Family Papers, Quaker Collections, Haverford College Library, Haverford, Penn.; Leonard P. Ayres to E. G. Dexter, 6 February 1908, "October 1902 July 1925" folder, box 2; "Free Speech Muzzled," *Boston Herald*, 9 February 1908, "Clippings 1907–46" folder, box 22, both in Leonard P. Ayres Papers, Library of Congress, Washington, D.C.; Leonard P. Ayres, *Laggards in Our Schools* (New York: Russell Sage, 1909), 7, 218.

23. Pamphile, "America's Policy-Making in Haitian Education," 107; Logan, "Education in Haiti," 447; Fr. Hippolyte, "Memorandum" (ms, 4 April 1928), folder 17, box 98, National Catholic Welfare Council/United States Catholic Conference Papers, American Catholic Historical Research Center, Catholic University, Washington, D.C.; "Report of the Educational Survey of Haiti," *School and Society*, 6 December 1930, fiche 001.546–1, Schomburg Clipping File, Schomburg Center; Balch, *Occupied Haiti*, 104.

24. James D. Anderson, *The Education of Blacks in the South, 1860–1935* (Chapel Hill: University of North Carolina Press, 1988), 104–105; Kliebard, *Schooled to Work*, 17–20. For a recent defense of Washington's educational program, see Wilson Jeremiah Moses, *Afrotopia: The Roots of African American Popular History* (Cambridge: Cambridge University Press, 1998), chap. 6, esp. pp. 181–183.

25. Diary entry, 12 February 1902, "1902. Honolulu High School" diary, folder 6, box 14, Chisholm Papers; Anderson, *Education of Blacks in the South*, 105; F. H.

Clowes to Vaughan MacCaughey, 21 January 1920, folder 15, box 62, RDE-HA; Eileen H. Tamura, *Americanization, Acculturation, and Ethnic Identity: The Nisei Generation in Hawaii* (Urbana: University of Illinois Press, 1994), 144.

26. Victor M. Buck, "Report of the Agricultural Institute 1926–1927" (ms), p. 2, folder 22; The Faculty of the Normal School, "Report of the Normal School for 1931" (ms), pp. 1–2, folder 23, both in box 9, BFM-West Africa; Fred G. Leasure, "My Personal Reactions on the Local Liberian Problem" (ms, rec. 24 May 1933), folder 6, box 119; Paul W. Rupel to Thomas Jesse Jones, 4 January 1937; Rupel to Anson Phelps Stokes, 11 January 1939, both in folder 1, box 120, all in Phelps-Stokes Collection.

27. James E. Fisher, *Democracy and Mission Education in Korea* (New York: Teachers College, 1928), 109; Frank W. Padelford, *Report on Christian Education in Burma* (n.p., 1932), p. 15, "Burma—Education—1930–39" folder, BIMSF; Manning Marable, "Ambiguous Legacy: Tuskegee's 'Missionary' Impulse and Africa during the Moton Administration," in *Black Americans and the Missionary Movement in Africa*, ed. Sylvia Jacobs (Westport, Conn.: Greenwood Press, 1982), 85; E. L. Hendricks to Cleland B. McAfee, 12 December 1932, folder 18, box 16, BFM-PCUSA.

28. Moses D. Flint, "My Experiences as a Teacher in the Philippines from 1900 to 1903," pp. 284–285, "Bureau of Education. Activities 1914. Early Experiences of American Teachers" binder, box 6, Marquardt Papers; Eugene P. Lyle Jr., "Our Experience in Porto Rico," *The World's Work* (n.p. [1905]), "General File: Puerto Rico—1901–1912—Printed" folder, box 189, Lindsay Papers; Balch, *Occupied Haiti*, 103; Arthur E. Lindborg, *Education in the Virgin Islands* (Washington, D.C.: U.S. Department of Interior, Office of Education, Leaflet No. 42, 1932), 1; Candida Custodio, "Climate" (ms, n.d. [1905]), "Student Papers (4)" folder, box 1, Frederick G. Behner Papers, Bentley Historical Library; "Education in Porto Rico," *Outlook* 66 (1 September 1900): 6.

29. Irene Mason Harper, "The Training School for Village Teachers, Moga," in Van Doren, ed., *Fourteen Experiments*, 8; W. O. Valentine, "Notes on Mr. Rose's Letter in Reply to Mr. Mornay Williams," enclosed with Valentine to James W. Franklin, 15 February 1917, "Philippines: Jaro Industrial School 1904–1917" folder, BIMSF; Kliebard, *Schooled to Work*, 122–125; G. F. Cranswick, "Community Middle School, Chapra," in Van Doren, ed., *Fourteen Experiments*, 70; William J. McKee, *New Schools for Young India: A Survey of the Educational, Economic, and Social Conditions in India with Special Reference to More Effective Education* (Chapel Hill: University of North Carolina Press, 1930), x.

30. Charles A. Glunz to A. W. Halsey, 8 January 1904, folder 25, box 1, Carson-PHS; A. Victor Murray, *The School in the Bush: A Critical Study of the Theory and Practice of Native Education in Africa* (London: Frank Cass, 1967 [1929]), 309.

31. Joseph A. Reaves, *Taking in a Game: A History of Baseball in Asia* (Lincoln: University of Nebraska Press, 2002), 91, 97; Janice A. Beran, "Americans in the Philippines: Imperialism or Progress Through Sport?" *International Journal of the History of Sport* 6 (1989): 70–74; H. S. Mead to Director of Education (n.d. [1913]), p. 336, "Bureau of Education. Activities 1914. Early Experiences of American Teachers" binder, box 6, Marquardt Papers; David P. Barrows, "Education in the Philippines" (ms, 1912), p. 14, "Philippine Islands—Education" folder, carton 6, David Prescott Barrows Papers, Bancroft Library, University of California-Berkeley;

Arthur L. Carson, *Silliman University 1901–1959* (Taipei: United Board for Christian Higher Education in Asia, 1965), 56; Ethel Clark Lewis, "Baseball in the Orient" (ms, n.d. [1920?]), enclosed with Lewis to Arthur L. Carson, 15 June 1960, folder 27, box 1, Carson-PHS.

32. Lewis, "Baseball in the Orient"; Mary H. Fee, *A Woman's Impressions of the Philippines* (Chicago: A. C. McClurg, 1910), 284–285; Carson, *Silliman University*, 56; George W. Dunlap, "The Missionary and His Baseball in Cebu," *Assembly Herald* (n.d. [1915]), folder 39, box 1, Carson-PHS; Tirso Garcia, "Athletic and Play Movement in the Philippines Public Schools" (ms, n.d.), p. 33, "Special Articles" binder, box 5, Marquardt Papers; Edwin Schoenrich, "An Interscholastic Basketball League for Porto Rico," *Porto Rico School Review* 4 (May 1920): 40, 38.

33. Walter W. Marquardt, "Physical Training in the Philippine Schools" (ms, n.d. [1922?]), "Articles 19–22" binder, box 7, Marquardt Papers; Gael Graham), *Gender, Culture, and Christianity: American Protestant Mission Schools in China, 1880–1930* (New York: Peter Lang, 1995), 44; letter by William F. O'Shea, April 1920, in *Maryknoll Mission Letters*, vol. 1 (New York: Macmillan, 1923), 200–201; Benjamin O. Wist, "Pahala School Playground," *Hawaii Educational Review* 2 (May 1914): 5; E. W. Koons, "Annual Report of the John D. Wells School (Kyung Sin Hakyo). May 19, 1930" (ms), p. 7, folder 47, box 7, Board of Foreign Missions—Korea Mission Record Group 140, Presbyterian Historical Society; Marion A. Beebe, "Moulmein, Burma" (ms, 11 January 1930), "Taunggyi Huldah Mix Girls School" folder, BIMSF.

34. Clifford Putney, *Muscular Christianity: Manhood and Sports in Protestant America, 1880–1920* (Cambridge, Mass.: Harvard University Press, 2003), 131; Garcia, "Athletic and Play Movement," 28–29; Amparo Santamaria Lardizabal, *Pioneer American Teachers and Philippine Education* (Quezon City: Phoenix Press, 1991), 92; Andrew W. Cain, "What do You Think of the Philippine Public School System?" *School and Home* 12 (November 1920), "Articles 19–22" binder, box 7, Marquardt Papers; Graham, *Gender, Culture, and Christianity*, 45; letter by Francis Ford, June 1922, in *Maryknoll Mission Letters*, vol. 2 (New York: Macmillan, 1927), 129; Florence H. Does, "After Two Years" (ms, 28 March 1919), p. 2, "Assam: Nowgong Girls Schools 1918 to 1945" folder, BIMSF; Catherine Ackerman, "Report of Girls' Hearthstone January-June 1934" (ms), folder 5, box 2, United Mission in Iraq Collection, Record Group 89, Presbyterian Historical Society.

35. Graham, *Gender, Culture, and Christianity*, 46; James Dale Van Buskirk, *Korea: Land of the Dawn* (New York: Missionary Education Movement of the United States and Canada, 1931), 119; Reaves, *Taking in a Game*, 93; Beran, "Americans in the Philippines," 71; "Spanish View of Education in the Philippines" *Literary Digest* 24 November 1923, file 3725A, box 512, BIA; Celia Bocobo-Olivar, *History of Physical Education in the Philippines* (Quezon City: University of the Philippines Press, 1972), 50.

36. Belle Sherwood Hawkes to "My dear little sister," 9 February 1893, Sarah Hawkes Papers, Record Group 116, Presbyterian Historical Society; Cora Bartlett, "Report of Iran Bethel" (ms, 1894), p. 6, folder 12, box 20, Board of Foreign Missions—Iran Mission [hereafter "BFM-Iran"], Record Group 91, Presbyterian Historical Society; Retta C. Macmillan, "Personal Report for 1923" (ms), folder 10, box 15, Board of Foreign Missions—Colombia Mission, Record Group 88, Presbyterian Historical Society; Esther Rhoads to Margaret Rhoads, n.d. [1918], "Letters

from Rhoads. May–December 1918" folder, box 13, Esther B. Rhoads Papers, Quaker Collection, Haverford College Library; Ruth Parker to Arthur J. Brown, 14 November 1929, folder 3, box 1, Parker Family Papers, Record Group 278, Presbyterian Historical Society; Harry Cole to "My dear Mother and Leon," 16 March 1902, "January–March 1902" folder, box 1, Harry N. Cole Papers, Bentley Historical Library.

37. Marius John, *Philippine Saga* (New York: House of Field, n.d. [1941]), 166–167; Helen P. Beattie, "American Teachers and the Filipinos," *Outlook* 78 (15 October 1904): 423; Herbert Priestley to "Dearest Mommy," 8 April 1902, "Transcriptions of Letters, April 1902" folder, Herbert I. Priestley Papers, Bancroft Library; n.a. (Walter M. Marquardt), "Teachers I Have Known" (ms, n.d.), p. 38, "Talks and Papers. 1922–1930" binder, box 6, Marquardt Papers; Philinda Rand to "My dear auntie," 14 September 1902, "Anglemyer, P.R. 1902" folder, box 1, Philinda Rand Anglemyer Papers, Arthur and Elizabeth Schlesinger Library, Radcliffe College, Cambridge, Mass.; Benigno Glodevisa Hinolan, "Cholera Not Poison," *Jaro Echo* 1 (September 1916): 1, "Philippines: Jaro Industrial School. 1910–1989" folder, BIMSF; Lewis S. Thomas to Director of Education, 2 August 1913, p. 347, "Bureau of Education. Activities 1914. Early Experiences of American Teachers" binder, box 6, Marquardt Papers.

38. H. S. Mead to Director of Education, n.d. [1913], p. 335, "Bureau of Education. Activities 1914. Early Experiences of American Teachers" binder, box 6, Marquardt Papers; Henry C. Brown to J. B. Pratt, 15 January 1912, folder 2, box 61, RDE-HA; letter by Anthony P. Hodgins, January 1921, *Maryknoll Mission Letters*, vol. 1, p. 351; Mary C. Johnson, "Girls' School Report. 1927–1928" (ms), p. 2, folder 10, box 20; "Personal Report of Annie Stocking Boyce. Teheran, Persia, July 1, 1927–June 30, 1928" (ms), p. 2, folder 12, box 18, both in BFM-Iran; Suellen Hoy, *Chasing Dirt: The American Pursuit of Cleanliness* (New York: Oxford University Press, 1995), 134–135; Sally Lucas Jean to Paul M. Pearson, 28 November 1932; Pearson to George H. Ivins, 8 December 1932, both in file 29–3, box 16, Virgin Islands Collection; Benjamin O. Wist, "Indigenous Culture and Some Implications for Education" (ms, 23 November 1948), p. 7, 10, "U.S. Trust Territories" folder, box 37, Benjamin Wist Papers, University Archives and Special Collections, University of Hawaii-Manoa, Honolulu, Hawaii.

39. Jonathan Zimmerman, *Distilling Democracy: Alcohol Education in America's Public Schools, 1880–1925* (Lawrence: University Press of Kansas, 1999), 131; Edmund B. Butterfield, "An Account of Lieutenant Gov. Mason Stone's Service in Organizing Schools in the Philippines," p. 21, Manuscript Miscellaneous File 160, Vermont History Center, Barre, Vt.; A. Edward Kelsey, "Turkish Officials Visit the Mission," *Ramallah Messenger* 1 (August 1904): 3; Paul Burgess et al. to Stanley White, 18 December 1916, folder 4, box 6, Board of Foreign Missions—Guatemala Mission, Record Group 157, Presbyterian Historical Society; Christina Jones, *The Untempered Wind: Forty Years in Palestine* (London: Longman, 1975), 11; L. W. Leavitt, "Report of Tripoli Boys School. 1926–1927" (ms, 1927), p. 1, folder 6, box 19, SMA; J. H. McLean to W. E. Browning, 1 September 1936, folder 23, box 4, Board of Foreign Missions—Chile Mission [hereafter "BFM-Chile"], Record Group 160, Presbyterian Historical Society; Edna Diffendorfer to "Dear Family," n.d. (April 1927), folder 1, box 1, Edna Diffendorfer Papers, Garrett-Evangelical Theological Seminary, Evanston, Ill.

40. Mary Cole to "Dear Folks at home," 28 August 1901, "August-September 1901" folder, box 1, Cole Papers; Walter M. Marquardt to Alice H. Marquardt, 13 June 1918, "Personal Letters. 1916–1918" binder, box 5, Marquardt Papers; Philinda Rand to ?, 21 September 1901, "Anglemyer, P.R. 1901" folder, box 1, Anglemyer Papers; George E. Carrothers, "Incidents in the Life of a Hoosier Schoolmaster: chap. IV. Philippines and Around the World" (ms, n.d. [1955?]), p. 15, folder 1, box 1, George Ezra Carrothers Papers, Bentley Historical Library; Edgar L. Morphet, "The Philippine Islands. Incidents" (ms, n.d. [1924]), p. 23, folder 3, box 3, Edgar L. Morphet Papers, Hoover Institution Archives, Stanford University, Palo Alto, Calif.; J. L. Hart to C. E. Maddry, 12 October 1933, fiche 9, Joseph Lancaster Hart Papers, International Mission Board Archives, Southern Baptist Convention, Richmond, Va.

41. Zimmerman, *Distilling Democracy*, 7–8; Clara B. Tingley, "Bassein, Burma" (ms, 12 January 1925), "Karens: Bassein—KoTha Boys High School" folder, BIMSF; Rosa E. Lee, "Day Schools," *Ramallah Messenger* 6 (March 1909): 4–5; Charlotte H. Brown, "Report of Sidon Girls School. July, 1924–July, 1925" (ms), p. 1, folder 18, box 17, SMA; Frank J. Bouick, "The Report of the Temperance Committee of the Chile Mission for the Year Ending September 1921" (ms), folder 11, box 1; Helen Isles Elmore, "In Pedro De Valdivia's Paradise (A Chronicle of Chile)" (ms, 1946), p. 8, folder 13, box 4, both in BFM-Chile.

42. See, for example, n.a. [Lois Wilson?] to "My dear friends," ? August 1929, folder 17, box 17, SMA; E. Grace Bullard to Miss McVeigh, 1 February 1928, "South India: Kavali Station and Middle School" folder, BIMSF.

43. Grace Strachan Roberts, "A School for Costa Rica," *Latin America Evangelist*, July-August 1955, frames 817–820; D. M. Howard to C. L. Berg, 19 March 1966, frames 759–60, both in microfilm reel 16, Latin American Mission Papers, Billy Graham Center Archives.

44. "History of the Work of the Maryknoll Sisters at Holy Rosary School, Likeip, Marshall Islands (ms, 1958), p. 1, Finding Aid 11, Maryknoll Fathers and Brothers Archives, Ossining, N.Y.; Hayden A. Duggan, "Final Report" (ms, n.d. [1968]), pp. 3–4, folder 19, box 17, NCC-DOM; Neil A. Boyer, "Ethiopia: Teaching and Much More," *Peace Corps Volunteer* 1 (March 1963): 14; "4,000 Peace Corps Opportunities in 44 Countries," *Peace Corps News* 2 (Spring 1963): 4; Arden Lampel, "Volunteers Around the World: The Peace Corps Is into Vocational Education," *American Vocational Journal* 47 (December 1972): 56–57; Roger L. Landrum, *The Role of the Peace Corps in Education of Developing Countries: A Sector Study* (Washington, D.C.: Peace Corps Information Collection and Exchange, Reprint Series R-49, 1984 [1981]), 33; "Educating for Development," *Peace Corps Times*, no vol. no. (July/August 1986): 13; Richard Bunce and Kenneth B. Platt, "Vocational Training as a Possible New Outreach Opportunity for Church and Mission in Iran" (ms, 1965), p. 7, folder 17, box 23, BFM-Iran.

45. Bunce and Platt, "Vocational Training," 2; James and Marie Kenney, "Progress Report of Volunteer Activities" (ms, 1 June 1968), p. 2, folder 19, box 17, NCC-DOM; Wayne D. Wardwell, "A Program of Technical Education for the Christian High School Located in Farrukhabad, U.P., India" (ms, 17 November 1952), folder 3; B. Freeman, "Christian Community Services Questionnaire. Western India Mission" (ms, 1952), p. 2, folder 3; A. E. Harper to Arthur H. Carson, 29 July 1953, folder 4, all in Box 20, Board of Foreign Missions—India Mission [hereafter "BFM-India"], Record Group 83, Presbyterian Historical Society.

46. M. D. Sargeant, "Career's Day," *U.C.S. Newsletter* 1 (December 1961), pp. 2–3, folder 13, box 20, BFM-India; Gordon Gaskill, "Our Stake in Liberia," *American Magazine*, July 1948, p. 62, folder 6, box 127, Phelps-Stokes Collection.

47. E. L. Pedersen to LeRoy Dodds, 27 April 1948, folder 1, box 20, BFM-India; Mary Helen Black, "Manual Work as a Part of the School Course" (ms, 20 May 1946), p. 4, folder 13, box 1, Mary Helen Black Papers, Record Group 213, Presbyterian Historical Society; Leonard Rieser to Nancy Nicalo and Jan S. F. van Hoogstraten, 24 November 1969, folder 19, box 17, NCC-DOM; Edward Robinson to Members of Board of Trustees, New York State Colonization Society, 30 April 1951, folder 5, box 326, Claude A. Barnett Papers, Chicago Historical Society, Chicago, Ill.

48. Robinson to Members of Board of Trustees, 30 April 1951, folder 5, box 326, Barnett Papers; Gary May, "Passing the Torch and Lighting Fires: The Peace Corps," in *Kennedy's Quest for Victory: American Foreign Policy, 1961–1963*, ed. Thomas G. Paterson (New York: Oxford University Press, 1989), 314.

49. James J. Shields Jr., "The Reports of the Phelps-Stokes Fund on Education in Africa and the Formation of a Theory of Community Development by the British" (ms, 4 May 1961), p. 6, fiche 001.524–6, Schomburg Clipping File; Francis Harry Hendrickson, "A Study of the Reactions of Selected Congo Missionaries toward Presumed Criticisms of Missionary Education in Africa" (Ed.D. diss., Teachers College Columbia University, 1964), 121, 154.

50. See, for example, J. L. Dodds to E. L. Peterson, 12 September 1948, folder 1; "The Strategic Place of the United Christian Schools in the Punjab and Its Contribution to the State and the Church" (ms, 24 February 1957), p. 4, folder 9, both in box 20, BFM-India.

51. Karen Schwarz, *What You Can Do For Your Country: An Oral History of the Peace Corps* (New York: William Morrow, 1991), 180–82, 185; T. Zane Reeves, *The Politics of the Peace Corps and VISTA* (Tuscaloosa: University of Alabama Press, 1988), 97–99.

52. Landrum, *The Role of the Peace Corps in Education*, 7, 25, 33–34; Schwarz, *What You Can Do For Your Country*, 183, 192.

53. *The Peace Corps Experience*, ed. Roy Hoopes (New York: Clarkson N. Potter, 1968), 134; Fritz Fischer, *Making Them Like Us: Peace Corps Volunteers in the 1960s* (Washington, D.C.: Smithsonian Institution Press, 1998), 41–43; Martin Benjamin, "Letters from a Peace Corpsman," *Symposium* [Union College, Schenectady, N.Y.], Summer 1963, "Ethiopia—Volunteer Information" folder, Collection 31, Peace Corps Volunteers Collection, National Anthropology Archives [hereafter "PC-NAA"], Museum Support Center, Smithsonian Institution, Suitland, Md.; Steve Wells, "Outward Bound." Retrieved November 10, 2004, from http://peacecorpswriters.org/pages/2000/0011/printvrs011/pv011pchist.html; memorandum to "All Peace Corps Programs" (n.d. [1963]); "Memo on Athletic Kit" (n.d. [1963]), both in "Peace Corps Athletic Kit" file, Vertical Files, Peace Corps Library, Washington, D.C.

54. Larry Olds letter, in *The TEA Experience*, ed. Judith Lindfors (ms, 2002, in possession of Brooks Goddard, Needham, Mass.); Francis Pollock, "A Boost for Athletics," *Peace Corps Volunteer* 2 (July 1964): 14; "Coaches, Teachers to Enter Indonesia Project Training," ibid. 1 (January 1963): 5; G. Mongeau, O.M.I., "Notre Dame Schools in the Philippines," *Worldmission* 5 (Summer 1954): 236–237; Brian Hindo, "Old School," *New Republic* (30 August 2004): 38; Schwarz, *What You Can*

Do For Your Country, 192; "Sangli Kindergarten and Primary School. Sangli, India" (ms, 1954), p. 1, folder 7, Box 20, BFM-India.

55. George P. Clarke to "Dear Mom and Pops," 20 September 1962, microfilm reel 1, George P. Clarke Papers, Wisconsin Historical Society, Madison, Wis.; Jim Stevens and Henry Scheinost, "COS Conference. Costa Rica VI" (ms, 5 August 1968), p. 18, "Costa Rica VI" folder, box 16, Close of Service Conference Reports, Peace Corps Records [hereafter "PC-COS"], Record Group 490, National Archives II; Bill Shurtleff, *Peace Corps Year with Nigerians*, ed. Hans Brinkmann (Frankfurt: Verlag Moritz Diesterweg, 1966), 39; Dan and Lisa Hebl, *Peace Corps Roller Coaster*, ed. Sharon Hebl (Eau Claire, Wis.: Heins Publications, 1994), 144–145.

56. Randall Barton to "Dear All," 5 October 1973, Randall Barton Papers, Collection No. 25, PC-NAA; Dan Ayala, "Stroke of Talent," *Peace Corps Volunteer* 1 (August 1963): 19.

57. See, for example, Stevens and Scheinost, "COS Conference. Costa Rica VI," 14; Schwarz, *What You Can Do For Your Country*, 192–193.

58. Gerard T. Rice, *The Bold Experiment: JFK's Peace Corps* (South Bend, Ind.: University of Notre Dame Press, 1985), 241–244.

59. Eleanor Margaret Rodgers, "The Use of Physical and Health Education on the Foreign Mission Field" (M.S. thesis, Wheaton College, Wheaton, Ill., 1956), 6.

60. M. Douglas Stafford, "COS Conference. Nigeria VII" (ms, 27 January 1966), p. 3, "Nigeria VII" folder, box 5, PC-COS; Diary entry, 1 November 1962, microfilm reel 1, David Matthes Papers, Wisconsin Historical Society; Roger McManus to "Mother and Dad," 1 December 1962, in Richard W. McManus, "The Story of a Peace Corps Volunteer. 'I Shall Never Forget' " (ms, n.d. [1964]), p. 37, General Collection, Peace Corps Library; Lynn and Mary Lou Linnman to "Dear Friends," 4 January 1963; Joan Carroll to R. Sargent Shriver, 9 July 1963, both in "Ethiopia—Volunteer Information" folder, Collection 31, PC-NAA; "Report for the Archives, M. Vincent on Hudson, N.Y., September 1964–June 1965" (ms), folder 3, box 10, Bahamas Collection, Sisters of Charity Archives, Mount St. Vincent College, Bronx, N.Y.

61. See, for example, Ernest G. Allen to T. H. Gibson, 25 January 1913, folder 13, box 59, RDE-HA; Arthur E. Lindborg to Benjamin Wist, 11 April 1933, "Samoan File: Correspondence 1933" folder, box 37, Wist Papers; Nancy Parker McDowell, *Notes from Ramallah, 1939* (Richmond, Ind.: Friends United Press, 2002), 62.

62. Sister Mary Frederick to "Dear Dad, Ginger, and Urban," 12 October 1969, "Correspondence 1952" folder; Sister Mary Anne, "Night Lights," *Bolivian Bulletin* 2 (October 1969), p. 3, "Bulletin 1968–1969" folder, both in box 2, Bolivia Collection, Record Group 12–09–10, Daughters of Charity Archives of the Northeast Province, Albany, N.Y.; Ed Smith, *Where To, Black Man?* (Chicago: Quadrangle, 1967), 155; Kay Ellen Aylor to Dear Corrine, 21 April 1965, "Ethiopia—Volunteer Information" folder, Collection 31, PC-NAA.

63. Hebl, *Peace Corps Roller Coaster*, 98–99.

64. Kevin Lowther and C. Payne Lucas, *Keeping Kennedy's Promise: The Peace Corps, Unmet Hope of the New Frontier* (Boulder, Colo.: Westview Press, 1978), 89, 148n10, 95.

65. Don Snow, "On English Teaching as Christian Service," *Church and Society* 3 (January–February 1998): 42.

3. Schooling for All?

1. W. T. Stead, *The Americanization of the World: The Trend of the Twentieth Century* (New York: Horace Markley, 1901), 385, 387, 184, 191.

2. "COLORED MISSIONARIES. Opinions of Individual Missionaries of the Gaboon and Corisco Mission" (ms, 1895), pp. 3–4, 16, folder 33; J. M. Patterson to Reginald Wheeler, 9 March 1926, folder 34, both in box 1, Board of Foreign Missions—West Africa Mission [hereafter "BFM-West Africa"], Record Group 142, Presbyterian Historical Society.

3. William T. Stead, *Americanizing Turkey* (n.p., n.d.), p. 6, "Pamphlets" folder, box 49, Outgrowths of Hampton Collection, Hampton University Archives, Hampton, Va.

4. Emily Rosenberg, "Rescuing Women and Children," *Journal of American History* 89 (September 2002): 456–465.

5. Flora Dodson to T. B. Ray, 22 November 1918, "Dodson, Flora (Miss) Ex Secy 1917–1938" folder, box 86, Flora Dodson Papers, Southern Baptist Historical Society and Archives, Nashville, Tenn.

6. R. Sargent Shriver, "Speech at Catholic Interracial Council" (ms, 1 June 1961), p. 2, Shriver file, box 14, Harris Wofford Papers, John F. Kennedy Library, Boston, Mass.; Shriver, "Statement Prepared for the American Association of School Administrators, Atlantic City, New Jersey, February 17, 1962" (ms), "Peace Corps Speeches-Sargent Shriver, 1961–63" binder, Peace Corps Library, Washington, D.C.

7. Vernon R. Dorjahn, "Transcultural Perceptions and Misperceptions in Sierra Leone," in *Cultural Frontiers of the Peace Corps*, ed. Robert B. Textor (Cambridge, Mass.: MIT Press, 1966), 183; Bill Wanlund, "Hearing-Impaired PCVs 'Sign Up' to Help Disabled," *Peace Corps Times* 3 (September–October 1980): p. 7, "Peace Corps—1980" folder, box 29, International Center on Deafness Collection, Gallaudet University Archives, Washington, D.C.

8. Louis H. Lisk to Director of Education, 27 September 1913, pp. 325–326, "Bureau of Education. Activities 1914. Early Experiences of American Teachers" binder, box 6, Walter W. Marquardt Papers, Bentley Historical Library, Ann Arbor, Mich.; W. W. Pettit, "Public Schools in the Philippines," *Southern Workman* 39 (October 1910): 532.

9. Lisk to Director of Education, p. 329; Walter W. Marquardt, "The Philippines Schools" (ms, 1922), p. 138, "Scrap Book. Talks and Papers. 1922–30" binder, box 6, Marquardt Papers; Harold Van Winkle, "Building Better Than They Knew," *Phi Delta Kappan* 36 (June 1955): 332, "American Teachers—Philippines" folder, box 8, Arthur R. Carson Papers, Hoover Institution Archives, Palo Alto, Calif.; Juan B. Huyke, "The Future Welfare of Puerto Rico from the Standpoint of Education" (ms, n.d. [1923]), folder 63, box 22, Board of National Missions: Educational and Medical Work/Health, Education and Welfare, Record Group 301.8, Presbyterian Historical Society; Mary E. Fleming, "The Changing Functions of Hawaii's Schools," *Hawaii Educational Review* 16 (April 1928): 213–214.

10. Edgar Allen Forbes, "American Teaching Around the World," *World's Work* (February 1908): 9864, 9867, "American Teaching Around the World" folder, Board of International Missions Subject Files [hereafter "BIMSF"], American Baptist Historical Society, Valley Forge, Penn.; Sushil Madhava Pathak, *American*

..ionaries and Hinduism: A study of Their Contacts from 1813 to 1910 (Delhi: Mun-
.iram Manoharlal, 1967), 105, 169–173; Eula Hutchison Sleeth, "History of the
Educational Work of the Presbyterian Church of America in India" (M.A. thesis,
University of Chicago, 1921), 2; John E. Cummings to Alvah Hovey, 18 September 1893, "Burma: Survey—Relation of Schools and Higher Education to Missionary Operations, Vol. I" folder, BIMSF.

11. For American attacks on prejudice in Latin America, see, for example, Ruth
Bradley to "Dear friends," 13 June 1923, folder 2, box 1, Ruth Winifred Bradley
Papers, Record Group 325; in the Mideast, S. D. Jessup, "Annual Report Gerard
Institute. 1928–1929" (ms), pp. 2–3, folder 4, box 15, Board of Foreign Missions—
Syria Mission, Record Group 90, both in Presbyterian Historical Society; and in
South Asia, A. E. Harper Jr., *The Village of Service* (New York: Board of Foreign
Missions, 1938), 9.

12. Sleeth, "History of the Educational Work," 7; Maina Chawla Singh, *Gender,
Religion, and 'Heathen Lands': American Missionary Women in South Asia, 1860s–1940s*
(New York: Garland, 2000), 60; Maza R. Evans to Minnie Sandberg, 19 July 1932,
"Assam: Golaghat Girls High School" folder, BIMSF.

13. Asa C. Watkins to R. J. Willingham, 29 September 1906, fiche 2, Asa Car-
rell Watkins Papers, International Mission Board Archives, Southern Baptist Convention, Richmond, Va.; Eunice Blackburn to "Dear Family," 4 December 1924,
folder 6, box 1, Eunice R. Blackburn Papers, Record Group 198, Presbyterian Historical Society; Margaret Doolittle, "Report of Tripoli Girls' School, 1925–1926"
(ms), p. 4, folder 8, box 19, Syria Mission Archives [hereafter "SMA"], Record
Group 115, Presbyterian Historical Society; Alice C. Reed interview (ms, 1969),
p. 44, China Missionaries Oral History Project, Manuscript Division, Columbia
University Libraries, New York; "Report of the Educational Committee" (ms, n.d.
[1924]), p. 2, "Burma-Education—1920–1929" folder, BIMSF; Mary Helm, "Report of the S. M. Wherry Middle School, Jagraon. 1935–36" (ms), pp. 1–2, folder
14, box 31, Board of Foreign Missions—India Mission [hereafter "BFM-India"],
Record Group 83, Presbyterian Historical Society.

14. "John Henry Manning Butler," *Journal of Negro History* 30 (April 1945): 243;
"Special Teachers—To Be Used on Further Advice" (ms, n.d. [1912]), file 42–07,
box 5, Bureau of Insular Affairs Records [hereafter "BIA"], National Archives II,
College Park, Md.; Governor's Advisory Committee on Education, *Survey of Schools
and Industry in Hawaii* (Honolulu: Printshop Company, 1931), 102; William Seraile,
"Black American Missionaries in Africa: 1821–1925," *The Social Studies* 58 (October
1972), p. 201, fiche 003.083–3, Schomburg Clipping File, Schomburg Center for
Research in Black Culture, New York Public Libraries; "Minutes of Conference on
Appointment of Colored Missionaries to Africa held February 7, 1927" (ms),
pp. 1–2; Robert E. Speer to W. E. B. Du Bois, 5 September 1928; Ernest W. Riggs
to W. R. Wheeler, 5 February 1927; Thomas S. Donohugh to W. R. Wheeler, 4
February 1927, all in folder 35, box 1, BFM-West Africa.

15. Seraile, "Black American Missionaries in Africa," 201; " 'How is Garvey'
Africans Ask Missionaries," *Philadelphia Bulletin*, 7 March 1928, fiche 003.083–1,
Schomburg Clipping File; "Extract of letter from W. C. Johnston to Mr. Wheeler
dated May 26, 1922" (ms); L. E. Smith to W. Wheeler, 7 March 1924, both in
folder 33; J. M. Patterson to Reginald Wheeler, 9 March 1926, folder 34, all in box
1, BFM-West Africa.

16. Henry C. Blair to Governor, 4 May 1918, folder 71–1918; Blair to Governor, 9 July 1919, folder 71–1919, both in box 45, Virgin Islands Records, Record Group 55, National Archives II; Alonzo G. Moron to Arthur Howe, 23 May 1934, "Virgin Islands—1934" folder, box 38, Arthur Howe Papers, Hampton University Archives, Humphrey, Va.

17. Jacqueline Goggin, *Carter Woodson: A Life in Black History* (Baton Rouge, La.: Louisiana State University Press, 1993), 16; Sister Anthony Scully, "The Philippines Challenge," *Negro History Bulletin* 44 (January–March 1981): 17; John Henry Manning Butler, "Early Experiences as a Teacher in the Philippines" (ms, 1914), pp. 237–39, "Bureau of Education. Activities 1914. Early Experiences of American Teachers" binder, box 6, Marquardt Papers; "John Henry Manning Butler," *Journal of Negro History* 30 (April 1945): 243–244.

18. Stephen Bonsal, "The Philippines—After an Earthquake," *North American Review* 174 (March 1902): 418; "The Bureau of Education," *Philippine Teacher* 1 (15 December 1904): 2; Aida Negron de Montilla, *Americanization in Puerto Rico and the Public School System, 1900–1930* (Rio Piedras, P.R.: Editorial Edil, 1971), 74, 55; Gael Graham, *Gender, Culture, and Christianity: American Protestant Mission Schools in China, 1880–1930* (New York: Peter Lang, 1995), 171–172; Edwin Parker to "Dear Friends of Roseland," 22 May 1924, folder 2, box 1, Parker Family Papers, Record Group 278, Presbyterian Historical Society; B. A. Hlaing to J. C. Robbins, 19 July 1919, "Moulmein: Judson Boys High School" folder, BIMSF.

19. James F. Smith, "Education in the Philippines," *Philippine Teacher* 1 (15 January 1905): 8; David P. Barrows, "Report of the General Superintendent of Education for the Philippine Islands for the Period September 1, 1902 to September 30, 1903," *Fourth Annual Report of the Philippine Commission*, pt. 3 (Washington, D.C.: Government Printing Office, 1904), 887–888; unidentified letter from American teacher, enclosed with D. H. McBride to Clarence R. Edwards, 26 June 1905, file 3140–26, box 322, BIA; *Report of the Commissioner of Education for Porto Rico to the Secretary of the Interior, USA* (Washington, D.C.: Government Printing Office, 1900), p. 12, "General File: Puerto Rico—Publications on Puerto Rican Education" folder, box 193, Samuel McCune Lindsay Papers, Manuscript Division, Columbia University Libraries; Eunice Blackburn to Dear Mabel, 2 July 1922, folder 4, box 1, Blackburn Papers; Mrs. W. W. Keefe to Irene Sheppard, 25 September 1934, folder 16, box 10, Board of Foreign Missions—Colombia Mission, Record Group 88; James W. Willoughby, "The United Mission in Iraq, 1924–1962. A Brief Historical Survey" (ms, 20 September 1962), p. 16, folder 27, box 2, United Mission in Iraq Collection, Record Group 89, both in Presbyterian Historical Society; George H. Scherer, "Annual Report of the American Mission High School, Shweir, Lebanon, for the School Year ending July 15, 1909" (ms), pp. 2–3, folder 10, box 17, SMA; Nancy Parker McDowell, *Notes from Ramallah, 1939* (Richmond, Ind.: Friends United Press, 2002), 18; Herbert Priestley to Dear Mother, 3 April 1902, "Transcriptions of letters, April 1902" folder, box 1, Herbert I. Priestley Papers, Bancroft Library, University of California-Berkeley; William B. Freer, *The Philippine Experiences of an American Teacher: A Narrative of Work and Travel in the Philippine Islands* (New York: Scribner, 1906), 105.

20. Willard B. Gatewood Jr., *Black Americans and the White Man's Burden, 1898–1903* (Urbana: University of Illinois Press, 1975), 324, 318; Kevin Gaines, "Black Americans' Racial Uplift Ideology as 'Civilizing Mission,'" in *Cultures of*

ed States Imperialism, eds. Amy Kaplan and Donald E. Pease (Durham, N.C.: Duke University Press, 1993), 437; Henry C. McDowell to Samuel B. Coles, 10 January 1925, folder HCM/Ang.2/10/2, box 3, Henry C. McDowell Papers; The Mc-Dowells to Dear Friend, 16 February 1920, folder TC/Afr.3/4/2, box 1, Talladega College Collection, both in Savery Library, Talladega College, Talladega, Ala.

21. n.a. [E. W. Koons], "Annual Report of the John D. Wells School—May 31, 1924 (ms), p. 2, folder 41; E. W. Koons, "Annual Report of the John D. Wells School. May 12, 1925" (ms), p. 1, folder 42, both in box 7, Board of Foreign Missions—Korea Mission, Record Group 140, Presbyterian Historical Society; E. M. Wright, "Resht Boy's School Annual Report. 1931–1932" (ms), p. 2, folder 3, box 20, Board of Foreign Missions—Iran Mission [hereafter "BFM-Iran"], Record Group 91, Presbyterian Historical Society; Edmund B. Butterfield, "An Account of Lieutenant Gov. Mason Stone's Service in Organizing Schools in the Philippines" (ms, n.d.), pp. 48–49, Manuscript Miscellaneous File 160, Vermont History Center, Barre, Vt.; Walter W. Marquardt to Miss Durham, 31 July 1914, p. 59, "Humorous, Personal Letters, Memoranda, Addresses" binder, box 5, Marquardt Papers; S. C. Newsom to Dear Sir, 18 October 1901, "Corres. 1901–1904" folder, box 1, Benjamin E. Neal Papers, George Arents Research Library, Syracuse University, Syracuse, N.Y.; American Teacher's Association of Puerto Rico petition, 24 February 1900, file 42–44; Eleanor P. Allen to Charles G. Dawes, 15 March 1900, file 42–42, both in box 5, BIA.

22. C. B. Fisher to Robert E. Speer, 12 May 1932, folder 25, box 19, BFM-Iran; Frederick Adolphus Price, Jr., application to Board of Foreign Missions, Methodist Episcopal Church (ms, 18 July 1936), folder 3, box 127, Phelps-Stokes Collection, Schomburg Center for Research in Black Culture; Esther Rhoads to Margaret Rhoads, 7 April 1933, "Letters from Rhoads March–June 1933" folder, box 18, Esther B. Rhoads Papers, Quaker Collection, Haverford College, Haverford, Penn.; Flora Dodson to T. B. Ray, 22 November 1918, "Dodson, Flora (Miss) Ex Secy 1917–1938" folder, box 86, Dodson Papers; Martha Wiley interview (ms, 1969), p. 111, China Missionaries Oral History Project.

23. Vaughan McCaughey, "Secondary Education in the Hawaiian Islands: A Survey, 1916–17" (ms), p. 16, folder 24, box 55, Records of the Department of Education [hereafter "RDE-HA"], Series 261, Hawaii State Archives, Honolulu, Hawaii; Mary Elspeth Fleming, "Pioneering in a Teacher's Paradise," in *Makers of Destiny, Hawaiian Style: The Lives of Pioneer Women Educators in Hawaii* (Honolulu: Delta Kappa Gamma Society, 1981), 82.

24. Mary J. Campbell, *One Hundred Girls of India* (Columbus, Ohio: Hann and Adair, 1900), 43; Henry Huizinga, "A Denominational Bombshell" (ms, 15 January 1917), p. 3, "Telugu Mission Educational Policy—H. Huizinga" folder, BIMSF; Annie W. Boyce, "Chapters from the Life of an American Woman in the Shah's Capital," pt. V (ms, n.d. [1924]), p. 2, folder 11, box 18, BFM-Iran; "The American Mission in Egypt. Its Educational Work" (ms, n.d. [1924]), p. 2, folder 29, box 21, United Presbyterian Church of North America, Board of Foreign Missions, Record Group 209, Presbyterian Historical Society; Leana A. Keans, "Sixty Years in the Narasaravupet School" (ms, 1942), p. 5, "South India: Narasaravupet: High School" folder, BIMSF.

25. Fred W. Atkinson, "Report of the General Superintendent of Public Instruction to the Secretary of Public Instruction for the Period From May 27, 1901

to October 1, 1901," *Report of the Philippines Commission to the Secretary of War*, pt. 2 (Washington, D.C.: General Printing Office, 1901), 534; diary entry, 3 February 1902, September 1901–July 30 1902 diary, "Diaries and Account Books 1901–1902" folder, box 1, Neal Papers; Burgess Shank, " 'Education in the Philippines': A Reply," *Gunton's Magazine* 24 (May 1903): 411; Eunice Blackburn to "Dear Family," 14 May 1922, folder 4, box 1, Blackburn Papers; Ethel Baker to Irene Sheppard, 15 April 1934, folder 17, box 6, Board of Foreign Missions—Guatemala Mission [hereafter "BFM—Guatemala"], Record Group 157, Presbyterian Historical Society; "Education in Porto Rico," *Boston Evening Transcript*, 11 April 1903, "General File: Puerto Rico—1901–1912—Printed" folder, box 189, Lindsay Papers.

26. Alice C. Reed interview, pp. 13–14; Grace Rowley interview (ms, 1970), p. 29, China Missionaries Oral History Project; "Synopsis of Pageant Given at Marissa, Ill., April 11, 1919" (ms, 1919), folder 23, box 1, Kate Alexander Hill Papers, Record Group 53, Presbyterian Historical Society; Graham, *Gender, Culture, and Christianity*, 42–43; Boyce, "Chapters From the Life," 5–6.

27. Martha Wiley interview, p. 26; Anna M. Donaldson, "Account of First Two years of Work in the Philippines," p. 258, "Bureau of Education. Activities 1914. Early Experiences of Teachers" binder, box 6, Marquardt Papers; "Report of Iran Bethel for the year 1926–1927" (ms), p. 3, folder 12, box 20, BFM-Iran.

28. "The Teaching Staff of the Public Elementary Schools of Hawaii. Advance Material from the Federal School Survey Report," *Hawaii Educational Review* 9 (February 1921): 175; Vaughan MacCaughey, "The Teacher Supply Situation in Hawaii," *School and Society* 12 (6 November 1920), 435; Mary Cole to "Dear Folks at Home," 24 July 1901, "July 1901" folder, box 1, Harry N. Cole Papers, Bentley Historical Library, Ann Arbor, Mich.; Fred W. Atkinson to Clarence R. Edwards, 30 September 1901, file 470–24, box 84; Department of Public Instruction, Bureau of Education, *Twenty-Fifth Annual Report of the Director of Education, January 1, 1924 to December 31, 1924* (Manila: Bureau of Printing, 1925), p. 16, no folder, box 510, both in BIA.

29. Gilbert S. Perez, *From the Transport Thomas to Sto. Tomas: The History of American Teachers in the Philippines* (n.p., n.d. [1949]), 21; Edwin Dexter to Clarence R. Edwards, Dec. ? 1909, file 42–54, box 5, BIA; diary entry, 16 September 1901, "September 1901–July 30 1902" diary, "Diaries and Account Books 1901–1902" folder, box 1, Neal Papers.

30. Hubert V. Everly interview, in *Public Education in Hawaii: Oral Histories*, vol. 1 (Honolulu: Center for Oral History, Social Science Research Institute, University of Hawaii at Manoa, 1991), 276; Philinda Rand to "Dear Katie," 31 August 1902, "Anglemyer, P.R. 1902" folder, box 1, Philinda Rand Anglemyer Papers, Arthur and Elizabeth Schlesinger Library, Radcliffe College, Cambridge, Mass.; Helen W. Kelsey to Superintendent and Commissioners, Department of Public Instruction, 9 July 1908, folder 31, box 55, RDE-HA.

31. May Faurote, n.t. (ms, 1914), pp. 265–266, "Bureau of Education. Activities 1914. Early Experiences of American Teachers" binder, box 6, Marquardt Papers; A. L. Case to H. W. Kinney, 28 September 1914, folder 4, box 62, RDE-HA; *Report of the Commissioner of Education for Porto Rico to the Secretary of the Interior, USA* (Washington, D.C.: Government Printing Office, 1902), p. 81, "General File: Puerto Rico—Publications on Puerto Rican Education" folder, box 193, Lindsay Papers.

32. Dana L. Robert, *American Women in Mission: A Social History of Their Thought and Practice* (Macon, Ga.: Mercer University Press, 1996), 184; Shirley S. Garrett, "Sisters All. Feminism and the American Women's Missionary Movement," in *Missionary Ideologies in the Imperialist Era: 1880–1920*, eds. Torben Christensen and William R. Hutchison (Aarhus, Denmark: Forlaget Aros, 1982), 221–224; Edward O. Stevens to Alvah Hovey, 3 November 1893, "Burma: Survey—Relation of Schools and Higher Education to Missionary Operations Vol. II" folder; Earnest Grigg to Hovey, 9 September 1893; F. T. Whitman to Hovey, 24 October 1893, both in "Burma: Survey—Relation of Schools and Higher Education to Missionary Operations Vol. I" folder, all in BIMSF.

33. John E. Cummings to Alvah Hovey, 18 September 1893, "Burma: Survey—Relation of Schools and Higher Education to Missionary Operations Vol. I" folder, BIMSF; Edward M. Haymaker to Stanley White, 30 November 1921, folder 4, box 6, BFM-Guatemala.

34. Nancy Scheper-Hughes, "The Way of an Anthropologist Companheira," in *Anthropology and the Peace Corps: Case Studies in Career Preparation*, eds. Brian E. Schwimmer and D. Michael Warren (Ames: Iowa State University Press, 1993), 101–102.

35. Robert Johnston, "Sit-ins Boring? Try Peace Corps," *Peace Corps News* 4 (Autumn 1968), Special College Supplement; Doug McAdam, *Freedom Summer* (New York: Oxford University Press, 1988), 187; "Snick Group in Guinea," *The Crier* [Peace Corps-Guinea] 1 (September 1964), p. 2, Peace Corps Library, Washington, D.C.; Jonathan Zimmerman, "Beyond Double Consciousness: Black Peace Corps Volunteers in Africa, 1961–1971," *Journal of American History* 82 (December 1995): 1022; *The Image* [Peace Corps-Ethiopia] 1 (November 1964), p. 2, Peace Corps Library.

36. Zimmerman, "Beyond Double Consciousness," 1008; Bill Moyers to Sargent Shriver, 15 May 1963, "Memos—To and From the Director" folder, box 41, Office Files of Bill Moyers, Lyndon Baines Johnson Library, Austin, Tex.; Paul Cowan, *The Making of an Un-American* (New York: Viking, 1967), 79–82; *Who's Who in the Peace Corps* (n.p., n.d. [1961]), p. 13, Margo F. Leining folder, box 8, Peace Corps Collection, Kennedy Library; Makonnen Desta, *History of Peace Corps Ethiopia* (n.p., 1976), 4–5; Richard Dudman, "A Presidential Assistant Moving from White House to African 'New Frontier' " *St. Louis Post-Dispatch*, 20 May 1962, "Peace Corps—Reading File" folder, box 6, Wofford Papers.

37. *Citizen in a Time of Change: The Returned Peace Corps Volunteer*, ed. Ernest Fox, George Nicolau, and Harris Wofford (n.p., 1965), 45; Dave Russel, "Civil Rights," *The Baobab* [Peace Corps-Senegal] 1 (May 1964), pp. 4–5, Peace Corps Library; Zimmerman, "Beyond Double Consciousness," 1011; Fritz Fischer, *Making Them Like Us: Peace Corps Volunteers in the 1960s* (Washington, D.C.: Smithsonian Institution Press, 1998), 180; David L. Szanton, "Cultural Confrontation in the Philippines," in Textor, ed., *Cultural Frontiers of the Peace Corps*, 36.

38. Fischer, *Making Them Like Us*, 161–167; David Berlew and Terence O'Donnell, "COS Conference. Iran VI" (ms, August 1967), p. 9, "Iran VI" folder, box 13, Close of Service Conference Reports, Peace Corps Records [hereafter "PC-COS"], Record Group 490, National Archives II; Szanton, "Cultural Confrontation in the Philippines," 51; Raymond L. Gold, *A Teaching Safari: A Study of American Teachers in East Africa* (Baltimore, Md.: PublishAmerica, 2004), 136.

39. "Guatemala" (ms, 1963), pp. 1, 4, folder 1; Maryknoll Sisters, untitled manuscript (ms, 26 October 1964), folder 5; Sister Mary Mildred, "Some Aspects of Monte Maria Work. November 1963–November 1964" (ms), pp. 4, 6, folder 5, all in box 1, Guatemala Collection, Maryknoll Fathers and Brothers Archives, Ossining, N.Y.

40. David A. Ratermann to Archbishop May, 10 August 1980, "Correspondence 1952–" folder, box 2, Bolivia Collection, Record Group 12–09–10, Daughters of Charity Archives of the Northeast Province, Albany, N.Y.; Angelyn Dries, O.S.F., *The Missionary Movement in American Catholic History* (Maryknoll, N.Y.: Orbis, 1998), 225; "Guatemala," 3; diary entry, 3 December 1962, microfilm reel 1, David Matthes Papers, Wisconsin Historical Society, Madison, Wis.

41. Robert A. Randall, "Similarities between Peace Corps and Anthropological Experience," in Schwimmer and Warren, eds., *Anthropology and the Peace Corps*, 92; Zimmerman, "Beyond Double Consciousness," 1016, 1018.

42. Carl Meacham, "Peace Corps Service in Liberia, 1965–66: Reflections of an African-American Volunteer," *Liberian Studies Journal* 15 (1990): 104, 90; Zimmerman, "Beyond Double Consciousness," 1021; Ed Smith, *Where to, Black Man?* (Chicago: Quadrangle Books, 1967), 105.

43. Unlike previous generations of Americans, missionary and Peace Corps officials zealously recruited African-Americans for overseas teaching slots in the post–World War II period. In 1952, for example, the National Council of Churches announced that its member mission boards were "actively seeking Negroes," as "proof of Christian brotherhood and of democracy's promises." Yet only forty African-Americans served in mainline Protestant missions worldwide, a fourfold increase from the pre–World War II era, but a tiny sliver of the overseas total. Likewise, Peace Corps officials were continually frustrated in their efforts to enlist African-Americans. The problem proved particularly embarrassing in African countries like Sierra Leone, where the first thirty-seven volunteers included just one black, while in Niger there were no African-Americans at all. Throughout the 1960s, the percentage of blacks in the Peace Corps would hover around 2 percent. By 1990, roughly 5,000 of the 130,000 Americans who had served in the Peace Corps, that is, about 4 percent, were African-American. *News from the National Council of Churches of Christ in the USA*, 16 June 1952, folder 6, box 393, Claude A. Barnett Papers, Chicago Historical Society, Chicago, Ill.; Zimmerman, "Beyond Double Consciousness," 1004–1005; "More Black Volunteers Sought by Peace Corps," unidentified clipping, n.d. [1969], "Minorities-Recruiting" file, Vertical Files, Peace Corps Library; Solomon Herbert, "Still the Toughest Job You'll Ever Love," *Black Enterprise* 20 (February 1990): 153.

44. "Confessions of a Portuguese Dodger Rooter," *Spectrum* [Peace Corps-Senegal] 1 (Winter 1965), p. 5, Peace Corps Library; Brent K. Ashabranner, *A Moment in History: The First Ten Years of the Peace Corps* (Garden City, N.Y.: Doubleday, 1971), 260.

45. See, for example, "This is the Peace Corps, Miss Jones!" *Sunday News* [University Park, Penn.], 20 August 1961, folder 61, box 195, National Catholic Welfare Conference/United States Catholic Conference Collection [hereafter "NCCC/USCC"], American Catholic Historical Research Center, Catholic University, Washington, D.C.; Arnold and Marian Zeitlin, untitled manuscript (ms, 1962), p. 10, "Ghana-Volunteer Information" folder, Collection 31, Peace Corps

Volunteers Collection, National Anthropology Archives [hereafter "PC-NAA"], Museum Support Center, Smithsonian Institution, Suitland, Md.; Arnold Zeitlin, *To The Peace Corps, With Love* (Garden City, N.Y.: Doubleday, 1965), 47; Helen Wilson and Jules Pagano, "COS Conference Report. Cameroon I" (ms, 22–24 May 1964), p. 2, "Cameroon I" folder, box 1, PC-COS.

46. Szanton, "Cultural Confrontation in the Philippines," 52; Ashabranner, *Moment in History*, 263; David Riesman, "Two Views," *Peace Corps Volunteer* 6 (October 1968): 4–5.

47. See, especially, Sara Evans, *Personal Politics: The Roots of Women's Liberation in the Civil Rights Movement and the New Left* (New York: Alfred A. Knopf, 1979).

48. Fischer, *Making Them Like Us*, 91, 100; Ivan Illich, "Mid-Term Report from Guidance Committee and Language Department" (ms, 13 August 1961), enclosed with Betsie Hollants to Rev. John Considine, 15 August 1961, folder 58, box 186, NCCC/USCC; Michael Sullivan, "Career Counseling for Single Women Missionaries," *Evangelical Missions Quarterly* 15 (January 1979): 31.

49. Fischer, *Making Them Like Us*, 99; Jonathan Zimmerman, "Crossing Oceans, Crossing Colors: Black Peace Corps Volunteers and Interracial Love in Africa, 1961–1971," in *Sex, Love, Race: Crossing Boundaries in North American History*, ed. Martha Hodes (New York: New York University Press, 1999), 521–522; Lawrence H. Fuchs, *"Those Peculiar Americans": The Peace Corps and American National Character* (New York: Meredith Press, 1967), 120–121.

50. Zimmerman, "Crossing Oceans, Crossing Colors," 521; Vincent J. D'Andrea, "Close of Service Conference. Philippines VII" (ms, 1964), p. 48, "Philippines VII" folder, box 2; Daniel A. Sharp and Henry U. Wheatley, "Close of Service Conference—Senegal" (ms, 4 June 1965), p. 6, "Senegal III" folder, box 5, both in PC-COS; Elizabeth Cobbs Hoffman, *All You Need is Love: The Peace Corps and the Spirit of the 1960s* (Cambridge, Mass.: Harvard University Press, 1998), 138; L. H. Mirel, "Close of Service Conference Kenya II" (ms, 2 March 1967), p. 16, "Kenya II" folder, box 8, PC-COS; James Carucci, "Peace Corps as Archaeology Field School," in Schwimmer and Warren, eds., *Anthropology and the Peace Corps*, 223.

51. Zimmerman, "Beyond Double Consciousness," 1024; diary entry, 29 November 1972, vol. 2, folder 1, Alfred T. Giannini Papers, Collection 8, PC-NAA; L. R. Satin, "Close of Service Conference. Afghanistan IV-B" (ms, 1–3 May 1966), pp. 3–4, "Afghanistan IV-B" folder, box 6, PC-COS; "Letter from Iran to the Peace Corps Director (1965)," in *Making a Difference: The Peace Corps at Twenty-Five*, ed. Milton Viorst (New York: Weidenfield and Nicolson, 1986), 58–59; Karen Schwarz, *What You Can Do For Your Country: An Oral History of the Peace Corps* (New York: William Morrow, 1991), 61.

52. Fischer, *Making Them Like Us*, 181; Bill Shurtleff, *Peace Corps Year with Nigerians*, ed. Hans Brinkmann (Frankfurt, Ger.: Verlag Moritz Diesterweg, 1966), 5; Carucci, "Peace Corps as Archaeology Field School," 223; Terence O'Donnell, "Supplementary Report on Iran VI Termination Conference," in David Berlew and Terence O'Donnell, "Close of Service Conference. Iran VI" (ms, August 1967), p. 27, "Iran VI" folder, box 13, PC-COS.

53. Lenore H. Lutz, "Personal Report—June 1956," pp. 1–2, folder 19, box 5, Korea Mission Papers, Record Group 197, Presbyterian Historical Society; Sister Emmanuel Schott, "Missionary Activities of the Daughters in Taiwan," *Mater Dei*

Provincialate News-Letter 16 (October 1984), pp. 5–7, "Taiwan ROC. Pamphlets, etc." folder, box 3, China/Taiwan Collection, Record Group 12–11–11/12; Sister Edwina, "Serving the Poor . . . The Audiology Institute of Cochambamba," *Echo,* April 1990, "Bolivia—Newspaper Clippings" folder, box 2, Bolivia Collection, Record Group 12–09–10, both in Daughters of Charity Archives of the Northeast Province; Annie J. Glocker, "American School For Girls. Annual Report 1951–1952" (ms), p. 2, folder 1, box 3, SMA; Kim E. Nielsen, *The Radical Lives of Helen Keller* (New York: New York University Press, 2004), 99, 111.

54. Frances M. Parsons, "First Deaf Peace Corps Volunteer Was Influenced to Join by President Kennedy," *Silent News,* October 1992, folder 1, Peace Corps Papers, Gallaudet University Archives [hereafter "PC-GUA"]; Mary Anne Dolan, "He Teaches Deaf in Ghana," *Washington Evening Star,* 24 August 1971, folder 1, Daniel Joseph Blessing Papers, Gallaudet University Archives; Joan Kelley, "Peace Corps Teaching Deaf in Philippines," *Woodland [Ill.] Democrat,* 31 March 1976, folder 1, PC-GUA; Mary Claveau Malzkuhn, "The Human Rights of the Deaf," in *The Deaf Way: Perspectives from the International Conference on Deaf Culture,* ed. Carol J. Erting et al. (Washington, D.C.: Gallaudet University Press, 1994), 782; Raghav Bir Joshi, "Nepal: A Paradise for the Deaf," ibid., 72; "Deaf Turtle Lake Woman Part of Third World Peace Corps Program," *Leader* [Washburn, N.Dak.], 20 August 1980, folder 1, PC-GUA; Roger L. Landrum, *The Role of the Peace Corps in Education in Developing Countries: A Sector Study* (Washington, D.C.: Peace Corps Information and Exchange, 1984 [1981]), 39.

55. Bill Wanlund, "Hearing-Impaired PCVs 'Sign Up' to Help the Disabled," *Peace Corps Times* 3 (September/October 1980): 1; Marie Greenstone to Frances Parsons, 10 January 1979, folder 7, box 2, Frances Parsons Papers, Gallaudet University Archives; Patricia Ross, "Nepali Sign Language Dictionary," *Peace Corps Times,* no volume number, January–February 1990, p. 15; Joshi, "Nepal: A Paradise for the Deaf," 73; Carole Olson, "Local Woman Improves Life and Language for the Deaf and Hearing Impaired in Mongolia," *Rock County Star Herald* [Luverne, Minn.], 7 December 1995, folder 1, PC-GUA.

56. Frances M. Parsons, "Education of the Deaf in the Philippines" (memorandum sent to Velma Linford, 19 June–1 July 1977), p. 10, folder 3, box 2, Parsons Papers; Aggrey A. Sawuka, "The Oppression of Deaf People as Cultural Minorities in Developing Countries," in Erting et al., eds., *The Deaf Way,* 794; "Deaf Education Program—Peace Corps/Philippines" (ms, 1982), p. 1, folder 1, PC-GUA; Katherine A. Jankowski, *Deaf Empowerment: Emergence, Struggle, and Rhetoric* (Washington, D.C.: Gallaudet University Press, 1997), 76–77; Malzkuhn, "The Human Rights of the Deaf," 781. On the history of the oralist/manualist debate in the United States, see Douglas C. Baynton, *Forbidden Signs: American Culture and the Campaign against Sign Language* (University of Chicago Press, 1996).

57. Marie Greenstone to Frances Parsons, 10 January 1979, folder 7, box 2, Parsons Papers; *Peace Corps: Special Education* (n.p., n.d. [1985]), General Collection, Canaday Library, Bryn Mawr College, Bryn Mawr, Penn.; "Deaf Education Program—Peace Corps/Philippines," 3; Fischer, *Making Them Like Us,* 181.

58. "About the Peace Corps." Retrieved December 6, 2004, from http://www.peacecorps.govt/index.cfm?shell=learn.whatispc.fastfacts; Janet Kalven, *Women Breaking Boundaries: A Grail Journey, 1940–1995* (Albany: State University of New York Press, 1999), 274.

59. Kalven, *Women Breaking Boundaries*, 265, 147.

60. *In the Classroom: Empowering Girls* (Washington, D.C.: Peace Corps Information Collection and Exchange Publication No. M0082, November 2001), 3, 16, 30, 66, 12, 68.

61. Dan and Lisa Hebl, *Peace Corps Roller Coaster*, ed. Sharon Hebl (Eau Claire, Wis.: Heins Publications, 1994), 163.

62. "Gay Peace Corps Volunteers 'Serve Everywhere,' " Peace Corps Press Release, 20 August 1999, *Peace Corps Online*, 19 August 2003. Retrieved December 6, 2004, from http://peacecorpsonline.org/messges/messages/2629/2015576.html. Earlier in its history, like most midcentury American institutions, the Peace Corps either ignored or actively tabooed homosexuality. At a training in the late 1960s, for example, a staff psychologist asked volunteer Alan Weiss if he had ever thought about homosexuality. Weiss lied and said no, assuming that "it would be death to answer in the affirmative." He was probably right. Later in the same training, psychologists told another male volunteer that his "feminity quotient" was too high. The volunteer demurred, arguing that his penchant for classical music and antipathy to contact sports "connoted nothing of the sort." But the psychologists were not persuaded. They eventually "deselected" the volunteer from the group, making it clear that "feminine" men—and, presumably, homosexual ones—were simply not welcome in the Peace Corps. Alan Weiss, *High Risk/High Gain: A Freewheeling Account of Peace Corps Training* (New York: St. Martin's, 1968), 31, 211–212, 246.

63. Eric Shea, "The Double Life of a Gay Volunteer in Kenya," *Lesbian, Gay, and Bisexual RPCVs NewsLetter*, November 2004. Retrieved December 6, 2004, from http://www.lgbrpcv.org/articles/11_04_ kenya.htm; Andrea Freygang, "Give Peace a Chance: Gay Community Members Face the Challenges of the Peace Corps," *The Weekly News* [Miami], 14 October 2004. Retrieved December 6, 2004, from http://www.twnonline.org/archive_twn/041014/041014_local_news_gays_in_the_peace_corps.html.

64. William R. Hutchison, *Errand to the World: American Protestant Thought and Foreign Missions* (Chicago: University of Chicago Press, 1987), 1.

Part II: American Critiques

1. Albert R. Hager, "The Educational Exhibit at the Philippine Exposition," *Philippine Teacher* 1 (15 February 1905): 21–23; Franz Boas, "The History of Anthropology" [1904], quoted in Richard Handler, "Boasian Anthropology and the Critique of American Culture," *American Quarterly* 42 (June 1990): 255.

2. M. de Montaigne, *Les Essais de Michel de Montaigne*, ed. P. Villery (Paris: Universitaires de France, 1978), 205, quoted in Clifford Geertz, *Available Light: Anthropological Reflections on Philosophical Topics* (Princeton: Princeton University Press, 2000), 45; untitled mimeograph, n.d. [1980], "Peace Corps (Simon Carmel)" folder, box 30, International Center on Deafness Collection, Gallaudet University Archives, Washington, D.C.

4. The Protective Garb of the "Job"

1. Helen P. Beattie, "American Teachers and the Filipinos," *Outlook* 78 (15 October 1904): 420.

2. *Letters from the Peace Corps*, ed. Iris Luce (Washington, D.C.: Robert B. Luce, 1964), 119.

3. *The Semi-Professions and Their Organization: Teachers, Nurses, and Social Workers*, ed. Amitai Etzioni (New York: Free Press, 1969); Dan C. Lortie, *Schoolteacher: A Sociological Study* (Chicago: University of Chicago Press, 1975); Marjorie Murphy, *Blackboard Unions: The AFT and the NEA, 1900–1980* (Ithaca, N.Y.: Cornell University Press, 1990); Victoria-Maria MacDonald, "The Paradox of Bureaucratization: New Views on Progressive Era Teachers and the Development of a Woman's Profession," *History of Education Quarterly* 39 (Winter 1999): 427–453.

4. *Teachers in the Peace Corps: From Rote to Reason* (n.p., n.d. [1968]), p. 11, "Peace Corps—Teaching" file, Vertical Files, Peace Corps Library, Washington, D.C.

5. Daniel W. Fulmer, "COS Conference Report. Tanzania Group VII" (ms, 18 January 1967), pp. 1–3, "Tanzania 64–05–07" folder, box 9, Close of Service Conference Reports, Peace Corps Records [hereafter "PC-COS"], Record Group 490, National Archives II, College Park, Md.

6. R. Freeman Butts, *American Education in International Development* (New York: Harper and Row, 1963), 79.

7. F. W. Atkinson, "The Teacher's Social and Intellectual Position," *Atlantic Monthly* 78 (April 1896): 534–538.

8. "Taxed $21,200 for Right to Teach Filipinos," unidentified clipping, 29 July 1901; "Root Objects to Teachers' Agents," unidentified clipping, 29 July 1901, both in file 470–28, box 84, Bureau of Insular Affairs Records [hereafter "BIA"], Record Group 350, National Archives II; Glenn Anthony May, *Social Engineering in the Philippines* (Westport, Conn.: Greenwood, 1980), 85; diary entry, 26 July 1901, "Syracuse-Manila" diary, "Diaries and Account Books 1901–1902" folder, box 1, Benjamin E. Neal Papers, George Arents Research Library, Syracuse University Library, Syracuse, New York; Mary Cole to "Dear Folks at Home," 24 July 1901, "July 1901" folder, box 1, Harry N. Cole Papers, Bentley Historical Library, Ann Arbor, Mich.; *The Log of the 'Thomas,' July 23 to August 21, 1901*, ed. Ronald P. Gleason (n.p., 1901), 54, 58; diary entry, 25 July 1901, "Diary 1/4" folder, box 1, Blaine Free Moore Papers, Library of Congress, Washington, D.C.

9. Geraldine Joncich Clifford, "Man/Woman/Teacher: Gender, Family, and Career in American Educational History," in *American Teachers: Histories of a Profession at Work*, ed. Donald Warren (New York: Macmillan, 1990), 294; Mary Cole to "Dear Folks at Home," 24 July 1901, "July 1901" folder, box 1, Cole Papers; Amparo Santamaria Lardizabal, *Pioneer American Teachers and Philippine Education* (Quezon City, Phil.: Phoenix Press, 1991), 7; Fred W. Atkinson to Clarence R. Edwards, 16 November 1901, file 470–26; W. S. Washburn to Edwards, 12 August 1904, file 470–147, both in box 84, BIA; *Eighth Annual Report of the Director of Education* (Manila: Bureau of Printing, 1908), p. 51, "Philippine Islands—Report to the Department of the Interior" folder, carton 6, David Prescott Barrows Papers, Bancroft Library, University of California-Berkeley.

10. *Eighth Annual Report of the Director of Education*, 51; *A Survey of the Educational System of the Philippine Islands* (Manila: Bureau of Printing, 1925), 71; Charles O. Walcutt to B. W. Anthony, 24 June 1913, file 3140–117, box 322, BIA; James S. Scott, "Report on work of obtaining American teachers in the United States. March 1 to May 18, 1921" (ms), pp. 2, 4, "Articles 1922" binder; William W. Marquardt

to Leonard Wood, 1 April 1922, "Articles Correspondence Philippines 1922" binder, both in box 7, William W. Marquardt Papers, Bentley Historical Library.

11. Edwin Dexter to Clarence R. Edwards, n.d. [1909], file 42–54, box 5, BIA; *Report of the Commissioner of Education for Porto Rico to the Secretary of the Interior, USA* (Washington, D.C.: Government Printing Office, 1900), p. 15, "General File: Puerto Rico—Publications on Puerto Rican Education" folder, box 193, Samuel McCune Lindsay Papers, Manuscript Division, Columbia University Libraries, New York; Edwin G. Dexter to M. Drew Carrel, 30 April 1912, file 42–105; E. W. Lord, "Department of Education of Porto Rico. Office of the Commissioner. San Juan. Circular of Information" (ms, n.d. [1900]), p. 2, file 42–46; E. M. Bainter to "Dear Madam," 10 May 1913, file 42–135, all in box 5, BIA.

12. "The Teaching Staff of the Public Elementary Schools of Hawaii. Advance Material from the Federal School Survey Report," *Hawaii Educational Review* 9 (February 1921): 174, 188; "Mainland Observer," "What's Wrong With Hawaii's Public Schools?" *Honolulu Advertiser*, 21 June 1919, file 9–4–31, box 624, Office of the Territories Records, Record Group 126, National Archives II; Frank McIntyre to Edwin Dexter, 7 December 1909, file 42–49; Dexter to Clarence R. Edwards, n.d. [1909], file 42–54, both in box 5, BIA; Vaughan MacCaughey, "The Teacher Supply Situation in Hawaii," *School and Society* 12 (6 November 1920): 434–435. Unlike the Philippines, which appointed teachers via the U.S. Civil Service Commission, Puerto Rico and Hawaii selected school staff without any federal examinations or assistance. Bureau of Education circular, n.d. [1907], enclosed with Elmer Ellsworth Brown to C. R. Edwards, 29 March 1907, file 3140–36, box 322, BIA.

13. Henry S. Townsend, "Recollections and Reflections of the Writer" (ms, n.d. [1935]), vol. 2, chap. 23, p. 8, Hamilton Hawaiian Collection, University of Hawaii-Manoa, Honolulu, Hawaii.

14. As David Labaree has shown, teachers in the United States moved frequently in order to improve their salaries and living conditions. Labaree, "Career Ladders and the Early Public High-School Teacher: A Study of Inequality and Opportunity," in Warren, ed., *American Teachers*, 164. For examples of teachers who moved between overseas territories, see J. B. Stearns to Willis T. Pope, 22 September 1911, folder 16, box 54, Records of the Department of Education, Series 261, Hawaii State Archives, Honolulu, Hawaii; "News Notes," *Hawaii Educational Review* 12 (March 1924): 125; Benjamin Wist to J. W. Moore, 8 May 1933, "Samoan File: Correspondence 1933" folder, box 37, Benjamin Wist Papers, University Archives and Special Collections, University of Hawaii-Manoa.

15. On teachers' skepticism of administrative authority in the United States during these years, see, for example, Murphy, *Blackboard Unions*, 23–45; Jonna Perrillo, "Beyond 'Progressive' Reform: Bodies, Discipline, and the Construction of the Professional Teacher in Interwar America," *History of Education Quarterly* 44 (Fall 2004): 337–363, esp. 356–358.

16. "Morphet Will Go to Philippines," *Fairmount News* [Indiana], 10 April 1922, folder 4, box 3; "Omar Khayam" [Edgar L. Morphet], "The Bureau of Likes and Dislikes," *Benedicto's Weekly* [Iolio, Phil.], 24 March 1923, "Publications" folder, box 5, both in Edgar L. Morphet Papers, Hoover Institution Archives, Stanford University, Palo Alto, Calif.

17. Khayam [Morphet], "The Bureau of Likes and Dislikes."

18. Edgar L Morphet, "Tin Can Orchestra" (ms, 18 December 1922), p. 2, folder 3, box 3, Morphet Papers.

19. May Faurote, untitled mss, n.d. [1914], pp. 264, 271, "Bureau of Education Activities 1914. Early Experiences of American Teachers" binder, box 6, Marquardt Papers.

20. Carter G. Woodson, *The Mis-Education of the Negro* (Washington, D.C.: Associated Publishers, 1933), 152–53; Leonard Ayres to Dear Ida, 17 January 1903, "1902–1930" folder, box 2, Leonard P. Ayres Papers, Library of Congress; E. G. Allen, "Vocational Education in the Rural Schools of Hawaii," *Hawaii Educational Review* 2 (May 1914): 2.

21. Philinda Rand to "Katie," 31 August 1902, "Anglemyer, P.R. 1902" folder, box 1, Philinda Rand Anglemyer Papers, Arthur and Elizabeth Schlesinger Library, Radcliffe College, Cambridge, Mass.; Helen French to "My dear Mamma," 19 March 1900, "March 1900" folder, box 1, Wood Family Papers, Rare Books and Manuscripts Division, Cornell University Libraries, Ithaca, N.Y.; William W. Marquardt to Hollister Marquardt, 8 February 1916, p. 198, "Humorous, Personal Letters, Memoranda, Addresses" binder, box 5, Marquardt Papers; Herbert Priestley to "Dear Mother," 4 October 1903, "Transcriptions of letters, October, 1903" folder, box 1, Herbert I. Priestley Papers, Bancroft Library.

22. Frank A. Butts to William W. Marquardt, 20 May 1915, p. 97, "Humorous, Personal Letters, Memoranda, Addresses" binder, box 5, Marquardt Papers; Harry Cole to "Dear Mother," 12 September 1901, "August-September 1901" folder, box 1, Cole Papers.

23. See, for example, Herbert Priestley to "Dearest Mother," 1 June 1902, "Transcriptions of letters, June 1902" folder, box 1, Priestley Papers; Louis D. Baun to ?, 20 April 1902, p. 39, "Serving America's First Peace Corps: Letters of Louis D. Baun. Written en route to, and from The Philippines. September 12, 1901—March 30, 1903" (ms, Bancroft Library); diary entry, 21 March 1902, "September 1901-July 30 1902" diary, "Diaries and Account Books 1901–1902" folder, box 1, Neal Papers; unidentified teacher letter, enclosed with D. H. McBride to C. R. Edwards, 26 June 1905, file 3140–26, box 322, BIA.

24. American Teacher's Association of Puerto Rico, untitled resolution, 24 February 1900, file 42–44, box 5, BIA; "Information which might be secured from the Acting General Superintendent" (ms, n.d. [1902]), "Material relating to the Philippines Commission, 1900–1907" folder, carton 2, Bernard Moses Papers, Bancroft Library.

25. Harry Cole to "Dear Leon," 21 October 1901, "October-November 1901" folder, box 1, Cole Papers.

26. Theodore de Laguna, "Education in the Philippines," *Gunton's Magazine* 24 (March 1903): 224; Stephen Bonsal, "The Philippines—After an Earthquake," *North American Review* 174 (March 1902): 419.

27. Herbert Priestley to "Dear Mommy," 16 August 1901, "Transcriptions of letters, July–August 1901" folder; Priestley to "Dearest Sissy," 4 September 1901; Priestley to "Dear Mother," 25 September 1901, both in "Transcriptions of letters, September 1901" folder; Priestley to "Dearest Mommy," 26 April 1902, "Transcriptions of letters, April 1902" folder; Priestley to "Dear Mother," 9 May 1902, "Transcriptions of letters, May 1902" folder; Priestley to "Dear Mother," 9 May 1903, "Transcriptions of letters, March 1903" folder, all in box 1, Priestley Papers.

28. Frederick W. Nash, "Educational Affairs in the Philippines," *Educational Review* 27 (March 1904): 232; Henry Parker Willis, *Our Philippines Problem: A Study of American Colonial Policy* (New York: Henry Holt, 1905), 228–229; n.a. [W. W. Marquardt], "Teachers I Have Known" (ms, n.d.), pp. 36–39, "Talks and Papers. 1922–1930" binder, box 6, Marquardt Papers; *Report of the Commissioner of Education for Porto Rico to the Secretary of the Interior, USA* (Washington, D.C.: General Printing Office, 1902), p. 81, "General File: Puerto Rico—Publications on Puerto Rican Education" folder, box 193, Lindsay Papers; Leonard P. Ayres to Ida, 15 June 1903, "1902–1930" folder, box 2, Ayres Papers.

29. Interview with Eileen Tam by Joe Rossi, 7 March 1991, in *Public Education in Hawaii: Oral Histories*, 2 vols. (Honolulu: Center for Oral History, Social Science Research Institute, University of Hawaii at Manoa, 1991), I: 139; Oma Little Duncan, "School on a Sugar Plantation," in *Makers of Destiny, Hawaiian Style: The Lives of Pioneer Women Educators in Hawaii* (Honolulu: Delta Kappa Gamma Society, 1981), 13; Interview with Virginia McBride by Rossi, 19 February 1991, in *Public Education in Hawaii: Oral Histories*, II: 335–336; Helen L. French to "Dear Papa and Mama," 3 December 1899, "November–December 1899" folder; French to "Dear Papa and Mamma," 3 January 1900; French to "Dear Mamma," 17 January 1900; French to "Dear Mamma," 29 January 1900, all in "January 1900" folder; French to "My dear Mamma," 1 May 1900, "April–May 1900" folder, all in box 1, Wood Family Papers.

30. Dr. Tiago, "Remnants and Floggings," p. 36, "Humorous, Personal Letters, Memoranda, Addresses" binder, box 5, Marquardt Papers; "Solons Urge Elimination of American Teachers to Avoid School Rows," *Philippine Herald*, 13 October 1930, file 3725A, box 512, BIA.

31. Burton S. John, "The Specific Problems Faced by the Missionary Educator in China," pp. 81–82; T. H. P. Sailer, "The Professional Training of the Educational Missionary," pp. 151–154; Edward D. Soper, "The Facilities Afforded in North American Institutions for the Adequate Preparation of Educational Missionaries," p. 129, all in *Report of a Conference on the Preparation of Educational Missionaries*, ed. Frank K. Sanders (New York: Board of Missionary Preparation, n.d. [1917]).

32. George Drach, "Discussion," in *Report of a Conference*, 202.

33. Dana L. Robert, *American Women in Mission: A Social History of Their Thought and Practice* (Macon, Ga.: Mercer University Press, 1996), 226–227.

34. Jane Hunter, *The Gospel of Gentility: American Women Missionaries in Turn-of-the-Century China* (New Haven, Conn.: Yale University Press, 1984), 36; Kathleen L. Lodwick, *Educating the Women of Hainan: The Career of Margaret Moninger in China, 1915–1942* (Lexington: University Press of Kentucky, 1995), 5; Clifford, "Man/Woman/Teacher," 309; Sailer, "The Professional Training of the Educational Missionary," 151; John Norman Hostetter, "Mission Education in a Changing Society: Brethren in Christ Mission Education in Southern Rhodesia, Africa, 1899–1959" (Ed.D. diss., State University of New York at Buffalo, 1967), 78; Henry C. McDowell to Ernest W. Riggs, HCM/Ang.2/11/4 folder, box 3, Henry C. McDowell Papers, Savery Library, Talladega College, Talladega, Ala.; Irene Sheppard to Jane Doolittle, 21 November 1929, folder 12, box 20, Board of Foreign Missions—Iran Mission [hereafter "BFM-Iran"], Record Group 91; Cleland B. McAfee to Norman E. Richardson, 12 May 1932, folder 4, box 4, PCUSA Board of

Foreign Missions, Secretaries' Files [hereafter "PCUSA-BFM"], Record Group 81, both in Presbyterian Historical Society.

35. Cleland B. McAfee to O. R. Sellers, 28 December 1931, folder 4, box 4, PCUSA-BFM; Katherine B. Ward interview (ms, 4 March 1970 and 12 January 1971), p. 2, China Missionaries Oral History Project, Manuscript Division, Columbia University Libraries; T. H. P. Sailer to Stanley White, 24 February 1914, folder 20, box 4, PCUSA-BFM; "Minute on Retirement of Professor Mabel Carney" (ms, n.d. [1942]), folder 388; "Course 62—Methods of Education in Foreign Lands" (ms, 1934), folder 383, both in box 28, Mabel Carney Papers, Hartford Seminary, Hartford, Conn.

36. Mabel Carney to Malcolm Pitt, 25 March 1942, folder 386, box 28, Carney Papers; Walter E. Hoffsommer, "The Training of the Educational Missionary During his First Period of Service on the Field and During His First Furlough," in *Report of a Conference on the Preparation of Educational Missionaries*, 161; "Facts Regarding the Instituto Ingles" (ms, 1922), folder 2, box 5, Board of Foreign Missions—Chile Mission [hereafter "BFM-Chile"], Record Group 160, Presbyterian Historical Society.

37. T. H. P. Sailer, *Report of the Committee on the Preparation of Educational Missionaries* (n.p., n.d. [1916]), p. 29, enclosed with Sailer to Ernest Burton, 13 September 1916, folder 8, box 25, Ernest DeWitt Burton Papers, Joseph Regenstein Memorial Library, University of Chicago; Esther B. Rhoads to Margaret Rhoads, 15 February 1923, "January–February 1923" folder, box 15, Esther B. Rhoads Papers, Quaker Collection, Haverford College, Haverford, Penn.

38. Esther Rhoads to Margaret Rhoads, n.d. [1917], "Letters from Rhoads. September 10–27, 1917" folder, box 13; Esther Rhoads to Margaret Rhoads, 4 February, no year, "Letters from Rhoads. n.d. ca. 1920s (2)" folder, box 14; Esther Rhoads to Margaret Rhoads, 19 September 1926, "Letters from Rhoads. March–September 1926" folder, box 16; Esther Rhoads to Caroline Rhoads, 9 February 1931, "Letters from Rhoads. 1931" folder, box 17, all in Rhoads Papers.

39. Esther Rhoads to "Dear Mother," 25 September, no year, "Letters from Rhoads. n.d. ca. 1920s (2)" folder, box 14, Rhoads Papers; "An English Teacher," *Ramallah Messenger* 3 (September 1906): 5; Alice W. Jones, untitled article, *Ramallah Messenger* 5 (June 1908): 6; Eunice R. Blackburn to "My dear Dr. Hollister," 6 November 1920, folder 2, box 1, Eunice R. Blackburn Papers, Record Group 198, Presbyterian Historical Society; Lucy Wiatt to Grace Maine, 19 August 1934, "Mandalay: Girls High School" folder, Board of International Missions Subject Files [hereafter "BIMSF"], American Baptist Archives Center, Valley Forge, Penn.; Jane Doolittle to Mrs. C. H. Corbett, 10 May 1932, folder 12, box 20, BFM-Iran.

40. Muriel Nichols to "Dear Home Folks," 28 May 1923, folder 6, box 1, Albert Sylvanus Nichols Papers, Billy Graham Center Archives, Wheaton College, Wheaton, Ill.; Edwin M. Wright, "Annual Report. Avicenna Middle School. 1936" (ms), p. 2, folder 25, box 19; Wright, "Resht Boys' School Annual Report. 1931–1932" (ms), folder 30, box 20, both in BFM-Iran.

41. Nancy Parker McDowell, *Notes from Ramallah, 1939* (Richmond, Ind.: Friends United Press, 2002), 18, 61–62; Ruth Bradley to "Dear friends," 10 September 1924; Bradley to "Dear friends," 28 March 1927, both in folder 2, box 1, Ruth Winifred Bradley Papers, Record Group 325, Presbyterian Historical Society;

"Report of Sophie S. Lanneau, Soochow, China for 2nd Quarter 1913" (ms), "Lanneau Sophie Stephens Ex Secy 1905–1918" folder, box 99, Sophie Stephens Lanneau Papers, Southern Baptist Historical Society and Archives, Nashville, Tenn.; "Report of Kathryn L. Dutton" (ms, 1943), folder 32, box 2, BFM-Chile.

42. "Personal Report of Esther M. Bartlett. 1937" (ms), folder 30, box 8, Board of Foreign Missions—West Africa Mission, Record Group 142, Presbyterian Historical Society; Arthur Judson Brown, *One Hundred Years: A History of the Foreign Mission Work of the Presbyterian Church of the U.S.A.*, vol. 1 (New York: Fleming H. Revell, 1936), appendix.

43. "Maryknoll Sisters History Project. Bolivia Region 1943–1958" (ms, 1994), p. 6, folder 21, box 2, Bolivia Collection, Maryknoll Fathers and Brothers Archives, Ossining, N.Y.; James F. Kearney, S.J., "Forming Leaders for Tomorrow?" *Jesuit Missions* 8 (November 1934), 265, 280; "Report of Cora M. Smith" (ms, 1937), p. 1, folder 26, box 2; "Report of Estella F. Daniel. Personal" (ms, 1936), folder 27, box 1, both in BFM-Chile.

44. Mary C. Alexander to T. B. Ray, 11 June 1923, "Alexander, Mary Charlotte Ex Secy 1920–35" folder, box 1, Mary C. Alexander Papers, Southern Baptist Historical Society and Archives; Sophie Lanneau to Charles E. Maddry, 21 March 1934, "Lanneau Sophie Stephens Ex Secy 1919–34" folder, box 99, Lanneau Papers; John E. Cummings to A. Hovey, 18 September 1893, "Burma: Survey—Relation of Schools and Higher Education to Missionary Operations Volume. I" folder; A. J. Rose to Hovey, n.d. [1893], "Burma: Survey—Relation of Schools and Higher Education to Missionary Operations Vol. II" folder, both in BIMSF.

45. Mission boards were reluctant to send single men into the field, fearing that men could not survive overseas without a spouse. By contrast, roughly one-third of female missionaries were single. In some countries, over half of them were unmarried. Lodwick, *Educating the Women of Hainan*, 2, 219n3; Michael P. Zirinsky, "Harbingers of Change: Presbyterian Women in Iran, 1883–1949," *American Presbyterians* 70 (Fall 1992): 175.

46. Eunice Blackburn to "Dear Family," 26 July 1925, folder 7, box 1, Blackburn Papers; Ellen A Tompkins, et. al. to Irene Sheppard, 11 December 1930; Sheppard to Tompkins et al., 30 December 1930, both in folder 8, box 11, Board of Foreign Missions, Colombia Mission, Record Group 88, Presbyterian Historical Society.

47. Henry C. McDowell to Alfred Lawless, 7 April 1924, HCM/Ang.2/9/2, box 2, McDowell Papers; "Report of Mrs. A. M. Alexander" (ms, 1936), folder 27, box 1, BFM-Chile; George Holcombe Lacy to R. J. Willingham, 12 January 1905, fiche 14; Lacy to Willingham, 7 September 1905, fiche 13, both in George Holcombe Lacy and Minnie Meek Lacy Papers, International Mission Board Archives, Southern Baptist Convention, Richmond, Va.; Henry C. McDowell to "My dear Friends," 26 September 1927, HCM/Ang.2/12/3; McDowell to Frank S. Brewer, 7 November 1928, HCM/Ang.2/13/2; McDowell to Alfred Lawless, 18 November 1928, HCM/Ang.2/13/2, all in box 3, McDowell Papers.

48. "Report of Kathryn L. Dutton" (ms, 1943), folder 32; "Report of Mrs. Robert B. Elmore" (ms, 1939), folder 28; "Report of Margaret Alexander" (ms, 1942), folder 31, all in box 2, BFM-Chile.

49. Esther Rhoads to Margaret Rhoads, 30 October 1930, "Letters from Rhoads. July–December 1930" folder, box 17, Rhoads Papers; Susan Anderson to

"J.A.," 20 July 1940, "Anderson Susan Area 1938–50" folder, box 2, Susan M. Anderson Papers, Southern Baptist Historical Library and Archives.

50. *The Peace Corps Experience*, ed. Roy Hoopes (New York: Clarkson N. Potter, 1968), 103.

51. *Eighth Annual Report of the Director of Education, July 1 1907 to June 30 1908* (Manila: Bureau of Printing, 1908), p. 51, "Philippine Islands—Report to the Department of the Interior" folder, carton 6, Barrows Papers; Harold Van Winkle, "Building Better Than They Knew," *Phi Delta Kappan* 36 (June 1955), p. 331, "American Teachers—Philippines" folder, box 8, Arthur R. Carson Papers, Hoover Institution Archives; "More Than Half of Volunteers Teach; 1400 in Secondary Schools Alone" *Peace Corps Volunteer* 1 (April 1963), 3; Roger L. Landrum, *The Role of the Peace Corps in Education in Developing Countries: A Sector Study* (Washington, D.C.: Peace Corps Information Collection and Exchange, 1984 [1981]), 7; Harlan Cleveland, Gerard J. Mangone and John Clarke Adams, *The Overseas Americans* (New York: McGraw-Hill, 1960), 83; Robert B. Tillman, "Report on the Proposal for an Office/Commission of Education in the D.O.M" (ms, April 1968), appendix, folder 7, box 8, National Council of Churches Papers, Division of Overseas Ministries [hereafter "NCC-DOM"], Record Group 8, Presbyterian Historical Society; *Opportunities Directory '71* (Downers Grove, Ill.: Short Terms Abroad, 1971), pp. 16–23, folder 4, box 10, Short Terms Abroad Papers, Billy Graham Center Archives; International Liaison, Inc., *The Response: Lay Volunteer Mission Opportunities, 1983–84*, 20th anniv. ed. (Washington, D.C.: n.p., 1983), folder 23, box 224, National Catholic Welfare Conference/United States Catholic Conference Collection [hereafter "NCWC/USCC"], American Catholic History Research Center, Catholic University, Washington, D.C.

52. *Teaching. Education Lays the Foundation for Human and Economic Development* (Washington, D.C.: Peace Corps, n.d. [1968], "Peace Corps—Teaching" file, Vertical Files, Peace Corps Library; Arnold Zeitlin, *To the Peace Corps, With Love* (Garden City, N.Y.: Doubleday, 1965), 24; Charles Peters, *Tilting at Windmills: An Autobiography* (Reading, Mass.: Addison Wesley, 1988), 123.

53. "A Peace Corps Test." Retrieved January 8, 2005, from http://peacecorpswriters.org/pages/2000/0005/printvers005/pv005pchist.htlml; Susan M. Anderson to "Dear J.A.," n.d. [1943]), "Anderson Susan Area 1938–50" folder, box 2, Anderson Papers; Helen L. Bailey and Herbert C. Jackson, *A Study of Missionary Motivation, Training, and Withdrawal (1953–1962)* (New York: Missionary Research Library, 1965), 30; C. R. Thayer to G. McLain, 4 February 1955; Thayer, "Report on Missionary A" (n.d. [1951]); Thayer, "Fred Russell" (rec. 12 September 1951); "Report on Candidate K" (n.d. [1951]), all in folder 27, box 24, Board of Foreign Missions—United Presbyterian Church of North America, Record Group 209, Presbyterian Historical Society. On the development and popularity of personality tests in the United States, see Annie Murphy Paul, *The Cult of Personality: How Personality Tests are Leading us to Miseducate Our Children, Mismanage Our Companies, and Misunderstand Ourselves* (New York: Free Press, 2004).

54. Fritz Fischer, *Making Them Like Us: Peace Corps Volunteers in the 1960s* (Washington, D.C.: Smithsonian Institution Press, 1998), 69, 75–76; Arnold Zeitlin, "Peace Corps Quiz Probes Aspirant," *Pittsburgh Post-Gazette*, 8 August 1961, "Ghana-Volunteer Information" folder, Collection 31, Peace Corps Volunteers Collection, National Anthropology Archives [hereafter "PC-NAA"], Museum

Support Center, Smithsonian Institution, Suitland, Md.; Alan Weiss, *High Risk/ High Gain: A Freewheeling Account of Peace Corps Training* (New York: St. Martin's, 1968), 211, 246, 231.

55. Fischer, *Making Them Like Us*, 43; "This is the Peace Corps, Miss Jones!" *Sunday News* [University Park, Penn.], 20 August 1961, folder 61, box 195, NCWC/USCC; William H. Hintz, "Close of Service Conference Report. Philippines 15" (ms, 22–24 June 1967), p. 7, "Philippines 15" folder, box 14; Willi Unsoeld and Richard A. Smith, "Close of Service Conference" (ms, 26 April 1965), p. 3, "Thailand VI" folder, box 6; Paul Sack and Andrew Hays, "Peace Corps Termination Conference. Somalia II" (ms, 18 May 1966), pp. 5, 7, "Somalia II" folder, box 9, all in PC-COS.

56. Fischer, *Making Them Like Us*, 33; "Peace Corps is Widening Its Role in Africa," *New York Times*, 31 March 1988, p. A11; John Rex, "Why Stay? A Point of View" (ms, 12 March 1964), p. 2, "Ethiopia—Volunteer Information" folder, Collection 31, PC-NAA; Sack and Hays, "Peace Corps Termination Conference. Somalia II," 4; *Teachers in the Peace Corps: From Rote to Reason* (Washington, D.C.: Peace Corps, n.d. [1968]), p. 1, "Peace Corps—Teaching" file, Vertical Files, Peace Corps Library; "Goal Seems Near for Peace Corps," *New York Times*, 24 September 1961, folder 61, box 195, NCWC/USCC.

57. "Corps Offers New Program for Teachers," *Peace Corps Volunteer* 2 (April 1964): 2; "33 Special-Term Missionaries to Go Overseas This Fall," *News from Board of Missions of the Methodist Church*, 9 July 1963, folder 5, box 393, Claude A. Barnett Papers, Chicago Historical Society; Theodore F. Fricke, "Rules and Regulations Pertaining to Candidates for Foreign Missions of the American Lutheran Church" (ms, n.d. [1949]), folder 12; American Baptist Foreign Mission Society and Woman's American Baptist Foreign Mission Society, "Suggested Standards in the Securing of Missionary Personnel" (ms, 19 November 1957), folder 11, both in box 2, R. Pierce Beaver Papers, Joseph Regenstein Memorial Library, University of Chicago; "A Look at Lay Missionary Groups" (ms, 1960), folder 58, box 194, NCWC/USCC; Janice Christina Smith, untitled statement, attached to "Friends Council on Education—Placement Service Blank" (12 January 1974), folder 6, box 5, Records of the Philadelphia Yearly Meeting—Japan Committee, Quaker Collection, Haverford College.

58. Mary Shannon questionnaire (ms, 1994), folder 1, box 3, Bolivia Collection; "Mission News Service" (ms, 1968), p. 4, folder 9, box 1, Mexico Collection, both in Maryknoll Fathers and Brothers Archives; William E. Gaymon, "COS Conference Liberia V" (ms, 6 February 1967), p. 4, "Liberia V" folder, box 8, PC-COS; "My Failure—the First Year. By a Peace Corps English Teacher," *Peace Corps—Ethiopia News*, n.d. (1963), p. 6, "Ethiopia—Volunteer Information" folder, Collection 31, PC-NAA; "Personal Report of Margaret S. C. Thomson (ms, 1958), folder 21, box 5, Korea Mission Papers, Record Group 197, Presbyterian Historical Society.

59. Julius A. Amin, *The Peace Corps in Cameroon* (Kent, Ohio: Kent State University Press, 1992), 121, 101; Mennonite Central Committee, *Teachers Abroad Program in Africa and Newfoundland* (n.p., n.d. [1967]), p. 3, folder 39, box 79, Evangelical Foreign Missions Association Papers, Billy Graham Center Archives; Omar Eby, *How Full the River* (Scottsdale, Pa.: Herald Press, 1972), 40; Nancy Chamberlayne, "Close of Service Conference Report. Cameroon III" (13 July 1966), p. 9, "Cameroon III" folder, box 6, PC-COS.

60. Raymond J. Smyke, "Problem of Teacher Supply and Demand," *Panorama* 3 (Winter 1961–62): 13; Paul Cromwell, "Close of Service Conference. Nigeria VII" (ms, 9 January 1966), p. 3, "Nigeria VII" folder; Daniel A. Sharp and Henry U. Wheatley, "Close of Service Conference—Senegal" (ms, 4 June 1965), p. 3, "Senegal III" folder, both in box 5, PC-COS; Donald S. Stroetzel, "The Other 49 Peace Corps," *Christian Herald*, n.d. [1967], folder 57, box 11, Short Terms Abroad Papers; Jan S. F. van Hoogstraten to Nancy Nicalo, 6 December 1968, folder 19, box 17, NCC-DOM; Eby, *How Full the River*, 38. On the Peace Corps and other Western volunteer agencies in the 1960s, see Elizabeth Cobbs Hoffman, *All You Need is Love: The Peace Corps and the Spirit of the 1960s* (Cambridge, Mass.: Harvard University Press, 1998), Chap. 3.

61. See, for example, Zeitlin, *To the Peace Corps, With Love*, 47; Eugene Bable, "Close of Service Conference. Cameroon I. Cameroon II" (ms, 8–13 June, 1965), p. 5, "Cameroon I and Cameroon II" folder, box 3; Daniel A. Sharp, "Report of Close of Service Conference. Ivory Coast III. Abidjan, April 15, 1965 (ms), "Ivory Coast III" folder, box 4, both in PC-COS; Frances M. Parsons, "First Deaf Peace Corps Volunteer Was Influenced to Join by President Kennedy," *Silent News*, October 1992, folder 1, Peace Corps Papers, Gallaudet University Archives, Washington, D.C.

62. Mark Harris, *Twentyone Twice: A Journal* (Boston: Little, Brown, 1966), 234; Jane Campbell, "Report on Close of Service Conference with Volunteers in Kaduna, Nigeria" (ms, 19 September 1963), p. 9, "Nigeria" folder, box 1; Thomas D. Scott and Gene Gordon, "Close of Service Conference—Morocco I" (ms, 7–10 August 1964), p. 4, "Morocco I" folder, box 2, both in PC-COS; Sharp and Wheatley, "Close of Service Conference—Senegal," 2; Jo Ann Cannon, "Cultural Map-Reading Applies to the Relationship between the European Community and Peace Corps in Malawi" (ms, n.d. [1964]), "Malawi-Peace Corps Folder #2" file, Vertical Files, Peace Corps Library.

63. "PEST CORPS. GO HOME!" *Peace Corps Volunteer* 5 (April 1967): 24; "An Observer," *Truth About the P.Corps* (New Delhi: People's Publishing House, 1968), 12, 18–19; Vincent J. D'Andrea, "Close of Service Conference. Philippine VII" (ms, 1964), p. 27, "Philippines VII" folder, box 2; John Starkey, "Close of Service Conference. Morocco III" (ms, 10 June 1966), p. 7, "Morocco III" folder, box 8, both in PC-COS; Theodore A. Braun, "Report on a Trip to Africa, April 5–May 17, 1964" (ms, 18 June 1964), p. 3, "TEA" folder, box 192, R. Freeman Butts Papers, Hoover Institution Archives; "HAVP Report. December 1971" (ms), p. 1, folder 18; Nancy Nicalo to Donald Mathews, 22 July 1969, folder 19, both in box 17, NCC-DOM.

64. Martin Benjamin, "Letters From a Peace Corpsman," *Symposium* [Union College, Schenectady, N.Y.], Summer 1963, p. 13, "Ethiopia-Volunteer Information" folder, Collection 31, PC-NAA; Raymond Gold, *A Teaching Safari: A Study of American Teachers in East Africa* (Baltimore, Md.: Publish America, 2004), 133; Butts, *American Education in International Development*, 76; *Making a Difference: The Peace Corps at Twenty-Five*, ed. Milton Viorst (New York: Wedienfeld and Nicolson, 1986), 36; Phillips Stevens Jr., "An Ethnographer Without Portfolio," in *Anthropology and the Peace Corps: Case Studies in Career Preparation*, eds. Brian E. Schwimmer and D. Michael Warren (Ames: Iowa State University Press, 1993), 29; Joseph S. Murphy and Paul Cromwell, "Close of Service Conference. Nigeria VII. Ibandan.

April 19–21, 1965" (ms), p. 6, "Nigeria VII" folder, box 5, PC-COS; Jack Presbis to All Volunteers, n.d. [1965], "Ethiopia-Volunteer Information" folder, Collection 31, PC-NAA.

65. Padraic Kennedy, "Report on Completion of Service Conference with Volunteers in Accra, Ghana" (ms, 6 December 1963), pp. 10, 4, "Ghana I" folder; Helen A. Wilson, "Close of Service Conference. Ghana II" (ms, 26–29 May, 1964), p. 3, "Ghana II" folder, both in box 2, PC-COS.

66. See, for example, Sharp, "Report of Close of Service Conference. Ivory Coast III," 9; Harris Wofford, "With 400 Volunteers in Haile Selassie's Court" (ms, n.d.), p. 36, "Ethiopia—Peace Corps, 1970–1977, folder #1" file, Vertical Files, Peace Corps Library; Peggy Anderson, "The Volunteer Experience: A Plea for Truth in Advertising," in *The Evaluation Reader: Selections from Evaluation Reports Published 1961–66 Describing and Attempting to Illuminate the Main Problems of the Peace Corps*, ed. Ann Anderson (Washington, D.C.: Peace Corps Office of Evaluation and Research, 1967), 48–55; William M. Baxter, "Close of Service Conference. Nigeria XIV. Secondary Education" (ms, 23 February 1967), pp. 11–12, "Nigeria XIV" folder, box 9, PC-COS.

67. Cynthia Courtney et al., "Close of Service Conference. Nigeria VII. Nsukka, Eastern Region. April 25–27, 1965" (ms), p. 3, "Nigeria VII" folder, box 5; William Gaymon et al., "Special Conference Report" (ms, 1966), p. 3, "Ethiopia III" folder, box 7, both in PC-COS; Dee McGuire, "Off the Compound," *Peace Corps Volunteer* 5 (March 1967): 20–21.

68. See, for example, Gaymon, "COS Conference Liberia V," 2; diary entries, 18 February 1969 and 8 May 1969, 1968–1970 diary, Peter V. Deekle Papers, Collection 10, PC-NAA; Braun, "Report on a Trip to Africa," 3.

69. See, for example, Efrem Sigel, "A Peace Corpsman Looks Back," in *The Peace Corps Reader* (Washington, D.C.: Peace Corps, 1968): 173; Richard Lipez, "Culture and the Classroom," in Anderson, ed., *Evaluation Reader*, 102–103; diary entries, 5 January 1972, 25 March 1972, and 13 May 1972, diary vol. 1, folder 1; diary entries, 17 January 1974, 4 February 1974, and 22 February 1974, diary vol. 3, folder 1, all in folder 1, box 1, Alfred T. Giannini Papers, Collection 8, PC-NAA.

70. Nathan Lindgren to "Mom and Dad," 26 September 1963, microfilm reel 1, Nathan Lindgren Papers, Wisconsin Historical Society, Madison, Wis.; Robert A. Randall, "Similarities between Peace Corps and Anthropological Experience," in Schwimmer and Warren, eds., *Anthropology and the Peace Corps*, 91; Sally Ruffino to "Everyone," 26 April 1964, folder 1, box 1, Sally Ruffino Papers, Collection 12, PC-NAA; Bable, "Close of Service Conference. Cameroon I. Cameroon II," 1.

71. Bable, "Close of Service Conference. Cameroon I. Cameroon II," 1; Julius Nimmons and Allan Kulakow, "Close of Service Conference. Uganda I" (ms, 23 February 1967), pp. 13–14, "Uganda I" folder, box 10; L. H. Mirel, "Close of Service Conference Kenya II" (ms, 2 March 1967), pp. 11–12, "Kenya II" folder, box 8, both in PC-COS; Fulmer, "COS Conference Report. Tanzania Group VII," 11; Bethany Rogers, " 'Better' People, Better Teaching: The Historical Tradition of the National Teacher Corps" (in author's possession).

72. In the 1960s and 1970s, over one-quarter of returning Peace Corps volunteers entered primary, secondary, or university-level teaching. Since roughly half of the total volunteer force during this period served as teachers overseas, it seems fair

to presume that at least half of the Peace Corps teachers went into educational careers in the United States. Gerard T. Rice, *Twenty Years of the Peace Corps* (Washington, D.C.: Peace Corps, 1981), 82; Landrum, *The Role of the Peace Corps in Education in Developing Countries*, 7.

73. *Teaching. Education Lays the Foundation for Human and Economic Development*, 16; Dean M. Gottehrer, "Teaching in the Ghetto," *Peace Corps Volunteer* 6 (July/August 1968): 19; *Teachers in the Peace Corps: From Rote to Reason*, 12; "My Failure—The First Year," 3; Deborah J. Seymour Oral History, tape 2, Deborah J. Seymour Collection, Billy Graham Center Archives.

74. "A Collection: Evaluation Comments on TEFL" (ms, n.d. [1969]), p. 3, "Peace Corps—TEFL, TESOL, Etc." file, Vertical Files, Peace Corps Library; *Peace Corps: Liberal Arts* (Washington, D.C.: Peace Corps, n.d. [1987]), General Collection, Canaday Library, Bryn Mawr College, Bryn Mawr, Penn.; Mary Anne Dolan, "He Teaches Deaf in Ghana," *Washington Evening Star*, 24 August 1971, folder 1, Daniel Joseph Blessing Papers; Joan Kelley, "Peace Corps Teaching Deaf in Philippines," *Woodland [Ill.] Democrat*, 31 March 1976, folder 1, Peace Corps Papers; Clyde Vincent to Frances Parsons, 28 March 1978, folder 7, box 2, Frances Parsons Papers, all in Gallaudet University Archives.

75. Thelma Ragsdale, "Teaching Problems of the Foreign Missionary: A Questionnaire Study" (M.A. thesis, Wheaton College, Wheaton, Ill., 1947), 98; Marilyn Mae Morley, "The Role of the Missionary Teacher in Modern Missions" (M.A. thesis, Wheaton College, Wheaton, Ill., 1964), 108, 117; Bradley Baurain, "Teaching English feeds a worldwide craving," *Evangelical Missions Quarterly* 28 (1992): 164; Donald B. Snow, *English Teaching as Christian Mission: An Applied Theology* (Scottdale, Penn.: Herald Press, 2001), 12, 67.

76. Karen Schwarz, *What You Can Do for Your Country: An Oral History of the Peace Corps* (New York: William Morrow, 1991), 275, 279, 285.

5. Going Global, or Going It Alone?

1. Edgar M. Wilson, "Minority Report of Committee on Government Grants" (ms, 1902), enclosed with Robert E. Speer to George Alexander, 6 February 1903, folder 7, box 23, Board of Foreign Missions—India Mission [hereafter BFM-India], Presbyterian Historical Society, Philadelphia, Penn. On the contentious history of federal aid to denominational schools for Native Americans in the late nineteenth century, see Francis Paul Prucha, *American Indian Policy in Crisis: Christian Reformers and the Indian, 1865–1900* (Norman: University of Oklahoma Press, 1976) and Robert H. Keller Jr., *American Protestantism and United States Indian Policy, 1869–1882* (Lincoln: University of Nebraska Press, 1983).

2. See, for example, John Witte Jr., "Introduction," in *Religious and Human Rights in Global Perspective: Religious Perspectives*, eds. John Witte Jr. and Johan D. van der Vyver (The Hague: Martinus Nijhoff Publishers, 1996), xxviii; Charles L. Glenn, *The Ambiguous Embrace: Government and Faith-Based Schools and Social Agencies* (Princeton: Princeton University Press, 2000), 99; Glenn, "Religion and Education: American Exceptionalism?" in *Making Good Citizens: Education and Civil Society*, eds. Diane Ravitch and Joseph P. Viteritti (New Haven, Conn.: Yale University Press, 2001), 297–325; Philip Jenkins, *The Next Christendom: The Coming of Global Christianity* (New York: Oxford University Press, 2002), 153.

3. H. W. Langheim to Arthur J. Brown, 26 May 1909; Charles R. Hamilton to Arthur J. Brown, 20 August 1909, both in reel 289, Presbyterian Church of the USA–Board of Foreign Missions, Philippine Mission Correspondence and Reports, Microfilm series [hereafter "Philippines Microfilm"], Presbyterian Historical Society.

4. Bette Novit Evans, *Interpreting the Free Exercise of Religion: The Constitution and American Pluralism* (Chapel Hill: University of North Carolina Press, 1997), 1; Warren A. Nord, *Religion and American Education: Rethinking a National Dilemma* (Chapel Hill: University of North Carolina Press, 1995), 111–120; "Encounters in Law, Philosophy, Religion, and Education," in *Curriculum, Religion, and Public Education: Conversations for an Enlarging Public Square*, ed. James T. Sears, with James C. Carper (New York: Teachers College Press, 1998), 33–34.

5. Sophie Lanneau to T. B. Ray, 2 February 1931, "Lanneau Sophie Stephens Ex Secy 1919–34" folder, box 99, Sophie Stephens Lanneau Papers, Southern Baptist Historical Society and Archives, Nashville, Tenn.

6. *Modernism and Foreign Missions: Two Fundamentalist Protests*, ed. Joel A. Carpenter (New York: Garland, 1988), 1–2; Joel A. Carpenter, "Propagating the Faith Once Delivered: The Fundamentalist Missionary Enterprise, 1920–1945" in *Earthen Vessels: American Evangelicals and Foreign Missions*, eds. Joel A. Carpenter and Wilbert R. Shenk (Grand Rapids, Mich.: William B. Eerdmans, 1990), 92, 99; Grant Wacker, "Second Thoughts on the Great Commission: Liberal Protestants and Foreign Missions, 1890–1940," ibid., 288; Richard V. Pierard, "Evangelical and Ecumenical: Missionary Leaders in Mainline Protestantism, 1900–1950," in *Re-Forming the Center: American Protestantism, 1900 to the Present*, eds. Douglas Jacobsen and William Vance Trollinger Jr. (Grand Rapids, Mich.: William B. Eerdmans, 1998), 170.

7. "Cosmopolitan" derives from the Greek words *kosmos* and *polis*; a cosmopolitan, then, is a "citizen of the world." Following John Tomlinson, this chapter associates *cosmopolitanism* with "a willingness to engage with the Other' and "an openness toward divergent cultural experiences." John Tomlinson, *Globalization and Culture* (Chicago: University of Chicago, 1999), 184–185. For other definitions and discussions of the concept, see Kristin Hoganson, "Cosmopolitan Domesticity: Importing the American Dream, 1965–1920," *American Historical Review* 107 (February 2002): 55–83; *Cosmopolitics: Thinking and Feeling Beyond the Nation*, eds. Pheng Chea and Bruce Robbins (Minneapolis: University of Minnesota Press, 1998); Martha C. Nussbaum, *For Love of Country: Debating the Limits of Patriotism* (Boston: Beacon Press, 1996); David A. Hollinger, *Postethnic America: Beyond Multiculturalism* (New York: Basic Books, 1995), 79–104; Ulf Hannerz, "Cosmopolitans and Locals in World Culture," in *Global Culture: Nationalism, Globalization and Modernity*, ed. Mike Featherstone (London: Sage Publications, 1990), 237–251.

8. E. S. Hume to Edgar M. Wilson, n.d. [1902], quoted in Wilson to Robert E. Speer, 21 November 1902, folder 7, box 23, BFM-India.

9. See, for example, Daniel T. Rodgers, *Atlantic Crossings: Social Politics in a Progressive Age* (Cambridge, Mass.: Harvard University Press, 1998); Penny von Eschen, *Race Against Empire* (Ithaca, N.Y.: Cornell University Press, 1997); Azza Salama Layton, *International Politics and Civil Rights Policies in the United States, 1941–1960* (Cambridge: Cambridge University Press, 2000).

10. Harry and Mary Cole to "My dear Mother and Leon," 16 March 1902, "January–March 1902" folder, box 1, Harry N. Cole Papers, Bentley Historical Library, Ann Arbor, Mich.

11. "Speech of Dr. Lindsay, Commissioner of Education, at the dedication of the Roosevelt Industrial School in Ponce, February 22nd 1904" (ms, 1904), p. 6, "General File: Puerto Rico—Photographs and artwork by Puerto Rican students, scrapbooks" folder, box 192, Samuel McCune Lindsay Papers, Manuscript Division, Columbia University Libraries, New York; Henry C. Blair to Governor, 4 May 1918, file 71–1918, box 45, Virgin Islands Records, Record Group 55, National Archives II, College Park, Md.; Homer C. Stuntz, *The Philippines and the Far East* (New York: Jennings and Pye, 1904), 190; Leonard Ayres to "Dear Mayblossom," 23 December 1902, "1902–1930" folder, box 2, Leonard P. Ayres Papers, Library of Congress, Washington, D.C.; May Faurote, untitled mss, n.d., p. 272, "Bureau of Education. Activities 1914. Early Experiences of American Teachers," binder, box 6, Walter W. Marquardt Papers, Bentley Historical Library; Vaughan MacCaughey, "Some Outstanding Educational Problems of Hawaii," *School and Society* 9 (25 January 1919): 102.

12. Mary Cole to "Dear Folks at home," 18 January 1902, "April–May 1902" folder, box 1, Cole Papers; Fred W. Atkinson, "Report of the General Superintendent of Public Instruction to the Secretary of Public Instruction for the Period From May 27, 1901 to October 1, 1901," *Report of the Philippines Commission to the Secretary of War*, part 2 (Washington, D.C.: General Printing Office, 1901), 541; Arthur E. Lindborg to Benjamin Wist, n.d. [1933], "Samoan File: Correspondence 1933" folder, box 37, Benjamin Wist Papers, University Archives and Special Collections, University of Hawaii—Manoa; E. Benjamin Oliver to Henry Blair, 25 September 1918, file 71–1918, box 45; H. J. Benedict to Director of Education, 1 November 1929, file 46–1929–30, box 19, both in Virgin Islands Records; Walter W. Marquardt, "Teachers I Have Known," p. 37; Marquardt, "Morals and Religion," pp. 88–89, both in "Talks and Papers. 1922–30" binder, box 6, Marquardt Papers.

13. Hiram Francis Fairbanks to Theodore Roosevelt, 10 June 1902, file 1534–13, box 201; n.a., "Protestant Ministers Running Philippine Public School System" (ms, 3 May 1902), pp. 1–3, file 470–41, box 84; Hugh J. Carroll to Elihu Root, 24 May 1902, file 1534–12, box 201; *Memorial Bearing Upon the Philippine Schools* (n.p., 16 July 1902), enclosed with Henry Moeller to Theodore Roosevelt, 11 August 1902, file 1534–16, box 201, all in Bureau of Insular Affairs Records [hereafter "BIA"], Record Group 350, National Archives II.

14. John Ireland to Clarence R. Edwards, 9 January 1903, file 3263, box 330, BIA; Frank T. Reuter, "American Catholics and the Establishment of the Philippine Public School System," *Catholic Historical Review* 49 (October 1963): 380; C. R. Edwards to William Loeb Jr., 2 July 1904, file 3263–39; William H. Taft to Henry M. Hoyt, 26 May 1902, enclosed with Hoyt to C. R. Edwards, 26 July 1901, file 3263–5, both in box 330, BIA; Judith Raftery, "Textbook Wars: Governor-General James Francis Smith and the Protestant-Catholic Conflict in Public Education in the Philippines, 1904–1907," *History of Education Quarterly* 38 (Summer 1998): 144–146.

15. Arthur J. Brown, *Report of a Visitation of the Philippine Mission of the Board of Foreign Missions of the Presbyterian Church in the United States of America* (New York:

Board of Foreign Missions of the Presbyterian Church in the USA, 1902), 52–53; Philip O'Ryan to William H. Taft, 8 November 1902; George M. Palmer to E. B. Bryan, 11 January 1903; William H. Taft, untitled mss, n.d. [1903], all in file 1534–58, box 201, BIA; David P. Barrows, "Religious Teaching Forbidden" (Bureau of Education circular No. 32, 11 March 1908), enclosed with H. W. Langheim to A. J. Brown, 18 May 1909, reel 289, Philippines Microfilm.

16. Arthur J. Brown to D. S. Hibbard, 30 September 1910, folder 22, box 1, Arthur Leroy Carson Papers, Record Group 59, Presbyterian Historical Society; Charles R. Hamilton to Arthur J. Brown, 20 August 1909, reel 289; Alix Pieters to Frank F. Ellinwood, 29 April 1903, reel 288; Charles E. Rath to A. J. Brown, n.d. (rec. 27 June 1904), reel 288, all in Philippines Microfilm; Stuntz, *The Philippines and the Far East*, 351–353; Robert W. Carter to A. W. Halsey, 5 October 1909, reel 289, Philippines Microfilm.

17. Charles R. Hamilton to Arthur J. Brown, 20 August 1909; H. W. Langheim to Brown, 26 May 1909, both in reel 289, Philippines Microfilm; Brown to David P. Barrows, 26 October 1910, "Brown, Arthur J." folder, box 12, David Prescott Barrows Papers, Bancroft Library, University of California-Berkeley.

18. Jonathan Zimmerman, *Whose America? Culture Wars in the Public Schools* (Cambridge, Mass.: Harvard University Press, 2002), 154; Charles R. Hamilton to Arthur J. Brown, 20 August 1909; James W. Graham to Arthur Brown, 18 December 1907, both in reel 289, Philippines Microfilm.

19. See, for example, Sushil Madhava Pathak, *American Missionaries and Hinduism: A Study of Their Contacts from 1813 to 1910* (Delhi: Munshiram Manoharlal, 1967), 143; A. C. Darrow, "A Tenasserim School of Industrial and Mechanical Trades in Moulmein Burma" (ms, 6 November 1918), p. 1, "Burma-Scheme for Tenasserim School" folder, Board of International Mission Subject Files [hereafter "BIMSF"], American Baptist Archives Center, Valley Forge, Penn.; n.a., "Anna Davis Industrial Department Report. 1913–14" (ms), p. 1, folder 31, box 7, Board of Foreign Missions—Korea Mission, Record Group 140 [hereafter "BFM-Korea"], Presbyterian Historical Society.

20. Emory Ross, "Memorandum on the Situation of Protestant Missions in Congo Belge" (ms, 1933), enclosed with Ross to J. H. Oldham, 21 February 1933, "Religious Liberty—CPC—1933" folder, box 8, Emory Ross Papers, Burke Library, Union Theological Seminary, New York; Fred R. Bunker to "My dear Friends," 10 December 1926, "1926" folder, box 2, African Collection [hereafter "AC-HU"], Hampton University Archives, Hampton, Va.; David G. Scanlon, "Introduction," in *Church, State and Education in Africa*, ed. David G. Scanlon (New York: Teachers College Press, 1966), 9–10, 13; Richard Heyman, "The Initial Years of the Jeanes School in Kenya, 1924–1931," in *Essays in the History of African Education*, eds. Vincent M. Battle and Charles H. Lyons (New York: Teachers College Press, 1970), 106; Fred R. Bunker to "My dear friends," 5 May 1914, "Reports, Newspapers, Articles, Etc." folder, box 4, AC-HU.

21. Jeffrey Cox, *Imperial Fault Lines: Christianity and Colonial Power in India, 1818–1940* (Stanford, Calif.: Stanford University Press, 2002), 190–191; Pathak, *American Missionaries and Hinduism*, 137–139; R. A. Hume, *A Wise Missionary Attitude Toward a Coming Demand for a Conscience Clause* (Poona: Scottish Mission Industries Co., 1916), 3; Arthur T. Mayhew, "Mission Education in India," *Missionary Review of the World* 53 (October 1930): 734; Frank W. Padelford, *Report on*

Christian Education in Burma (n.p, n.d. [1932]), p. 2, "Burma—Education—1930–39" folder, BIMSF; Eula Hutchison Sleeth, "History of the Educational Work of the Presbyterian Church of America in India" (M.A. thesis, University of Chicago, 1921), 110; n.a., *Confidential Bulletin for Missionary School Managers of the American Baptist Foreign Mission Society, Issued by the Education Committee* (n.p, n.d. [1925?]), "Burma—Education—1920–1929" folder, BIMSF.

22. Henry Huizinga, "Our Educational Policy in the Baptist South India Mission, A Rejoinder" (ms, 24 January 1917), p. 6, "Telugu Mission Educational Policy—H. Huizinga" folder, BIMSF; Timothy Walch, *Parish School: American Catholic Parochial Education from Colonial Times to the Present* (New York: Crossroad, 1996), 152; Padelford, *Report on Christian Education in Burma*, 17, 29.

23. Henry Huizinga, "A Denominational Bombshell" (ms, 15 January 1917), p. 3, "Telugu Mission Educational Policy—H. Huizinga" folder, BIMSF; Huizinga, "Our Educational Policy in the Baptist South India Mission," 6; C. A. Nichols to Alvah Hovey, 8 March 1894, "Burma: Survey—Relation of Schools and Higher Education to Missionary Operations Vol. II" folder, BIMSF; W. J. Wanless to Robert Speer, November ? 1902, folder 7, box 23, BFM-India.

24. Braham Datt Bharti, *A Short History of Subversion and Sabotage of Indian Education by Christianism* (New Delhi: Erabooks, 1990), 19–22; Board of Foreign Missions of the Presbyterian Church, USA, *For Conscience' [sic] Sake* (n.p., 1924), 10; "Study Made of Government Grants to 'Mission Institutions' " (ms, 2 January 1948), pp. 1–2, enclosed with J. L. Hooper to Board Members and to the Executive Council, 1 July 1952, folder 3, box 20; Emily L. Peterson to Robert E. Speer, 26 September 1924, folder 8, box 23, both in BFM-India.

25. Mrs. S. J. Broadwell to A. J. Brown, 22 November 1917; F. W. Warne et al. to "Dear Brethren," 15 April 1921, both in folder 7, Box 23, BFM-India.

26. Pierard, "Evangelical and Ecumenical," 154–155; W. T. Mitchell to Robert E. Speer, 14 November 1923, folder 8, box 23, BFM-India. See also Ray C. Smith, "Memorandum on the Conscience Clause as it relates to Isabella Thoburn College" (ms, n.d. [1922]), enclosed with Smith to Speer, 29 May 1922, folder 7, box 23, BFM-India.

27. Alice B. Van Doren, *Projects in Indian Education: Experiments in the Project Method in Indian Schools* (Calcutta: Associated Press, 1930), 17; William J. McKee, *New Schools for Young India: A Survey of the Educational, Economic, and Social Conditions in India with Special Reference to More Effective Education* (Chapel Hill: University of North Carolina Press, 1930), ix; Robert E. Speer to H. A. Whitlock, 25 August 1924; Speer to Emily L. Peterson, 19 August 1924, both in folder 8, box 23, BFM-India.

28. James C. Manry to Robert E. Speer, 10 September 1934; William Paton to E. D. Lucas, 9 April 1924, enclosed with Lucas to Speer, 10 April 1924; H. A. Whitlock to Speer, 3 April 1924, all in folder 8, box 23, BFM-India.

29. Pierard, "Evangelical and Ecumenical," 160; Robert E. Speer to J. J. Lucas, 27 August 1934, folder 8, box 23; "Report of a Special Committee on the Conscience Clause Adopted by the General Board, April–May 1934" (ms), enclosed with E. Graham Parker to Speer, 20 May 1934, folder 8, box 23, both in BFM-India.

30. "Agenda for the meeting of the Group on Religious Liberty" (ms, 19 January 1932), "Church State-3" folder, box 105, Robert E. Speer Papers, Speer

Library, Princeton Theological Seminary, Princeton, N.J.; n.a., "Some Notes on Universal Religious Liberty" (ms, n.d. [1935?]), pp. 6–7, folder 16, box 12, BFM-Korea.

31. Robert T. Bryan, "The Mission Appraisal Commission" (ms, n.d. [1933]), p. 2, "Bryan Robert T. Ex Secy 1931–38" folder, box 11, Robert T. Bryan Papers, Southern Baptist Historical Society and Archives; Sophie Lanneau to T. B. Ray, 2 February 1931; Lanneau to C. E. Maddry, 26 March 1933, both in "Lanneau Sophie Stephens Ex Secy 1919–34" folder, box 99, Lanneau Papers.

32. Alice C. Reed interview (ms, 1969), pp. 32, 35, 74; Netta P. Allen interview (ms, 1970–71), pp. 34, 37, both in China Missionaries Oral History Project, Manuscript Division, Columbia University Libraries.

33. Commodore B. Fisher, "When the Government Forced the Issue: Facing the Problem of National Control of Mission Schools in Hamadan, Persia," *Missionary Review of the World* 56 (March 1933): 138; "The Girls' Boarding and Day School. Tabriz Station—Persia Mission" (ms, October 1932), p. 2, folder 10, box 20; R. L. Steiner, "Annual Report. Boys School of Meshed. June 1930" (ms), p. 3, folder 2, box 20; C. B. Fisher, "The Avicenna Middle School, Hamadan. Annual Report 1939–1940" (ms), p. 2, folder 25, box 19; W. J. Ellis to Robert E. Speer, 9 December 1927, folder 4, box 25; Charles A. Pittman to H. D. Griswold, 19 April 1928, folder 5, box 25, all in Board of Foreign Missions—Iran Mission [hereafter "BFM-Iran"], Record Group 91, Presbyterian Historical Society.

34. Eunice Blackburn to Dearest Family, 24 February 1935, folder 16, box 1, Eunice R. Blackburn Papers, Record Group 198; Blackburn to Irene Sheppard, 27 December 1940, folder 24, box 24, Board of Foreign Missions—Mexico Mission [hereafter "BFM-Mexico"], Record Group 87, both in Presbyterian Historical Society; C. E. Maddry to David H. LeSueur, 21 September 1933, fiche 3, David H. LeSueur Papers, International Mission Board Archives, Southern Baptist Convention, Richmond, Va.

35. Interview with Miriam Bell Dickason (ms, 1983), p. 9, manuscript no. C272, Presbyterian Historical Society; John J. Jarrett, "Question: Which of the present means employed brings greatest Evangelical results?" (ms, n.d. [1935?]), pp. 1–2, folder 10, box 15, Board of Foreign Missions, Colombia Mission, Record Group 88, Presbyterian Historical Society; L. K. Anderson to Hester F. Trivette, 25 February 1941; Anderson to Eunice Blackburn, 6 February 1941, both in folder 24, box 24, BFM-Mexico.

36. L. K. Anderson to Eunice Blackburn, 6 February 1941, folder 24, box 24, BFM-Mexico; In Soo Kim, *Protestants and the Formation of Modern Korean Nationalism, 1885–1920* (New York: Peter Lang, 1996), 65; James E. Adams to H. W. Guthrie, 17 August 1915, folder 4, box 12, BFM-Korea; Michael Breen, *The Koreans: Who They Are, What They Want, Where Their Future Lies* (New York: St. Martin's, 1999), 108; Peter van Lierop, "The Development of Schools Under the Korea Mission of the Presbyterian Church in the USA, 1919–1950" (Ph.D. diss., University of Pittsburgh, 1955), 45, 101–102; Floyd E. Hamilton, "Missionary Studies in the Far East. Korea. Part IX," *Independent Board Bulletin* 4 (November 1938): 7.

37. The most complete account of the shrine controversy is Sung-Gun Kim's, "The Shinto Shrine Issue in Korean Christianity Under Japanese Colonialism," *Journal of Church and State* 39 (Summer 1997): 503–521. See also Allen D. Clark, "A Study of Religion and the State in the Japanese Empire with Particular Reference

to the Shrine Problem in Korea" (Ph.D. diss., Princeton Theological Seminary, 1939); van Lierop, "The Development of Schools Under the Korea Mission," 176–204.

38. Breen, *The Koreans*, 111–112; Harold H. Henderson, "Annual Report for 1934–35" (ms), p. 4, folder 52, box 7; E. W. Koons, "John D. Wells School. Annual Report. May 30, 1938" (ms), p. 4, folder 28, box 7; Blanche I. Stevens, "Report of the Osyung Girls' Academy, Syenchun, Korea, 1937–1938" (ms), p. 9, folder 28, box 7; J. G. Holdcroft to C. B McAfee, 18 December 1935, folder 14, box 12; Harold H. Henderson, "To Bow or Not to Bow? Being the 30th Annual Report of the Kisung Academy. Taiku, Chosen. 1936–1937" (ms), folder 54, box 7, all in BFM-Korea.

39. John Z. Moore to Ralph E. Diffendorfer, 29 March 1937, roll 621, Vol. 3, Microfilm Edition of the Missionary Files, United Methodist Church [hereafter "UMC"], UMC General Commission on Archives and History, Madison, N.J.; Wi Jo Kang, *Christ and Caesar in Modern Korea: A History of Christianity and Politics* (Albany: State University of New York Press, 1997), 64; T. S. Soltau, "Notes on the Shrine Problem" (ms, 6 October 1935), p. 1; J. G. Holdcroft to C. B. McAfee, 7 October 1935, both in folder 14, box 12, BFM-Korea; "Reply of the Chosen Mission to Re-Thinking Missions—Second Section" (ms, 1933), pp. B, H, folder 19, box 16, Board of Foreign Missions—Presbyterian Church of the USA, Record Group 81, Presbyterian Historical Society.

40. J. G. Holdcroft to C. T. Leber, 8 April 1938, folder 25, box 12, BFM-Korea; George S. McCune, " 'Thou Shalt Have No Other Gods Before Me,' " *Presbyterian Tribune* 53 (20 January 1938): 8; Horace H. Underwood, " 'Render Unto Caesar the Things that are Caesar's,' " ibid., 10; Shawn Francis Peters, *Judging Jehovah's Witnesses: Religious Persecution and the Dawn of the Rights Revolution* (Lawrence: University Press of Kansas, 2000), 1, 10; James M. McCutcheon to Peter K. Emmons, 20 October 1937, folder 21; Willis Lamont to J. L. Hooper, 19 June 1940, folder 33, both in box 12, BFM-Korea. Three years after the Supreme Court upheld compulsory flag-salutes, the Court reversed itself. See *West Virginia Board of Education v. Barnette* 319 U.S. 624 (1943).

41. Willis Lamont to J. L. Hooper, 19 June 1940, folder 33, box 12, BFM-Korea; "The Flag Salute Case," *Christian Century* 57 (19 June 1940): 791; H. H. Underwood to C. B. McAfee, 5 February 1936; Mrs. H. H. Underwood to McAfee, 7 April 1936, both in folder 16, box 12, BFM-Korea.

42. James B. Moore to Frank T. Cartwright, 20 October 1939, roll 621, Vol. 3, UMC. For similar complaints among liberal Presbyterians, charging that "paternalist" conservatives neglected Korean viewpoints, see "Letter from Miss Schultz and Mr. Mack" (ms, 21 October 1938), folder 27, box 12, BFM-Korea.

43. For evidence about the mixed nature of Korean opinion on the shrine issue, see Horace H. Underwood to Charles T. Leber, 8 June 1937, folder 20; Allen D. Clark to J. L. Hooper, 21 November 1938, folder 26, both in box 12, BFM-Korea; "Rioting in a Korean Mission School," *Sunday School Times* 79 (19 June 1937): 445–446; C. Darby Fulton, *Star in the East* (Richmond, Va.: Presbyterian Committee of Publication, 1938), 188–189, 195–196.

44. "Letter from Dr. D. B. Avison dated October 31, 1938" (ms); Charles Allen Clark to J. L. Hooper, 5 November 1938, both in folder 26, box 12, BFM-Korea; "The Official 'Presbyterian Board' and the Shrine Situation in Korea," *Independent*

Board Bulletin 6 (June–July 1940): 3; Myrtle Pike to BFM, 28 April 1938; Mr. D. L. Keith to BFM, 16 May 1938; Marion E. Dodge to BFM, 22 May 1938, all in folder 28, box 12, BFM-Korea.

45. "The Shift from Evangelism," *Independent Board Bulletin* 1 (October 1935): 6; Floyd E. Hamilton, "Missionary Studies in the Far East. Korea. Part IX," ibid. 4 (November 1938): 8; "Dr. J. Gordon Holdcroft, Famed Missionary, Appointed by Board," ibid. 6 (January–February 1940): 3–4, 31; William H. Chisolm, "Letter from Dr. Chisolm to 'Dear Friend,' " (ms, 11 April 1940), p. 3, folder 33, box 12, BFM-Korea; Joel A. Carpenter, *Revive Us Again: The Reawakening of American Fundamentalism* (New York: Oxford, 1997), 29.

46. "Report on Subsidy Questionnaire" (ms, 1950), pp. 1–2, "Congo: Education. Subsidies. Revolving Funds" folder, BIMSF; Rhoda Armstrong, "Teaching Them," *Congo News Letter* 43 (July 1952): 9; James Cavin, "Report of the Superintendent of Schools. July 1947" (ms), p. 1, folder 59, box 10; Rene Ryter, "Superintendent of Schools—1948–49" (ms), p. 2, folder 7, box 11; "Report of Foulassi Station. 1944" (ms), p. 4, folder 39, box 10, all in Board of Foreign Missions—West Africa Mission [hereafter "BFM-West Africa"], Presbyterian Historical Society.

47. Rene Ryter, "Superintendent of Schools. Report 1954–55" (ms), p. 4, folder 80, box 11, BFM-West Africa; "Minutes of the Conference on Evangelical Responsibility in the Lands of the Caribbean" (ms, 3 December 1951), p. 2, folder 31, box 5, National Council of Churches Papers, Division of Overseas Ministries [hereafter "NCC-DOM"], Record Group 8, Presbyterian Historical Society.

48. "Government Subsidies Research" (ms, 8 May 1952), pp. 14, 16, 8, 12, 2, enclosed with J. L. Hooper to Board Members and to the Executive Council, 1 July 1952, folder 3, box 20, BFM-India; Raymond J. Smyke, "Problem of Teacher Supply and Demand," *Panorama* 3 (Winter 1961–62): 13; "Peace Corps in West Cameroon," *Christianity Today* 9 (1 January 1965): 29.

49. Richard Dodson, "Congo-Leopoldville," in Scanlon, ed., *Church, State, and Education in Africa*, 87; Allan G. Marsh, "Education and Schools. Tanganyika" (ms, June 1955), p. 1, folder 18, box 16, Africa Inland Mission Papers [hereafter "AIM"], Billy Graham Center Archives, Wheaton College, Wheaton, Ill.; Sophie De La Haye, "God is Honored in Liberia," *Africa Now* 20 (January–March 1964): 10; "Report of the School of the Circonscription of the South" (ms, 1957), p. 3, folder 20, box 12, BFM-West Africa; W. Harold Fuller, "Harvest in the Classroom," *Africa Now* 25 (April–June 1965): 5.

50. Marybeth Rupert, "The Emergence of the Independent Missionary Agency as an American Institution, 1860–1917" (Ph.D. diss., Yale University, 1974), 203; "The Shift from Evangelism," *Independent Board Bulletin* 1 (October 1935): 6.

51. Division of Foreign Missions, National Council of Churches of Christ, "North American Protestant Missionaries—Their Affiliations" (ms, 1952); R. Pierce Beaver, "The Southern Baptists" (ms, April 1953), p. 1, both in folder 13, box 4, NCC-DOM.

52. During the pre–World War II era, colonial authorities sometimes required the AIM to establish a school in exchange for a residential permit. But these schools languished for lack of trained personnel, often dragging unwilling missionaries—particularly women—into the classroom. In the 1930s, British officials even closed several Kenyan AIM schools for failing to maintain a proper instructional staff. Dana L. Robert, *American Women in Mission: A Social History of Their Thought and*

Practice (Macon, Ga.: Mercer University Press, 1996), 226–227; David P. Sandgren, *Christianity and the Kikuyu: Religious Divisions and Social Conflict* (New York: Peter Lang, 2000), 49, 132.

53. Emma M. Mathys and Margaret E. Hartsock, "Questionnaire No. 5. Subject: School Work" (ms, 1946), pp. 4–6, folder 13, box 13, AIM; Howard W. Ferrin, "How Shall We Serve the Sugar?" *Inland Africa* 32 (September–October 1948): 6; "The African At School," ibid. 31 (September–October 1947): 10; Eleanor Loizeaux, "A Study of the Relative Value of Evangelism, Education, and Medical Work in Pioneer Fields in Africa" (M.A. thesis, Wheaton College, Wheaton, Ill., 1940), 98, 43–44; Janet M. Wingerd, "From the Regions Beyond," *Inland Africa* 32 (May–June 1948): 14.

54. Tanganyika Annual Conference Minutes, June 1955, folder 18, box 16; Earl A. Winsor, "Notes on Education Situation. Congo Field—January 1950" (ms), folder 26, box 10, both in AIM.

55. "The African At School," 8; Allan G. Marsh, "A Memorandum From the Tanganyika Field" (ms, 1957–58), folder 1, box 28; Howard W. Ferrin to Ralph T. Davis, 13 July 1953, folder 18, box 16, both in AIM.

56. William L. Downey to "Dear Brother Maynard," 5 May 1942, enclosed with Downey to Ralph T. Davis, 8 August 1942; "Minutes of the Conference at Nasa Station, July 18–20 1942" (ms), both in folder 10, box 20, AIM.

57. Winsor, "Notes on Education Situation"; Mathys and Hartsock, "Questionnaire No. 5," 5; Francis Harry Hendrickson, "A Study of the Reactions of Selected Congo Missionaries Toward Presumed Criticisms of Missionary Education in Africa" (Ed.D. diss., Teachers College, Columbia University, New York, 1964), 67–68.

58. Marsh, "A Memorandum From the Tanganyika Field"; Marsh, "Report of the Education Department. African Inland Mission (Tanganyika). January, 1956–June, 1957" (ms), folder 15, box 28; Marsh to General Secretary, 24 March 1959, folder 18, box 16, both in AIM.

59. Kenneth Richardson, *Garden of Miracles: A History of the Africa Inland Mission* (London: Victory Press, 1968), 162; "Studies in Belgium for Congo Missionaries," *Inland Africa* 33 (November–December 1949): 13; Clara L. Bentley, untitled memorandum, 7 July 1948, folder 3, box 12; H. Wakelin Coxill to Mesdames et Messeurs, 3 September 1949, folder 26, box 10; Earl A. Winsor, "Notes on Congo Educational Matters" (ms, 18 September 1949), folder 26, box 10; Winsor to J. B. Henry, 24 October 1951, folder 4, box 12; Minutes of International Conference meeting, 10–14 September 1956, folder 16, box 12, all in AIM; Hendrickson, "A Study of the Reactions of Selected Congo Missionaries," 54.

60. Allan and Elizabeth Marsh to "Dear Friend," 20 Jan. 1966, folder 2, box 39; Allan Marsh to Paul Beverly, 19 December 1969, folder 15, box 28, both in AIM.

61. Edward Arnesen, "Schools Grow Christians," *Inland Africa* 42 (March–April 1958): 6.

62. Carol Carlson, "No Supreme Court 'Ruling' in Kenya," *Eastern Challenge* 1 (November–December 1962): 1–2.

63. Joyce Johnson, "Education Work in Kenya," *Inland Africa* 41 (November–December 1957): 4.

64. Hendrickson, "A Study of the Reactions of Selected Congo Missionaries," 67; "Memorandum Prepared by the Educational Consultation of the East Lake

Division of the Lake Missions Education Council" (ms, 2 May 1961), folder 14, box 28, AIM.

65. Especially after World War II, Catholic commentators often noted that the same Protestants who rejected state funds for parochial schools in the United States gladly accepted state aid to their own mission schools overseas. See, for example, "School Aid in Basutoland," *America* 73 (7 July 1945): 266–267; "At Home and Abroad," ibid. 105 (20 May 1961): 302; Virgil C. Blum, S.J., *Freedom in Education: Federal Aid for ALL Children* (Garden City, N.Y.: Doubleday, 1965), 187–188.

66. Mae and Martin Duggan, "Fight for Freedom," in *Educational Freedom and the Case for Government Aid to Students in Independent Schools*, eds. Leo Ward and Daniel D. McGarry (Milwaukee: Bruce Publishing Co., 1966), 203; William Willoughby, "Parochial School Crisis Fuels State Aid Debate," *Christianity Today* 13 (28 March 1969): 37–38; Kenneth D. Wald, *Religion and Politics in the United States*, 3rd ed. (Washington, D.C.: Congressional Quarterly Press, 1997), 207. In the South, especially, Protestant demands for state-aided private schools were also linked to "massive resistance" against court-ordered desegregation in the public schools. See Michael W. Fuquay, "Civil Rights and the Private School Movement in Mississippi, 1964–1971," *History of Education Quarterly* 42 (Summer 2002): 159–180.

67. According to sociologist Robert Wuthnow, Christian conservatives stress America's superior, divinely sanctioned purpose in the world; liberals, by contrast, focus less on the nation than on "humanity"—and human rights—at large. On church–state issues, however, conservatives point to other nations' practices as superior to the United States'; indeed, they argue, these international models can help America *reclaim* its divine role. Robert Wuthnow, "Divided We Fall: America's Two Civil Religions," *Christian Century* 105 (20 April 1988): 398; Wuthnow, *The Restructuring of American Religion: Society and Faith Since World War Two* (Princeton: Princeton University Press, 1988), 244–245.

68. Dean M. Kelley, "An Outline of Relations Between Church and State in American Society" (ms, 1961), p. 4, folder 14; "Minutes of Consultation on Approaches to Government with Special Reference to the World Outreach of the Church" (ms, 17 February 1961), p. 3, folder 12, both in box 36, National Council of Churches Papers, Division of Christian Life and Mission, Record Group 6, Presbyterian Historical Society; James E. Wood Jr., "Editorial: Church, State, and Missions," *Journal of Church and State* 7 (Autumn 1965): 324–325.

69. See, for example, Stephen V. Monsma and J. Christopher Soper, *The Challenge of Pluralism: Church and State in Five Democracies* (Lanham, Md.: Rowman and Littlefield, 1997), 216; Glenn, *The Ambiguous Embrace*, 270–271; Jerome J. Hanus, "An Argument in Favor of School Vouchers," in Jerome J. Hanus and Peter W. Cookson, Jr, *Choosing Schools: Vouchers and American Education* (Washington, D.C.: American University Press, 1996), 89–92; David W. Kirkpatrick, *Choice in Schooling: A Case for Tuition Vouchers* (Chicago: Loyola University Press, 1990), 50–51, 61, 99–100.

70. In June 2002, the U.S. Supreme Court upheld a 1995 Ohio program that provided vouchers worth up to $2,250 to low-income Cleveland families who patronized private and parochial schools. Florida established a similar program across the state in 1999, offering $4,000 to students in schools that have failed state assessment tests for two of four years. Advocates hope the Supreme Court decision

[*Zelman v. Simmons-Harris*] energizes voucher plans in other states, where the reform has fared poorly: since 1999, voters in four states have rejected voucher measures while legislatures in four other states have done the same. Mark Walsh, "Supreme Court Upholds Cleveland Voucher Program," *Education Week*, 27 June 2001, p. 1; *Zelman v. Simmons-Harris*, Case No. 00–1751, argued February 20, 2002, decided June 27, 2002; John Gehring, "Voucher Battles Head to State Capitals," *Education Week*, 10 July 2002, p. 1.

71. Mark Walsh, "Public Sees Role for Religion in Schools," *Education Week*, 17 January 2001, p. 1; Walsh, "Patriotism and Prayer: Constitutional Questions are Muted," ibid., 10 Oct. 2001, p. 1; Zimmerman, *Whose America?*, 160–185; James W. Fraser, *Between Church and State: Religion and Public Education in a Multicultural America* (New York: St. Martin's, 1999), 198–208, 217–221; Monsma and Soper, *The Challenge of Pluralism*, 127–128.

72. David Scanlon, "Church, State, and Education in Sub-Saharan Africa: An Overview," *International Review of Education* 9, no. 4 (1963–1964): 442.

6. Ambivalent Imperialists

1. Edgar Allen Forbes, "American Teaching Around the World: The Vast Intellectual Empire of Government Teachers and Protestant Missionaries Working Under Many Flags," *World's Work*, February 1908, "American Teaching Around the World" folder, Board of International Missions Subject Files [hereafter "BIMSF"], American Baptist Historical Society, Valley Forge, Penn.

2. Henry S. Townsend, "Recollections and Reflections of the Writer" (ms, n.d. [1935]), 2:5, Hamilton Hawaiian Collection, University of Hawaii-Manoa, Honolulu, Hawaii.

3. John Bellamy Foster, Harry Magdoff, and Robert W. McChesney, "Kipling, the 'White Man's Burden,' and U.S. Imperialism," in *Pox Americana: Exposing the American Empire*, eds. Foster and McChesney (New York: Monthly Review Press, 2004), 14–15, 19.

4. On Americans' recurrent insistence that they are *not* a colonial power—or that they are different from all other colonial powers—see Paul A. Kramer, "Empires, Exceptions, and Anglo-Saxons: Race and Rule Between the British and United States Empires, 1880–1810," *Journal of American History* 88 (March 2002): 1315–1353; Michael Adas, "From Settler Colony to Global Hegemon: Integrating the Exceptionalist Narrative of the American Experience into World History," *American Historical Review* 106 (December 2001): 1692–1720; Adas, "Improving on the Civilizing Mission? Assumptions of United States Exceptionalism in the Colonization of the Philippines," in *The New American Empire: A 21st Century Teach-In on United States Foreign Policy*, eds. Lloyd C. Gardner and Marilyn B. Young (New York: New Press, 2005), 153–181; Amy Kaplan, " 'Left Alone with America': The Absence of Empire in the Study of American Culture," in *Cultures of United States Imperialism*, eds. Amy Kaplan and Donald E. Pease (Durham, N.C.: Duke University Press, 1993), 3–21.

5. On Americans' long-standing antipathy toward overseas revolutions—and their ambivalent attitude toward decolonization—see, especially, Michael E. Hunt, *Ideology and United States Foreign Policy* (New Haven: Yale University Press, 1987), 92–124; *The United States and Decolonization: Power and Freedom*, eds. David Ryan

and Victor Pungong (New York: St. Martin's, 2000); Mary Ann Heiss, "The Evolution of the Imperial Idea and United States National Identity," *Diplomatic History* 26 (Fall 2002): 511–540.

6. John Fousek, *To Lead the Free World: American Nationalism and the Cultural Roots of the Cold War* (Chapel Hill: University of North Carolina Press, 2000).

7. On the concept of cultural imperialism in American historical scholarship, see Jessica C. E. Gienow-Hecht, "Shame on US? Academics, Cultural Transfer, and the Cold War—A Critical Review," *Diplomatic History* 24 (Summer 2000): 465–502.

8. For the argument that Peace Corps teachers, especially, spread American cultural imperialism in the Third World, see Gary May, "Passing the Torch and Lighting Fires: The Peace Corps," in *Kennedy's Quest For Victory*, ed. Thomas G. Paterson (New York: Oxford, 1989), 284–316; for a reply, see Fritz Fischer, *Making Them Like Us: Peace Corps Volunteers in the 1960s* (Washington, D.C.: Smithsonian Institution Press, 1998), 126.

9. Diary entry, 5 January 1972, diary volume 1, folder 1, box 1, Alfred T. Giannini Papers, Collection 8, Peace Corps Volunteers Collection, National Anthropology Archives [hereafter "PC-NAA"], Museum Support Center, Smithsonian Institution, Suitland, Md.

10. Diary entry, 3 February 1972, diary volume 1, folder 1, box 1, Giannini Papers.

11. Socorro Marques, "Laffayatte" [sic] (n.d. [1905]), "Student Papers" folder; Gregarior Elezar ? (unintellig.), "Philippine Government" (n.d. [1905]), "Student Papers (4)" folder; Vincente Villaricaud ? (unintellig.), "If Philippine [sic] had been independent" (n.d. [1905]), "Student Papers (3)" folder; Rufina Alma, "Oration" (n.d. [1905]), "Student papers" folder, all in box 1, Frederick G. Behner Papers, Bentley Historical Library, Ann Arbor, Mich.

12. On "civilization" as a theme in American imperialism, see Frank Ninkovich, *The United States and Imperialism* (Malden, Mass.: Blackwell, 2001), 48–90; Anders Stephanson, *Manifest Destiny: American Expansionism and the Empire of Right* (New York: Hill and Wang, 1995), 80–81; Kevin Gaines, "Black Americans' Racial Uplift Ideology as 'Civilizing Mission,' " in Kaplan and Pease, *Cultures of United States Imperialism*, 433–455.

13. Philinda Rand Anglemyer, untitled manuscript, n.d. [1940], p. 9, "Anglemyer, P.R. Memorabilia" folder; "Summary Written by PRA During WWII" (ms, n.d. [1918]), p. 5, "Anglemyer, P.R. T.S. of Misc., Diaries" folder, both in box 1, Philinda Rand Anglemyer Papers, Arthur and Elizabeth Schlesinger Library, Radcliffe College, Cambridge, Mass.; Louis H. Lisk to Director of Education, 27 September 1913, p. 329, "Bureau of Education Activities 1914. Early Experiences of American Teachers" binder, box 6, Walter W. Marquardt Papers, Bentley Historical Library; Helen P. Beattie, "American Teachers and the Filipinos," *Outlook* 78 (15 October 1904): 424; "Educational Advance in the Philippines," *Christian Science Monitor*, 3 June 1916, file 3725A, box 512, Bureau of Insular Affairs Records [hereafter "BIA"], Record Group 350, National Archives II, College Park, Md.

14. Geronima T. Pecson and Maria Racelis, *Tales of the American Teachers in the Philippines* (Manila: Carmelo and Bauermann, 1959), 77; Mary Bonzo Suzuki, "American Education in the Philippines, the Early Years: American Pioneer Teachers and

the Filipino Response, 1900–1935" (Ph.D. diss., University of California-Berkeley, 1991), 89.

15. Leonard P. Ayres to Milan Ayres, 26 October 1902, "1902–1930" folder, box 2, Leonard P. Ayres Papers, Library of Congress, Washington, D.C.; Edith Algre De Gutierrez, *The Movement Against Teaching English in Schools of Puerto Rico* (New York: University Press of America, 1987), 46; *Report of the Commissioner of Education for Porto Rico to the Secretary of the Interior, USA* (Washington, D.C.: General Printing Office, 1900), p. 14, "General File: Puerto Rico—Publications on Puerto Rican Education" folder, box 193, Samuel McCune Lindsay Papers, Manuscript Division, Columbia University Libraries, New York, New York.

16. For varied discussions of teachers as exponents "civilization," see Burgess Shank, " 'Education in the Philippines': A Reply," *Gunton's Magazine* 24 (May 1903): 408; Daniel Logan, "Education in the Hawaiian Islands," *North American Review* 165 (July 1897): 23; "Education in Porto Rico," *Outlook* 66 (1 Sept. 1900): 6; Emanuel Hurwitz, Jules Menacker, and Ward Weldon, *Educational Imperialism: American School Policy and the U.S. Virgin Islands* (Lanham, Md.: University Press of America, 1987), 37.

17. Helen James diary, 1903, p. 1, folder 7, box 14, Frank and Helen Chisholm Papers, Special Collections, Emory University, Atlanta, Ga.; Edmund B. Butterfield, "An Account of Lieutenant Gov. Mason Stone's Service in Organizing Schools in the Philippines," p. 43, Manuscript Miscellaneous File No. 160, Vermont History Center, Barre, Vt.

18. Arthur Floyd Griffiths, "Educational Problems in Hawaii," *Independent* 67 (30 December 1909): 1478; Levona P. Newsom, "The Filipino at School," *Outlook* 72 (18 October 1902): 412; Edward W. Capen, "Lecture IV. Problems of Industrial Training" (ms, n.d. [1920]), folder 246, box 21, Edward Warren Capen Papers, Hartford Seminary, Hartford, Conn.

19. George M. Briggs, "Are the Schools in the Philippines Meeting the Demands in Respect of Industrial and Technical Training?" (ms, n.d. [1911]), p. 3, "1911, B (Bouve-Brown)" folder, box 29, Smiley Family Papers, Quaker Collections, Haverford College Library, Haverford, Penn.; Eugene A. Gilmore, "A Discourse on True Education," *The Philippine Collegian*, 8 November 1926, file 3725A, box 512, BIA; "Education in Porto Rico," *Boston Evening Transcript*, 11 November 1903, "General File: Puerto Rico—1901–1912—Printed" folder, box 189, Lindsay Papers.

20. Oscar V. Campomanes, "Casualty Figures of the American Soldier and the Other: Post-1898 Allegories of Imperial Nation-Building as 'Love and War,' " in *Vestiges of War: The Philippine-American War and the Aftermath of an Imperial Dream, 1899–1999*, eds. Angel Velasco Shaw and Luis H. Francia (New York: New York University Press, 2002), 138; Harry Cole to Commander Worcester and Major Allen, 10 January 1902; Cole to Mother and Leon, 16 February 1902; Mary Cole to "Dear Folks at home," 26 January 1902, all in "January–March 1902" folder, box 1, Harry N. Cole Papers, Bentley Historical Library.

21. William Dinwiddie, "Teaching the Filipinos," *Munsey's Magazine* 30 (March 1904): 809.

22. Henry Parker Willis, *Our Philippine Problem: A Study of American Colonial Policy* (New York: Henry Hot, 1905), 244n; David P. Barrows, "Report of the Director of Education," *Seventh Annual Report of the Philippine Commission. 1906*, pt. 3

(Washington, D.C.: Government Printing Office, 1907), 345; Gutierrez, *The Movement Against Teaching English*, 55, 61, 68–69; Aida Negron de Montilla, *Americanization in Puerto Rico and The Public School System, 1900–1930* (Rio Piedras, P.R.: Editorial Edil, 1971), 140; Adrian Hull, "The 'English Problem,' " *San Juan Review* 2 (June 1965), fiche 001.570–1, Schomburg Clipping File, Schomburg Center for Research in Black Culture, New York Public Libraries.

23. Bonifacio S. Salamanca, *The Filipino Reaction to American Rule, 1901–1913* (n.p.: The Shoestring Press, Hamden, Conn., 1968), 84; n.a. to M. G. Brumbaugh, 2 October 1904; Brumbaugh to William Howard Taft, 17 December 1904, both in file 3140–23, box 322, BIA.

24. Theodore de Laguna, "Education in the Philippines," *Gunton's Magazine* 24 (March 1903): 221, 229; "Education in the Philippines," *Springfield Daily Republican*, 13 March 1903, "Philippines Commission: 1903" folder, carton 2, Bernard Moses Papers; "Filipino Education," *Springfield Weekly Republican*, 19 April 1906, "Philippines" folder, carton 21, David Prescott Barrows Papers, both in Bancroft Library, University of California-Berkeley.

25. Letter from unidentified teacher, n.d. [1905], enclosed with D. H. McBride to Colonel R. Edwards, 26 June 1905, file 3140–26, BIA; Ella L. Austin to W. H. Babbitt, 13 October 1908, folder 21, box 59, Records of the Department of Education [hereafter "RDE-HA"], Series 261, Hawaii State Archives, Honolulu, Hawaii; "Education in Puerto Rico," *Outlook* 66 (1 September 1900): 6; H. P. Wood to Governor, 25 May 1932, reel 31, Records of the Government of American Samoa, microfilm ed., Federal Archives and Records Center, San Bruno, Calif.; Luther Harris Evans, "Unrest in the Virgin Islands," *Foreign Policy Reports* 9 (27 March 1935), "Articles About the Virgin Islands" folder, box 15, Paul M. Pearson Papers, Friends Historical Library, Swarthmore College, Swarthmore, Penn.

26. Herbert Priestley to "Dearest Mother," 9 June 1902, "Transcriptions of Letters, June 1902" folder, box 1, Herbert I. Priestley Papers, Bancroft Library; F. W. Cheney, "El Mujer" (n.d. [1920?]), "Humorous, Personal Letters, Memoranda, Addresses" binder, box 5, Marquardt Papers; George Ezra Carrothers, "A Sojourn in the Philippines, by a Hoosier Schoolmaster" (ms., n.d. [1955?]), p. 20; Carrothers, "Incidents in the Life of a Hoosier Schoolmaster: Ch. IV. Philippines and Around the World" (ms, n.d. [1955?]), p. 15, both in box 1, George Ezra Carrothers Papers, Bentley Historical Library; Louis D. Baun to parents, 11 February 1902, in "Serving America's First Peace Corps: Letters of Louis D. Baun" (ms, n.d.), General Collection, Bancroft Library; P. Law to H. W. Babbitt, 20 January 1909, folder 31, box 55, RDE-HA; Virginia McBride interview with Joe Rossi, 19 February 1991, in *Public Education in Hawaii: Oral Histories*, 2 vols. (Honolulu: Center for Oral History, Social Science Research Institute, University of Hawaii at Manoa, September 1991), II:335–36.

27. Gilbert S. Perez, *From the Transport Thomas to Sto. Tomas: The History of American Teachers in the Philippines* (n.p., n.d. [1949]), 14; Walter W. Marquardt, "Teachers I Have Known," (ms, n.d.), p. 39, "Talks and Papers. 1922–1930" binder, box 6, Marquardt Papers; diary entry, 9 March 1902, September 1901–July 30 1902 diary, "Diaries and Account Books 1901–1902" folder, box 1, Benjamin E. Neal Papers, George Arents Research Library, Syracuse University; Pecson and Racelis, *Tales of the American Teachers*, 148–151; David P. Barrows, "Report of the Superintendent of Education," *Sixth Annual Report of the Philippine Commission*, pt. 4

(Washington, D.C.: General Printing Office, 1906), 518. On the relationship between *ladrones* and the Filipino anti-American insurgency, see Brian McAllister Linn, *The Philippine War, 1899–1902* (Lawrence: University Press of Kansas, 2000), 193.

28. Harry Cole to "Mother and Leon," 30 June 1902, "April–May 1902" folder, box 1, Cole Papers; letter from unidentified teacher, n.d. [1905], enclosed with D. H. McBride to Clarence R. Edwards, 26 June 1905, file 3140–26, BIA.

29. Harry Cole to "Mother and Leon," 16 March 1902, "January–March 1902" folder, Cole Papers.

30. Bessie Charry Fonvielle McDowell, "Educational and Recreational Features of Umbundu Culture" (M.A. thesis, Kennedy School of Missions, Hartford Seminary, 15 April 1931), 7–10, 54–55.

31. See, for example, Fred R. Bunker to "My dear friends," 5 May 1914, "Reports, Newspapers, Articles" folder, box 4, African Collection, Hampton University Archives [hereafter "AC-HU"], Hampton, Va.; Thomas Jesse Jones, *Education in East Africa* (New York: Phelps-Stokes Fund, 1925), 80.

32. See, for example, Richard Glotzer, "The Career of Mabel Carney: The Study of Race and Rural Development in the United States and South Africa" (ms, August 1995), pp. 15, 17, folder 388, box 28, Mabel Carney Papers, Hartford Seminary; M. Claire Bailey, "American School for Girls. 1946–1947" (ms), p. 2, folder 1, box 3, Syria Mission Archives [hereafter "SMA"], Record Group 115, Presbyterian Historical Society.

33. John J. Considine, M.M., *Across a World* (Maryknoll, N.Y.: Catholic Foreign Mission Society of America, 1942), 64.

34. *Report of the Committee on the Preparation of Educational Missionaries* (n.p., n.d. [1916]), enclosed with T. H. P. Sailer to Ernest D. Burton, 13 September 1916, folder 8, box 25, Ernest DeWitt Burton Papers, Joseph Regenstein Memorial Library, University of Chicago; Paul W. Rupel, "The Building of an Indigenous Christian Community in Africa" (ms, 3 April 1935), p. 1; Thomas Jesse Jones to Rupel, 12 April 1935, both in folder 9, box 119; Rupel to Jones, 4 January 1937, folder 1, box 120; Frederick Adolphus Price application to Board of Foreign Missions, Methodist Episcopal Church, 18 July 1936, folder 3, box 127, all in Phelps-Stokes Collection, Schomburg Center for Research in Black Culture.

35. Helen Young, "Resht Girls' School—Section I. June 1933–January 1934" (ms), p. 3, folder 4, box 20, Board of Foreign Missions—Iran Mission [hereafter "BFM-Iran"], Record Group 91, Presbyterian Historical Society; ? to "My dear friends," August 1929, folder 17, box 17, SMA; Alice B. Van Doren, *Christian High Schools in India: Being the Report of a Survey Conducted on Behalf of the National Christian Council of India, Burma, and Ceylon* (Calcutta: YMCA Publishing House, 1936), 61; Rachel H. Seagrave, "Notes on the Evaluation Report with reference to the schools in Taunggyi, Shan States, Burma" (ms, n.d. [1936]), "Taunggyi Huldah Mix Girls School" folder, BIMSF; "Report of the Frank James Industrial School for the Year 1926" (ms), p. 2, folder 19, box 9, Board of Foreign Missions—West Africa Mission [hereafter "BFM-West Africa"], Record Group 142, Presbyterian Historical Society; Fred R. Bunker to "My dear friends," 5 May 1914, "Reports, Newspapers, Articles, Etc." folder, box 4, AC-HU.

36. Alice B. Van Doren, *Lighten to Lighten: The Hope of India. A Study of Conditions Among Women in India* (West Medford, Mass.: Central Committee on the

United Study of Foreign Missions, 1922), 39; Henry C. McDowell to Dear Friend, 22 September 1921, HCM/Ang.2/6/3, box 2, Henry C. McDowell Papers, Savery Library, Talladega College, Talladega, Ala.; "Statement Concerning the Rights of American Missionaries in Cameroun" (ms, June 1922), folder 15; Victor Agagneur, "Circular Relating to the DECREE Concerning the Private Instruction of Natives in the A.E.F.," trans. E. A. Ford (ms, n.d. [1921]), folder 19, both in box 1, BFM—West Africa.

37. Albert D. Helser, *Education of Primitive People* (New York: Negro Universities Press, 1969 [1934]), 31.

38. In their colonies, as in several states back home, Americans barred instruction in non-English languages from parochial as well as public schools. "History of Catholic Education in the Philippines" (ms, n.d. [1925]), folder 6, box 1, Philippines History Collection, Maryknoll Fathers and Brothers Archives, Ossining, N.Y.; William G. Ross, *Forging New Freedoms: Nativism, Education, and the Constitution, 1917–1927* (Lincoln: University of Nebraska Press, 1994), Chaps. 1–4. In 1923, the U.S. Supreme Court struck down state laws that prohibited non-English languages in parochial schools. *Meyer v. Nebraska*, 262 U.S. 390 (1923).

39. Jones, *Education in East Africa*, 19.

40. McDowell, "Educational and Recreational Features of Umbundu Culture," 5; John Norman Hostetter, "Mission Education in a Changing Society: Brethren in Christ Mission Education in Southern Rhodesia, Africa, 1899–1959" (Ed.D. diss., State University of New York at Buffalo, 1967), 42; Christian Ngoumbas of the Presbyterian Mission to Directors of Board of Foreign Missions, 10 February 1934, folder 23, box 1, BFM-West Africa.

41. Lizbeth Hughes, "Taunggyi, Burma" (ms, 30 June 1930), "Taunggyi Huldah Mix Girls School" folder, BIMSF; Gael Graham, *Gender, Culture, and Christianity: American Protestant Mission Schools in China, 1880–1930* (New York: Peter Lang, 1995), 60; Henry C. McDowell to Enoch F. Bell, HCM/Ang.2/6/4, box 2, McDowell Papers; Charlotte H. Brown, "Report of Sidon Girls School. July 1924–July 1925" (ms), folder 18, box 17, SMA; Margaret Doolittle to Margaret Hodge, 25 April 1927, folder 6, box 15, Board of Foreign Missions—Syria, Record Group 90, Presbyterian Historical Society.

42. James E. Fisher, *Democracy and Mission Education in Korea* (New York: Teachers College Columbia University, 1928), 90–91, 99–100.

43. n.a., "Report of Iran Bethel for the year 1926–1927" (ms, 1927), folder 12, box 20, BFM-Iran; Frederick J. Libby, *To End War: The Story of the National Council for Prevention of War* (Nyack, N.Y.: Fellowship Publications, 1969), 35–36; n.a., "Moga Training School" (ms, 1936), p. 2, folder 20, box 33, Board of Foreign Missions—India Mission [hereafter "BFM-India"], Record Group 83, Presbyterian Historical Society; Nancy Parker McDowell, *Notes from Ramallah, 1939* (Richmond, Ind.: Friends United Press, 2002), 17; Frederick Adolphus Price application to Board of Foreign Missions, Methodist Episcopal Church, 18 July 1936, folder 3, box 127, Phelps-Stokes Collection.

44. E. W. Koons, "John D. Wells Academy" (ms, 1917), p. 5, folder 34; Samuel A. Moffett, "Report of Boys' Academy (Pyengyang)" (ms, 1924), p. 1, folder 41; Harold H. Henderson, "Annual Report. Taiku Boys' Academy. 1923" (ms), p. 1, folder 28, all in box 7, Board of Foreign Missions—Korea Mission, Record Group 140, Presbyterian Historical Society; "Extract of letter from H. C. Velte, India

Council, 11/26/1930" (ms), folder 14, box 30, BFM-India; Edith Crisenberry, "Semi-Annual Report Letter" (ms, 16 March 1932), "Assam: Nowgong Girls School 1918 to 1945" folder; Alice Thayer to "Dear Folks at home," 1 March 1931, "Mandalay: Girls High School" folder, both in BIMSF.

45. A. R. Bryan to "Dear George and Winifred," 17 September 1930, folder 17, box 25; Irene Harper to Arthur W. Packard, 7 December 1938, folder 20, box 33; C. S. Vaughan to "Dear Brethren," 4 July 1930, folder 14, box 30; "India Expels U.S. Cleric," *New York Times*, n.d. [1944]), folder 14, box 30, all in BFM-India.

46. Albert Ravenholt, "Miss Stewart—'Our Teacher!' " *American Universities and Field Staff Letter*, 8 August 1958, "American Teachers—Philippines" folder, box 8, Arthur R. Carson Papers, Hoover Institution Archives [hereafter "Carson-Hoover"], Stanford University, Palo Alto, Calif.

47. Harland Cleveland, Gerard J. Mangone, and John Clarke Adams, *The Overseas Americans* (New York: McGraw-Hill, 1960), 83; Division of Foreign Missions, National Council of Churches, "North American Protestant Foreign Missionaries. Classified by Assignments" (ms, 1952), folder 13, box 4, National Council of Churches Papers, Division of Overseas Ministries [hereafter "NCC-DOM"], Record Group 8, Presbyterian Historical Society; Most Rev. G. Mongeau, O.M.I., "Notre Dame Schools in the Philippines," *Worldmission* 5 (Summer 1954): 236–237; Emery DesRochers to Lee Sanborn, 8 May 1961, folder 61, box 195, National Catholic Welfare Conference/United States Catholic Conference Collection [hereafter "NCWC/USCC"], American Catholic History Research Center, Catholic University, Washington, D.C.

48. Friar Patrick O'Connor, "Filipino Public School Officials Concerned Over Possible Religious Proselytism by Peace Corps Members," *NCWC News Service*, 21 August 1961, folder 61, box 195, NCWC/USCC; Beulah Heaton, "The Policy of the Education Committee of the Conservative Baptist Mission of the Philippine Islands" (ms, n.d. [1965]), folder 23, box 2, Committee to Assist Missionary Education Overseas Collection, Billy Graham Center Archives, Wheaton College, Wheaton, Ill.; Howard Whitman, "God's Foreign Agents," *Redbook*, December 1954, folder 9, box 3, R. Pierce Beaver Papers, Regenstein Library, University of Chicago; "The Missionaries," *Wall Street Journal*, 14 August 1961, folder 8, box 189, NCWC/USCC.

49. Fischer, *Making Them Like Us*, 38; R. S. Shriver, "Speech Prepared for Delivery by Robert Sargent Shriver, Jr., Director, Peace Corps, to the Student National Education Association, Atlantic City, New Jersey, June 29, 1961" (ms), 10; Shriver, "Statement Prepared for the American Association of School Administrators, Atlantic City, New Jersey, February 17, 1962" (ms), p. 3, both in "Peace Corps Speeches—Sargent Shriver, 1961–1962" binder, Peace Corps Library, Washington, D.C.; Harris Wofford, "With 400 Volunteers in Haile Selassie's Court" (ms, n.d.), p. 38, "Ethiopia—Peace Corps. 1970–1977—folder #1" file, Vertical Files, Peace Corps Library.

50. "US sent first 'Peace Corps' to the Philippines in 1901," *Chronicle* [Manila], 19 August 1963; Vic Barranco, "Honoring America's First PCVs—the Thomasites," *Examiner*, 26 March 1966, both in "American Teachers—Philippines" folder, box 8, Carson-Hoover; Fred Eggan lecture notes, n.d. [1962?], folder 20, box 22, Philippine Studies Program Records, Regenstein Library, University of Chicago; John S. Noffsinger, "A teacher for Bayombong," *Peace Corps Volunteer* 3

(October 1965): 22–25; "John Noffsinger Dead; Peace Corps Official," *Washington Post*, 5 May 1966, "Peace Corps News" binder, Peace Corps Library.

51. See, for example, Frederick W. Nash, "Education in the Philippines," *Educational Review* 22 (October 1901): 235; Fred W. Atkinson, "Education in the Philippines," *Outlook* 70 (5 April 1902): 939; "Banquet to Doctor Barrows," *Manila Times*, 11 October 1909, "Philippines" folder, carton 21, Barrows Papers; Kenneth M. Dedrick, "Teaching," *Porto Rico School Review* 6 (September 1921): 38; William W. Marquardt to Leonard Wood, 1 April 1922, "Articles Correspondence Philippines 1922" binder, box 7, Marquardt Papers.

52. "The Missions Go Native," *Newsweek*, 27 April 1959, fiche 003.083-2, Schomburg Clipping File; Cleveland et al., *Overseas Americans*, 91; Kenneth I. Brown, "Letter to a Young Missionary," *World Outlook*, April 1964, fiche 003.086-8, Schomburg Clipping File; Janet Kalven, *Women Breaking Boundaries: A Grail Journey, 1940–1995* (Albany: State University of New York Press, 1999), 147; Jonathan Zimmerman, "Religious bigotry," *Atlanta Constitution*, 16 November 1999.

53. On this point, see especially William R. Hutchison, *Errand to the World: American Protestant Thought and Foreign Missions* (Chicago: University of Chicago Press, 1987), as well as the essays collected in the special issue on "Missionaries, Multiculturalism, and Mainline Protestantism," *Journal of Presbyterian History* 81 (Summer 2003).

54. Gerald Ditz to Howard Schomer, 25 September 1969; A. Stafford Clayton to Schomer, 9 October 1969, both in folder 7, box 8, NCC-DOM.

55. Sally Ruffino to "Dad," 6 May 1964, folder 1, box 1, Sally Ruffino Papers, Collection 12, PC-NAA; Bernard F. Meyer, "Third World Library: Mark Seminar Library Annex. Opened at Easter, 1969" (ms); Meyer, untitled manuscript, enclosed with Bernard F. Meyer to Sister de Sales, 21 September 1969, both in folder 23, box 6, Rogers College Archives, Maryknoll Fathers and Brothers Archives; *The IVS Experience: From Algeria to Vietnam*, ed. Stuart Rawlings (Washington, D.C.: International Voluntary Services, 1992), 89.

56. Sisters Mary Duffy and Nancy Donovan to "Dear Sisters," 29 June 1973, folder 7, box 1, Mexico Collection, Maryknoll Fathers and Brothers Archives.

57. Michael E. Latham, *Modernization as Ideology: American Social Science and 'Nation Building' in the Kennedy Era* (Chapel Hill: University of North Carolina Press, 2000), 143; "A Collection: Evaluation Comments on TEFL" (ms, n.d. [1969]), pp. 1–2, "PC—TEFL, TESOL, Etc." file, Vertical Files, Peace Corps Library; "3 Quit Peace Corps in Turkey, Calling Jobs Meaningless," *New York Times*, 7 December 1969, p. 113.

58. Karen Schwarz, *What You Can Do For Your Country: An Oral History of the Peace Corps* (New York: William Morrow, 1991), 124; James and Margaret Goff, *In Every Person Who Hopes* (New York: Friendship Press, 1980), 61; Ivan Illich, "The Seamy Side of Charity," *America* 116 (21 January 1967): 90; Gerald M. Costello, *Mission to Latin America: The Successes and Failures of a Twentieth Century Crusade* (Maryknoll, N.Y.: Orbis, 1979), 50, 171.

59. Elizabeth Cobbs Hoffman, *All You Need is Love: The Peace Corps and the Spirit of the 1960s* (Cambridge, Mass.: Harvard University Press, 1998), 119; "An Observer," *Truth About the Peace Corps* (New Delhi: People's Publishing House, 1968), 14; "PEST CORPS. GO HOME!" *Peace Corps Volunteer* 5 (April 1967): 24; Elizabeth Cobbs Hoffman, "Diplomatic History and the Meaning of Life," *Diplomatic History*

21 (Fall 1997): 513–514; "Book by Nkrumah Attacks the U.S.," *New York Times*, 31 October 1965, p. 13; Arnold Zeitlin, *To the Peace Corps, With Love* (Garden City, N.Y.: Doubleday, 1965), 150; "Anti-U.S. Feelings Up in Philippines," *New York Times*, 11 December 1969, p. 17.

60. Alex Shakow, "Remarks on the Decision to Withdraw from Indonesia" (1965), in *Making a Difference: The Peace Corps at Twenty-Five*, ed. Milton Viorst (New York: Weidenfeld and Nicolson, 1986), 128; "Who Wants the Peace Corps?" *Newsweek*, 29 June 1970, folder 17, box 84, Paul R. Hanna Papers, Hoover Institution Archives.

61. On this point, see especially Hoffman, "Diplomatic History and the Meaning of Life," 516.

62. Irene Teagarden, "Annual Narrative Report. Sidon Girls' School. 1946–1947" (ms), p. 1, folder 18, box 17, SMA; Roger McManus to Aunt Anna, 20 October 1962, quoted in Richard W. McManus, "The Story of a Peace Corps Volunteer. 'I Shall Never Forget' " (ms, n.d. [1964?]), p. 29, General Collection, Peace Corps Library; Vincent J. D'Andrea, "Close of Service Conference. Philippines VII" (ms, 1964), p. 48, "Philippines VII" folder, box 2, Close of Service Conference Reports, Peace Corps Records [hereafter "PC-COS"], Record Group 490, National Archives II; Marjorie Pfankuch to "Dear Mom, Dad, and Jud," 23 October 1962, reel 1, Marjorie Pfankuch Papers, Wisconsin Historical Society, Madison, Wis.; Fred Eggan, "Relations with Teachers," undated lecture notes [1962?], folder 20, box 22, Philippine Studies Program Records. On Coca-Cola as a symbol of American cultural dominance, see Reinhold Wagnleitner, *Coca-Colonization and the Cold War: The Cultural Mission of the United States in Austria after the Second World War* (Chapel Hill: University of North Carolina Press, 1994), and Rob Kroes, "American Empire and Cultural Imperialism: A View from the Receiving End," in *The Ambiguous Legacy: United States Foreign Relations in the "American Century,"* ed. Michael J. Hogan (New York: Cambridge University Press, 1999), 506.

63. E. Gordon Dalbey Jr., "The Technicolored Christian," *Practical Anthropology* 15 (January–February 1968): 86; Mark Harris, *Twentyone Twice: A Journal* (Boston: Little, Brown, 1966), 218–19.

64. Mennonite Central Committee, *Teachers Abroad Program in Africa and Newfoundland* (n.p., n.d. [1967]), pp. 9–10, folder 39, box 79, Evangelical Foreign Missions Association Papers, Billy Graham Center Archives; Gordon Gaskill, "Our Stake in Liberia," *American Magazine* (July 1948), folder 6, box 127, Phelps-Stokes Collection; Kalven, *Women Breaking Boundaries*, 266.

65. Paul S. Slawson and John Groebli, "Close of Service Conference. Togo (Teachers and Fishermen)" (ms, 1964), pp. 4–5, "Togo" folder, box 3, PC-COS; Dalbey, "The Technicolored Christian," 87; Chester J. Jump, "The Christian Gospel and African Culture," *Practical Anthropology* 6 (January–February 1959): 32.

66. Matthew Frye Jacobson, *Barbarian Virtues: The United States Encounters Foreign Peoples at Home and Abroad* (New York: Hill and Wang, 2000), 231; unidentified Peace Corps teacher, quoted in Joe D. Kimmins, "Peace Corps—Central African Republic" (ms, 1975), p. 3, folder 1, box 1, Joe Kimmins Papers, Collection 15, PC-NAA.

67. Paul G. Hiebert, *Anthropological Reflections on Missiological Issues* (Grand Rapids, Mich.: Baker, 1994), 55, 59, 63–64.

68. Gertrude H. Rose to James W. Franklin, 23 January 1917, "Philippines: Jaro Industrial School 1904–1917" folder, BIMSF; Deborah Chadsey, untitled report (ms, n.d.), enclosed with Chadsey to "Dear Miss Nicalo, Mr. Van Hoogstraten et al.," 10 September 1970, folder 18, box 17, NCC-DOM.

69. On this point, see Samantha M. Shapiro, "All God's Children," *New York Times Magazine*, 5 September 2004, pp. 46–51. For other surveys of anthropology in American missions, see Charles R. Taber, *The World is Too Much With Us: 'Culture' in Modern Protestant Missions* (Macon, Ga.: Macon University Press, 1991); Taber, *To Understand the World, Save the World: The Interface Between Missiology and the Social Sciences* (Harrisburg, Penn.: Trinity Press International, 2000); Charles H. Kraft, *Anthropology for Christian Witness* (Maryknoll, N.Y.: Orbis, 1996).

70. Eric Friedman, "A Letter from Bulgaria," Retrieved September 12, 2004, from http://peacecorpswriters.org/pages/2000/0003/prntvers003/pv003letbulg.html.

Epilogue

1. George W. Bush, "Address to a Joint Session of Congress and the American People" (September 20, 2001), Retrieved March 13, 2005, from http://www.whitehouse.gov/news/releases/2001/09/20010920–8 html.

2. For scholars' citations of the Bush speech, see, for example, Michael H. Hunt, "In the Wake of September 11: The Clash of What," *Journal of American History* 89 (September 2002): 419; Clyde Prestowitz, *Rogue Nation: American Unilateralism and the Failure of Good Intentions* (New York: Basic Books, 2003), 35; James M. McCormick, "The Foreign Policy of the George W. Bush Administration," in *High Risk and Ambition: The Presidency of George W. Bush*, ed. Steven E. Schier (Pittsburgh, Penn.: University of Pittsburgh Press, 2004), 206–207.

3. Henry R. Luce, "The American Century" [1941], in *The Ambiguous Legacy: United States Foreign Relations in the "American Century,"* ed. Michael J. Hogan (New York: Cambridge University Press, 1999), 25, 20.

4. John Gray quoted in Jedediah Purdy, *Being America: Liberty, Commerce, and Violence in an American World* (New York: Knopf, 2003), 43.

5. For recent examples of such claims, emphasizing America's denigration of other cultures across time and space, see Michael Adas, "From Settler Colony to Global Hegemon: Integrating the Exceptionalist Narrative of the American Experience into World History," *American Historical Review* 106 (December 2001): 1696–1697; Adas, "Improving on the Civilizing Mission? Assumptions of United States Exceptionalism in the Colonization of the Philippines," in *The New American Empire: A 21st Century Teach-In on United States Foreign Policy*, eds. Lloyd C. Gardner and Marilyn B. Young (New York: New Press, 2005), 174; Michael E. Latham, *Modernization as Ideology: American Social Science and "Nation Building" in the Kennedy Era* (Chapel Hill: University of North Carolina Press, 2000), 5, 212.

6. See, for example, Rachel Waltner Goossen, *Women Against the Good War: Conscientious Objection and Gender on the American Home Front, 1941–1947* (Chapel Hill: University of North Carolina Press, 1997); James Tracy, *Direct Action: Radical Pacifism from the Union Eight to the Chicago Seven* (Chicago: University of Chicago Press, 1996); Penny von Eschen, *Race Against Empire* (Ithaca, N.Y.: Cornell

University Press, 1997); Michael S. Foley, *Confronting the War Machine: Draft Resistance During the Vietnam War* (Chapel Hill: University of North Carolina Press, 2003).

7. Two studies that do acknowledge overseas Americans' ambivalence—and that parallel my own argument—are William R. Hutchison, *Errand to the World: American Protestant Thought and Foreign Missions* (Chicago: University of Chicago Press, 1987), and Fritz Fischer, *Making Them Like Us: Peace Corps Volunteers in the 1960s* (Washington, D.C.: Smithsonian Institution Press, 1998).

8. "This is the Peace Corps, Miss Jones!" *Sunday News* [University Park, Penn.], 20 August 1961, folder 61, box 195, National Catholic Welfare Conference/United States Catholic Conference Collection, American Catholic History Research Center, Catholic University, Washington, D.C.

9. For a recent and clear statement on this subject, see Howard Gardner, "How Education Changes: Considerations of History, Science, and Values," in *Globalization: Culture and Education in the New Millennium*, eds. Marcello M. Suarez-Orozco and Desiree Baolian Qin-Hilliard (Berkeley and Los Angeles: University of California Press, 2004), 238.

10. As Alfred E. Eckes Jr. and Thomas W. Zeiler write in their survey of the subject, the term "globalization" first appeared in a 1983 article in the *Harvard Business Review*. See Eckes and Zeiler, *Globalization and the American Century* (New York: Cambridge University Press, 2003), 1.

11. For reminders of this obvious but oft-overlooked point, see Jessica C. E. Gienow-Hecht, "Shame on US? Academics, Cultural Transfer, and the Cold War—A Critical Review," *Diplomatic History* 24 (Summer 2000): 492; Richard Pells, "Who's Afraid of Steven Spielberg?" ibid., 497–498.

12. Latham, *Modernization as Ideology*, 212–213. Like most scholars of these subjects, Latham derives his conclusions by examining the architects of such policies—mainly politicians, diplomats, and academicians. To his credit, he acknowledges that "not all Americans shared the vision of their nation presented by modernization." But he goes on to assert that dissent from the vision "remained comparatively rare in an America that had not yet begun the ask the fundamental questions that the Vietnam War would eventually push to the center of national debate." I disagree. Well before Vietnam, the culture concept itself made overseas Americans deeply skeptical of the linear, confident, and ethnocentric assumptions that undergirded the American Century. Latham, *Modernization as Ideology*, 18.

13. James Patton, "An American in Fiji" (ms, n.d. [1971]), p. 12, General Collection, Peace Corps Library, Washington, D.C.

14. Robert D. Dean, *Imperial Brotherhood: Gender and the Making of Cold War Foreign Policy* (Amherst: University of Massachusetts Press, 2001), 171–179; Elizabeth Cobbs Hoffman, *All You Need Is Love: The Peace Corps and the Spirit of the 1960s* (Cambridge, Mass.: Harvard University Press, 1998), 16–22; Fischer, *Making Them Like Us*, 32–60.

15. Clifford Geertz, *Available Light: Anthropological Reflections on Philosophical Topics* (Princeton: Princeton University Press, 2000), 12–13; Kathleen Hall, "Understanding Educational Processes in an Era of Globalization: The View from Anthropology and Cultural Studies," in *Issues in Education Research: Problems and Possibilities*, eds. Ellen Condliffe Lagemann and Lee S. Shulman (San Francisco: Jossey-Bass, 1999), 148.

16. Here I follow the analysis in John Tomlinson, "Interests and Identities in Cosmopolitan Politics," in *Conceiving Cosmopolitanism: Theory, Context, and Practice,* eds. Steven Vertovec and Robin Cohen (New York: Oxford University Press, 2003), 246.

17. Fischer, *Making Them Like Us,* 171–172; Jonathan Zimmerman, "Beyond Double Consciousness: Black Peace Corps Volunteers in Africa, 1961–1971," *Journal of American History* 82 (December 1995): 1024.

18. Zimmerman, "Beyond Double Consciousness," 1001; Zygmunt Bauman, *In Search of Politics* (Stanford, Calif.: Stanford University Press, 1999), 202.

19. On the educational challenges of diversity and complexity in a globalized world, see Suarez-Orozco and Qin-Hilliard, *Globalization,* esp. 4–6.

20. Helen A. Wilson, "COS Conference. Gahana II" (ms, 26–29 May, 1964), p. 3, "Ghana II" folder, box 2, Close of Service Conference Reports, Peace Corps Records, Record Group 490, National Archives II, College Park, Md.; *Destination: Poland* (Washington, D.C.: U.S. Peace Corps, 1999), 19; William Jones memoir, n.t., in *The TEA Experience,* ed. Judith Lindfors (ms, 2002, in possession of Brooks Goddard, Needham, Mass.).

21. "The Peace Corps . . . or Service as a Missionary?" *Presbyterian Survey* (July 1963), p. 23, folder 38, box 11, Short Terms Abroad Papers, Billy Graham Center Archives, Wheaton College, Wheaton, Ill.

22. See, for example, Jonathan Zimmerman, "The White House and World Opinion," *Boston Globe,* 3 March 2005.

23. Mark Twain, *The Innocents Abroad* (New York: Signet, 1966 [1869]), 484.

24. Twain, *Innocents Abroad,* 197, 47, 193.

25. Philinda Rand Anglemyer, untitled manuscript, n.d. [1940?], p. 2, "Anglemyer, P. R. Memorabilia" folder, Philinda Rand Anglemyer Papers, Arthur and Elizabeth Schlesinger Library, Radcliffe College, Cambridge, Mass.; Jurgen Osterhammel, *Colonialism: A Theoretical Overview,* trans. Shelley L. Frisch (Princeton: Markus Wiener, 1997), 102.

26. R. Freeman Butts, "Confidential Notes by R. Freeman Butts" (ms, 1961), p. 2, "First Impressions of TEAers in Africa" folder, box 193, R. Freeman Butts Papers, Hoover Institution Archives, Palo Alto, Calif.

27. See, e.g., Ian Tyrrell, "American Exceptionalism in an Age of International History," *American Historical Review* 96 (October 1991): 1031–1055; George M. Fredrickson, "From Exceptionalism to Variability: Recent Developments in Cross-National Comparative History," *Journal of American History* 82 (September 1995): 587–604; Michael Kammen, *In the Past Lane: Historical Perspectives on American Culture* (New York: Oxford University Press, 1997), 169–98; Mary Nolan, "Against Exceptionalism," *American Historical Review* 102 (June 1997): 769–774; Daniel T. Rodgers, "Exceptionalism," in *Imagined Histories: American Historians Interpret the Past,* eds. Anthony Molho and Gordon S. Wood (Princeton: Princeton University Press, 1998), 21–40.

28. On the international roots and development of so-called progressive educational reform, see, for example, W. F. Connell, *A History of Education in the Twentieth Century World* (New York: Teachers College Press, 1980); *Kindergartens and Cultures: The Global Diffusion of an Idea,* ed. Roberta Wollons (New Haven: Yale University Press, 2000); William J. Reese, "The Origins of Progressive Education," *History of Education Quarterly* 41 (Spring 2001): 1–24.

29. Trevor B. McCrisken, *American Exceptionalism and the Legacy of Vietnam: United States Foreign Policy Since 1974* (New York: Palgrave Macmillan, 2003), 2.

30. Seymour E. Moon, "African Education—Old and New," *Missionary Review of the World*, December 1933, fiche 001.524–1, Schomburg Clipping File, Schomburg Center for Research in Black Culture, New York Public Libraries.

31. See, for example, Tyrrell, "American Exceptionalism," 1034; Daniel T. Rodgers, *Atlantic Crossings: Social Politics in a Progressive Age* (Cambridge, Mass.: Harvard University Press, 1998), 3, 502–508; Adas, "From Settler Colony to Global Hegemon," 1696.

32. Mark Twain, *Following the Equator: A Journey Around the World* (New York: Oxford University Press, 1996 [1897]), 340, 343.

33. See *Mark Twain's Weapons of Satire: Anti-Imperialist Writings on the Philippine-American War*, ed. Jim Zwick (Syracuse, N.Y.: Syracuse University Press, 1992).

34. *The IVS Experience: From Algeria to Vietnam*, ed. Stuart Rawlings (Washington, D.C.: International Voluntary Services, 1992), 163.

Index

Harvard University Press is a member of Green Press Initiative
(greenpressinitiative.org), a nonprofit organization working to
help publishers and printers increase their use of recycled paper
and decrease their use of fiber derived from endangered forests.
This book was printed on 100% recycled paper containing
50% post-consumer waste and processed chlorine free.